ANTISEMITISM AND THE

The Tauber Institute Series for the Study of European Jewry

JEHUDA REINHARZ, *General Editor*
CHAERAN Y. FREEZE, *Associate Editor*
SYLVIA FUKS FRIED, *Associate Editor*
EUGENE R. SHEPPARD, *Associate Editor*

The Tauber Institute Series is dedicated to publishing compelling and innovative approaches to the study of modern European Jewish history, thought, culture, and society. The series features scholarly works related to the Enlightenment, modern Judaism and the struggle for emancipation, the rise of nationalism and the spread of antisemitism, the Holocaust and its aftermath, as well as the contemporary Jewish experience. The series is published under the auspices of the Tauber Institute for the Study of European Jewry—established by a gift to Brandeis University from Dr. Laszlo N. Tauber—and is supported, in part, by the Tauber Foundation and the Valya and Robert Shapiro Endowment.

For the complete list of books that are available in this series, please see https://brandeisuniversitypress.com/series/tauber

*SCOTT URY and GUY MIRON, editors
Antisemitism and the Politics of History

JEREMY FOGEL
Jewish Universalisms: Mendelssohn, Cohen, and Humanity's Highest Good

STEFAN VOGT, DEREK PENSLAR, and ARIEH SAPOSNIK, editors
Unacknowledged Kinships: Postcolonial Studies and the Historiography of Zionism

JOSEPH A. SKLOOT
First Impressions: Sefer Hasidim and Early Modern Hebrew Printing

*MARAT GRINBERG
The Soviet Jewish Bookshelf: Jewish Culture and Identity Between the Lines

SUSAN MARTHA KAHN
Canine Pioneer: The Extraordinary Life of Rudolphina Menzel

ARTHUR GREEN
Defender of the Faithful: The Life and Thought of Rabbi Levi Yitshak of Berdychiv

*A Sarnat Library Book

ANTISEMITISM

and the POLITICS *of* HISTORY

Edited by SCOTT URY *and* GUY MIRON

A SARNAT LIBRARY BOOK

BRANDEIS UNIVERSITY PRESS

Waltham, Massachusetts

An earlier version of this volume was
originally published in Hebrew as:
אנטישמיות: בין מושג היסטורי לשיח ציבורי
(*Antishemiyut: ben musag histori lesiah tsiburi*)
© 2020 by Zalman Shazar Center, Jerusalem
All translation rights reserved

For permission to reproduce any of the material in this book, contact
Brandeis University Press, 415 South Street, Waltham MA 02453,
or visit brandeisuniversitypress.com

This publication was made possible through the generous support of
Brandeis University's Bernard G. and Rhoda G. Sarnat Center for
the Study of Anti-Jewishness, which aims to promote a deeper
understanding of anti-Jewish prejudice, as well as Jewish and
non-Jewish responses to this phenomenon, from both a historical
and contemporary perspective.

The volume's publication was also supported by the Stephen Roth
Institute for the Study of Contemporary Antisemitism and Racism,
Tel Aviv University, with generous contributions by the Sybil Shine
Memorial Trust, London, and anonymous private donors, as well as
the Koret Center for Jewish Civilization, Tel Aviv University.

LIBRARY OF CONGRESS CATALOGING-IN-PUBLICATION DATA
available at https://catalog.loc.gov/
cloth   ISBN 978-1-68458-179-5
paper   ISBN 978-1-68458-180-1
e-book   ISBN 978-1-68458-181-8

5 4 3 2 1

To our partners
Noa
and
Shoshana

Contents

Acknowledgments   xi

I · INTRODUCTORY CONSIDERATIONS

1 Antisemitism: On the Meanings and Uses of
  a Contested Term   1
  SCOTT URY *and* GUY MIRON

2 Thinking about "Antisemitism"   33
  DAVID ENGEL

II · METHODOLOGICAL EXPLORATIONS

3 History and Noise   45
  AMOS MORRIS-REICH

4 Erotohistoriography: Sensory and Emotional
  Dimensions of Antisemitism   65
  SUSANNAH HESCHEL

5 Toward Entanglement   87
  STEFANIE SCHÜLER-SPRINGORUM

III · PREMODERN CONTEXTUALIZATIONS

6 Separation, Judeophobia, and the Birth of the "Goy":
  The Chicken and the Egg   105
  ADI M. OPHIR *and* ISHAY ROSEN-ZVI

7 Antisemitism and Islamophobia:
A Medieval Comparison   127
YOUVAL ROTMAN

8 The Term "Antisemitism" as a Category for
the Study of Medieval Jewish History   147
TZAFRIR BARZILAY

IV · MODERN CONTESTATIONS
9 "Feverish Preference": Philosemitism,
Anti-antisemitism, and Their Critics   167
OFRI ILANY

10 Cautious Use of the Term "Antisemitism"—
for Lack of an Alternative: Interwar Poland
as a Test Case   187
GERSHON BACON

11 America and the Keyword Battle Over "Antisemitism"   207
ELI LEDERHENDLER

12 "Fog in Channel—Continent Cut Off?": Remarks on
Antisemitism, Pride, and Prejudice in Britain   227
ARIE M. DUBNOV

13 A Retreat from Universalism: Opposing and
Defining Antisemitism and Islamophobia
in Britain, ca. 1990–2018   251
DAVID FELDMAN

V · POST-HOLOCAUST RUMINATIONS
14 In Defense of the Concept of "Antisemitism"
in Holocaust Studies   281
HAVI DREIFUSS

15 "Antisemitism" as a Question in Holocaust Studies   299
AMOS GOLDBERG *and* RAZ SEGAL

16 Is There Christian Antisemitism?: The History of
an Intra-Catholic Debate, 1965–2000   319
KARMA BEN-JOHANAN

VI · CONCLUDING EXPLANATIONS

17 Can the Circle Be Broken?   339
DAVID ENGEL

Select Bibliography   361
Contributors   367
Index   373

Acknowledgments

IT IS OUR PLEASURE to thank the many colleagues, friends, and family members who accompanied us in the long process of conceiving, editing, translating, and publishing both the original Hebrew version of this volume, *Antishemiyut: ben musag histori lesiah tsiburi* (*Antisemitism: Historical Concept, Public Discourse*), and now the revised, English-language volume, *Antisemitism and the Politics of History*.

This book began as the result of two parallel, intersecting research projects, the first undertaken by volume co-editor Guy Miron at the Open University of Israel, which was designed to prepare an updated Hebrew textbook for a remote, online course on antisemitism in the nineteenth century, and the second, a research project conducted by Scott Ury, the volume's other co-editor, on the politics of antisemitism, which was developed during his tenure as director of Tel Aviv University's (TAU) Stephen Roth Institute for the Study of Contemporary Antisemitism and Racism.

Informal conversations over coffee and at various academic venues regarding our common interests led us to propose to the Historical Society of Israel's Hebrew-language journal *Zion* a special issue on David Engel's provocative article regarding the concept of antisemitism. Moshe Rosman, who was one of the journal's editors at the time, wisely guided us throughout the process of developing, editing, and publishing a special volume of *Zion* with more than twenty contributions. The other editors of *Zion*, Shmuel Feiner, Miriam Frenkel, Nadav Na'aman, Vered Noam, and Michael Toch, also contributed to the review process, particularly in regard to submissions that went beyond our immediate fields of expertise as scholars of modern Jewish history, as did Miriam Eliav-Feldon, who was chair of the Historical Society of Israel at the time. We are also deeply indebted to Yehezkel Hovav, the phenomenal in-house editor at *Zion* and the Zalman Shazar Center, whose input and assistance was absolutely indispensable to the production of the

Hebrew volume, and to Michal Sagie, director of the Zalman Shazar Center, and Haya Paz Cohen, head of the Shazar Center's publishing house, who ensured that the special issue of *Zion* would also be published as an independent volume in Hebrew.

Although not directly involved in the production of either the Hebrew or the English volumes, David Engel was kind enough to humor our curiosity and patient enough to prepare thoughtful introductions and responses to both volumes, even when the process threatened, at times, to career off course.

Amos Morris-Reich, the current director of TAU's Roth Institute, took the initiative to secure the funds necessary for the production of a revised, English version of the original Hebrew volume, and we are grateful to members of the Roth Institute's International Board for procuring funding from the Sybil Shine Memorial Trust in London as well as from a number of anonymous, private sources in the United States. This volume's publication was also supported by Tel Aviv University's Koret Center for Jewish Civilization and its academic director, Youval Rotman. In addition to this institutional backing, we are indebted to staff members at the Roth Institute, including Julija Levin, Riva Mane, and Eitan Rom, whose dedicated efforts have helped create a vibrant, dynamic discourse regarding the study of antisemitism at Tel Aviv University and beyond.

Our efforts to publish an English translation were encouraged by the lively public debate that the Hebrew volume produced on the pages of Israel's leading newspaper *Haaretz*; engaging podcast conversations like the one hosted by the *Tel Aviv Review*; public discussions regarding the volume that were sponsored by the Historical Society of Israel and the Zalman Shazar Center, Israel's Ministry of Education, and Tel Aviv University's Department of Jewish History; and panel discussions at the 2022 Association for Jewish Studies (AJS) Conference in Boston.

Ten of this volume's seventeen chapters were translated with care by Elli Fischer, a scholar of Jewish intellectual and cultural history. Bessie Goldberg, a scholar of modern literature and culture based in Toronto, sagely edited the entire manuscript, and Madeline Levy, a PhD student at Harvard University's Committee on the Study of Religion, undertook the task of streamlining the notes and helping prepare the bibliography and manuscript for publication.

Careful readings by Yehuda Mirsky and David Myers led us to Brandeis University Press, where Sylvia Fuks Fried has proven to be a dedicated and supportive editor with a unique eye for both scholarly detail and the larger academic horizon. Situated down the hall from Sylvia's office in Brandeis's Lown Building, Eugene Sheppard provided us with the insightful comments and critical encouragement necessary to move this project forward in a constructive fashion. Time and again, working and interacting with Sylvia, Eugene, and other faculty and staff at Brandeis and Brandeis University Press has demonstrated the benefits of publishing with a university press staffed by dedicated professionals who are willing to engage with, challenge, and listen to their authors.

While preparing and translating this collected volume has been a laborious task for its editors, it has been, perhaps, no less trying for their families and partners who have lived vicariously with both the Hebrew and English versions of this volume for years and have heard far more than they ever cared or dared to know about the different definitions, interpretations, and debates over antisemitism, both within Israeli academia and beyond. We can only imagine what the many half-conversations regarding the various dilemmas that inevitably arose as both of these editions came together sounded like to our partners, Noa and Shoshana, who, as classic participant-observers, were both distinctly removed from and inevitably a part of the larger process of exploration, contemplation, collation, and now publication. We dedicate this volume to them, without whom it would never have seen the light of day.

SCOTT URY
GUY MIRON

I
INTRODUCTORY CONSIDERATIONS

1

Antisemitism
On the Meanings and
Uses of a Contested Term

SCOTT URY *and* GUY MIRON

I N HIS THOUGHT-PROVOKING ESSAY from 2009 that serves as the
starting point of this volume, the historian David Engel analyzes the
concept of "antisemitism" and the way that it is used, both in scholarly
research and in the wider public discourse. According to Engel, the
concept of antisemitism currently speaks simultaneously to a wide
range of historical, social, and political phenomena. For example, the
very same term is used to describe tensions and hostilities between
Jews and Christians in ancient times, blood libels against Jewish
communities in the Middle Ages and the early modern period, the
rise of national movements with distinct anti-Jewish agendas in late-
nineteenth-century eastern and central Europe, and the mass murder
of millions of Jews on the part of the Nazis and their collaborators in
the middle of the twentieth century. At the same time, the very same
term, antisemitism, is also used to describe moments of social exclusion, insults, or bullying toward Jews on the part of their neighbors,
coworkers, or fellow students, and, in recent years, the vocal, at times
angry, arguments regarding the State of Israel, its policies, and even
its very existence.[1] As the Israeli doyen of Holocaust studies Yehuda
Bauer conceded over a decade ago:

> The term *antisemitism* is, as many of us realize, the wrong term for
> what we try to describe and analyze.... It makes a mess of research
> projects, as it interferes with the task of differentiation. Yet we

1

all use it, simply because we have not come up with the proper terminology.[2]

In light of observations by Engel, Bauer, and other thinkers, the question arises: Can one historical concept represent so many different phenomena accurately?[3] Perhaps Engel is correct in his claim that the widespread use of the term "antisemitism" in both historical research and the public discourse renders it an empty vessel that ultimately tells us much more about the person using the term in the present than the person or phenomenon in the past that it claims to represent.[4] Surveying the study of antisemitism, Engel notes that generations of scholars have "persuaded themselves that the concept 'antisemitism' was not something that they had invented, adopted, and defined for their own purposes but was instead a tangible quality possessing an objectively true, permanent meaning inscribed in an identifiable feature of the natural world."[5] If the past is, indeed, a foreign country, then perhaps we are all, at a certain point and time, chronological colonialists, inevitable children, or, perhaps, even unavoidable prisoners of the present, who repeatedly foist our own fears, foibles, and fantasies on distant lands and peoples past, comfortably protected by the very fact that those for whom we portend to speak are no longer able to respond.

These and many other questions lie at the center of this collection of essays, which is based on a special four-issue volume of the Historical Society of Israel's Hebrew-language journal, *Zion*, that was published in the fall of 2020.[6] Inspired by Engel's intervention and other critical works that have appeared over the past few years, scholars specializing in different periods and aspects of Jewish history were asked to consider whether or not "antisemitism" is, indeed, a useful tool of historical analysis.[7] In addition to responding to Engel's provocative challenge to scholars to refrain from using the term "antisemitism" in future studies, contributors were asked to propose potential solutions that the wider community of scholars might be able to employ as part of ongoing efforts to overcome the many methodological, intellectual, political, and ethical problems that arise from the widespread, oftentimes unreflexive, use of the same concept in both historical research and public debates.[8] The response to our initial inquiries was overwhelmingly positive, reflecting a desire among many academics in Israel and abroad to explore and probe these questions and to wrestle with the intellectual, ethical, and political dilemmas that they pose. As a result, the original Hebrew volume included more than twenty chapters from a variety of scholars and perspectives regarding many of the dilemmas associated with research on anti-Jewish attitudes and actions in a range of historical periods and geographic regions. Some of the contributors to the Hebrew volume dwelled at length on Engel's comments while others used his essay as a starting point to raise additional issues. Due to considerations of space, the current volume includes revised versions of seventeen of the original twenty-two chapters, including an abbreviated introductory essay as well as an updated response by David Engel that concludes the volume.

At its core, this volume is designed to promote academic and intellectual debate and exchange that will help promote new approaches to the study of antisemitism, the various uses of the term, and the ramifications, both intellectual and political, of these and related endeavors. When we began the process of turning to a number of leading scholars of Jewish history based in Israel, Europe, and North America, it was clear to us that the many different people involved in the production of this volume—the authors of individual chapters, the editors of the journal *Zion*, external readers of different essays, and us, the editors of this special volume—would never come to a consensus regarding many of the core questions and central debates involved in the study of antisemitism.

Despite, or perhaps because of, the many differences of opinions and perspectives, we hope that the current collection will help advance research and discussion regarding the various meanings and uses of the concept of antisemitism, including those related to its history, nature, and, even, its future. Was Robert S. Wistrich, one of the leading scholars of antisemitism over the past two generations, correct in describing antisemitism as "the longest hatred"?[9] If so, were other, equally prominent scholars of Jewish history based in Israel, such as Shmuel Ettinger, similarly accurate in their position that antisemitism was a historically unique phenomenon, and that it was pointless, if not fundamentally errant, to compare it to other forms of racism and prejudice?

What about the parallel usage of the very same term—anti-semitism—in contemporary public and political spheres as well as the repeated, perhaps simply inevitable, influence of these politically charged debates on academic research? To what extent do public debates regarding antisemitism influence efforts by scholars to understand, research, and write about anti-Jewish attitudes and actions?[10]

Lastly, how should scholars respond to the wide range of emotions that often accompany and at times inflame academic research and public discussions of antisemitism? Can we separate the emotional aspects of antisemitism from scholarly research on the topic as a historical, contemporary, and, in many cases, deeply personal phenomenon? Or is antisemitism, always and already, an emotionally charged and politically fraught field of intellectual inquiry that individual authors and the wider scholarly community quite simply need to acknowledge, confront, and negotiate, each in their own way?

Good scholarship builds upon, responds to, and advances the work of other scholars, and the present volume eagerly joins the growing discourse on these and related questions by an array of gifted scholars based at Israeli, European, and North American universities. In 2018, the scholar of French intellectual history and of antisemitism Jonathan Judaken edited a roundtable discussion in the leading historical journal *The American Historical Review* entitled "Rethinking Anti-Semitism."[11] In his thought-provoking introduction to that collection, Judaken claimed that unlike other scholarly realms like the study of race or gender, scholars of antisemitism often refrain from asking critical questions regarding the history, uses, and implications of scholarship in the field.[12] The *AHR* issue edited by Judaken includes seven additional articles regarding fundamental questions that contemporary scholars of antisemitism often encounter, including those related to the connection between antisemitism and other forms of racism, the relationship between the study of antisemitism and gender studies, and the politics of studying antisemitism.[13] Moreover, while the contributors to the *AHR* volume didn't arrive at any consensus regarding these and other questions, they did agree, if even implicitly, that the time had come to undertake a critical reassessment of the field as part of the larger intellectual and scholarly processes designed to further our understanding of the study of antisemitism, in particular, and its relationship to the study of Jewish and non-Jewish histories, in general.

This position reflects a growing sense of frustration among many scholars regarding the current state of the field and the looming impression that the study of antisemitism over the past few generations has coalesced around a number of fundamental postulates, many of which are accepted far more often than they are questioned.[14] As the leading scholar of medieval history David Nirenberg notes in the early pages of *Anti-Judaism: The Western Tradition*, "History can easily become unreflective, pathological, impeding criticism rather than furthering it."[15] The following analysis of current trends in the study of antisemitism argues that a dominant perspective on the study of antisemitism has emerged over the past generation or two, and that the time has come to review and critique many of the fundamental assumptions upon which this body of research lies.[16]

The first fundamental postulate upon which the dominant approach to antisemitism is often based is the assumption that antisemitism has a long, autonomous history, one that stretches in a seemingly uninterrupted fashion from ancient times to today.[17] This assumption is tied to another underlying assumption that has coalesced over the past few decades that views the Holocaust not only as the height (or nadir) of the long history of antisemitism but also as the almost logical, if not at times seemingly inevitable, conclusion of thousands of years of anti-Jewish sentiment. The central place of the Holocaust as the culmination of antisemitism's history leads to the third component in the dominant approach in the field today, one that claims—at times explicitly, at times implicitly—that antisemitism is not only different from other forms of group hatred and racism but also that because of these fundamental differences there is no point (and according to some authors it is even deeply flawed) to study antisemitism alongside other forms of racism or prejudice. The fourth point critical to the current approach to the study of antisemitism is what is often referred to as the "new antisemitism," a view that points to angry debates regarding the State of Israel, its policies, and, at times, its very existence as another chapter in the long history of antisemitism. In addition to these four fundamental postulates that inform and shape the current study of antisemitism, we should add one additional element that often characterizes research on antisemitism: the emotional, charged nature of the academic discourse and public debates regarding the topic.

On the one hand, the central role that these fundamental assumptions fulfill in a range of influential studies of antisemitism has helped construct a dominant approach to the field, one whose influence is apparent in scholarship, conferences, articles, and volumes, including this collection. Indeed, the study of antisemitism and related phenomena owes a great deal to these and other studies. On the other hand, the construction, solidification, and institutionalization of the field of "antisemitism studies" over the past two generations or so reflects a certain intellectual conservativism, one that may simultaneously inhibit the development of new perspectives and approaches. Hence, our goal in publishing this collection is to encourage and promote a critical analysis and discussion of many of the core assumptions in the study of antisemitism that are often bypassed by readers, students, and scholars.

Lastly, as we refer to in the subtitle of this essay, "On the Meanings and Uses of a Contested Term," antisemitism means many things to many people, both as the topic of academic research and as the subject of heated political debates in Israel, in Jewish communities outside of Israel, and across the globe. This is the last and perhaps the most important point that we wish to note in regard to current research on antisemitism: the constant, seemingly unavoidable, and perhaps inevitable tension between academic scholarship and the political realm, a tension that each scholar, student, and reader needs to acknowledge and come to terms with as he or she addresses, researches, and speaks about antisemitism.

Current Approaches, Central Debates, Open Questions

Seventy years ago, in the shadow of the Second World War and the horrors of the Holocaust and in the midst of the Cold War, scholars in the United States, Israel, and other centers fervently debated the connection between antisemitism in the twentieth century and earlier expressions of anti-Jewish animus.[18] At the center of these debates stood the critical question regarding the historical continuity of antisemitism, on one hand, and the role that scholars, in particular historians, often assign to changing social and political circumstances, on the other. Supporters of the latter, modernist approach were struck by and emphasized the radical differences between the racial antisemitism that had come to dominate antisemitism in the twentieth century and the religious basis of what was often referred to as a premodern "anti-Judaism," hostility toward the religion of Judaism that often revolved around long-running religious disputes, in particular those between Christians and Jews. Hannah Arendt, one of the most important intellectual figures of the twentieth century whose experience as a German-Jewish émigré scholar seemed to embody the very problems she analyzed so brilliantly, was a staunch supporter of the modernist approach to the study of anti-semitism. In the preface to her sweeping, daring 1951 analysis regarding the swift and disastrous collapse of the tower of cards often referred to as modernity, *The Origins of Totalitarianism* (which dedicated its entire first part to the study of antisemitism), Arendt presented an unflinching, caustic critique of the school of "eternal antisemitism." In particular, she criticized the logic underpinning its fundamental point regarding the "unbroken continuity of persecutions, expulsions, and massacres from the end of the Roman Empire to the Middle Ages, the modern era, and down to our time" that were "frequently embellished by the idea that modern antisemitism is no more than a secularized version of popular medieval superstitions...."[19]

Despite the far-reaching influence of Arendt and other scholars who advocated this approach, many central studies of antisemitism published over the past generation or two have adopted the opposite position by maintaining that antisemitism has a long, continuous history dating back to ancient times. This, for example, was the approach embraced by Robert S. Wistrich, who was the director of the Hebrew University's Vidal Sassoon International Center for the Study of Antisemitism from 2002 until his death in 2015. An incredibly prolific scholar, Wistrich wrote a number of important studies on anti-semitism that revolved around the position that modern antisemitism represented a direct continuation of earlier expressions of anti-Jewish sentiment that date back to ancient times. As he states unequivocally in his massive and definitive 2010 tome *A Lethal Obsession: Anti-Semitism from Antiquity to the Global Jihad:*

> There has been no hatred in Western Christian civilization more persistent and enduring than that directed against the Jews. Though the form and timing that outbursts of anti-Jewish persecution have taken throughout the ages have varied, the basic patterns of prejudice have remained remarkably consistent.[20]

Over the past few decades, the approach advocated by Wistrich and other scholars has become a central part of the dominant interpretation of antisemitism and has helped shape a number of influential studies, including those by prominent scholars like Anthony Julius, Dina Porat, Alvin Rosenfeld, and others.[21] Hence, despite the criticism of some of the more polemical aspects of his works, Wistrich's many studies and his influential position as the longtime head of one of the most important academic centers for the study of antisemitism helped fortify and bolster his position regarding antisemitism's long, continuous history.

The emphasis that Wistrich and many of his contemporaries have placed on antisemitism's long, continuous history is related to the second major point that often shapes current scholarship in the field: the inherent, at times inevitable, connection between antisemitism and the Holocaust. In the wake of the cataclysmic events of the Second World War, scholars began to view antisemitism in a different light, oftentimes emphasizing or even conflating the two phenomena—the history of antisemitism and the Holocaust. Part of these developments were related to accompanying debates in the realm of Holocaust studies between the "functionalist" school and the "intentionalist" camp, the latter of which emphasized the place of antisemitism in the implementation of the Final Solution. As a result of these and other factors, more and more scholars began to view antisemitism as a social or a historical phenomenon that led to and culminated in the Holocaust.[22] However, while scholars from the realm of Holocaust studies continue to debate the extent to which antisemitism was a "necessary" factor leading to the extermination of most of the Jews in Nazi-occupied Europe, there is far less debate regarding the narrative place of and the reciprocal role played by the Holocaust in the study of antisemitism.[23]

Prevailing conceptions regarding the long history of antisemitism and its seemingly inevitable culmination in the Holocaust serve as the basis for the third core point informing, forging, and defining the study of antisemitism today: the ostensibly unique nature of antisemitism and the not-infrequent opposition—or at the very least hesitancy (both implicit and explicit)—to comparing antisemitism to other forms of racism or prejudice. Here, as well, the current understanding and study of antisemitism is radically different from how important scholars and institutions approached these and related questions several generations ago. Immediately after the Second World War, the American Jewish Committee (AJC) initiated an ambitious research project designed to decipher and explain the Nazis' rise to power, the implementation of "the Final Solution," and the road to Auschwitz as well as the place of antisemitism, in particular, and racism, in general, in these seemingly unprecedented processes. Published under the larger series title of *Studies in Prejudice*, prominent scholars of modern society like Theodor Adorno, Max Horkheimer, and Bruno Bettelheim wrote a number of influential works that repeatedly emphasized the general, and some would even claim universal, aspects of hatred and prejudice directed at Jews.[24] While *Studies in Prejudice* was deeply influenced by the AJC's diasporist Jewish agenda at the time as well as the approach of many of the central figures involved in the project, antisemitism was repeatedly framed, researched, and presented in the series as a sociological or historical phenomena related to the onset of modernity, and not as an integral part of the field of knowledge that would soon become established as "Jewish history," let alone the newly anointed realm of research that has recently received the appellation of "antisemitism studies."

Although these studies were incredibly influential, scholars in Israel like Shmuel Ettinger, a leading historian of East European Jewry and a central figure in Israeli academic and public life in the 1960s, 1970s, and 1980s, vehemently opposed the approach undertaken in the AJC's *Studies in Prejudice* series. In a critical essay that appeared as the lead in the influential collection *Antisemitism Through the Ages* (which was first published in 1980 in Hebrew and then translated and published in English by the Hebrew University's Vidal Sassoon Center in 1988 as one of its first books in the Center's publication series, *Studies in Antisemitism*), Ettinger bitterly critiqued (Jewish) scholars in the United States and elsewhere who adopted general or universal approaches to the study of antisemitism.[25] Here and elsewhere, Ettinger would highlight the misguided efforts by "psychologists, sociologists and historians to find some general significance in antisemitism, and in some extreme cases, to discover something universal in it."[26] After summarizing works by Arendt, Adorno, and other leading thinkers, Ettinger declared that these and other studies of antisemitism "miss the target" by adopting comparative or general approaches to the phenomenon.[27] According to Ettinger, the various attempts to compare antisemitism to other forms of racism or prejudice, or to study antisemitism within a wider, comparative context, were intellectually baseless, if not ethically bankrupt. In the spirit of the "Jerusalem school" of Jewish history that he embraced, helped solidify, and lived by, Ettinger was fundamentally opposed to any analysis that approached antisemitism as a general, universal problem, and, in doing so, turned "Jews into a marginal or even a casual element" in the course of history.[28] Here, and elsewhere, Ettinger maintained that the deep-seated connection between antisemitism's historical continuity and its unique historical, social, and political nature defied simple comparisons.

> Explanations of this sort deal very little with the question of the Jews' specific character or even with their status in the surrounding society, and direct most of their attention to the psychological, social, or political structure of the surrounding majority peoples. Such explanations from the outset turn Jews into a marginal or even a casual element, and by doing so, make the problem one of explaining the phenomenon in the framework of world history rather than as a factor in Jewish history.[29]

Despite long-running scholarly debates between advocates of the historically continuous, uniqueness camp and those supporting the comparative or contextual approach to the study of antisemitism, the position advocated by Ettinger, Wistrich (who Ettinger helped bring to the Hebrew University from London in 1982), and other scholars has become increasingly dominant over the past few decades as more and more scholars frame antisemitism as a unique historical and social phenomenon that belongs far more to the realms of Jewish studies or Jewish history than to parallel academic fields like sociology, psychology, or the study of racism.[30]

The noticeable divide between the study of antisemitism and the study of anti-Black racism over the past few decades helps illustrate this point. On the one hand, the development of the study of race and racism as new, autonomous fields of inquiry and knowledge in North American academia in the 1960s, 1970s, and 1980s led many scholars of prejudice and racism to focus increasingly on anti-Black racism and less on comparative studies of this and other, potentially related phenomena. The exponential growth of Jewish studies in Israel and North America during this same period similarly contributed to the growing divide between the study of anti-Black racism and research on antisemitism. One trend that illustrates these developments was the creation of new research centers at different universities that were dedicated specifically to the study of antisemitism. In addition to early institutes that were created at the Hebrew University of Jerusalem (1982), the Technical University in Berlin (1982), and Tel Aviv University (1991), a second wave of academic centers was inaugurated in the early twenty-first century at Yale University (2005, 2011), Indiana University, Bloomington (2009), Birkbeck, University of London (2010), and in Winnipeg, Canada (2010). As a reflection of these intellectual and scholarly trends, all of these research institutes—save for Tel Aviv University's Stephen Roth Institute—were dedicated to the study of antisemitism as a distinct historical or social phenomenon.

Designed to advance the study of antisemitism, these different centers—stretching from Jerusalem to Berlin and from London to Bloomington, Indiana—helped fortify the nature and limits of the field as one that was designed both to advance the academic study of antisemitism in the past and to combat anti-Jewish sentiments and attitudes in the present. This dual role as both academic research centers and forums for public activity and intervention is apparent in the public profile and activities of many of these institutes. However, the twinning of the scholarly and public agendas also contributes to the tendency to study antisemitism as a unique social, political, and historical problem. As a result of this mixing of academic and contemporary concerns, several of these centers—including but not only the one at Yale University and the one at Birkbeck—have been embroiled in acrimonious public disputes regarding the political implications of their research and programming, highlighting further the extent to which many of these institutes and their stated topic of research—antisemitism—are viewed as scholarly enterprises with distinctly public agendas.[31]

The tendency to view antisemitism as a separate social, political, and religious phenomenon is also reflected in the book series or academic journals that some of these centers support. Indiana University Press (IUP) has an active book series titled *Studies in Antisemitism* that is connected directly to the center in Bloomington, Indiana, and IUP is also home to the relatively new journal *Antisemitism Studies*, which is based in and run out of the research center in Winnipeg.[32] Unlike the *Studies in Prejudice* series that the American Jewish Committee administered immediately after the Second World War, these publishing projects approach antisemitism as a distinct historical and social phenomenon, one that is, by its very definition, separated and insulated from parallel, potentially related realms of scholarly inquiry.[33] As the website for the journal *Antisemitism Studies* declares, the biannual periodical "provides the leading forum for scholarship on the millennial phenomenon of antisemitism, both its past and present manifestations."[34]

The central place and influential role of these institutions and their affiliated publication platforms have encouraged recent generations of scholars to approach antisemitism as a unique phenomenon that dwells within an independent field of research—a scholarly echo chamber, as it were. Indeed, even research students or scholars who might want to examine antisemitism as part of the larger discourse on racism or prejudice or from a comparative perspective would have some degree of difficulty integrating such projects into the intellectual framework that has come to dominate these and other institutions and the discourse they have helped construct and maintain, for better and for worse.

Here, as well, many of the debates regarding antisemitism's ostensible uniqueness are influenced by parallel discussions regarding the advantages and disadvantages involved in comparing the Holocaust to other instances of genocide.[35] Hence, over the past few generations, the spirited struggle by Shmuel Ettinger and other scholars to separate the study of antisemitism from other forms of racism has passed from a debated topic to an academic standard, one that receives additional, intellectual scaffolding and support from the different research centers and publication projects grounded in several fundamental assumptions regarding antisemitism's separate, if not unique, nature. For better and for worse, the current academic discourse regarding antisemitism now embraces much clearer academic lines than the exchanges that characterized the field some fifty years ago. Of course, every success story demands its own price.

Shmuel Ettinger's career as a revered figure in Israeli academia who regularly integrated his academic interests and his political activities highlights further the underlying tension between the scholarly study of antisemitism and contemporary political debates. Similar to such seminal scholars of East European Jewry as Simon Dubnow and his doctoral advisor at the Hebrew University, Ben-Zion Dinur, Ettinger saw little problem mixing scholarship and politics, especially when they both served the interests of the (Jewish) nation. Not by chance, the Hebrew biography penned by his former student Jacob Barnai was titled *Shmuel Ettinger: Historian, Teacher, Public Figure*.[36]

The ease with which Ettinger mixed scholarship and politics highlights the fourth point around which current research on antisemitism is often shaped and, in turn, defined: the deep, underlying connection between academic research and contemporary political concerns. Here, as well, Ettinger's approach in the 1960s, 1970s, and 1980s foreshadowed important developments in the field. Much like Ettinger, who dedicated a great deal of time and energy to researching antisemitism in eastern Europe and Russian lands alongside his political activity on behalf of Soviet Jewry at the height of the Cold War (including public campaigns against anti-Zionism), the last few decades have seen a noticeable increase in research and discussion regarding a topic that is central to both scholarly and political discussions, the "new antisemitism." According to this interpretation, the State of Israel, the history of

Zionism, and the conflict between Israel and its neighbors play an increasingly central role in current expressions of antisemitism.[37]

Ettinger himself contributed directly to these developments through a series of publications that bound antisemitism in the Soviet Union to a growing campaign against Zionism in the 1970s and 1980s. In the eyes of Ettinger and other observers, the two were not only interrelated but were also best understood as part of the same, larger phenomenon. As he declared in a pamphlet published under the auspices of the World Zionist Organization's Department of Information, "It is here that the relationship between anti-Semitism and anti-Zionism becomes obvious, for all denials notwithstanding, they are clearly one and the same and even resort to similar images and claims."[38]

In response to these developments, a growing number of scholars and activists (and those who similarly blur these ostensibly sacrosanct lines) from the other side of the political spectrum have called for the separation between research on the history of antisemitism and the emotionally charged debates regarding the State of Israel, the conflict between Israel and the Palestinians, and their connection, or lack thereof, to antisemitism. However, here as well, calls for the separation of history from politics are not without their own political implications or motivations. Time and again, the study of antisemitism resembles a scholarly hall of mirrors, from which there may very well be no true escape.

While there are a number of examples that reflect this trend of mixing scholarship and politics, none is as illustrative as the many studies published by Robert Wistrich. Repeatedly, Wistrich's works demonstrate the extent to which the realm of research and the world of politics are deeply intertwined with one another and the degree to which this tension shapes this particular realm of academic inquiry. As Judaken noted ironically in his introduction to the *AHR* roundtable, "Contemporary discussions about anti-Semitism have consequently become a battlefield, with scholarship caught in the crossfire."[39]

In the current academic battlefield of studying antisemitism, Wistrich's position was clear and unequivocal: A new form of antisemitism had arisen and taken hold over the past decades, one that directs its hatred and bile toward the State of Israel as the "collective

Jew." According to Wistrich and other observers, activists and organizations from the political left (including Jewish and Israeli ones) frequently employ the language and rhetoric of anti-Zionism to mask (or even to advance) traditionally anti-Jewish sentiments and attitudes.[40] This interpretation serves as the basis for one of Wistrich's last major works, which he published under the provocative title of *From Ambivalence to Betrayal: The Left, the Jews, and Israel*. Wistrich opens the volume with a canonical definition of the central characteristics and dangers of the "new antisemitism," including its growing conflation with anti-Zionism.[41] "The 'new' antisemitism involves the denial of the rights of the Jewish people to live as an equal member within the family of nations. In that sense contemporary antisemitism above all targets Israel as the 'collective Jew' among the nations."[42]

The position advocated by Wistrich and many other scholars and activists that anti-Zionism should be considered a central part of the "new antisemitism" has led to much protest on the part of historians and intellectuals in Israel and elsewhere.[43] From their perspective, one can protest and even oppose Zionism—and certainly many of Israel's policies—without falling prey to concepts or dabbling in language that derive from or reify antisemitic tropes.

This position has been embraced and advocated by one of the leading scholars of gender and literary theory today, Judith Butler of the University of California at Berkeley. Over the past decade or so, Butler has dedicated much intellectual energy to exploring and explicating her position on these issues, and has even published a book on the topic, *Parting Ways: Jewishness and the Critique of Zionism*.[44] Here and elsewhere, Butler maintains emphatically that anti-Zionism is not antisemitism, and that it actually represents an integral part of the Jewish intellectual tradition.[45] Pointing to the deeply political aspects of these debates, Butler notes that *Parting Ways* was written with the express purpose of debunking "the claim that any and all criticism of the State of Israel is effectively anti-Semitic."[46]

On many levels, the debate between Wistrich and Butler and their respective camps repeats earlier disputes between Ettinger and Arendt, in which a senior scholar in Israel who fervently supports Jewish nationalism and Zionism squares off against a leading female

Jewish critic of Israel who advocates for a diasporic, if not a universal, approach to Jewish society and life in the fractured, post-Holocaust universe. In fact, in one of his last essays (which was published post-humously and, therefore, probably not proofread by him), Wistrich not only criticizes Butler's universal approach to these questions but also points to Arendt's influence on her thinking. As in many other cases, Wistrich's razor tongue is absolutely unequivocal. Writing about Butler's critique of Jewish nationalism (Zionism), he charges that "such selective humanism, claiming to speak in the name of a universalistic Diaspora-oriented Judaism, can hardly claim to be 'ethical.'"[47]

The pitched battles regarding the many connections (or, alternatively, vast differences) between anti-Zionism and antisemitism and accompanying discussions regarding what is and is not acceptable public discourse regarding the State of Israel and its policies are connected to another critical aspect of the "new antisemitism": the place and origins of anti-Jewish and antisemitic attitudes in critiques of Israel in the Muslim world. Like many other scholars, Wistrich maintains that such developments reflect the larger transition of antisemitism from Christian Europe to the Islamic Middle East over the last fifty years. According to Wistrich and other advocates of this viewpoint, the sources of such tensions can often be found in Islam itself. According to these and other, similar interpretations, the conflict between Israel and its neighbors should not be understood as a political one revolving around disputed territories and limited resources but, rather, as a modern expression of an age-old, ongoing religious conflict that represents yet another chapter in "the longest hatred." As Wistrich declares in *A Lethal Obsession*:

> Terrorist exultation over violence, death, and destruction has been a key feature of Islamofascism from the outset and is intimately connected to the 'annihilationist' character of jihadi anti-Semitism.... In examining the virulent anti-Semitism of the contemporary Muslim world, one cannot ignore this more general propensity to violence nor the radically dysfunctional nature of so many Muslim societies confronted with the cultural and political challenges of globalization. Islam has remained a religion of the sword, prizing

military virtues, expanding primarily through conquest and holy war...the concept of nonviolence has virtually no place in its doctrine or practice.[48]

The position advocated by Wistrich and other scholars has been the subject of much criticism from other researchers, in particular those who embrace, or, at the very least, are sympathetic to the opposing school of thought. As part of these debates, Daniel Schroeter, a leading scholar of Jewish society in North African lands, published a critical analysis of the concept "Islamic antisemitism" in the 2018 *AHR* roundtable edited by Judaken.[49] Throughout his piece, Schroeter traces the origins of the concept and comes to the conclusion that the study of "Islamic antisemitism" is often influenced by the Israeli-Palestinian conflict as well as the manner in which key scholars like Wistrich, Rosenfeld, and others understand the conflict.

One example he points to is the case of Norman Stillman, another leading scholar of Jewish history in Muslim lands, whose work often points to the connection between anti-Jewish attitudes in the Arab and Muslim worlds and the conflict between Israel and its neighbors, including the Palestinians.[50] According to Stillman's analysis, "The birth of the state of Israel, the Palestinian refugee problem, and the resounding military defeats of 1948, 1956, and 1967 hardened and embittered Arab attitudes toward Jews generally. All of the libels and canards of European antisemitism now took on a greater resonance than ever and became commonly accepted in both elite and popular circles...This imported ideology was combined in a more or less integrated fashion with the most negative aspects of traditional Islamic anti-Judaism."[51]

Surveying central works by Wistrich, Rosenfeld, and other scholars on "Islamic antisemitism," Schroeter comes to the conclusion that many of these works are little more than political treatises masquerading as academic scholarship. Similar to Wistrich's language, Schroeter spares no punches: "This deeply flawed scholarship fails to distinguish between scholarly analysis, political advocacy, and propaganda. Many writers, including some of the leading historians of anti-Semitism, have become active publicists in a political campaign aimed at exposing the threat of Islam to Israel and the Western world. Some scholars have joined forces with organizations, lobby groups, think tanks, governmental agencies, and centers that monitor, collect, and publish data on what they consider to be 'Islamic anti-Semitism.'"[52] Moreover, while not all scholars of antisemitism in the Muslim world adopt positions as dogmatic as those espoused by Wistrich and others, these and other works demonstrate the deep-seated and potentially inevitable intersection as well as the recurrent interference between scholarly research on antisemitism and contemporary political considerations regarding the ongoing conflict between Israel and its neighbors.[53]

In fact, the repeated intersection and, indeed, pervasive sense of confusion between the academic realm and political considerations characterizes work by scholars in both academic camps. As Schroeter notes, "Both scholars of 'Islamic anti-Semitism' and their critics consequently reflect the competing and clashing narratives of Israel/Palestine, trapped in the legitimizing logic of their respective political positions and ideologies."[54]

If Schroeter is indeed correct, then the question arises: What does all this say about the current state of research on antisemitism? Or to paraphrase David Engel's essay: Does contemporary research on antisemitism reflect the historical phenomena being examined or the hefty weight of contemporary political concerns? Moreover, what influences a particular author (or reader) more when they set out to write (or read) about the past: historical sources or a scholar's intentions, temperament, or worldview? Similar to Engel's reference to the adventures of Humpty Dumpty, scholars of antisemitism repeatedly find themselves falling off their high-perched walls, tumbling to the ground, and crashing into pieces, unable—despite all of their noble efforts—to put together a convincing, holistic, unadulterated account of the past. As William Faulkner reminds us, "The past is never dead. It's not even past."

The difficulty involved in separating political positions from academic research and the incessant slip-sliding between the two only adds to the confusion and tension between the academic and the public discourses on antisemitism. As Wistrich noted ironically in his mammoth study from 2010, *A Lethal Obsession*, "Anti-Zionism has never been completely identical to anti-Semitism, but some thirty years ago it began to fully crystallize as its offspring and heir. At times it even seems like its Siamese twin."[55] Hence, many of those who research the "new antisemitism" or antisemitism in the Muslim world will claim that there is simply no way to separate between the two spheres because contemporary campaigns against the State of Israel and its (Jewish) supporters are infused with antisemitic language, allusions, and symbolism. However, even if one accepts this claim, it still does not resolve the intellectual and academic dilemmas posed by the underlying tension in the field between contemporary political debates and scholarly research as well as many of the questions raised by David Engel.

The potentially unavoidable collision between contemporary debates and academic research on antisemitism brings us to the question of emotions. Over the past few years, scholars of Jewish history have begun to explore the emotional realm in both historical research and historiography. Works by Derek Penslar, Orit Rozin, and others on the emotional aspects of the history of Zionism and the history of modern Israel have demonstrated that both the past and debates regarding the past are full of emotions, and the history and study of antisemitism is no exception.[56] It is sufficient to read only a few of the central works in the field (including those by Wistrich and Rosenfeld, on one side, and Butler and Judaken, on the other) to note the emotional overtones that characterize and, at times, seem to drive research on antisemitism, as even the most scholarly of approaches to the topic often elicit heated responses from an array of researchers who take part in spirited, at times angry, debates on the subject.

What isn't clear to us—as researchers, authors, and members of a loosely bound community of scholars—is how and to what extent these emotional undertones influence the various ways that scholars research, write, read, teach, and understand antisemitism. Indeed, almost every Jew in Israel and many of those living outside of Israel not only have a myriad of opinions about what antisemitism is but also a range of personal experiences or memories—either from actual individual encounters or those that were internalized from the historical record—related to the phenomenon. Much like many other central topics in modern Jewish history—Zionism and the State of Israel, the Holocaust, gender—antisemitism is anything but an abstract topic from a distant place and time for many observers. Thus, for many scholars of antisemitism, these questions are simultaneously historical and contemporary, personal and collective, past and present. As a result of such intense connections to the topic, individual responses often inject a range of emotions into discussions, including a mixture of sadness, anxiety, frustration, and even a fair amount of anger (or rage).

Moreover, even though it remains unclear exactly how these emotional undercurrents impact academic research, it is clear that emotions can steer research in one of several directions. One the one hand, strong sentiments can help advance research forward, giving an otherwise isolated scholar a much-needed sense of mission, meaning, and urgency. On the other hand, the emotional aspects of these scholarly endeavors might also intimidate others from raising questions or pursuing topics that might potentially offend other people's sensitivities, thus leading them to refrain (both consciously and subconsciously) from challenging accepted conventions and reigning consensus. This point touches upon a fundamental tension for many practitioners of Jewish studies (and perhaps other ethnic studies fields as well) between the social norms and accepted truisms that often help fortify ethnic or religious communities, on the one hand, and the scholarly pursuit of intellectual questions that aspires to push the boundaries of reigning preconceptions and their historical trajectories, on the other.

Aware of these and other tensions, the current volume is designed to go beyond (or at the very least to challenge) many of the reigning academic and communal truisms that shape and define the study of antisemitism. At the same time, while the volume includes contributions from a range of scholars based in Israel, Europe, and North America, the vast majority of these contributors are scholars of Jewish studies, and many, although not all of the volume's contributors, also identify as Jews, Jewish Israelis, or both. In this and other ways, the volume represents (and some may say also perpetuates) the very problem that it aims to resolve. Despite these and other inevitable limits of discourse and community, our hope is that the range of opinions and perspectives presented in the volume will add to the current debates regarding the study of antisemitism as both a topic of scholarship and a political phenomenon, and, in doing so, underscore the need to reconsider the very usefulness of the concept of antisemitism as a tool of historical analysis.

Antisemitism: A Useful Category of Historical Analysis?

This collection begins with a brief introduction by David Engel in which he reflects upon his original essay from 2009 and delineates the academic debate that has unfolded since then.[57] The fourteen substantive chapters in the volume address the subject from a variety of historical and theoretical perspectives and are organized into four separate sections.

The first section includes three articles that discuss broader theoretical and historiographical questions. Amos Morris-Reich presents Engel's thesis as an example of a contemporary historian acting as an educator who reevaluates that which is often taken for granted by questioning how his audience relates to a concept and calls for them to reexamine it. Morris-Reich's contribution also touches on a tension that runs throughout this volume between presenting Engel's discussion of antisemitism to a broader readership—and thus responding to the pressures placed on contemporary scholars to be "relevant"—and Engel's decision to address this subject within the context of the professional, scholarly discourse. Regarding Engel's call to refrain from using the concept of "antisemitism" in scholarly research, Morris-Reich argues that avoiding the term can actually harm the historian's ability to analyze and detail complex historical phenomena. Instead, he calls for scholars to analyze antisemitism amid the various historical, cultural, and linguistic factors—what he coins as "noise"—taking place at the same time and in the same historical and intellectual contexts.

Susannah Heschel's article offers an especially critical response to Engel's thesis, claiming that his approach ultimately absolves scholars from discussing the long durée of antisemitism. Heschel compares how many historians use the term "antisemitism" with how others use "racism," especially within the context of American history and the study of racism. Through this comparison, Heschel shows how here, too, despite the many questions raised by the use of a larger concept for understanding historical phenomena across generations, discussions regarding anti-Black racism can help deepen our understanding of anti-semitism. Another critical aspect of Heschel's analysis is her turn to the emotional aspects of antisemitism and her call for scholars of anti-semitism to implement lessons from the realm of "erotohistoriography" in their study of antisemitism and its impact on Jews. Drawing from the history of emotions, gender studies, and works dealing with anti-Black racism, Heschel's call to study the emotional aspects of anti-Jewish rhetoric and actions (in particular pogroms), as well as their traumatic impact on the Jewish men and women who were assaulted and raped in these moments of violence, suggests a new path that may help scholars move beyond many of the methodological dilemmas raised by Engel and other observers.

In contrast to Morris-Reich and Heschel, Stefanie Schüler-Springorum adopts a position that is far more sympathetic to Engel's viewpoint. Schüler-Springorum examines the development of anti-Jewish sentiments in several distinct eras and countries, starting with medieval Christian Spain and continuing on to modern Britain and Germany. Her article shows that in each of these cases, hatred of Jews and their exclusion as "others" is intimately bound to hostility toward and exclusion of other marginalized groups: Muslims in Spain, Catholics in Britain, and women in Germany. These diverse contexts and their far-reaching ramifications, argues Schüler-Springorum, can be clarified and understood only by means of comparative historical frameworks that stretch far beyond the narrow limits imposed on us by the study of anti-Jewish attitudes and hatred as a distinct phenomenon through the binding prism and concept of "antisemitism."

As part of our efforts to promote exchange among a range of scholars, this volume includes contributions from historians who research earlier periods in Jewish history alongside those who focus on the modern era. Addressing ancient and medieval histories, the three articles in the volume's next section shed light on and enrich discussions revolving around the question of antisemitism's historical continuity and the impact of historical contexts. The article by Adi M. Ophir and Ishay Rosen-Zvi offers readers an original and critical analysis of the history of Jews' self-separation from their wider environment. The article examines the connection between isolation and mutual suspicion in the ancient world and presents the tension between attempts to portray such differences as normative representations of intergroup relations and more essentialist accounts that highlight some of the deeper anxieties regarding the very meaning and impact of difference. The article raises a number of fascinating questions regarding the role that Jews did or did not play as historical agents in shaping the discourse that ultimately separated Jews from non-Jews in the period and offers a perspective that differs radically from the traditional view of antisemitism, which tends to portray Jews as passive victims who played a negligible role in shaping their political world and historical fate.

The next piece by Youval Rotman provides an analysis of the different concepts and terms used to describe Jews, Muslims, and Pagans in the Byzantine world. Throughout this article, Rotman shows, based on a close study of Byzantine historiography and hagiography as well as an analysis of the religio-political struggle in the Byzantine world against emergent Islam, how the hatred of Jews in this era began to fill an important role in Byzantine political culture, one that often had little connection to Jews themselves.

Tzafrir Barzilay's essay concludes this section with a discussion of violence by Christians against Jews in the Middle Ages. Focusing on the utility of concepts like "antisemitism" and "anti-Judaism," Barzilay argues against the tendency to describe the history of the Jews in the Middle Ages as that of a persecuted minority struggling against what Wistrich coined as "the longest hatred." Unlike many other studies of the topic, Barzilay joins those scholars who adopt Salo Baron's call to eschew the narrative of Jewish suffering and recommends that historians view Jewish society as part of the larger Christian environment.

The volume's next section includes five case studies devoted to the many challenges related to examining relations between Jews and non-Jews in different modern societies. Ofri Ilany begins this section with an eye-opening discussion of the concept of philosemitism, a topic that is discussed far less than antisemitism in scholarly and public realms. Ilany surveys the history of the concept and the often contradictory meanings that were given to it in the context of German history and society from the late eighteenth century until today, suggesting a need to reexamine and rethink the impact and place of the philosemitic discourse.

In his chapter on interwar Poland, Gershon Bacon accepts, on one hand, David Engel's conclusion regarding the scholarly inflation of the term "antisemitism" and joins Engel's call to use the term more judiciously. That said, Bacon also analyzes a range of historical materials from the period to demonstrate how many Jews related to "antisemitism" in interwar Poland and argues that many of them refer to "antisemitism" as one of the central problems of their time. In Bacon's view, the different historical sources available demand that contemporary scholars accept and use the term "antisemitism," especially because it was used by so many historical subjects.

Turning to the United States, Eli Lederhendler claims that, while Engel's call for scholars to focus on specific historical contexts and to avoid using the term "antisemitism" may be suitable for some limited case studies, the strategy of avoiding the term is simply unsuitable for understanding and describing larger historical events and developments. Turning to the study of race, ethnicity, and "whiteness," Lederhendler demonstrates the need to take race and racism into account when studying anti-Jewish animus in the United States and shows how this scholarship can help advance our understanding of the American Jewish experience. That said, Lederhendler echoes Bacon's approach by arguing that anti-Jewish expressions and outbursts in the United States should still be examined through the conceptual lens of antisemitism because this was how such moments were often perceived and discussed by Jews themselves.

Returning back across the Atlantic, articles by Arie M. Dubnov and David Feldman examine the history of enmity toward Jews in modern Britain. Inspired by Engel's challenge, each author emphasizes the many problems entailed by the widespread use of antisemitism as a tool of historical analysis. Dubnov surveys the history of the twin concepts of "antisemitism" and the "Jewish question" in British English and uses this discussion as a springboard to explore the complex relationship between Zionism and the British Empire, on one hand, and the connection between antisemitic and philosemitic viewpoints, on the other. Feldman presents an equally compelling analysis that compares hostilities toward Jews and Muslims (Islamophobia) over the past few decades, thus posing another, pressing challenge regarding the ostensible uniqueness of antisemitism. Dubnov and Feldman relate, each in their own way, to public aspects of the conceptual debate and discuss whether and to what extent different attempts to define antisemitism and the public campaigns against it are based on universal or parochial values.

The following section contains three articles that address the usefulness of the concept of antisemitism in the study and memory of the Holocaust. Havi Dreifuss connects her discussion of Engel's essay to the question of defining and explaining the Nazis' systematic murder of most of Europe's Jews, the Holocaust. Dreifuss claims that despite the many differences between the murder of Jews in Nazi Germany and events in other parts of occupied Europe, the many commonalities involved in these violent acts far outweigh the differences between them. As a result, any linguistic or methodological attempts to circumvent— and therefore diminish—the common aspects of this wider historical experience would inevitably lead to the blurring of the historical record. For Dreifuss, this position is critical in regard to both the Holocaust and the study of antisemitism.

In their contribution, Amos Goldberg and Raz Segal express deep reservations regarding the usefulness of the concept of antisemitism as a tool for understanding the collection of events known as the Holocaust. From their article it emerges that although antisemitism is a necessary ingredient for explaining the origins of the Holocaust, it is not a sufficient, determining factor. Moreover, according to Goldberg and Segal, it is simply not possible to understand the genocide of the Jews without considering the broader context of the nationalist and imperialist violence taking place both within and outside of Germany at the time. Their article concludes with a critical discussion of what they view as the politicized uses of antisemitism today. Here they point to political developments in contemporary Hungary as well as current debates regarding the International Holocaust Remembrance Alliance's (IHRA) 2016 "working definition of antisemitism."

This section closes with an article by Karma Ben-Johanan that juxtaposes two approaches to antisemitism undertaken by leaders in the post-Holocaust Catholic Church. The conservative approach to Jews and antisemitism ascribed the Church's anti-Jewish positions to mistaken Christian interpretations of the Old Testament, according to which the Jews were cursed and ceased to be the chosen people. The more "progressive" approach to these questions, according to Ben-Johanan, maintained that Christianity was plagued by antisemitism from the time of the New Testament. According to Ben-Johanan, the main differences between these two approaches are reflected in one's understanding of modern antisemitism, in general, and Nazi antisemitism, in particular, as well as the question of the Church's responsibility for both of these developments.

The volume concludes with a response by David Engel in which he addresses many of the claims raised in the volume's different contributions and highlights the tension between the academic study of antisemitism and spirited discussions of the phenomenon in the public sphere. Pointing to some of the responses and criticisms of the Hebrew volume that appeared on the pages of the Hebrew-language daily *Haaretz*, Engel clarifies and reiterates his opposition to the commonly held viewpoint that "*all* instances of adversity Jews have ever faced are best understood as" representatives of the same phenomenon, "antisemitism." He continues this line of thought by noting, much like Yehuda Bauer and other observers, that despite the many advances in the study of antisemitism, contemporary research has "failed to generate any consensus among scholars about which of the various" definitions of antisemitism should be accepted as the definitive interpretation of the term.[58] As part of his efforts to elaborate on and clarify these and related points, Engel proposes that scholars differentiate between "thinking about 'antisemitism' as the thought or behavior of 'antisemites' and thinking about it as a feature of Jews' own experience."[59] These parameters guide Engel through a thoughtful response that not only engages many of the critiques raised in this volume but also offers additional food for thought for scholars, students, and readers.

Several Concluding Thoughts
Regarding the Study of Antisemitism

While our discussion of these questions is bound to the current volume, the scholarly and intellectual discussion of these issues is far from complete. Ultimately, we hope that the scholarly, ethical, and political questions that the volume raises and debates will enhance awareness and sensitivity among historians and other scholars to the many dilemmas involved in turning to and using the concept of antisemitism, as well as other, similarly broad concepts and supercategories, to detail and explicate a range of historical, religious, and social phenomena. For scholars of the humanities, for whom language is very often the most important material they study and also the basic tool with which they craft their studies, this awareness and sensitivity is particularly vital. In cases like those related to the study of antisemitism, where the term enjoys such widespread use in both academic and public discourses, it is all the more important.

NOTES

1. David Engel, "Away from a Definition of Antisemitism: An Essay in the Semantics of Historical Description," in *Rethinking European Jewish History*, ed. Jeremy Cohen and Moshe Rosman (Oxford: Littman Library of Jewish Civilization, 2009), 30–53, esp. 46–47 and 51–53.

2. Yehuda Bauer, "Problems of Contemporary Antisemitism," in *Varieties of Antisemitism: History, Ideology, Discourse*, ed. Murray Baumgarten, Peter Kenez, and Bruce Thompson (Newark: University of Delaware Press, 2009), 315, 315–27. Italics in original. Also note the comment by Marcus that antisemitism is an "unquestionably problematic" term. Kenneth L. Marcus, *The Definition of Anti-Semitism* (New York: Oxford University Press, 2015), 9.

3. Also see Gavin I. Langmuir, *Toward a Definition of Antisemitism* (Berkeley: University of California Press, 1990), 311–52; Yehuda Bauer, "In Search of a Definition of Antisemitism," in *Approaches to Antisemitism: Context and Curriculum*, ed. Michael Brown (New York: American Jewish Committee, 1994), 10–23; and, Marcus, *The Definition of Anti-Semitism*, 1–55.

4. Engel, "Away from a Definition of Antisemitism," 34–35 and 44.

5. Ibid. 44.

6. Scott Ury and Guy Miron, eds., *Antishemiyut: ben musag histori lesiah tziburi* (Jerusalem: Shazar Center, 2020).

7. Here, and throughout this volume, we are borrowing from the seminal work on the study of gender, Joan Wallach Scott, "Gender: A Useful Category of Historical Analysis," chap. 2 in *Gender and the Politics of History* (New York: Columbia University Press, 1999), 28–50.

8. Engel, "Away from a Definition of Antisemitism," 52–53.

9. Robert S. Wistrich, *Antisemitism: The Longest Hatred* (New York: Pantheon Books, 1991).

10. Scott Ury, "Strange Bedfellows? Anti-Semitism, Zionism, and the Fate of 'the Jews,'" *American Historical Review* 123, no. 4 (October 2018): 1151–71.

11. Jonathan Judaken, guest ed., *"AHR* Roundtable: Rethinking Antisemitism," *American Historical Review* 123, no. 4 (October 2018). Also see Sol Goldberg, Scott Ury, and Kalman Weiser, eds., *Key Concepts in the Study of Antisemitism* (Cham, Switzerland: Palgrave Macmillan, 2021).

12. Jonathan Judaken, "Rethinking Anti-Semitism: Introduction," *American Historical Review* 123, no. 4 (October 2018): 1122–38.

13. See, for example, David Feldman, "Toward a History of the Term 'Anti-Semitism,'" *American Historical Review* 123, no. 4 (October 2018): 1139–50; Stefanie Schüler-Springorum, "Gender and the Politics of Anti-Semitism," *American Historical Review* 123, no. 4 (October 2018): 1210–22.

14. Judaken, "Introduction," 1122–23.

15. David Nirenberg, *Anti-Judaism: The Western Tradition* (New York: W. W. Norton, 2013), 11.

16. See Judaken's learned essay "Anti-Semitism, Modern," Oxford Bibliographies Online, www-oxfordbibliographies-com.ezp-prod1.hul.harvard.edu/display/docu ment/obo-9780199840731/obo-9780199840731-0072.xml?rskey=AXJLhd&result=9.

17. See Nirenberg, *Anti-Judaism,* 7, 11, 85, 91, 459, 463; Wistrich, *Antisemitism: The Longest Hatred.*

18. See Jacob Katz, *From Prejudice to Destruction: Anti-Semitism, 1700–1933* (Cambridge, MA: Harvard University Press, 1980).

19. Hannah Arendt, *The Origins of Totalitarianism* (San Diego: Harcourt Brace Jovanovich, 1979), xi.

20. Robert S. Wistrich, *A Lethal Obsession: Anti-Semitism from Antiquity to the Global Jihad* (New York: Random House, 2020), 79.

21. Anthony Julius, *Trials of the Diaspora: A History of Anti-Semitism in England* (Oxford: Oxford University Press, 2010), esp. xxiv, 8, 97, 357, 359, 441, 483, 538, 583; Dina Porat, "The International Working Definition of Antisemitism and Its Detractors," *Israel Journal of Foreign Affairs* 5, no. 3 (2011): 93–101, esp. 93–94, 99–100; Alvin H. Rosenfeld, ed., *Deciphering the New Antisemitism* (Bloomington: Indiana University Press, 2015); Alvin H. Rosenfeld, "Introduction," in *Resurgent Antisemitism: Global Perspectives,* ed. Alvin H. Rosenfeld (Bloomington: Indiana University Press, 2013), 1–7, esp. 6; Alvin H. Rosenfeld, "The End of the Holocaust and the Beginnings of a New Antisemitism," in *Resurgent Antisemitism: Global Perspectives,* 521–33, esp. 525, 528, 529; Pierre-André Taguieff, *La nouvelle judéophobie* (Paris: Mille et une nuits, 2002); Michel Wieviorka, *The Lure of Anti-Semitism: Hatred of Jews in Present-Day France,* trans. Kristin Couper Lobel and Anna Declerck (Leiden: Brill, 2007).

22. Robert S. Wistrich, *Laboratory for World Destruction: Germans and Jews in Central Europe* (Lincoln: University of Nebraska Press, 2007).

23. See Doris L. Bergen, "Nazism," in *Key Concepts in the Study of Antisemitism*, 173–86.

24. Theodor W. Adorno et al., *The Authoritarian Personality* (London: Verso, 2019); Leo Lowenthal and Norbert Guterman, *Prophets of Deceit: A Study of the Techniques of the American Agitator* (New York: Harper, 1949). Also see Jack Jacobs, *The Frankfurt School, Jewish Lives, and Antisemitism* (New York: Cambridge University Press, 2015), 82–102.

25. See *Studies in Antisemitism*, Vidal Sassoon International Center for the Study of Antisemitism, https://sicsa.huji.ac.il/studies-antisemitism-series.

26. Shmuel Ettinger, "Jew-Hatred in Its Historical Context," in *Antisemitism Through the Ages*, ed. Shmuel Almog, trans. Nathan H. Reisner (Oxford: Pergamon, 1988), 1. The original Hebrew volume appeared as Shmuel Almog, ed., *Sin'at-yisra'el ledoroteha: kovets ma'amarim* (Jerusalem: Shazar Center, 1980). For another, similar critique by Ettinger of Arendt and other thinkers, see Ettinger, "Conclusion," in *Anti-Semitism in the Soviet Union: Its Roots and Consequences*, 3 vols., ed. Jacob M. Kelman and Shmuel Ettinger (Jerusalem: Hebrew University of Jerusalem, 1979), 1: 202, 202–207.

27. Ettinger, "Jew-Hatred in Its Historical Context," 7.

28. Ettinger, "Jew-Hatred in Its Historical Context," 6. For a discussion of the "Jerusalem school" of Jewish studies, see David N. Myers, *Re-inventing the Jewish Past: European Jewish Intellectuals and the Zionist Return to History* (New York: Oxford University Press, 1995).

29. Ettinger, "Jew-Hatred in Its Historical Context," 6.

30. On the relationship between Ettinger and Wistrich, see Y. Barnai, *Shmuel Ettinger: Historion, moreh ve-ish tsibur* (Jerusalem: Shazar Center, 2011), 146.

31. See the following articles regarding controversies at research centers at Yale, Birkbeck, and Berlin, respectively: Jeffrey Herf, "Why Did Yale Close, Then Open, a Center for Studying Anti-Semitism?," *The New Republic*, July 4, 2011, https://new republic.com/article/91257/yale-anti-semitism-center; Lee Harpin, "Pears Foundation Removes Name from Antisemitism Institute," *Jewish News*, April 7, 2021, www.jewishnews.co.uk/pears-foundation-removes-name-from-antisemitism-institute; Itay Mashiach, "In Germany, a Witch Hunt Is Raging Against Critics of Israel: Cultural Leaders Have Had Enough," *Haaretz*, December 10, 2020, www.haaretz.com/israel-news/2020-12-10/ty-article-magazine/.highlight/in-germany-a-witch-hunt-rages-against-israel-critics-many-have-had-enough/0000017f-dbod-dfof-a17f-df4fa21b0000.

32. See *Studies in Antisemitism* (Indiana University Press), https://iupress.org/sea rch-results-grid/?keyword=antisemitism&series=studies-in-antisemitism.

33. A list of more than twenty-five books and volumes published between 1987 and 2015 as part of the Vidal Sassoon International Center for the Study of Antisemitism's book series *Studies in Antisemitism* can be found at https://sicsa.huji.ac.il/studies-antisemitism-series. Almost all of the works (twenty-six out of twenty-seven) examine antisemitism as a distinct form of prejudice and hatred. One exception to this

larger scholarly trend is *Critical Studies of Antisemitism and Racism*, a relatively new series published by Palgrave and connected to the Birkbeck Centre for the Study of Antisemitism in London. *Key Concepts in the Study of Antisemitism*, which was co-edited by one of the co-authors of this article, was published as part of this series. See *Critical Studies of Antisemitism and Racism* (Palgrave Macmillan), https://link. springer.com/series/15437.

34. *Antisemitism Studies* (Indiana University Press), https://iupress.org/journals /antisemitismstudies.

35. See Omer Bartov, "Genocide and the Holocaust: Arguments over History and Politics," in *Lessons and Legacies XI* (Evanston, IL: Northwestern University Press, 2014), 5–28; Donald Bloxham, "Comparison and Contextualization in the Study of the Holocaust," *Dapim: Studies on the Shoah* 25 (2011): 321–30; A. Dirk Moses, "Conceptual Blockages and Definitional Dilemmas in the 'Racial Century': Genocides of Indigenous Peoples and the Holocaust," *Patterns of Prejudice* 36, no. 4 (2002): 7–36.

36. Barnai, *Shmuel Ettinger*.

37. See Jonathan Judaken, "So What's New? Rethinking the 'New Antisemitism' in a Global Age," *Patterns of Prejudice* 42, nos. 4–5 (2008): 531–60; Brian Klug, "Interrogating 'New Anti-Semitism,'" *Ethnic and Racial Studies* 36, no. 3 (2013): 468–82; Arnold Forster and Benjamin R. Epstein, *The New Anti-Semitism* (New York: McGraw Hill, 1974), esp. chaps. 8–11; Earl Raab, "Is There a New Anti-Semitism?," *Commentary* 57, no. 5 (1974): 53–55; Scott Ury, "The Epitome of Evil: On the Study of Antisemitism in Cold War Eastern Europe and Beyond," *East European Jewish Affairs* 50, no. 3 (2020): 322–38.

38. Shmuel Ettinger, *Anti-Semitism in Our Time* (Jerusalem: World Zionist Organization, 1982), 17.

39. Judaken, "Introduction," 1124.

40. Robert S. Wistrich, "Jewish Anti-Zionism: From Critique to Delegitimization," in *Anti-Judaism, Antisemitism, and Delegitimizing Israel*, ed. Robert S. Wistrich (Lincoln: University of Nebraska Press, 2016), 135–47; Robert S. Wistrich, *Parallel Lines: Anti-Zionism and Antisemitism in the 21st Century* (Jerusalem: Hebrew University, 2017), 6–16; Alvin H. Rosenfeld, *"Progressive" Jewish Thought and the New Anti-Semitism* (New York: American Jewish Committee, 2006).

41. See the fascinating interview with the current director of the Anti-Defamation League (ADL), Jonathan Greenblatt: Isaac Chotiner: "Is Anti-Zionism Anti-Semitism?" *The New Yorker*, May 11, 2022, www.newyorker.com/news/q-and-a/is-anti -zionism-anti-semitism.

42. Robert S. Wistrich, *From Ambivalence to Betrayal: The Left, the Jews, and Israel* (Lincoln: University of Nebraska, 2012), 1. Rosenfeld echoes Wistrich's lead: "Typically expressing itself in objections to Jewish particularism and, especially, in efforts to demonize and delegitimize Jewish national existence in the State of Israel, this new version of Judeophobia is at the core of much of today's anti-Jewish hostility."

Rosenfeld, "Introduction," in *Resurgent Antisemitism*, 3. See also Porat, "The International Working Definition of Antisemitism."

43. For a particularly scathing critique of scholarship on the "new antisemitism," see Antony Lerman, *Whatever Happened to Antisemitism?: Redefinition and the Myth of the 'Collective Jew'* (London: Pluto Press, 2022), chap. 5.

44. Judith Butler, *Parting Ways: Jewishness and the Critique of Zionism* (New York: Columbia University Press, 2012).

45. Judith Butler, "No, It's Not Anti-Semitic: The Right to Criticise Israel," *London Review of Books* 25, no. 16 (August 2003): 19–21, www.lrb.co.uk/v25/n16/judith-butler /no-its-not-anti-semitic.

46. Butler, *Parting Ways*, 1.

47. Wistrich, "Jewish Anti-Zionism," 140.

48. Wistrich, *Lethal Obsession*, 71–72.

49. Daniel J. Schroeter, "'Islamic Anti-Semitism' in Historical Discourse," *American Historical Review* 123, no. 4 (October 2018): 1172–89.

50. Ibid., 1176.

51. Norman A. Stillman, "Anti-Judaism and Antisemitism in the Arab and Islamic World Prior to 1948," in *Antisemitism: A History*, ed. Albert S. Lindemann and Richard S. Levy (Oxford: Oxford University Press, 2010), 220. Also see Norman A. Stillman, "Islamic Anti-Semitism," in *New Dictionary of the History of Ideas*, ed. Maryanne Cline Horowitz (New York: Charles Scribner's Sons, 2005), v. 1, 103–105; Norman A. Stillman et al., "Anti-Judaism/Antisemitism/Anti-Zionism," in *Encyclopedia of Jews in the Islamic World*, vol. 1 (Leiden: Brill, 2010), 221–40.

52. Schroeter, "'Islamic Anti-Semitism,'" 1173. See, for example, Robert S. Wistrich, *Muslim Anti-Semitism: A Clear and Present Danger* (New York: American Jewish Committee, 2002). Also see Dina Porat, "The 'New Anti-Semitism' and the Middle East," in *Islamophobia and Anti-Semitism*, ed. Hillel Schenker and Ziad Abu-Zayyad (Princeton, NJ: Marcus Wiener, 2006), 38–40.

53. See, for example, Esther Webman, "Discourses on Antisemitism and Islamophobia in Arab Media," in *Antisemitism, Racism and Islamophobia*, ed. Christine Achinger and Robert Fine (New York: Routledge, 2017), 105–21; Webman, "The Challenge of Assessing Arab/Islamic Antisemitism," *Middle Eastern Studies* 46, no. 5 (2010): 677–97.

54. Schroeter, "'Islamic Anti-Semitism,'" 1174. Schroeter refers to Gilbert Achcar, *The Arabs and the Holocaust: The Arab–Israeli War of Narratives* (New York: Metropolitan Books, 2009); Norman G. Finkelstein, *Beyond Chutzpah: On the Misuse of Anti-Semitism and the Abuse of History* (Berkeley: University of California Press, 2005); Alvin H. Rosenfeld, ed., *Deciphering the New Antisemitism*; Wistrich, ed., *Anti-Judaism, Antisemitism and Delegitimizing Israel*.

55. Wistrich, *Lethal Obsession*, 62.

56. See Uffa Jensen und Stefanie Schüler-Springorum, eds., "Gefühle gegen Juden,"

Geschichte und Gesellschaft 39, no. 4 (2013); Derek Jonathan Penslar, "What's Love Got to Do with It?: The Emotional Language of Early Zionism," *Journal of Israeli History* 38, no.1 (2020): 25–52; Orit Rozin, "Infiltration and the Making of Israel's Emotional Regime in the State's Early Years," *Middle Eastern Studies* 52, no. 3 (2016): 448–72; Scott Ury, "The Generation of 1905 and the Politics of Despair: Alienation, Friendship, Community," in *The Revolution of 1905 and Russia's Jews*, ed. Stefani Hoffman and Ezra Mendelsohn (Philadelphia: University of Pennsylvania Press, 2008), 96–110.

57. Engel, "Away from a Definition of Antisemitism."

58. David Engel's essay "Can the Circle Be Broken?," 340, 343.

59. Ibid., 339.

2
Thinking about "Antisemitism"

DAVID ENGEL

In 2009 I published an essay entitled "Away from a Definition of Antisemitism."[1] I wrote it as part of an ongoing effort, begun more than two decades before, to determine how I might best think and write about the invidious stereotypes, defamations, discriminatory legislation, social exclusion, acts of political delegitimation, economic restrictions, and violence that I encountered in many of the aspects of Jewish history that stood and continue to stand at the center of my interest. Initially, following common practice, and without giving the matter much thought, I had referred to nearly all of these instances as manifestations of something called "antisemitism." However, I soon began to sense that neither the term nor the concept it appeared to signify helped me describe and analyze the parts of the past in which I was most interested with the clarity and the precision I sought.

At first, I attributed that sense to a difficulty in assigning the concept firm boundaries, a difficulty that many before me had noted. As early as 1923 a Dutch Zionist activist, Fritz Bernstein, had complained that whereas "an ordinary person...can distinguish with complete confidence between a live cat and a dead one..., one cannot determine with the same degree of certainty whether an incident that many people regard as unquestionably antisemitic really deserves that designation or not."[2] But did that fact by itself pose a problem? After all, human language is full of words signifying abstractions that elude exact definition but are nevertheless broadly intelligible to the people who use them. Surely, I could count upon that broad intelligibility to convey the content I sought to convey.

But I couldn't. In my early research on the Jewish question in Polish politics during the Second World War, I encountered numerous situations of a sort Bernstein had described: "There has not been even a single antisemitic occurrence whose antisemitic character has not been simultaneously denied. ... Jews too ... often stubbornly and even vehemently reject its antisemitic character, even though every bystander regards it as a clearly antisemitic episode."[3] Bernstein's work offered no way to resolve such disagreements. Nor did any of the numerous other theories or definitions of "antisemitism" that had been put forth in the meantime. I found myself hard-pressed to justify, for example, terming or not terming "antisemitic" the 1942 statement of a senior Polish diplomat, Stanisław Kot, to a group of Jewish leaders that his government would consider their request to assist Polish Jews facing death under German occupation only after they issued a declaration in favor of Poland's territorial claims vis-à-vis the Soviet Union. Kot maintained that Jews possessed unusual power over public opinion in Britain and the United States and that they should use it on Poland's behalf if they expected Poland to do the same for them.[4] The invocation of Jewish power or influence has long been considered an expression of "antisemitism." But it turned out that the person invoking it was a distinguished historian who had published a seminal piece of research debunking a common negative stereotype about the history of Jews in Poland.[5] He had also assisted at least two promising young Jewish scholars facing career discrimination.[6] Those actions were widely held, in his day and later, to reflect the opposite of "antisemitism"—"philosemitism." To complicate matters further, several Polish Jewish leaders had recently intimated to key Polish government figures that they were prepared to place what they portrayed as their considerable influence in the West (using the ostensibly "antisemitic" stereotype) at the disposal of Polish interests, with the understanding that a political payoff for them would be forthcoming.[7] And in the end, Kot actually *did* convey the Jewish requests to his government and recommend in their favor without quid pro quo. On the other hand, he had told a different group of Jewish leaders in 1940 that there were too many Jews in Poland and that most would have to leave the country once German occupation ended—a position normally associated with "antisemitic" politics.[8] The notion of "antisemitism" thus seemed not to be an especially serviceable tool for understanding the range of Kot's behavior with regard to Jewish matters.

I soon found that it could actually confound understanding of the documentary traces of that behavior. I showed the reports of Kot's 1942 statement to two senior colleagues, both accomplished historians expert in the politics of the Jewish question in Poland before and during the Second World War. One doubted their veracity: Since, as he claimed to know, Kot was not an "antisemite," he could not have put forward an "antisemitic" calumny about Jewish power. Hence, my colleague reasoned, the documents must have misrepresented his words. The second scholar reached a different conclusion from the same premise: Kot was not an "antisemite"; therefore, he could not have manifested "antisemitism" in his demand that Jews employ their power to Poland's benefit. Consequently, his move should be interpreted as an unfortunately distasteful act of political hardball in the service of his government, one that his position required him to take against his own personal feelings.

Unfortunately, neither they nor I had any empirical basis for affirming or denying either interpretation. None of us knew of any evidence testifying to what Kot felt about Jews in his heart of hearts. None of us possessed any trace of what had passed through his mind during his meeting with the Jewish leaders. Instead, both interpretations were inferred from a hidden assumption: that "antisemitism" is manifested only by "antisemites." But the sole basis any of us had for declaring that the diplomat was not an "antisemite" was the fact that he had not been identified with the political circles to which Polish Jews customarily attached the label (roughly, parties and organizations that placed the exclusion of Jews from the central institutions of Polish life among their most prominent demands). Moreover, although my two colleagues appeared to agree about an essential property of "antisemites" (advocacy in the political arena of a particular type of relations between Jews and non-Jews), they differed fundamentally in their understanding of what constituted "antisemitism": For the first, "antisemitism" was manifest *inherently* in certain utterances, whereas for the second, a given utterance could be taken as an instance of "antisemitism" or not according to the circumstances in which it was made and the intent that stood behind it. Of course, other interpretive possibilities were imaginable: "Antisemites" might express their convictions other than publicly through party identification; "philosemites" might become "antisemites" over time; Kot may simply have been advising his Jewish interlocutors about the sort of argument they would need to mount when facing government officials who had the authority, which he lacked, to act on their request; he may have believed that he was help-ing them by doing so and have felt good about it. The only basis my colleagues could adduce for preferring their interpretations over any of these was what they professed to know about "antisemitism" in general. But each claimed to know something different. I was confused.

Eventually I found a practical solution, of which more later. I also located some likely sources of the confusion through lexicographical study of how the word "antisemitism" had been used over time.[9] My 2009 essay presented the results of that investigation. To summarize briefly: Contrary to widespread belief, the word was *not* coined by Wil-helm Marr in 1879. It gained currency in the early 1880s in Germany to designate a particular set of demands for legislation aimed at mitigating damage that proponents believed had been caused by that country's 1871 removal of all restrictions on civil and political rights based upon religion. It did not signify any coherent set of ideas or beliefs; the suf-fix "ism" denoted activity (à la "baptism," "plagiarism," or "vandal-ism"), not ideology. In particular, it was not used—again, contrary to a common assertion—to indicate "opposition to Jews" based on race instead of religion. Proponents of the legislation soon applied the word to similar demands in other countries, as well as to the arguments adduced in their favor. The German *Jewish* press extended the usage even farther, applying the label to all manner of perceived threats to Jewish security present and past. That move brought two results that most Jews evidently thought beneficial: It allowed the experience of earlier generations to guide present Jewish responses, and it helped brand "antisemitism" as an irrational prejudice from a bygone era, a "misplaced bit of medievalism," as Theodor Herzl termed it, with no legitimate place in a modern, civilized world.

The negative branding campaign was effective—not at eliminating ongoing breaches of Jews' safety and well-being, to be sure, but at least at making the label "antisemite" one that perpetrators of those breaches were keen to avoid.[10] However, the same features that contributed to the success of this campaign appear to have created the conceptual muddle that has vexed scholars for the past hundred years. The campaign's effectiveness grew together with its ability to employ "antisemitism" as a single pejorative with which to tar as many perceived threats to Jewish security as possible. That ability was enhanced, in turn, by representing all occurrences tagged "antisemitism" as sharing essential elements beyond Jews' perception of them as threatening. Jewish spokesmen began to adduce such elements from as early as 1882, positing a diseased mental state, a "spirit of hostility" toward people not of "one's own kind," as the primordial force behind every "antisemitic" act or utterance. That ostensible force was labeled "antisemitism" as well, leading to the word's rapid reification. "Antisemitism" was henceforth figured as a thing, one that could perform actions in its own right, independently of any human agent: "It" could, by itself, "raise its head," "jump" from place to place, "celebrate," spread, rise, decline, change its shape, emerge, reemerge, or, like the recently discovered tubercle bacillus, mutate into more or less "virulent" strains.[11] However, unlike tuberculosis and other physical diseases produced by bacteria, which could be defined without ambiguity and whose existence could be infallibly confirmed or refuted by the microbe's presence or absence, the newly posited mental disease of "antisemitism" possessed no unambiguous physical referents. It was not subject to differential diagnosis. Its presence or absence in any situation could not be detected with any certainty. Hence Bernstein's conundrum; hence my own difficulty in characterizing Stanisław Kot's behavior in 1942; and hence my colleagues' inability to resolve it.

Bernstein had tried to work around the problem. He understood that the only way he could make any general statements about "antisemitism" was to limit the word's usage to a predefined set of cases. He chose a behavioral criterion—"dealing more favorably with a non-Jew [than with a Jew] under identical circumstances."[12] He acknowledged that this procedure could not make it possible to determine whether a given incident deserved inclusion in his set of cases or not, but he evidently believed that a sufficient number of cases could be identified clearly enough to permit him to establish the phenomenon's "essence."[13] Six decades later the historian Gavin Langmuir made a similar move using a different criterion, not behavioral but mental—"socially signif-icant chimerical hostility" toward Jews, with "chimerical" designating beliefs that "attribute with certitude to an outgroup characteristics that have never been empirically observed," like portraying Jews with horns or charging that they commit ritual murder.[14] Langmuir under-stood that the set of cases he labeled "antisemitism" was smaller than Bernstein's, but he asserted that his more restrictive standard was necessary for answering the questions, "What is antisemitism, when did it start, and why?"[15] In other words, the work-around had only pushed the difficulty from the level of individual cases to the level of definition. Moreover, each definition generated a circular argument: Different "essences" of "antisemitism" were derived from different sets of cases, each preselected for shared essential features.

Not that the selection criteria were arbitrary. Bernstein and Lang-muir formulated their definitions and chose their cases differently because they wanted to know different things. Bernstein hoped to iden-tify a set of social conditions that generated "antisemitic" behavior (by his definition) and to trace its etiology. By contrast, Langmuir sought the origins of a set of cognitive structures that he associated with the Nazi Holocaust. That fact rendered the apparent conflict between their definitions illusory. In effect, each used "antisemitism" as an algebra student might use the letter "x"—as a symbol for the value of a vari-able under investigation. For Bernstein, "antisemitism" was a stand-in for certain behaviors; Langmuir used the same symbol to represent certain beliefs. Had each used "x" instead of "antisemitism," no one would likely have perceived any difficulty in their choice of the same symbol to designate different qualities. Nor would anyone likely have imagined that, by solving for his unknown, as it were, either would have discovered any essential quality of the letter "x." Hence defining "antisemitism" in a way that could compel acceptance by revealing its indisputable essence was as insoluble a problem as squaring the circle. That Bernstein, Langmuir, and legions of other scholars have been persuaded nonetheless that they could solve it suggests that perhaps the reification process begun in the 1880s has misled them to believe that they were dealing not with a symbol but with an actual natural phenomenon.

That was the gist of the 2009 essay, presented here with some additional commentary and illustration. The findings of the investigation that had generated it also showed me a way out from the practical problem of how to deploy "antisemitism" in my own writing. The ongoing effort to attach the label to an ever-widening range of perceived threats to Jews had given the word much more connotative than denotative worth; it favored judgment over descriptive precision. But whereas descriptive precision was one of my scholarly aims, judgment wasn't. Hence the word offered me little if any added scholarly value. Why, then, use it at all?

To answer the question, I began an experiment: I would eliminate the word "antisemitism" from my professional vocabulary and see what happened. I would not simply substitute a different word for it (say, "Judeophobia" or "Jew-hatred"). Instead, I would convey what I observed with as much specificity and with the most narrowly focused descriptors available. A numerus clausus law, for example, would be called just that, or at most "discriminatory legislation." A blood libel would be labeled only as such, certainly no more than as an example of Langmuir's "chimeria." That practice, I thought, would leave open to empirical investigation the question of the precise relation between blood libels and a given numerus clausus law, whereas labeling both as manifestations of "antisemitism" implied a significant relationship a priori. I did not reject the possibility of a connection; I merely required evidence of it. In the same way, I would use no descriptor for Polish diplomat Stanisław Kot's behavior beyond what available evidence allowed, without the aid of inferences drawn from any overarching concept that the word "antisemitism" might suggest.

The experiment has gone on long enough to report its results. Since 1990 I have not used the word "antisemitism" in any of my writing when speaking in my own voice. In the interval I have published a career's worth of books and articles, most on relations between Jews and non-Jews in the modern era, many on the Holocaust. To my surprise, I have found no difficulty speaking about derogatory representations of Jews, emotional revulsion from them, invidious discrimination, or violence against them without either the word or any of the concepts it has signified. Moreover, no one seems to have noticed; as far as I know, I have not been criticized for gainsaying "antisemitism" in my scholarship or for giving it short shrift. Finally, I have almost always been able, using contextual clues, to translate others' use of "antisemitism" into more descriptively precise terms.

Many have asserted that "antisemitism" is an imperfect term but still must be used, for there is no available alternative. The results of my experiment render that claim false. Those who speak of "antisemitism" do so not by necessity but by choice. The choice requires justification. I have justified my choice to refrain from employing the word or the concept and from pursuing its definition. I await my colleagues' justifications for doing otherwise.

NOTES

1. David Engel, "Away from a Definition of Antisemitism: An Essay in the Semantics of Historical Description," in *Rethinking European Jewish History*, ed. Jeremy Cohen and Moshe Rosman (Oxford: Littman Library of Jewish Civilization, 2009), 30–53.

2. Quoted in ibid., 49.

3. Ibid.

4. See David Engel, "The Polish Government-in-Exile and the Holocaust: Stanisław Kot's Confrontation with Palestinian Jewry, November 1942-January 1943—Selected Documents," *Polin* 2 (1987): 269–309.

5. Stanisław Kot, *Polska, rajem dla Żydów, piekłem dla chlopów, niebem dla szlachty* (Warsaw, 1937).

6. Anna Landau-Czajka, *Syn będzie Lech....Asymilacja Żydów w Polsce międzywojennej* (Warsaw: Neriton, 2006), 99.

7. See, for example, David Engel, "Hahashpa'ah hapolitit shel yahadut ha'olam be'einei misrad hahuts hapolani, detsember 1940," *Gal-Ed* 24 (2015): 107–13.

8. Dariusz Stola, *Nadzieja i zagłada: Ignacy Schwarzbart—żydowski przedstawiciel w Radzie Narodowej RP (1940-1945)* (Warsaw: Oficyna Naukowa, 1995), 73.

9. By "lexicographical study" I mean something different from a study of the word's etymology, of which there were many. I was interested not in the morphological elements from which the word was constructed but in the word's pragmatic deployment in discourse after its construction.

10. See Laura Engelstein, *The Resistible Rise of Antisemitism: Exemplary Cases from Russia, Ukraine, and Poland* (Waltham, MA: Brandeis University Press, 2020), esp. 18–20, 169–76.

11. For the source of the quoted words (except "virulent," which is a later collocation), see Engel, "Away from a Definition," 45.

12. Fritz Bernstein, *Der Antisemitismus als Gruppenerscheinung: Versuch einer Soziologie des Judenhasses* (Königstein im Taunus: Jüdischer Verlag, 1980), 24.

13. Ibid., 14.

14. Gavin I. Langmuir, *Toward a Definition of Antisemitism* (Berkeley: University of California Press, 1990), 334, 336, 341.

15. Ibid., 1. Langmuir did not mention Bernstein by name, but he explicitly rejected a similar categorization, 317.

II

METHODOLOGICAL
EXPLORATIONS

3
History and Noise

AMOS MORRIS-REICH

DAVID ENGEL'S ESSAY on the development of the concept of antisemitism, perhaps the most important essay on the history of antisemitism to have appeared in the past decade or two, touches, directly and implicitly, on core questions concerning the work of contemporary historians of antisemitism. One aspect that reflects the power and significance of Engel's essay is that rather than isolating or distinguishing antisemitism from other subjects, Engel links dilemmas in the study of antisemitism with broader dilemmas that historians encounter today. He accomplishes this on several levels, starting with where he chose to publish the essay, continuing to his treatment of practical and material aspects of the work of contemporary historians, and culminating with the essay's educational message. The path by which Engel guides readers through the dilemmas of the historian—that is, the ethics that dictate how the historian ought to proceed—is, in my opinion, even more important than his conclusion, namely, that he avoids using the term "antisemitism" in his research and publications.[1]

In the first part of my essay, I analyze the contents of Engel's essay, the forum in which it was published, the educational perspectives it implies, and how Engel deals with the dilemmas of the contemporary historian. In the second part, I discuss antisemitism in greater detail by distinguishing between "antisemitism" as a signifier, concept, or category, and "antisemitism" as a historical phenomenon. I claim that the logic that Engel uses throughout his essay leads to a conclusion that differs from the one he reaches.

45

Form, Content, and Message in David Engel's Essay

I first encountered a reference to Engel's essay a year or two after its publication. Though the citation was clear, I quickly discovered that it is not that easy to obtain a copy of the essay, as it was published in a relatively marginal platform (a platform that no Israeli university would count toward promotion). Did Professor Engel anticipate that so many historians would deem his essay to be so valuable and significant? If he had known, would he have published it elsewhere? In my view, there is a connection between the forum in which Engel chose to publish his essay—an essay that reflects and synthesizes decades of his work as a historian—and the positions he develops within it. The disparity between the essay's importance, which emerges clearly from the reactions it triggered within the wider community of historians, and the fact that it was published in a relatively obscure forum undermines the accepted attitude in the academic world, namely, that the prestige of the publishing platform correlates perfectly with the scholarly value of the publication.

The essay's mode of publication can be seen as a speech act related to the dilemmas that Engel addresses in his essay. The historian's dilemmas are visible in the essay in two ways and from two perspectives that are linked to one another: The first is the demand that the historian "be relevant," and the second is what can be called the "natural language trap." Both perspectives are reflected in how the essay was published, as the volume in which it appeared was not intended for a broad audience, but for the small and predetermined community of professional historians.

In today's prevailing academic culture, there is pressure on humanities scholars, and especially historians, to be relevant. This pressure is applied both from without and from within the community of historians. This state of affairs rests on the assumption that the work of historians is not sufficient, on its own, to justify the cost of their employment. Aside from their employment as teachers, the fruits of their efforts—that is, their scholarly output—brings no, or at least insufficient, public benefit. One expression of this pressure is expressed in the expectation that historians publish op-eds in newspapers, thus demonstrating that the work of historians can have contemporary relevance.[2]

For historians of Jewish history, what could be more attractive or relevant to the *New York Times*, the *Guardian*, or *Haaretz* than an op-ed on antisemitism, a topic that is always on the public agenda? The problem is that when historians are invited to write opinion columns for the *New York Times*, they must meet the newspaper editors' expectations concerning the nature of the article. It goes without saying that it must conform to the paper's political and journalistic agenda, but, more importantly in the present context, it must meet expectations about what history is, as well as accommodate related ontological and epistemological assumptions. As a result of these larger developments, historians must also adapt their work to the significant differences between an academic journal and a newspaper article; newspapers leave no room for systematically laying out and delving into methodological considerations, and it is impossible to enter the thicket of scholarly and historiographical traditions or the historian's epistemological deliberations (and reservations) about the applicability of the work.

Perhaps most importantly of all, in our context, is the historian's educational role in thickening and hardening, or loosening and unraveling, her own cognitive categories: addressing questions that constitute the fundamental techniques of the historical discipline. A newspaper op-ed must be written so that the lay reader—the reader who can manage clever crossword puzzles, who is educated but not a trained, professional historian—can, and more importantly, would want or at least be willing to engage with it. Newspaper readers must be able to understand the op-ed without the effort (and aggravation) demanded by an academic article in a discipline in which they have little or no training.

Although Engel's essay was published in a narrow academic forum, the question of addressing the broader public clearly preoccupies him, and he recognizes the difficulty of aspiring to simultaneously address the public and the community of professional historians. Engel recognizes this difficulty and does not attempt to resolve it, to find some harmonious way to offer his knowledge to the community of historians while also making it accessible to lay audiences. On the contrary, he sharpens the dilemmas faced by historians. Whatever personal decisions we make as historians, our choices have a price. We can speak to the broader public, but then we must speak to it in its language and be responsive to its expectations; or we can speak the language of historians, at the cost of giving up on the broader public. I appreciate Engel's strategy of sharpening the dilemma, and no less, his decision in favor of professional, academic discourse that does not ignore the high price of professionalism. If historians must choose between speaking to the broader public or speaking in the specific language of historians, they must choose the latter option.

Engel expresses his choice in the theoretical introduction of his essay. Astronomers who had to decide whether to speak to the broader public in common language using popular categories or to use the specific technical language of their discipline chose to remain true to the terminology of their field. If, according to the scientific standards of their field, Pluto is too small to be considered a planet, then it follows that they must "demote" Pluto and remove it from the list of planets. Yet, their decision alienated them from the broader public, for every child knows that Pluto is a planet within our solar system. Historians who want and are even expected to speak to the broader public face a similar dilemma that is perhaps even more acute, as historians face two problems. First, historians in Israel and around the world are expected—more than astronomers or chemists are expected—to justify their existence by addressing the public at large. They are perceived as experts, and the public wants to hear their views, though in a manner that matches popular expectations, cognitive categories, and knowledge. These expectations are often far removed from the demands that guide historians within their own discipline; sometimes they are even at odds with them.

The second problem, which poses an even greater challenge, is that the professional language of historians is a natural language like the language of the broader public, in contrast to mathematicians, for example, who use a formal language. This has ramifications for the broader public's understanding and response to a published text, as well as for the public's sense that it has or has not understood what a given text signifies. In the case of a text in the mathematical language of formal notations, the public, untrained in this language, does not expect to understand it and presumes that this inability originates with its own lack of the requisite knowledge and training. However, in the case of a text composed in the same language spoken by the broader public, like historical writings in Hebrew or English, the public either supposes that it understands the text, or, if it does not, that the historian has not been clear. The broader public does not understand that the meaning of the signifier within their language differs from the meaning of the same signifier within the professional jargon of historians. This is the trap of natural language, language that is shared by historians and the wider public, and it also divides them. Here we begin to approach the thread that I wish to pursue from Engel's essay relating to "antisemitism" as a signifier, a category, and a phenomenon.

Antisemitism as a Signifier, Category, and Phenomenon

When an astronomer writes "Pluto" and a historian writes "antisemitism," the broader public presumes that it knows the subject, as it speaks the same language. The public recognizes the signifiers, knows their meanings, and presumes that the familiar meaning is what is intended by the astronomer or historian. However, it is harder for historians than astronomers to explain the difference between their use of signifiers and the meaning of the same signifiers in natural language. For example, the signifier "antisemitism" is not only a signifier in (informal) natural language, but also a part of the audience's experiential, conceptual, social, and political world. Its semantic meaning is unstable; it shifts with the movements of the historical ground, within the different historical and political contexts of its usage, which, according to the historian's definition, are biased and political. Therefore, the differences in meaning remain less visible to the broader audience than the difference between its use of "Pluto" and the quantifiable, formal measurements of the astronomer vis-à-vis Pluto.

Let us say that something happened in France or the United States, and in its wake a historian is asked to write an op-ed on antisemitism for the *New York Times*. Let us presume that the historian understands his task to be the need to clarify the connection between the signifier "antisemitism" and the historical, analytical category of antisemitism and discussing the methodological ramifications of this clarification for a historian of modern Jewish history. It is almost certain that the historian does not fully understand what the editors want and quite likely that whatever he writes will not be published. He may never be asked to write for the newspaper again. But even if such a text were published in the newspaper, it is reasonable to presume that the newspaper's readers would understand it in a manner entirely different from how an academic audience would. I suppose that the newspaper's audience would interpret such an article as bearing a clever message maintaining that antisemitism does not exist as a historical phenomenon. Yet we historians would understand that the scholar's aims are completely at odds with this claim. That is, the same words are likely to mean completely different things in academic and journalistic contexts.

This gap between academic and popular publications pertains directly to the dilemmas of the current generation of historians. The public thirsts for history, but the public's understanding of the substance of history differs greatly from that of the historian in recent generations. What the historian actually addresses—what is seen as an academic discipline that justifies the training, time, energy, and resources that are invested in it—is very different from what the broader public understands and is interested in as history. The most important aspect of this gap, in my view, is hard to articulate because it is subtle and usually implied: This is the role of the historian as a teacher.

The popularity of Yuval Noah Harari's *Sapiens: A Brief History of Humankind* is perhaps the best illustration of the public thirst for history.[3] This book has garnered millions of readers in dozens of languages around the world. Harari has managed to bring history to a very broad audience, and this is no small feat. However, we can also conclude from the book's tremendous success that the public is interested in a specific style of history, one that is very different from Engel's. Harari's book presents the public with a continuous version of history, whereas Engel lingers precisely on the twists and turns of the historian's work, the range of his discretion, and the ramifications of his decisions on the historical picture he presents to readers. Harari's readers stand directly before history. Engel forces his readers to acknowledge that there is no direct, unmediated access to the past. These are two different and even opposing views of history and also of the historian's role as an educator.

What is the educational role of the historian in today's world? The historian embodies a set of values, and the way that she treats the historical past within a specific context teaches her students or colleagues not only something about the subject but also, for example, something about knowledge in general and the importance of consistent, methodical self-criticism. The dilemma raised by Engel's essay is that professionals are unable to bring to the broader public the knowledge integrated into their training as historians, even when they are invited to express their views on public platforms. Ultimately, the fragility and instability of historical knowledge is in very little public demand as educational merchandise.

From these observations I now turn to a more detailed discussion of the explicit topic of Engel's essay: antisemitism. My point of departure is what he writes at the end of his essay, namely, that after decades of activity as a historian of Polish Jewry, he reached the conclusion that it is best to refrain from using the signifier "antisemitism." This conclusion can be interpreted in different ways depending on how one understands the relationship between the signifier—the word "antisemitism"—the historical and analytical concept and category of "antisemitism," and the historical phenomena under study. One interpretation, which can be called a "soft" approach, is that Engel claims that antisemitism as an ahistorical category cannot explain historical phenomena, even if it was part of how the "actors" or "agents" perceived the reality surrounding them. According to this interpretation, Engel negates the historian's use of "antisemitism" as an atemporal category or concept but does not refrain from using the signifier "antisemitism" when it appears within the historical materials that the historian is examining. What is negated here is not the existence of the phenomenon of antisemitism, nor of the signifier "antisemitism," but only the idea that the concept or category of "antisemitism" is static or that it crosses different eras and contexts.

A "stronger" interpretation is that Engel advocates avoiding not only the ahistorical category but also the signifier "antisemitism" even though he does not mean that antisemitism does not exist as a phenomenon. Engel has been dealing as a historian for decades with questions relating to the darkest periods of modern Jewish history—periods that cannot be understood without antisemitism. It is thus possible to see here a connection between his views on antisemitism and the role of the historian as an educator. If Engel reaches the conclusion that it is better to avoid the signifier "antisemitism" and give up attempts to define the category or concept because the benefits of such attempts are outweighed by their costs, then what can we learn from this? This conclusion is neither intuitive nor self-evident. It demands that the reader *think* about Engel's decision, about how Engel arrived at it, and about its implications for other contexts. An educator, of course, is not a demagogue; Engel does not try to force us to accept his conclusions. Rather, he leads us through the web of his own considerations, forcing the reader to think nonintuitively and emphasizing the historian's mediation on the way to his conclusion. This process illustrates the more general educational aspect of the historian's work with respect to the study of the past and the production of knowledge. This educational aspect can be called "de-idealization."

Engel's de-idealization reminds me of Max Weber's wonderful lecture, published posthumously as the essay "Science as a Vocation."[4] Weber begins his discussion with the material conditions of the scientist's work. He describes the scientist not as the embodiment of an ideal quest for truth, but as a human being who prosaically turns to a scientific career within given material and institutional circumstances. Weber then leads his audience to the inherent temporality and temporariness of scientific knowledge. He goes further, directing his lecture to an audience of emotionally, philosophically, and politically confused young students, an audience that has come to hear from the era's greatest intellectual that if they cannot find their destiny in the defeated German nation, then they can at least find it in science. Weber refuses to accede to the audience's expectations and give it what it wants to hear. Engel does something similar with antisemitism, which, as a phenomenon, signifier, and concept, is central, within our contemporary circumstances, to understanding Jewish history in general and modern Jewish history specifically.

This de-idealization is built into the trail through which Engel leads us in his essay, and it is tightly bound to the educational aspect that I discussed above. The educational aspect of the historian's work is not entrenched within an idea or a message that can be articulated wholly and positively within a book or an article. Instead, this educational aspect only takes place through the process of learning, turning to knowledge, and locating oneself vis-à-vis knowledge, reflexivity, and reservations about what we can know and about what benefit can (or cannot) be derived from this knowledge.

The educational aspect finds expression in the training of historians and in the values imparted through this training. It pertains to issues that occupy historians in their actual work, issues that constitute a large part of their work. It relates to existing historical corpora, how they shape what historians can ask about them, and the empirical lacunae entailed by them. It touches on the implications of these lacunae for the questions that historians choose to pose (specifically these and not others), what they deem important, and how they justify their choices. The educational aspect also pertains to the methodological considerations that occupy historians and the stakes of their methodological choices at the great or small junctions of deliberation and interpretation.

These methodological considerations are all expressions of the mediation between the historian and history. They are embedded in various layers of the historian's routine work and in that of the community of historians. They are embedded in the peer-review process and other pragmatic aspects of historians' work. This process forces historians to conform to the professional standards, conventions, metrics, and expectations of the field. Built into them is the recognition and understanding that the study of history is an unending process of clarification that is itself dynamic and historic, and that philosophical perspectives about history, society, culture, and humanity are embedded within it.

The dynamic or dialectic of idealization is built into both scientific work and the work of the historian. In a scientific context, idealization is a necessary form of abstraction, of separating the phenomenon studied, observed, or explained from the surrounding "noise"—that which manifests with the studied phenomenon but does not seem to be essential to it. This, for example, is what the scientist does in the laboratory by creating controlled work conditions; this is the approach of the phenomenologist who gradually separates and isolates the essence of the observed phenomenon, and this is why illustrations of organs in medical texts are not realistic: precisely to sharpen the appearance of the organ so that the student can better recognize and identify it in the patient's body. Every scientist does this; scientists differentiate the primary from the secondary because they need abstraction to better define the primary phenomenon that is their focus. There is no scientific work without idealization.

De-idealization is derived from this; it can be understood only within the necessity of idealization in scientific research. De-idealization means recognizing that it is impossible to fully differentiate the phenomenon from the "noise." Paradoxically, its importance is rooted in the fact that science, ideally, contains an element of hesitation or compromise. Thus, there is a dialectical moment within de-idealization stemming from the fact that, with respect to knowledge about the question or phenomenon studied, what constitutes a retreat on one plane is likely to be progress on a different, perhaps more important plane. De-idealization is the recognition that within both the essence of the phenomenon studied (ontology) and the study itself (epistemology), the ability to separate the primary from the secondary, the essence from the "noise," is limited.

That Engel refrains not only from defining the concept of "antisemitism" but even from using it implies a perspective on the dialectic between idealization and de-idealization in the work of the historian. That is, every attempt to refine antisemitism—to separate it from the "noise" that accompanies it in history, to define it one way or another—is doomed to failure. Engel's conclusion is, therefore, that historians studying histories interwoven with antisemitism should not try to isolate it from the "noise" with which it manifests. They must accept that the form of its manifestation does not allow for refinement and definition, and that, moreover, any attempt to reach such a definition will do more harm than good.

This conclusion, the fruit of decades of research, seems consistent with the other aspects of the essay that I discussed above: the marginal platform in which the essay was published, the mode of writing that does not shy away from the historian's mediation between the reader and history, and the de-idealization of both the phenomenon studied and the historian as researcher. This conclusion is also in keeping with the dilemma of the historian who seeks, nowadays, to reach a broader audience that includes nonspecialists. Engel's dilemma and decision do not stem from the historian's condescension toward the nonhistorian public. On the contrary, they stem from the historian's humility in light of endemic limitations within professional historical discourse, in light of the historian's inability to speak the same way to all audiences, and in light of the historian's limited place in contemporary culture. Engel's conclusion is that he must refrain from using "antisemitism" as a concept or category, or, according to the "strong" interpretation of his claim, even from using it as a signifier. He recommends that other historians adopt his conclusions.

I certainly understand Engel's conclusion, and it is consistent with everything pertaining to idealization and de-idealization in his essay. Nevertheless, I think that a different conclusion emerges from Engel's own methods and words, a conclusion that agrees with Engel's perspective on idealization and de-idealization but differs in its position on how episodes and phenomena in Jewish history can be addressed without the concept or category of antisemitism. It seems to me—and I will at least try to demonstrate—that it is impossible to understand antisemitic phenomena without a suitable category and signifiers because these three elements—phenomena, signifier, and category— have maintained reciprocal relationships throughout Jewish history.

There are historical contexts in which avoiding the term "antisemitism" is clearly faulty. This is the case, for example, in the history of branches of knowledge, science, or culture that were themselves saturated with representations of Jews, Jewish difference, Judaism, and antisemitism. In such contexts, avoiding the term "antisemitism" means avoiding a signifier, category, or concept that is built into the given discourse, field, or context. In such cases, avoiding the term is akin to omitting part of the historical picture. The past—like the present—is saturated with interests and with interested parties. Interests and biases are an essential part of the picture that historians wish to approximate in their efforts to better describe, understand, and explain. In such contexts, how members of an era understood dialogue partners, ideas, representations, and conventions is essential to the historian's understanding. If historians avoid using the term "antisemitism" in instances where members of the period in question perceive its presence, then they omit a component of the past reality and harm their ability to reconstruct it.

These, however, are relatively straightforward cases. Harder cases touch on the relationship between the signifier "antisemitism" and the historical category "antisemitism." Neither the signifier nor the category is historically stable, and the changing relationship between them is relevant to understanding many phenomena throughout the length and breadth of Jewish history. Engel's conclusion about not using the concept "antisemitism" is opposed to historical methodologies developed in the latter half of the twentieth century—such as historical semantics, the methodology developed by Reinhart Koselleck in the field of the history of political concepts in the German language (and antisemitism certainly meets that definition). The category of "antisemitism," according to Koselleck's interpretation, is not the instances or historical phenomena in which antisemitism is interwoven, nor is it the signifier "antisemitism." Rather, it is the historical, social, conceptual, or intellectual conditions that form the varying ground, background, horizon, and contours of the signifier, the category, and the social phenomena. If we do not assume the existence and variability of such a category, then the historical manifestations it is interwoven within and the meanings that can be extracted from the signifiers linked to it will remain opaque and impossible to understand.

Historical semantics is very similar to the philosophical-historical analytical framework developed by Quentin Skinner in the field of the history of political philosophy in the English language, and both are similar to the historical epistemology developed in the last generation by Lorraine Daston, who engages in the history of science.[5] All these analytical frameworks share the attempt to understand the changing reciprocal relations between signifiers and the political, social, and conceptual ground on which they stand. The historical ground is changing and unstable, but it is also vital to understanding the connection between phenomena, signifiers, and concepts.

These three conceptual frameworks also share an understanding that there is never harmony between phenomena, signifiers, and concepts, which means that the work of the historian is to trace their changing relationships within historical reality. Thus, if we try to think about antisemitism using their methods, it becomes clear that we can be content neither with the philological analysis of the signifier through the historical evolution of its meaning nor with the methods of the history of ideas, that is, the reconstruction of the opinions of these or those thinkers about antisemitism as a concept. Rather, we would have to triangulate among the world of social phenomena, the changing meanings of signifiers, and the changing ground under the concept or category. Only this triangulation enables the conceptual analysis of a phenomenon.

These three—signifier, category, and phenomenon—maintain reciprocal relationships; no one can be understood without the other two. Accordingly, the category "antisemitism" is necessary to understand the signifier "antisemitism" and related historical incidents and phenomena, even if the category is not ahistorical or fixed. I believe that such an approach follows more directly from Engel's analysis than does his dramatic conclusion. This approach also emphasizes, once again, the historian's view of his work: Only he can explain the relationship among the three. In the context of the study of antisemitism, it seems to me that the two volumes by Saul Friedländer on Nazi Germany and the Jews constitute a clear example of the sort of triangulation that I describe here.[6]

The complex relationship between context, the signifier "antisemitism," and the category "antisemitism" can be seen, for example, in the history of science and medicine—more specifically, in the concepts of race and eugenics during the Second Reich. In retrospect, the father of German eugenics, Wilhelm Schallmayer, belongs to the contemporary trend of the racialization and biologization of society and culture. This trend marked Jews as biologically different from the non-Jewish German populace. This biologization was an integral part of the historical category of "antisemitism" within nineteenth- and twentieth-century history. However, no antisemitism can be attributed to Schallmayer: He worked on a team with Jewish colleagues, most of whom were doctors; he did not view himself as hostile to Jews, and certainly not as an antisemite; and he was not viewed as an antisemite by his Jewish colleagues. Thus, the signifier "antisemitism" is external and foreign to this historical phenomenon, namely, eugenics.

A change within the category "antisemitism" is also needed to understand the polymath Felix von Luschan, the great (non-Jewish) Austrian archaeologist, ethnographer, and linguist. Von Luschan developed a theory that Jews are descendants of the ancient Hittites who lived in regions of Asia Minor, what is now Turkey. His contemporaries understood very well that his views stemmed from his rejection of the antisemitic claim that Jews, from a racial perspective, are Semites. Today it is difficult to avoid ascribing ambivalence about modern Jews to von Luschan. However, he was not an antisemite and was not seen as an antisemite within his environment, not even among his Jewish interlocutors. On the contrary, he explicitly wrote and acted against political antisemitism. Many viewed him as a friend and supporter of Jews, to the extent that long after his death, Arthur Ruppin referred to him in his publications as *"mori ve-rabi"*—"my master and teacher"— a term of reverence traditionally reserved for rabbinic mentors. In this context, as in the case of Schallmayer, the important element is not the signifier "antisemitism" but changes within the philosophical, scientific, and cultural conditions in which historical phenomena rife with antisemitism occurred, and in which the signifier "antisemitism" can indeed be found.

The complex reciprocity underlying the relationship between antisemitism as a category or concept, a signifier, and a phenomenon can be seen when we move from Schallmayer and von Luschan to Eugen Fischer, who is considered the founder of the field of human heredity. Along with the slightly older Schallmayer and von Luschan, Fischer belongs to the broad historical trend that witnessed the biologization and racialization of social and cultural phenomena. Fischer was unquestionably no friend of the Jews, and Jews did not perceive him as their friend. But it was only much later, following Germany's invasion of Poland in 1939, that Fischer used explicitly antisemitic signifiers and his language became more radicalized. My point is that this later stage of using antisemitic signifiers cannot be understood outside the changes wrought to the category "antisemitism," which, in this case, manifested in the biologization of Jews, their religion, their culture, and their language—in other words, in every aspect of their material constitution.

Nevertheless, comparing Schallmayer and von Luschan to Fischer reveals different relationships between the category and the signifier: Schallmayer and von Luschan are part of a change in antisemitism as a category, a change that constitutes a necessary condition for understanding the signifiers and phenomena in Fischer's context. There are many more examples of this, but the main idea that I am pointing out is the incongruity between the category, the signifier, and the phenomenon, all three of which are necessary for historical understanding of the phenomenon of antisemitism in each and every case. If we omit even one of them, the resulting historical analysis will be, in a fundamental historical sense, weaker and more deficient.

The analysis of historical phenomena thus hinges not only on the historian's understanding of the relationship between signifier and category. It also necessitates an understanding of how the historian perceives the historical actors' understanding of the relationship between the signifier and the category. Today's historian understands the attitudes of Schallmayer and von Luschan toward antisemitism (the relationship between the category and the signifier) differently than how they and their contemporaries understood them, and historical and sociological understandings of actors' subjectivity have changed as well.

In today's civic-political environment, the subjective perspective within an objective portrayal is clearly important. This is made explicit in Great Britain, where the subjective feelings of minorities (of which Jews are an example) constitute an important component of surveys designed to investigate objective levels of discrimination. This follows from the view that subjective experience is essential to what the survey seeks to measure. Hence, the feeling of Jews that certain ways of speaking about the Holocaust or the State of Israel are infected with antisemitism is an indicator that they are indeed so. In other words, the historian should be attentive to the voices of historical subjects and should be sensitive to their subjective perceptions.

This changing subjectivity is a component of a complete historical portrayal. That is, without this subjective component, it is impossible to understand the history of the racialization of Jews or the changing relations between Poles and Jews. Yet even if the historian must consider how people of the period understood the events around them, she is not bound to that understanding. Ruppin did not think that von Luschan was linked to antisemitism; a later historian can see how von Luschan's activities were part of a trend to biologize and racialize Jews, without which it is impossible to understand Fischer, who, without a shadow of a doubt, is part of the history of antisemitism.

It is important to emphasize that the goal of my analysis is methodological and heuristic, not judgmental. Understanding the changing reciprocal relationship between signifiers and categories in a given historical context enables the examination of their shifting meaning throughout history. Such a framework allows for a view that antisemitism is historical in a multilayered sense; its meaning can change, occasionally beyond recognition, both diachronically and synchronically. The changes are never just semantic, features of the signifiers or what they signify; they manifest a dynamic historical category that changes throughout history and that is necessary for understanding historical contexts and phenomena.[7]

Changes in the category "antisemitism" can be detected only by cross-referencing semantics with social circumstances. This view of Koselleck's is similar to that of Jeffrey Alexander, an American Jewish sociologist who developed cultural sociology. Alexander emphasizes— not from the perspective of the concepts, but from the "other side"—that the discursive frameworks of the possible meanings of signifiers and concepts themselves change throughout history, sometimes unrecognizably.[8] The historian tracing how people of a certain period judged the self-expression of scientists or producers of culture does not do so from her own, contemporary perspective, but by reconstructing the discursive and symbolic structures of the period studied. The historian's interest in how people of a certain period were judged by their contemporaries does not mean that she accepts these judgments; instead, she regards them as necessary for historical contextualization. It follows that, contra Engel's conclusion but consistent with the internal logic of his presentation, the historian cannot avoid the category or concept "antisemitism" if she wants to understand the signifiers and contexts she is studying. For without the category and concept, all she has before her is a random collection of events. The historian cannot relinquish the category "antisemitism," not because she strives to define it, but because it is impossible to understand history without it.

Conclusion

I conclude with another comment about broader trends in the contextualization of antisemitism over an extended period of time. If nineteenth-century historians viewed history as the product of necessity, and twentieth-century historians—at least in the latter half of the century—tended to view history in terms of contingency, coincidence, and randomness, historians of the twenty-first century view history as the gray area between these two extremes. Even if history is not inevitable in nineteenth-century terms, neither is it completely free of structure, direction, and inherent tendencies. In other words, its uncertainty is not equally open-ended in all directions.

The final reference in Engel's essay is to David Nirenberg's first book, *Communities of Violence*. Engel praises Nirenberg and views him as a fellow traveler. It seems that the approach that Engel takes in his essay is closer to Nirenberg's approach in this book than to that in his second book, *Anti-Judaism: The Western Tradition*, which appeared after the publication of Engel's essay.[9] Comparing two objects emphasizes and draws immediate attention to the differences between them. In the title of this book, Nirenberg takes care not to use the word "antisemitism," and also distinguishes his approach from that of Robert Wistrich, for example. However, he nevertheless tends to recognize the constant presence—beyond temporal and local contexts—of a tendency and structure within and throughout Western history. True, Nirenberg does not define a transhistorical concept or category, but it seems that he acknowledges something of the sort. In *Anti-Judaism*, then, Nirenberg presents the opposite of the approach that he takes in his first book, *Communities of Violence*.

Yet one only has to zoom out just a little bit to recognize that the two books have several things in common. Their commonality can be described in terms of the dynamic of de-idealization: The commonality can be found in the swing of the pendulum from the contingency and non-inevitability of history, which characterizes twentieth-century historical thinking, to the other extreme, which views history as stable and even inevitable. There are historians claiming that, by measurable indices (economic, social, and even cultural), one cannot speak of antisemitism in Western societies today, and so they implicitly or explicitly offer a new view of the world, one that differs greatly from that of pre–World War II history.

Yet we must recognize that whether the historian strives for a definition or avoids it, history is not entirely free of relatively stable structures, patterns, and tendencies. This insight may have no place in public, political discourse, but it is part of the educational role played by professional historians as they navigate the shifting grounds and relationships between antisemitism, Jewish history, and history in general.

NOTES

1. David Engel, "Away from a Definition of Antisemitism: An Essay in the Semantics of Historical Description," in *Rethinking European Jewish History*, ed. Jeremy Cohen and Moshe Rosman (Oxford: Littman Library of Jewish Civilization, 2009).

2. Jo Guldi and David Armitage, *The History Manifesto* (Cambridge: Cambridge University Press, 2014).

3. Yuval N. Harari, *Sapiens: A Brief History of Humankind*, trans. John Purcell and Haim Watzman (New York: Harper, 2015).

4. Max Weber, "Science as a Vocation," in *The Vocation Lectures*, ed. David Owen and Tracy Strong, trans. Rodney Livingstone (Indianapolis, IN: Hackett, 2004), 1–31.

5. Reinhart Koselleck, *The Practice of Conceptual History: Timing History, Spacing Concepts*, trans. Todd Samuel Presner (Stanford, CA: Stanford University Press, 2002); Reinhart Koselleck, *Futures Past: On the Semantics of Historical Time*, trans. Keith Tribe (New York: Columbia University Press, 2004); Quentin Skinner, *The Foundations of Modern Political Thought: Volume I: The Renaissance* (Cambridge: Cambridge University Press, 1978); Quentin Skinner, *Volume II: The Age of Reformation* (Cambridge: Cambridge University Press, 1978); Lorraine Daston, *Classical Probability in the Enlightenment* (Princeton, NJ: Princeton University Press, 1995); Lorraine Daston and Peter Galison, *Objectivity* (Boston: Zone Books, 2007).

6. Saul Friedländer, *Nazi Germany and the Jews: Volume 1: The Years of Persecution, 1933–1939* (New York: HarperCollins, 1997); Saul Friedländer, *Nazi Germany and the Jews, 1939–1945: The Years of Extermination* (New York: HarperCollins, 2007).

7. See, first and foremost, the lexicon of basic historical concepts that Koselleck initiated and edited: Otto Brunner, Werner Conze, and Reinhart Koselleck, eds.,

Geschichtliche Grundbegriffe: Historisches Lexikon zur politisch-sozialen Sprache in Deutschland (Stuttgart: Klett-Cotta, 2004).

8. Jeffrey C. Alexander, *The Civil Sphere* (Oxford: Oxford University Press, 2006).

9. David Nirenberg, *Communities of Violence: Persecution of Minorities in the Middle Ages* (Princeton, NJ: Princeton University Press, 1996); Nirenberg, *Anti-Judaism: The Western Tradition* (New York: W. W. Norton, 2013).

4
Erotohistoriography
Sensory and Emotional Dimensions of Antisemitism

SUSANNAH HESCHEL

David Engel asks if the term "antisemitism," when applied to a variety of incidents, distracts us from the uniqueness of each and fosters a generalization that distorts rather than illuminates. Because the term can refer to hostilities ranging from discrimination to violence, hostilities based on political, racial, or religious grounds, and hostilities that were not intended or perceived as such, it gives rise to a "conceptual muddle." The term "antisemitism" becomes essentialized and reified, Engel argues, as if it were a causal agent: Jews are attacked because of antisemitism. Engel is correct: Blaming "antisemitism" for denigrating language, images, or even violence directed against Jews and Judaism shifts agency from human beings to an ideological construct. Used that way, antisemitism functions as one of the long-discredited "covering laws" that fail to explain.

Yet Engel goes too far in asserting that "no necessary relations among particular instances of violence... can be assumed."[1] Scholars of racism would never make a similar claim, nor would a scholar of race view the term "racism" as a socio-semantic error. The enslavement of Black Africans by American whites in the eighteenth and nineteenth centuries has a clear and essential relationship to the lynching of Emmett Till in 1955 and the growing mass incarceration and police murders of Black Americans today. Denying a link between discrete acts ignores the trajectory of racism, fails to recognize the tenacity of white people's loathing of people of color, and blinds us to the depth and longevity of racism—indeed blinds us to racism as the fundamental axis of the United States.

Racism and antisemitism are not identical, though some of their manifestations are similar; for example, aspects of the 1921 "race riots" in Tulsa bear similarities to the pogroms in eastern Europe in the 1880s. Neither occurred in a vacuum; images and ideas about Blacks and Jews instill a thick, sticky cultural "knowledge" that is hard to eradicate. "Once established in the mind-set," writes the philosopher Charles W. Mills, "influence is difficult to escape, since it is not a matter of seeing the phenomenon with the concept discretely attached but rather of seeing things through the concept itself."[2] Hostility toward Jews has a *longue durée*, influencing not only recurrent violence against Jews but also unarticulated motivations that shape the social fabric. Antisemitism is its own tool of power, a weapon that is of lethal danger to Jews and of considerable danger to non-Jews as well; antisemitism can fuel misogyny, and right-wing anti-Black racism in the United States usually coexists with antisemitism.

Antisemitism's chameleon quality demonstrates its significance: No matter whether right-wing or left-wing, nationalist or communist, Christian or secular, antisemitism remains a powerful tool for rhetoric, action, and emotion. Significantly, it is precisely the ability to conceal or disguise themselves that gives both racism and antisemitism power. Yet similarities are not explanations; as Shulamit Volkov argues, antisemitism forms the background for National Socialism but does not explain it.[3] Antisemitic and racist violence are increasing, but antisemitism and racism do not explain why this is happening at this moment.

In their famous analysis, Frankfurt School theorists combined social critique and psychoanalytic theory to understand the appeal of antisemitism and its links to fascism. More recent methods developed by scholars of anti-Black racism and of gender theory might deepen our understanding of the tenacity of antisemitism. In particular, scholars of anti-Black American racism include the traumatic impact of racism on Black people in ways that scholars of antisemitism generally do not. Saidiya Hartman writes of the "erotics of terror" in her studies of American enslavers, taking us beyond social constructionism and theatricality.[4]

Drawing on Hartman's work and that of Frankfurt School theorists,

I propose that scholars of antisemitism include an "erotohistoriography" in their analyses of antisemitism and its impact on Jews. I borrow the term from the queer theorist Elizabeth Freeman (though she uses it in a very different context)[5] to question the deeply embodied emotional and sensory pleasures antisemites derive from their racist beliefs and actions, and to analyze the Jewish trauma antisemitism creates. I use the term "erotohistoriography" to encompass the range of theorizations developed by scholars of anti-Black racism, the history of emotions, affect theory, feminist theory, psychoanalysis, whiteness studies, critical race theory, and theories of religion. These theorizations point to the gendered and sexualized aspects of antisemitism in its various manifestations, whether theological or political, in images or with violence. Freeman speaks of erotohistoriography as "a politics of unpredictable, deeply embodied pleasures that counters the logic of development" and shapes historical consciousness.[6] Her formulation offers a logic to the illogic of antisemitic eruptions and the gratification they offer.

Anti-Black racism and antisemitism fortify each other so that antisemitism cannot be studied in a vacuum. Blacks, Jews, and Asians face the "invisibility" of whiteness and gentile-ness. Neither is simply a matter of skin color or being a "non-Jew." More than identities, they are privileged property that is defended at all costs against policies that promote anti-racism, feminism, gay marriage, and other politically progressive principles of equality and human rights, policies that white supremacists blame Jews for promoting. Right-wing white nationalism justifies itself with antisemitism;[7] "white nationalists see a Jewish stranglehold on American society that fuels multiculturalism and feminism and hence accelerates white extinction, constituting the largest obstacle to the white ethnostate."[8] Jews are denounced for replacing whites, Black achievements are condemned as undermining the social fabric, and antisemitic associations of Jews with disease are projected onto Asians. The Left focuses primarily on condemning the State of Israel and anyone associated with Zionism and identifying Jews with imperialism and colonialism. As conspiracy theories skyrocket, Jews are blamed by the Right and the Left for AIDS, the 9/11 attacks, running ISIS, and controlling global finance.

Antisemitism and racism are not only about negative depictions of degeneracy, but also about creating a fear of being vulnerable to that degeneracy. That fear overrides all other political concerns and demands the expulsion of the dangerous people. Together, antisemitism, anti-Black, and anti-Asian racism constitute the foundation of white supremacist ideology enacted in gendered and sexualized aggression. Indeed, some whites in the United States vote against their own economic interests to keep benefits from Black Americans. Antisemitism reconfigures Christian identity as the anti-Jew "who can remain a Christian only by never mingling with Jews."[9]

What is antisemitic pleasure? The continued appeal of antisemitic tropes suggests a deeper, hidden level of desire that requires attention to understand the gratification antisemitism seems to provide and the reasons for its persistent power. Scholarly attention to affect, emotion, gender, sexuality, and their resonances in the body and senses points to the erotic pleasure experienced in the verbal and physical cruelty of racism and antisemitism; such investigations are also erotohistoriography. Racist expressions are not concrete and logical but slippery and contradictory. Enslaved Africans were often entrusted with the highest responsibilities—caring for white children, for example—yet at the next moment falsely accused of raping white women, then sadistically tortured or lynched by their white enslavers.[10] That Jesus was a Jew at times connected the two religions, but at times was perceived as threatening to Christian uniqueness and denied.[11] Although Jesus became the phallic signifier of the West, on the cross he was female: pierced, wounded, and bleeding.

Engel is correct that antisemitism does not exist in a straight historical line of continuity. Rather than abandon the term, however, I suggest a different way of conceptualizing antisemitic history. Drawing from the theorist of queer temporalities, José Esteban Muñoz, I suggest that antisemitism is never enclosed by a chronological trajectory; rather, antisemitism is better conceptualized as a reservoir of possibility waiting to be activated by the present.[12] In the unconscious, time is not linear, and there antisemitism lives in its nest of fantasies, waiting to be activated. Myths, images, and ideas of the past can erupt in the present, and Nietzsche's genealogical analysis of ruptures and eruptions rather than lines of continuity should be marshalled to understand how antisemitism works. Antisemites are experienced by their victims as revivifications of the past; in the realm of the imagination, the present is experienced as a revival of the past.

Historians may identify proximate causes of each event, but gene-alogies mobilized by antisemites are experienced by their victims as revivifications of the past; in the realm of the imagination, the present is experienced as a revival of the past. Thus we can understand Shylock's insistence on his bond resurrecting Christian fantasies of Jews as carnal, legalistic, and lacking mercy. Only rarely are the language and images of antisemitism new and original; they recreate what has already been articulated in the past, revivifying hostility. Hartman writes, "I, too, live in the time of slavery, by which I mean I am living in the future created by it."[13] Both Jews and antisemites live in the future created by the past, heirs to a history they may not consciously recognize.

The Violence of Silence

Whereas Eichmann was antisemitic without being vocal, antisemitism can be voiced without being enacted. Think of the loud antisemitic voices of influential ideologues who never killed a Jew—such as Richard Wagner, Heinrich von Treitschke, H. S. Chamberlain, Father Charles Coughlin, or Henry Ford. They never physically attacked a Jew, but they shaped a rhetoric of emotion and language that revivified older motifs, creating a cultural ethos for modern use, whether in the Third Reich or contemporary American political campaigns that associate Jews and money. Only rarely are the language and images of antisemitism new and original; they recreate what has already been articulated in the past, reinscribing trauma as they revivify hostility.

The past can also exist as silence in the present, for example in the omission or denial of racist and antisemitic history. Racist words do not inevitably lead to violence, and violence can occur in the supposed "absence" of racist rhetoric; that is, racist rhetoric is embedded in the imagination and does not require verbal articulation to spur violence. We now know that Adolf Eichmann was antisemitic, though he did not rant against Jews, and that the "banality of evil" that Hannah Arendt identified was not banal.[14] Eichmann kept his antisemitism quiet during the trial, and we wrongly assume that the power of antisemitism lies in its public display, as if it doesn't exist if it is kept secret.[15] Yet as a "desk murderer," Eichmann's secret antisemitism was intensified. By enacting indifference through silence, Eichmann relegated Jews to the status of nonhumans outside the realm of the ethical, and his anti-semitism annihilated millions of Jews.[16]

In postwar interviews, the "ordinary men" of Nazi police battalions who murdered Jews in eastern Europe also did not rant against Jews, nor did Franz Stangl, commandant of Treblinka, who was convicted of the murder of 900,000 Jews.[17] Their denial of antisemitism as their motive for murdering Jews is disingenuous, as if Jews are not even wor-thy of being hated. Secret, silent antisemitism has its own power. Not rowdy and enthusiastic, it is seductively quiet and self-possessed, aloof, cultivating an air of mystery, yet easily genocidal. Nazi antisemitism was loud and vociferous, not silent, yet silence about antisemitism's role in Nazism continues in some scholarship.

Even when subtle, rhetoric can have a murderous impact because language possesses affect that is often long lasting. Think of the thou-sands of Black Americans who were tortured and lynched by white men and women, often right after Sunday church services. No political rallies or racist rants in church led a community of white men, women, and children to capture, torture, and murder a Black man (or woman), yet such violence could occur after Gospel readings and hymn singing.[18] Did whites consider lynching Black people a response to Christian wor-ship? Christian religious services were also held at Nazi concentration camps, led by pastors and priests. Presumably nothing was spoken explicitly at these religious services against Blacks or Jews to encourage their murder. Motivations may not be verbalized and thus elude the most careful empiricist historian. We might instead consider motiva-tion aroused in a different, emotional register: Attending a religious service affirms a sense of moral self-righteousness that overrides moral inhibition, social convention, and laws against murder, and generates social cohesion. Even when racist rants were absent from the church service, lynching was no less a racist act, and the murder of Jews by *Einsatzgruppen* was no less antisemitic if the murderers claimed they were simply following orders. Rhetoric does not require articulation in the moment but can be revivified as unspoken passions demanding fulfillment.

Antisemitism as Intimacy

Numerous studies have detailed the language and images of anti-semitism; scholars in nearly every discipline have detailed the various functions of antisemitism—economic, political, religious, psychologi-cal. Yet the overriding question is: What makes racism and antisemitism so appealing and tenacious? Conventional correlations of finances, social status, and educational level with racist beliefs fail to explain the ability of racism to override issues of personal relevance, such as jobs, health care, or education. That leads to a deeper register: The tenacity of racism makes us wonder what deeper gratifications it offers, and at what intimate level it has hitched itself to our minds. Antisemitism arises not because Jews are "other," but because Jews are felt too inti-mately, as evidenced in the explosion of antisemitic violence against neighbors in a pogrom or in the spontaneous murder of the Jews in the village of Jedwabne, Poland. Medieval Christian hostility was not directed toward a distant religion, but toward Judaism, the foundation of Christian beliefs and the religion of Jesus and Paul; no other two religions stand in such intimate relationship.

While intimacy may generate empathy, it may also enhance sadistic gratification. The "erotics of race" points to the pleasure experienced in the sadism of racist denigration, a feeling of transgression and excite-ment that seems to overcome, at least temporarily, self-denigration. Enslavement was governed not only by economics and politics, but also by a dangerous, racist sadism that is deeply ingrained and difficult to eradicate. Indeed, race is a concept we learn from society, a social category of identity that becomes "integral to a deep sense of self," as the psychoanalyst Farhad Dalal, among others, argues.[19] Antisemitism, too, is a regime of emotion demanding gratification. Antisemitic ide-ology is seductive, all the more so when antisemitism spreads—we are more likely to find antisemitism appealing when it is widespread in our society.

Religion turns the present into the future of the past. Watching the Christian passion play at Oberammergau (Germany) in 1934, the audience, seeing Jesus hoisted onto the cross, screamed, "There he is. That is our Führer, our Hitler!"[20] Hitler as Christ was crucified but also resurrected to resurrect the German *Volk*. As a theologian wrote, "Here [with Hitler] God Himself is dealing with the German people."[21] Theologians spoke of "Führer Jesus" and described Hitler as "God's agent [*beauftragter*] in our day,"[22] declaring, "Our *Volk* is in a struggle against the satanic powers of world Judaism."[23] Religion encourages the present to participate in the *Heilsgeschichte* (salvation history) of the past. Pastor Julius Leutheuser wrote, "The Reich of the Germans is for us similar to the eternal Kingdom of God. For us, belief in Germany is a touchstone of our faith in God. Our love of Germany is a measure of our love for the Eternal...It was for us as if Christ had traveled through Germany and Adolf Hitler was his mouth."[24] If the Jews killed Christ, then Hitler became the Christ who promised revenge against them, fulfilling Christian Heilsgeschichte. Love of God became devotion to Hitler.

Precisely the affect underlying antisemitism makes it powerful, haunting us because after a while, ideas and images become entrenched in the unconscious and terribly difficult to extricate. Like hidden bias or implicit racism, unconscious antisemitism concealed as unconscious fantasies can explode as violent attacks on Jews. Dracula, the mythic vampire from Transylvania in Bram Stoker's eponymous novel, is a figure that both conceals and transmits antisemitic tropes.[25] Though Dracula is not identified as a Jew, blood sucking, as a metaphor for usury, has long been coded as "Jewish." Penetrating the bodies of "innocent women" by sucking their blood, Dracula turns them into vampires and enacts the fear of the Christian West: Infection with Jewish blood that can only be stopped by the Christian cross. Here the Jew is a male rapist; Christians are virginal women. The Jew does not inject his semen but, like an animal, draws blood with his biting mouth and makes his victim drink his blood, turning her into a vampire, the Christian becoming a Jew. Precisely that fear of the dangerous male Jew who will suck Christian blood expresses the terror that Christianity itself is a baptized Judaism that might at any moment return to its fallen state of Judaism.

Rape

In her book on the pogroms that took place in eastern Europe after World War I, the historian Irina Astashkevich concludes that "the mass rape of Jewish women occurred in at least two-thirds of pogroms and often involved the majority of the Jewish female population in the victimized community... tens if not hundreds of thousands of Ukrainian Jewish women were victims of sexual violence and many more Jewish men and women witnessed it."[26] This evidence includes women's own accounts and investigations by journalists and writers in the aftermath, especially of the Kishinev pogrom of 1903. Women, some pregnant, some with young children, wrote and dictated reports of being assaulted in horrific ways, often multiple times by many men, including neighbors. Some were then shamed and rejected by their husbands and families—with rabbinic approval—reinforcing the goal of mass rape: the destruction of the community.[27] Some women became pregnant, and the children born of rape were often abandoned; some women died by suicide. The consequences lasted for generations. Though women gave detailed testimony of the horrific rapes they endured, "a pall of silence stifle[d] the public discourse."[28]

The shame thrown on these women continues in the disregard of rape in some contemporary historical scholarship. For example, a recent volume regarding pogroms in eastern Europe includes the statement: "In addition, thousands of women were raped."[29] And nothing more. Another historian asserts, without citing evidence, that "while rapes undoubtedly did occur, they were not a widespread phenomenon. In particular they were not accompanied by murder and mutilation."[30] In another recent study of emotions among pogrom perpetrators as well as Jewish efforts at armed self-defense, the word "rape" does not even appear.[31]

Some contemporary scholars who mention rape present women as passive victims, reproducing the influential Jewish literary and political responses to Kishinev that viewed the Jewish collective as dishonored, passive victims of violence. The Hebrew poet Hayim Nahman Bialik, for example, used rape as a metaphor for the "national and sexual weakness" of Jews, as did Zionists and socialists.[32] In their view, the Jewish collective usurps the role of the raped female without questioning the gendered politics of shame and the violence of rape; as in Judaism itself, the women victims have no voice about their own experience.

Rape mutilates women's lives in every imaginable way and affects the lives of their families as well, including men, because rape is a sexualized tool of political violence; precisely the body part with which women express love is now subjected to horrific violence. Rape tells a woman: Your body does not belong to you; "rape is the essence of unfreedom."[33] The consequences of the brutality include death, disease, painful and permanent deformities, infertility, incontinence, and constant pain. The emotional consequences of rape shatter a woman's sense of self. "History is what hurts," writes Frederic Jameson, and historians should be attentive to that hurt.[34]

Religiocide

Pogroms are violent riots with multiple aims—rampant, uncontrolled destruction and looting, beating, raping, and killing without compunction. They function as public theater, spectacles whose purpose is to humiliate and degrade. Economic tensions may have been a spark, but the destructiveness did not enrich the perpetrators. Most striking is pogrom intimacy: violence directed against neighbors and friends, for instance a Jewish woman raped by a Christian man whom she had cradled as an infant.

In medieval Europe, Christians attacked Jews, often claiming retaliation for alleged desecrations of Christianity. In the modern period, Judaism was attacked for causing social degeneration. Rape emphasizes intimacy and adds an extra dimension: Assaulting women with rape is also religiocide, an attack meant to destroy Judaism. Like those of most religions, Judaism's gender binary and laws regarding sexuality and purity are foundational, starting with the Bible and Talmud. Rabbinic law discusses the vagina more than any other single body part and has meticulous regulations concerning heterosexual intercourse; violating the laws of menstrual impurity, for example, is punished by being banned from heaven after death. Rape also attacks Judaism's purity codes of gender and sexuality, the heart of the religion. Pogrom rapists knew they were polluting Judaism: "It seems like you haven't slept with a Gentile yet. Now you will know the taste of one."[35] Mass-perpetrator rape, especially in the context of widespread violence, seeks the shame and destruction of women, their families and communities, and also targets their religion; it is genocidal and it is also "religiocidal." The Marquis de Sade presented sexual debauchery as achieving its greatest pleasure when it occurs in a church, shaming Christianity. Mass rape in a pogrom enacted a comparable scene: defiling Judaism by raping women.

Antisemitism as Seduction

Erotohistoriography signifies not only attention to emotions and feelings of hate, disgust, or envy in antisemitic texts, but also to the seductive way antisemites win adherents and the pride and glory they cultivate in their followers. The strategy of *Mein Kampf* is a good example of antisemitic seduction. Opening with a friendly, welcoming description of his youth in Linz, Hitler then brings the reader to Vienna, a city he describes as innocent and blissful, with both glittering wealth and revolting poverty. He expresses sympathy for readers who had hoped for more in their lives, addressing them with understanding and empathy. Vienna is an amazing political, intellectual, and economic center, Hitler writes, yet sadly divorced from the vitality of German nationalism and beset by two dangers: Marxists and Jews. Jewish dangers, described in vivid and horrific detail, intensify with each chapter, matched by the rhythm of the narrative, which grows increasingly rapid and ugly. Gaining readers' confidence, Hitler defines their problem: the Jews, a destructive force that brings down individuals as well as the collective German people, Europe, and the superior Aryan race. Hitler claims to have arrived in Vienna without prejudice. His slate was clean: His exposure to actual Jews, he writes, led him to antisemitism, not any preconceived prejudices. Even as he promotes the repugnance of

Jews, he teaches his bourgeois readers that they, like him, are free of bias and are instead experiencing a natural, sensory response to the repugnant sight, smell, and behavior of Jews. *Mein Kampf* presents itself as a *Bildungsroman*, a genre of educational and moral self-cultivation, via antisemitism.[36]

Not limited to hating Jews, antisemitism can become an all-encompassing identity, a "cultural code."[37] Jew-hating offers the eroticized excitement of violating liberal morals, blaspheming norms of behavior, having a secret knowledge of Jewish conspiracies and danger, and creating new political consensus. As secret knowledge, antisemitism stimulates pride, a sense of superiority, and the thrill of creating a new and revolutionary movement. The impact on Jews is complex, gendered, and sexualized, as women and men play different roles in the antisemitic heteronormative economy. That females are already coded as flesh shifts the antisemitic gendering. Male Jews are sexually abnormal in the antisemitic script, whereas Jewish women are portrayed as perfidiously seductive, objects of dangerous desire. Simone de Beauvoir explained that "the erotic experience is one that most poignantly reveals to human beings their ambiguous condition."[38] The ambiguity revealed by the erotic is illustrated in many literary sources, among them *The Merchant of Venice*, in which Lorenzo desires Jessica, the daughter of Shylock, until he marries her and realizes that her blood remains Jewish despite her conversion to Christianity and will therefore contaminate his children. Jessica is trapped between being rejected as a Christian convert and being locked in her father's house, a symbol of Jewish patriarchy.

As an eroticized object, both flesh and spirit, Jews are enemies and lovers, hated and yet desired as the mysterious object of hate, requiring us to consider the role of fantasies in shaping the racial imagination. Vibrancy and boredom, culture and filth are linked to the presence and absence of Jews; racism, like sex, is about mind and body and frequently linked to the "excess" of what it despises. William Faulkner writes in his novel *Absalom, Absalom!*: "There is something in the touch of flesh with flesh which abrogates, cuts sharp and straight across the devious intricate channels of decorous ordering, which enemies as well as lovers know because it makes them both."[39] Antisemites do not turn away from Jews but are relentlessly obsessed with Jews. The so-called "research" institutes of the Third Reich promoted the loathing of Jews, while constantly publishing books, curating exhibits, and talking endlessly about Jews and Judaism.[40] Similarly, a mixture of loathing and envy stands at the heart of Christian attitudes: Though Jesus is a Jew and not a Christian, Judaism had to be repudiated for Christianity to come into being. While Jesus the Jew is revered by Christians as divine, Christian theologians sometimes denigrate Judaism, expressing shame over Christianity's Jewish origins.[41] After World War II, the loathing and envy of Jews mutated into a loathing and envy of antisemitism. Yet even as antisemitism was repudiated, the erotic kept it in place with a mixture of repulsion and attraction, hatred and desire, indifference and passion; antisemitism itself functioned as the Jew. Precisely that dual quality assures the tenacity of both racism and antisemitism.

The historian Alexandra Cuffel has pointed to gendered emotions of disgust that were cultivated by medieval religious polemics: "Describing one's opponent and his or her religion as disgusting and polluted... [evokes] a gut-wrenching emotional antipathy that is closely linked to a variety of other feelings: fear, contempt, hatred."[42] Joseph Goebbels, Reich minister of propaganda, who, with Hitler, "forcefully advocated" Jews wearing the yellow star, explained in November 1941 that "every Jew is our enemy," a "parasite" responsible for the war, and that wearing the yellow star is "a hygienic prophylaxis to hinder the Jew from worming into our ranks."[43] The claims of religion on the body easily led to a gendering of antisemitic emotion and an association of Jews with carnal impurity, gender inversion, and sexual perversion that was intended to provoke revulsion and portray Jews as undermining "decent society."

Afropessimists, such as Frank Wilderson and Tendayi Sithole, argue that Blacks are nonlife in the white mind:[44] "Afro-Pessimism explains the ongoing racial fantasies of black criminality and parasitism through a critical analysis of modernity and its construction of blackness as non-human."[45] Antisemites view Jews as parasites but locate their criminality in a Jewish power that brings death. Whereas modern capitalism created itself through the enslavement of Black flesh, modern secularism, which is Christianity in a new form, turned Jews into a racialized, life-threatening carnality that must be annihilated.

Jews not only kill the spirit of religion, as St. Paul wrote, but Jews also killed God himself in Christ.[46] When Achille Mbembe writes that the State of Israel is the greatest necropower in the world, he is speaking as a Christian theologian in secularized terms: Jews are the sign of death.[47]

Antisemitism as Soundscape

Ideological formulations of antisemitism are important, but so is sensory experience, including sound. As Christina von Braun asks, how does an idea become transformed into the corporeal?[48] In their analysis of Richard Wagner's *Judaism in Music*, Uffa Jensen and Stefanie Schüler-Springorum identify emotions that are "unconscious, negative, and very much present."[49] Such emotions are effectively created through images of Jews in Wagner's operas and his careful calibration of music, text, and dramaturgy. His Bayreuth audiences received not a verbal instruction in antisemitism, but a subtle and deeply powerful emotional experience. For the audience, the powerfully sensory experience of the operas went beyond aesthetics and emotions to become felt as physical; antisemitic myths became lodged in the bodies of the viewers. In Otto Weininger's notorious 1903 text, *Geschlecht und Charakter*, von Braun finds that Weininger transfers "an *idea* of Jewishness into Jewish *corporeality* while at the same time turning Jewishness into an individual *psychological* trait."[50] The idea becomes a body, and bodies are gendered and sexualized. Combining studies of gender theory and antisemitism, von Braun emphasizes the role of erotic fantasy in antisemitic discourse that sometimes turns the "Jew" into a female sacrificial figure and at other times into a sexually abnormal, sometimes voracious, male figure. Weininger identified Jews with femininity and used antisemitism as a powerful tool to denigrate and humiliate women and used misogyny to express his loathing of Jews.

The musicologist Ruth HaCohen has traced the juxtaposition of the assumption that Christians produce harmonious music and claims that Jews only produce noise.[51] Churches are places of beautiful music while synagogues are places of ugly clamor. If Christians appreciate beautiful sounds, Jews can neither produce nor appreciate musical instruments or the voice as tools of divine worship. If Jews are allegedly impervious to the aesthetics of sound, then they are subjected to the horrors of sound. A pogrom was not only an attack against human beings and property; it was also a theater of horrific sounds. Erotohistoriography calls us to examine the sensory effects of pogroms. What is captured by bodily senses—seen, heard, tasted, and smelled—has an "effect on the human sensorium, on the affects, sensibilities, and perceptual habits of its vast audience."[52] Numerous Jewish testimonies, diaries, and memoirs describe a chaotic horror created by the violence.[53] Consider the sounds: Both attackers and Jewish victims heard people screaming, property shattered, glass broken, and cries of fear, horror, pain, and death. Were these sounds sadistically gratifying to the attackers? For Jews listening to the sounds of friends, family, and neighbors being beaten, tortured, raped, and murdered and of property smashed and set on fire, a pogrom was a horrific emotional experience of aural as well as physical violence. Such sounds are never forgotten, nor are the other sensory experiences—the smell of blood, the sight of destruction, the taste of death.

The soundscape of a pogrom can be more powerful than words. A pogrom does not disseminate ideas or promote an ideology, and its impact lies well beyond the physical destruction, the injuries caused, and the number of people killed. Antisemitism is not communicated by words alone; sound is another of its vehicles. Attention to the soundscape by historians would capture a neglected element of subjective experience and provide evidence for continuities or changes over time in the perpetrators' strategies and the nature of the assaults.

We might also consider the sound of an antisemitic rally, such as the German American Bund rally of twenty thousand at Madison Square Garden in 1939 to support Hitler, or the tiki torch parade in Charlottesville, Virginia, in 2017 where marchers proclaimed, "The Jews will not replace us," or the thrill and thunderous applause that greeted Hitler. A remarkable description exists of the euphoria at a 1936 rally in a forest in Saxony: "After singing an old hymn, 'Wer jetzig Zeiten leben will' [Who wants to live in current times], with militaristic overtones, there came a hushed pause, and then jubilant applause" to greet the speaker who described the heroism of Germans in the face of their enemies. "Once again," he intoned, "there is an assault against the West, unleashed by the Bolsheviks of the world, behind whom stands the Jew, and the Germans are once again the Reich *Volk*....Our *Volk* has been chosen to halt the avalanche of the Bolsheviks and the Jews on behalf of the entire West—and therefore in its deepest sense the word receives its meaning: the German *Volk* are the Anti-Jews [*Gegenvolk der Juden*]!"[54] Defeating Jews would transform Germans and restore their heroic identity; just describing that victory brought jubilation and pride, as conquering Jews would restore a German social order and recognize Germans as truly chosen.

Militarism, jubilance, and heroism create a sense of pride in hating Jews and seeking their destruction. Just as the Jew is the anti-Christ, the German is the anti-Jew. Here again we see that dual quality of attraction and repulsion, of wanting to appropriate the mantle of chosenness while loathing Jews. Antisemitic emotion generates duality by inducing sensory revulsion and offering the relief of redemption through exorcizing or eradicating Jews. Attacking Jews can also assuage fears. The line between Christianity and Judaism is thin, and the Christian horror of possibly turning into a Jew always lurks.

In *The Merchant of Venice*, this fear is expressed by Shylock's servant, Launcelot, "I am a Jew if I serve the Jew any longer" (2:2.106–7), and by Antonio, "The Hebrew will turn Christian: he grows kind" (1.3.175). Within Protestantism, sinfulness and Jewishness are equated, as in John Donne's *Holy Sonnet XI*. The Jews killed Jesus once, the poem says, but Christians, by sinning, kill Jesus every day. In Chaucer's *Prioress's Tale*, the Jews are wicked in ways that are inhuman and opposed to the Virgin Mary's purity; to Donne, the Jew is a sinner, and in sinning the Christian becomes the despised Jew deserving punishment. Building on Pauline theology, Martin Luther's definition of Judaism as "works righteousness" meant that Jews, by definition, were not spiritual and lacked a moral compass, a tradition that Kant translated into philosophical terms: Judaism is heteronomy; obedience, not morality. Rejecting or destroying Jews would be a moral act protecting Christianity; cruelty to Jews is not sinful in Christian terms because cruelty is Jewish. That claim was voiced by some postwar Christian theologians in Germany who wrote that the Holocaust exemplified Jewish morality and by the historian Ernst Nolte who called the Holocaust an "Asiatic barbarism."[55]

Conclusion

During the first decades after the Holocaust, antisemitism became a taboo, and the shame that antisemites imposed on Jews was transferred to antisemites themselves. Just as antisemites had described Jews as a disease, a virus that spreads, antisemitism was now described using the same imagery and terminology. Non-Jews were now told to be ashamed of antisemitic teachings and their consequences in the Holocaust. Yet shame is an incendiary emotion, one that is not easily tolerated and can generate dangerous rage and revenge. On the Left, non-Jews and antisemites are now rejecting the imposed shame, and conservatives demand that Jews either return to the status of the shamed or join the Christian world in becoming the shamers of others—that is, in self-elevation through the debilitation of others: gaining the control of biopolitics through authoritarian regimes.

Demagogues are successful in engineering shame so that hatred of others becomes a source of pride. Passions once aroused cannot easily be quashed but can be rerouted. Enslavement may have been rendered illegal in the United States, but the sadism that drove it continues to demand gratification. Today's authoritarian, racist governments and political movements foster fascination with Nazism and are growing within democratic countries, along with antisemitism. Religious teachings insist on the immorality of racism, laws restrict and punish sadistic actions, and education defines goals and strategies, but overcoming the sadism that desires antisemitism eludes those methods. The sadistic gratification that gives racism and antisemitism their power requires a complex redress, a redirection of the sensory experience to find gratification through nonsadistic pleasures. The trauma of antisemitic violence on Jews has not been fully addressed by historians, and the lacuna has disturbing political consequences, such as the manipulation or feigned ignorance of antisemitic trauma to establish political alliances.

Hartman notes that for African Americans, even after enslavement became illegal, the trauma of violence, degradation, and abjection remained ensconced emotionally in the individual, fortified by Jim Crow social norms, politics, and law. She writes, "The whip was not abandoned; rather, it was to be internalized."[56] For enslaved people, to be beaten was the pain of violence and the constant dread of it. Antisemitism's power, too, lies in its threat as well as its enactment. Yet there is an important distinction between internalized trauma and the political invocations of trauma to justify redirecting antisemitism to other racist regimes and ignoring the gender politics that make mass-perpetrator rape an increasingly widespread tool of genocidal violence against women.

Finally, we might also ask about the experiences of the scholar: What are the emotional consequences of studying scenes of terror, rhetoric of hatred, threats and acts of violence and murder? Nijah Cunningham writes, "Each time I pick up [Saidiya Hartman's book] *Scenes of Subjection*, I am made to rediscover the enduring legacies of slavery as an uncanny illumination of the present. That rediscovery is as much a remembering as it is a kind of touch, a 'sentient relation to an animating alterity' (Butler 2004, 191) that is retrospectively sensed, felt, known."[57] Studying antisemitism inevitably prompts a strong emotional response in the scholar, as when we contemplate the question: What does a pogrom sound like? The emotional impact of reading documents describing atrocities, hearing ideologues screaming hatred of Jews, and interviewing survivors and perpetrators is not without personal consequences, as I have experienced in examining Nazi-era archives. The trauma of history elicits emotional and visceral reactions in the historian and challenges our cognitive modes of historical interpretation. The emotions creating and perpetuating antisemitism and racism ultimately haunt the lives of scholars as we struggle to understand and overcome their legacies and continued presence within our societies.

NOTES

Many thanks to my colleagues who offered insightful advice while I was preparing this article, especially Gilah Kletenik, Tarek El-Ariss, Shaul Magid, Mark Massa, and Emily Oliveira.

1. David Engel, "Away from a Definition of Antisemitism: An Essay in the Semantics of Historical Description," in *Rethinking European Jewish History*, ed. Jeremy Cohen and Moshe Rosman (Oxford: Littman Library of Jewish Civilization, 2009), 53.

2. Charles W. Mills, "White Ignorance," in *Race and Epistemologies of Ignorance*, ed. Shannon Sullivan and Nancy Tuana (Albany: SUNY Press, 2007), 27.

3. Shulamit Volkov, "Antisemitism as a Cultural Code: Reflections on the History and Historiography of Antisemitism in Imperial Germany," *The Leo Baeck Institute Year Book* 23, no. 1 (January 1978): 25–46.

4. Saidiya Hartman, *Scenes of Subjection: Terror, Slavery, and Self-Making in Nineteenth-Century America* (New York: Oxford University Press, 1997), 85.

5. Elizabeth Freeman, *Time Binds: Queer Temporalities, Queer Histories* (Durham, NC: Duke University Press, 2010).

6. Elizabeth Freeman, "Time Binds, or, Erotohistoriography," *Social Text* 23, nos. 3–4 (Fall–Winter 2005): 57–68. See also Sharon Patricia Holland, *The Erotic Life of Racism* (Durham, NC: Duke University Press, 2012).

7. Eric Ward, "Skin in the Game: How Antisemitism Animates White Nationalism," *The Public Eye*, June 29, 2017, https://politicalresearch.org/2017/06/29/skin-in-the -game-how-antisemitism-animates-white-nationalism. In the manifesto of the terrorist who targeted Black people in Buffalo and murdered ten Black people on May 14, 2022, "the antisemitic rants . . . are much more prevalent than his focus on the Black community." The manifesto claims that "Jewish groups wield all the power, including in bringing Africans to America in the first instance." Tahir Abbas et. al., "The Buffalo Attack—An Analysis of the Manifesto," International Centre for Counter-Terrorism, May 18, 2022, https://www.icct.nl/publication/buffalo-attack-analysis-manifesto.

8. Alexandra Minna Stern, *Proud Boys and the White Ethnostate: How the Alt-Right Is Warping the American Imagination* (Boston: Beacon Press, 2019), 68–69.

9. Leo Löwenthal and Norbert Guterman, *Prophets of Deceit: A Study of the Techniques of the American Agitator* (London: Verso, 2021), 121.

10. James Goodman, *Stories of Scottsboro* (New York: Vintage, 1995), 221.

11. Susannah Heschel, *The Aryan Jesus: Christian Theologians and the Bible in Nazi Germany* (Princeton, NJ: Princeton University Press, 2008).

12. José Esteban Muñoz, *Cruising Utopia: The Then and There of Queer Futurity* (New York: New York University Press, 2009).

13. Saidiya Hartman, *Lose Your Mother: A Journey along the Atlantic Slave Route* (New York: Farrar, Straus and Giroux, 2007), 133.

14. Hannah Arendt, *Eichmann in Jerusalem: A Report on the Banality of Evil* (New York: Viking, 1963).

15. Jacques Derrida and Maurizio Ferraris, *A Taste for the Secret*, trans. Giacomo Donis (Cambridge: Polity, 2001); Chris Danta, "Derrida and the Test of Secrecy," *Angelaki: Journal of the Theoretical Humanities* 18, no. 2 (July 2013): 61–75.

16. Bettina Stangneth, *Eichmann before Jerusalem: The Unexamined Life of a Mass Murderer*, trans. Ruth Martin (New York: Alfred A. Knopf, 2014).

17. Christopher Browning, *Ordinary Men: Reserve Police Battalion 101 and the Final Solution in Poland* (New York: HarperCollins, 1992); Gitta Sereny, *Into That Darkness: An Examination of Conscience* (New York: Vintage Books, 1974).

18. James Cone, *The Cross and the Lynching Tree* (Maryknoll, NY: Orbis, 2011); George Yancy, *Black Bodies, White Gazes: The Continuing Significance of Race in America* (Lanham, MD: Rowman and Littlefield, 2017).

19. Farhad Dalal, *Race, Colour and the Processes of Racialization: New Perspectives from Group Analysis, Psychoanalysis and Sociology* (Hove, UK: Brunner-Routledge, 2002), 157–58.

20. Heschel, *The Aryan Jesus*, 279.

21. Walter Grundmann, *Totale Kirche im totalen Staat*, vol. 3, *Kirche im Dritten Reich* (Dresden: O. Günther, 1934), 71.

22. "Bericht über die Arbeitstagung der 'Deutschen Christen' Gruppe Rheinland," *Briefe an deutsche Christen*, 3:8 (1934), 144–46. All translations are mine.

23. Walter Grundmann, "Das Messiasproblem," in *Germanentum, Christentum und Judentum: Studien zur Erforschung ihres gegenseitigen Verhältnisses*, ed. Walter Grundmann (Leipzig: Georg Wigand, 1943), 379–412.

24. Julius Leutheuser, *Die deutsche Christusgemeinde: der Weg zur deutschen, Nationalkirche* (Weimar: Verlag Deutsche Christen, 1935).

25. J. Halberstam, "Technologies of Monstrosity: Bram Stoker's 'Dracula,'" *Victorian Studies* 36, no. 3 (1993): 333–52.

26. Irina Astashkevich, *Gendered Violence: Jewish Women in the Pogroms of 1917 to 1921* (Boston: Academic Studies Press, 2018), xiii. On rape as a tool of genocide, see Elissa Bemporad, "Memory, Body, and Power: Women and the Study of Genocide," in *Women and Genocide: Survivors, Victims, Perpetrators*, ed. Elissa Bemporad and Joyce W. Warren (Bloomington: Indiana University Press, 2018), 1–16.

27. Astashkevich, *Gendered Violence*, 131.

28. Gur Alroey, "Sexual Violence, Rape, and Pogroms, 1903-1920," *Jewish Culture and History* 18, no. 3 (2017): 313–30, 325. Also see Mikhal Dekel, "'From the Mouth of the Raped Woman Rivka Schiff,' Kishinev, 1903," *Women's Studies Quarterly* 36, no. 1 (2008): 199–207; Iris Milner, "'In the City of Slaughter': The Hidden Voice of the Pogrom Victims," *Prooftexts* 25, nos. 1–2 (Winter/Spring 2005): 60–72.

29. Jonathan Dekel-Chen, David Gaunt, Natan M. Meir, and Israel Bartal, eds., "Introduction," in *Anti-Jewish Violence: Rethinking the Pogrom in East European History* (Bloomington: Indiana University Press, 2011), 9.

30. John D. Klier, *Russians, Jews, and the Pogroms of 1881-1882* (Cambridge: Cambridge University Press, 2011), 83.

31. Stefan Wiese, "'Spit Back with Bullets!' Emotions in Russia's Jewish Pogroms, 1881-1905," *Geschichte und Gesellschaft* 39, no. 4 (October–December 2013): 472–501.

32. Michael Gluzman, "Pogrom and Gender: On Bialik's Unheimlich," *Prooftexts* 25, nos. 1–2 (Winter/Spring 2005): 39–59.

33. Jamieson Webster, "The Rape Joke as Ur-Joke," *Studies in Gender and Sexuality* 18, no. 4 (2017): 269–73, 269.

34. Fredric Jameson, *The Political Unconscious: Narrative as a Socially Symbolic Act* (Ithaca, NY: Cornell University Press, 1981), 102.

35. Steven J. Zipperstein, *Pogrom: Kishinev and the Tilt of History* (London: Liveright Publishing Corporation, 2018), 74.

36. Susannah Heschel, "Being Adolf Hitler: *Mein Kampf* as Antisemitic *Bildungsroman*," in *Hitler's Mein Kampf and the Holocaust: A Prelude to Genocide*, ed. John J. Michalczyk, Michael S. Bryant, and Susan A. Michalczyk (New York: Bloomsbury, 2022), 185–96.

37. Volkov, "Antisemitism as a Cultural Code."

38. Simone de Beauvoir, *The Second Sex*, trans. Constance Borde and Sheila Malovany-Chevallier (New York: Alfred A. Knopf, 2010), 56.

39. William Faulkner, *Absalom, Absalom!* (New York: Random House, 1936), 115.

40. Dirk Rupnow, *Judenforschung im Dritten Reich. Wissenschaft zwischen Politik, Propaganda und Ideologie* (Baden-Baden: Nomos, 2011).

41. From the earliest historiography on Christian origins, Christian scholars explained how the early followers of Jesus purified their movement of Jewish accretions.

42. Alexandra Cuffel, *Gendering Disgust in Medieval Religious Polemic* (Notre Dame, IN: University of Notre Dame Press, 2007), 7.

43. Wolfgang Gerlach, *And the Witnesses Were Silent: The Confessing Church and the Persecution of the Jews*, trans. Victoria J. Barnett (Lincoln: University of Nebraska Press, 2000), 127-29; Edward Timms, ed., *Anna Haag and Her Secret Diary of the Second World War* (Bern: Peter Lang, 2015), 135; Eberhard Röhm and Jörg Thierfelder, *Juden, Christen, Deutsche, 1933-1945*, vol. 4, pt. 1 (Stuttgart: Calwer Verlag 2004), 30, n. 16.

44. Frank B. Wilderson III, *Afropessimism* (New York: Liveright, 2020); Tendayi Sithole, *The Black Register* (Cambridge: Polity, 2020).

45. Zahi Zalloua, "Afro-Pessimism with Žižek," *Intertexts* 23, nos. 1–2 (Spring–Fall 2019): 44–64, 44.

46. 2 Corinthians 3:6; Romans 7:10; Acts 2:36; Acts 3:14-15; 1 Thessalonians 2:14-15.

47. Achille Mbembe, "Necropolitics," trans. Libby Meintjes, *Public Culture* 15, no. 1 (2003): 11-40.

48. Christina von Braun, "Und der Feind ist Fleisch geworden: Der rassistische Antisemitismus," in *Der Ewige Judenhaß*, ed. Christina von Braun and Ludger Heid (Berlin: Philo Verlag, 2000), 149-213.

49. Uffa Jensen and Stefanie Schüler-Springorum, "Gefühle gegen Juden: Die Emotionsgeschichte des modernen Antisemitismus," *Geschichte und Gesellschaft* 39, no. 4 (December 2013): 413-42, 415.

50. Christina von Braun, "Gender and Antisemitism," in *The Routledge History of Antisemitism*, ed. Mark Weitzman, Robert J. Williams, and James Wald (New York: Routledge, forthcoming).

51. Ruth HaCohen, *The Music Libel Against the Jews* (New Haven, CT: Yale University Press, 2011).

52. Charles Hirschkind, *The Ethical Soundscape: Cassette Sermons and Islamic Counterpublics* (New York: Columbia University Press, 2006), loc. 125, Kindle.

53. See, for example, the two-volume book published in 1910, *Die Judenpogrome in Russland*, ed. A. Linden (Leo Motzkin) (Cologne: Jüdischer Verlag, 1910), and Timothy Snyder, *Bloodlands: Europe between Hitler and Stalin* (New York: Basic Books, 2010).

54. *Christenkreuz und Hakenkreuz*, 9 (September 1936): 11–12. *Wer jetzig Zeiten leben will / Muß haben ein tapfers Herze, Es sein der argen Feind so viel / Bereiten ihm groß Schmerze*. Whoever wants to live today / Must have a brave heart; There are so many wicked enemies / Ready to give him monumental pain.

55. Christa Mulack maintains that Jewish adherence to divine commandments is equivalent to Nazi obedience to the criminal orders of their superiors. She describes the Holocaust as the triumph of Jewish patriarchal ethics over the feminist morality taught by Jesus; thus, Jews are made the victims of their own religion. Christa Mulack, *Jesus: der Gesalbte der Frauen* (Stuttgart: Kreuz Verlag, 1987), 155–56. Ernst Nolte famously wrote, "Did not the National Socialists, did not Hitler perhaps commit an 'Asiatic' deed only because they regarded themselves and those like them as potential or real victims of an 'Asiatic' deed?" Ernst Nolte, *Frankfurter Allgemeine Zeitung*, June 6, 1986.

56. Hartman, *Scenes of Subjection*, 140.

57. Nijah Cunningham, "The Nonarrival of Black Freedom (c. 12.6.84)," *Women and Performance: A Journal of Feminist Theory* 27, no. 1 (2017): 112–20. The citation is from Judith Butler, "Merleau-Ponty and the Touch of Malebranche," in *The Cambridge Companion to Merleau-Ponty*, ed. Taylor Carman and Mark B. N. Hansen (Cambridge: Cambridge University Press, 2004), 181–205. In footnote 2, Cunningham writes that his interpretation is "a slight variation of and deviation from Hartman's and Frank Wilderson's provocative description of *Scenes of Subjection* as an allegory of the present." See Saidiya V. Hartman and Frank B. Wilderson III, "The Position of the Unthought," *Qui Parle* 13, no. 2 (2003): 183–201, 190.

5
Toward Entanglement

STEFANIE SCHÜLER-SPRINGORUM

"THOSE WHO WOULD codify the meanings of words fight a losing bat-tle, for words, like the ideas or things they are meant to signify, have a history." This is the first sentence of Joan Wallach Scott's pathbreaking article, "Gender: A Useful Category of Historical Analysis."[1] What the North American scholar, writing in 1986, had in mind and eventually succeeded in instigating was to take the linguistic turn seriously. She warned of its shortcomings and offered positive suggestions about the possibilities for further study in a field—gender history—that was and still is heavily imbued with identity building, morals, and politics.

Given the fact that this description would work just as well for the ongoing debates on historical and contemporary antisemitism, it is not by chance that Joan Scott's article influences this volume's goal of discussing the challenge posed by David Engel in his seminal essay of 2009. Being utterly unsatisfied with conventional historical writing about and attempts to define antisemitism, Engel elaborates on "how constituting antisemitism as an object of historical study, in whatever form and according to whatever parameters, has diverted and will likely continue to deflect historians from potentially fruitful ways of investigating the specific incidents, texts, laws, visual artefacts, social practices and mental configurations that that rubric customarily subsumes."[2]

The core of his text can thus be described as a passionate call for context, for a "thick description," in the Geertzean sense, of events where, verbally or physically, "people behaved violently towards Jews," whose interconnectedness "across time and space," however, has never been demonstrated.[3] For those of us who come from fields in which a certain identity of our objects of study "across time and space" is taken for granted—like "Jewish studies" or "gender history"—Engel's call to

87

eschew antisemitism altogether as a "ready-made category" that disguises more than it explains is unsettling at first glance.[4] However, his compelling argument might indeed have a positive effect on research in all those fields, not only because questioning one's own basic assumptions, categories, and definitions is always a healthy enterprise, but also because scrutiny of an assumed interconnectedness is precisely what might lead to new insights.

I will therefore proceed the opposite way. Instead of delivering a thick description of one anti-Jewish incident in time, I will pursue certain "ghosts"[5] that come up time and again in different disguises, or put differently, look for entanglements of diverse resentments in the *longue durée* of modern European history. This means that I will look for anti-Jewish feelings in various countries and in various historical periods and describe how they are linked to other forms of hatred. I will start my rather eclectic journey in the geographical region that for almost eight hundred years was home to the three monotheistic religions: the Iberian Peninsula. While the Spanish experience in early modernity allows for a discussion of the intersection of ethnicity and religion, the second part of this essay will examine both the idealized treatment of these questions in nineteenth-century British and German literature as well as the different ways that Jews actively positioned themselves within these political debates. Not by chance, it seems, this positioning within the economically aspiring and culturally dominating middle class is heavily gendered, and it is precisely the gendered imagery of what we might legitimately call "modern antisemitism" that will be analyzed in the third part of this essay.

Sepharad

The Spanish early modern era that started with the expulsion of the Jews in 1492 has for a long time been presented as the zenith of religiously based anti-Jewish persecution. This interpretation, however, overlooks the impact of the blood purity laws that for four centuries barred Christians of Jewish origin (Marranos) or Muslim origin (Moriscos) from entering the higher echelons of the state, like universities, administration, military orders, and, of course, positions within the Santo Oficio itself. Given the ongoing persecution by the Inquisition against those who were considered "unclean" and therefore heretics, investigating the blood purity of someone who wanted to access university, for example, could result not only in educational or professional discrimination but also in death for him and his family, including its distant members—even when all of them had been Christians for centuries. One presumed Jewish or Muslim ancestor could thus ruin the lives of dozens or even hundreds of people.

It is worth noting that while the racist practice of the blood purity laws was directed more against persons of Jewish background, it was the Christian population of Muslim ancestry that was finally expelled altogether in 1609. Thus Max Hering Torres, María Elena Martínez, and others have presented important works that argue for a nuanced approach to premodern Spanish "notions of difference" or racisms "in plural form,"[6] one that, in Hering Torres's words, "may question the idea of racism as a linear process."[7]

While this approach is strikingly similar to that of David Engel, another literary scholar, Geraldine Heng, goes back even further into history: She formulates a new interpretation of the linkage between religion and racism in the European Middle Ages, one that might help us understand the entanglement of anti-Jewish and anti-Muslim concepts of difference, as it is manifested in the blood purity laws. In her view, the category of "race" is always a "response to ambiguity,"[8] and here a central role is assigned to religion as a key source of authority in the European medieval context, a role similar to that of science in modernity: "It is important to note that religion—the paramount source of authority in the Middle Ages—can function both socioculturally *and* biopolitically, subjecting people of a detested faith, for instance, to a political hermeneutics of theology that can biologize, define and essentialize an entire community as fundamentally, and absolutely different in an inter-knotted cluster of ways."[9]

Like Heng, the Belgian anthropologist Christiane Stallaert, who examines Spanish blood purity laws from an ethnological perspective, stresses the role of religion as the principal authority and of the Inquisition as the driving force behind the racially grounded nation building in Spain.[10] The scholar of Romance languages Georg Bossong elaborates on the effects of the Inquisition: "As an institution of coldly and systematically rationalized, bureaucratized repression, it was a powerful and efficient instrument for suppressing any manner of free thought, any mode of being different." He concludes that "the fear of its power permeated Spanish society, extending into the most minute reticulations, and led to a total process of uniformity, at least on the surface."[11] In this context, the blood purity laws were thus fundamental as the groundwork for the distinctions promoted by the Inquisition between "good" and "evil," "right" and "wrong," and later "Spanish" and "non-Spanish."

Proceeding from these interpretations, the German historian Bettina Voss suspects that it was specifically the lengthy eight-hundred-year Muslim presence on the Iberian Peninsula that underpinned and justified the intransigence of Spanish strategies of distancing and "othering" in subsequent centuries. Being labeled a "Moor" functioned as the "most effective basis of antagonism" for Christian Spain, while at the same time Jews were the concrete targets for the implementation of these "strategies of distancing."[12] The hostility and antagonism toward both Jews and Muslims run, as Stefan Schreiner sees it, "like a red thread" through European-Christian history: "It is thus not surprising that in Christian anti-Islamic polemics up into the modern era, not only were the same 'arguments' put forward that can be found in Christian anti-Jewish polemics. Rather... 'Jews' and 'Muslims' virtually became interchangeable concepts."[13]

Thus, what Gil Anidjar initially identified only for the nineteenth century had already emerged in the early modern era in Europe: "the invention of the Semites," that discursive element "whereby whatever was said about Jews could equally be said about Arabs, and vice versa."[14] This category was repeatedly grounded and bolstered anew by religious arguments, while at the same time deeply engraved into European social memory by means of racist exclusion and brutal persecution on the one hand—the Inquisition was officially active until 1834—and a new perceived "threat" from the "East" on the other, the Turks or later the Ottoman Empire. Thus, it is hardly surprising that during the Enlightenment and indeed well into the nineteenth century, both Jews and Muslims were regarded as "Orientals," as "Asian," in sum, as Europe's "Other."

There are obvious political reasons for the comparatively little attention this linkage has been given in the historiography on Judaism and
Islam. Historians who stressed the racist content of the Spanish blood
purity laws, such as Benzion Netanyahu and Yosef H. Yerushalmi,
consciously aligned them with Nazi Germany, largely ignoring their
anti-Muslim dimension.[15] By contrast, Edward Said was accused of
having intentionally avoided coming to critical terms with German
Orientalism, because precisely there the parallels with antisemitism
would have emerged with particular clarity. However, Said expressly
emphasizes this connection in the introduction to *Orientalism*: "I have
found myself writing the history of a strange, secret sharer of Western
anti-Semitism. That anti-Semitism and, as I have discussed it in its
Islamic branch, Orientalism resemble each other is a historical, cultural,
and political truth."[16] Even if he himself did not pursue this "secret
nexus," the discussions around his book stimulated an entire series of
suggestions for making that linkage fruitful for a post-colonial-inspired
history of knowledge and discourse[17] and for European Jewish history
as well.[18] For our purpose here, however, it should be enough to state
that the racist core of premodern Judeophobia linked it intimately to
other forms of hatred that, taken together, served the Christian nation-
building process that started in Spain at the beginning of what we have
come to call "the Modern Age."

Great Britain

Jewish communities north of the Pyrenees remained conscious of
the centuries-old racist core of their shared exclusion from Christian
Europe.[19] As the literary scholar Michael Ragussis pointed out some
time ago, for intellectuals of the nineteenth century, "Spain" represented a kind of "historical laboratory" in which one might experiment
ad libitum with questions of race and religion—albeit in telling national
variations.[20] In Germany, for example, fascination with Sephardic culture stimulated the cultural creativity of German Jews, as John Efron
has recently shown.[21] He and Carsten Schapkow attribute the special attraction of Spanish Jews for German Jewry to the possibility of
understanding "Iberian-Sephardic culture as a model for successful

integration of Jews into a non-Jewish majority society, as equal partners in the cultural conversation," and of imagining themselves or their own Spanish mirror image as intercultural intermediaries.[22]

Virtually all nineteenth-century German popular or academic treatments of Sephardic Jewry revolved to a certain extent around the Jewish sense of self, of an identity strung between the tensions of adaptation and preservation. This focus may well have been due to German society's specific impositions on Jews to assimilate over the course of the long period of civic emancipation as well as to the precarious situation of German Jews springing from that difficult framework in which they were caught between social advancement and political inequality. Interestingly, the obvious enemy threatening Jewish or Marrano existence, the representatives of Christianity, remained in the background of the German version of *Sepharad*.[23]

This peculiar gap becomes all the more clear if one looks at the British-Jewish tradition of literature on the Sephardim, which according to Ragussis dealt far more with the aspect of exclusion in Iberian-Jewish history and with the tension between its religiously and racially grounded legitimation.[24] This different frame of interpretation seems explainable by the self-confidence of British Jewry that was in the process of emancipation and could afford to name and denounce the religious grounds of the persecution of Iberian Jews and converts.[25] However, it could only do so as long as this accusation referred to a certain variant of Christianity, namely Roman Catholicism.

As David Feldman has noted, the history of Jewish anti-Catholicism in Victorian England has been given scarcely any attention to date.[26] In order to understand this rather surprising link between British Protestantism and Judaism, one must go back to the decades after the French Revolution, when the evangelical movement, originally an impulse for renewal within the Anglican Church, developed a decidedly anti-liberal attitude. This was manifested not only in an increasingly aggressive anti-Catholicism but also, together with millenarian expectations, in intensified efforts to convert Jews. Thus, the London Society for the Promotion of Christianity amongst the Jews increasingly concentrated its activities at the beginning of the nineteenth century on Jewish women.[27] Women were considered especially receptive, because they had a poor religious education, and they were considered highly emotional and thus open to the torrent of Romantic stories of conversion that descended upon the British reading public in the first half of the nineteenth century. In these stories, it was women who, in unprecedented numbers, wrote for women—and Jewish female writers responded, as Nadia Valman has shown.[28] They often did so, however, by using the Marrano experience to rail against any form of forced conversion and, indirectly but clearly, by employing "evangelical cultural codes" to upgrade the value of Judaism.[29]

This "discursive identification between Judaism and Protestantism," went hand in hand with defining a common enemy: the Catholic Church.[30] The ingredients of these stories about Marranos and the Inquisition—torture, greed, and perversion—were all too familiar to the reading public at the time through dozens of highly popular gothic novels, all imbued with a virulent anti-Catholicism.[31] Their readers, the British middle classes, were still under the shock of the Catholic Emancipation Act of 1829 that granted active and passive voting rights to the religious minority, while still prohibiting, for example, the use of religious clothing in public. In the ensuing decades, a huge number of books, pamphlets, and leaflets appeared that targeted the purported superstitions of Roman Catholics and questioned their loyalty to the state. "Popery" was one of the most abusive anti-Catholic expletives in British discourse of the nineteenth century, and, in the words of D. G. Paz, "anti-Catholicism was an integral part of what it meant to be a Victorian."[32]

In view of these clear front lines in religious combat, it is hardly surprising that British Jews enthusiastically accepted the offer of integration that enabled them to stage themselves as rational, patriotic, and liberal.[33] The fact that anti-Catholicism in the mid-nineteenth century was a much more powerful social force than British animosity toward Jews may have contributed to that blind spot that in retrospect is so conspicuous: namely, the parallel between anti-Catholicism and anti-Judaism.[34] As Feldman stresses, for some pioneering evangelical thinkers, the figure of the rabbi was just as problematic as that of the Catholic priest because both stood as non-authorized intermediaries between God and humankind. Rabbinism was supposedly "Jewish popery," or vice versa; the papacy was nothing other than "Gentile Rabbinism," as the head of the Evangelical Mission and professor of Hebrew and rabbinical literature at King's College in London, Alexander McCaul, argued.[35]

In the somewhat lower precincts of popular anti-Catholicism prevalent in novels, pamphlets, and caricatures, Catholics were portrayed either as uneducated yokels mainly interested in sex, money, and power, or, on the other hand, they were highly intelligent conspirators, who strove to eventually rule the world via influence in education and other state institutions.[36] While these images are already strikingly similar to anti-Jewish tropes, even more surprising is the way conversos are depicted in novels written by Jewish writers. All the descriptions of Sephardic grandeur centered around "secret Jews": Jews who occupied high and even the highest state positions as Christians and only feigned their religious ardor while remaining loyal exclusively to their true faith. These literary fantasies perpetuated, albeit unintentionally, antisemitic core convictions or revitalized and renewed them for the modern context as negative stereotypes of Jewish deception, disloyalty, stealth, and conspiracy. By offering these historically rather distorted portrayals of Sephardic existence, Jewish writers were walking a tightrope, balancing precariously upon that very thin line separating understanding for the ambivalent position of the purported crypto-Jews from anti-Jewish feelings of resentment.[37]

British-Jewish writers and intellectuals were seduced into turning a blind eye to the dangerous similarity between the two discourses of exclusion by the suggestive offer of quasi self-inscription into the ranks of the British nation via anti-Catholicism. That they sometimes even actively participated in the creation of vile anti-Catholic images was probably fostered by the fact that, from a Jewish perspective, there were good reasons to be skeptical, to say the least, about the Catholic Church.

Germany

A similar but still different mechanism can be found when we cross the channel to Germany and focus on a more intimate entanglement, namely the one between anti-Jewish discourse and gender.[38] At the beginning of the period under discussion stood the Enlightenment with its promise of universal equality. By around 1800, demands for female and Jewish emancipation had led male Christian intellectuals to provide ever so eloquent reasons for the breach of this promise: Women and Jewish men became the target of groundless accusations.[39] It was not by chance that the Jewish women of the famous Berlin and Viennese salons, a little island of idealized social, religious, and gender equality, bore the brunt of the anti-Jewish discourse of the period, probably for the only time in the long history of Judeophobia. This discourse, however, was closely entangled with an anti-feminist one: First and foremost, the femininity of the salon ladies was denied, the standard reproach against educated women. Letters, pamphlets, and plays from the period are replete with malicious representations of educated women and Jewish women behaving improperly.[40]

However, with the demise of the literary salons and the advent of the Restoration in the wake of the anti-Napoleonic wars, Jewish women vanished from the antisemitic discourse. Nationalist ideologues writing after 1815 focused on arguments for excluding Jewish men from the community of citizens of the state. One of the leading anti-feminist arguments for excluding women from citizenship was fitness for military service, closely linking service in the army and the concomitant rights of a citizen that emerge from this obligation. While the exclusion of women from civil rights seemed easily explained by compulsory military service, this was not at all clear in the case of male Jews. On the contrary, between 1780 and 1810, there was vehement debate on this in different circles, as reflected in expert reports and opinions. There were certainly doubts about the desirability of male Jews as soldiers, but these were in general connected with the religious and cultural otherness ascribed to them that would endanger military homogeneity.[41] The advocates of compulsory military service for Jews argued for Jewish inclusion by citing certain especially masculine qualities ascribed to the Jewish character that still resembled older images from *Sepharad*: "The Jew's blood is fiery oriental," wrote one Prussian state official, "and he has a lively imagination. All this is a sign of manly strength if it is put to use and implemented."[42]

It is important to note that in the early nineteenth century, the physical ability and fitness for conscription of Jewish males was not doubted, and Jewish masculinity was not yet called into question. It was only after the victory over Napoleon that Jews once again came under focus among the precursors of German nationalism. Now, doubts also emerged about whether Jews were really physically fit for military service; a key argument was their supposed proclivity for being flat-footed. This purported minor malformation was used to mark Jews as unfit to serve in military ranks. As Sander Gilman has pointed out, 1815 to 1848 was a period of liberal citizens' militias and the glorification of the foot soldier as a hero. The alleged flat foot would render sustained marching difficult and thus served as concrete proof of the inability of the Jewish male to integrate into the community of able-bodied citizens of the state.[43]

Nonetheless, the physical exclusion and segregation of the male Jewish body did not emerge in a comprehensive way until the last third of the nineteenth century, when "the Jew" was construed as the counterimage to the classical "Greek" ideal of masculine beauty. This ideal suggested the unity of the perfect body and the perfect spirit or intellect. Only in the last decades of the century were Jewish men consistently sketched as "effeminate," unmanly and unmilitary, chubby and wimpish, and sufferers of flat feet, a flat chest, and poor posture. They supposedly gesticulated "like women" or homosexuals. Mentally, they were considered prone to melancholy or hysteria, but were also deemed immoral, devoid of character, manipulative, mendacious, and unpredictable. At the same time, like women in general, they were deemed devoid of self-control and subject to their base carnal desires. Jewish men were characterized as both hypersexual and feminized. Antisemitic representations of the Jewish male were ambivalent about Jewish potency and impotence, just as they persistently blurred distinctions between the genders. In contrast with earlier discriminations and exclusions, these venomous attacks on male Jewish gender identity were now, at the turn from the nineteenth to the twentieth century, firmly anchored in the body and supposedly substantiated by science as fundamentally organic in origin, precisely akin to the parallel bourgeois discourse about the polar genders and their biologically different characters.[44] Both femininity and Jewishness were reimagined as justifications for inequalities within the enlightened framework of theoretical civic equality.

By the end of the nineteenth century, normality and deviance were defined in medical, biological, and psychological terms. The result was unambiguous: The norm was male, heterosexual, and Christian; by contrast, deviance was female, homosexual, and Jewish. Antisemitism, homophobia, and misogyny thus had become closely entangled within the anti-modern vision of a clearly demarcated and hierarchically structured society.

Muslims, Catholics, and Women

On our journey from Spain to the British Isle and over to Germany, we have encountered Jews and other minorities who suffered similar exclusions and resentments. These entanglements are most obvious, albeit very little researched, in Inquisition Spain. In England, British Jews engaged actively in anti-Catholic propaganda in order to secure a safe place in Victorian society—something that would not have worked, for example, in Germany with its tradition of confessional diversity, even though Jewish liberals did support Bismarck's "culture war" on German Catholics, most likely for related reasons. Gendered exclusion is similar, but fundamentally different in its interwovenness with minority and majority groups: Women are not a minority but half of both the victimizing and the victim's collective, and at the same time femininity serves as the social marker for a lower status in general.

How, then, can we make sense of these entangled mechanisms if we follow David Engel and do not presume that there is some underlying assumption of an "eternal antisemitism" in its various disguises? First of all, my examples clearly show that there is no such thing as a linear development of anti-Jewish feeling from "realistic hostility" to "xenophobic" to "chimerical," as Gavin Langmuir has argued.[45] Judeophobia always could be and has been everything at the same time: racist, xenophobic, and chimerical—but the same is true for anti-Muslim panic in the seventeenth century, the anti-female witch craze in the eighteenth century, anti-Catholic resentment in the nineteenth century, and last but not least, homophobic violence in the twentieth century.

So maybe we should ask the question the other way around and analyze, as Jean Delumeau has done, the imagery of collective anxieties in Europe. Over centuries and in radically different contexts, people used such imagery to make sense of the calamities surrounding them from all sides. Those fearsome images in innumerable reproductions could be interrelated *ad libitum*: Devils, witches, Jews, heretics—they all pursued a grand plan, conspired in subterranean caverns, indulged in perverse lusts, and conjured worldwide conspiracies of power over and over again.[46] Apparently, the Enlightenment and the age of reason brought an end to what were redefined as "superstitions," but not an end to the existential anxieties, which from then on tended to be internalized. The new means to fight them were no longer collective burnings of heretics, but rather the good conscience and moral behavior of the individual—which were, needless to say, heavily gendered.[47]

If we follow Zygmunt Baumans's concept of proteophobia as a hatred against those who blur established binary categories, "who send out contradictory signals as to proper conduct and are behaviorally confusing,"[48] then we might indeed have an explanation for the emotional excess of anti-Jewish resentment in modernity.[49] However, at least in the twentieth century, hate and violence were directed with similar energy against homosexuals and certain women—"reds," "partisans," or "race defilers."[50] I am thus convinced that we can only understand the emotional impact produced by this modern, internalized fear of ambivalence when we become aware of its rootedness in the longing for clear-cut gender identities and images of sexuality, a longing that apparently becomes easily entangled with other forms of resentment—something that does not augur well for the twenty-first century, as can already be observed.

NOTES

1. Joan W. Scott, "Gender: A Useful Category of Historical Analysis," *American Historical Review* 91, no. 5 (1986): 1053–75.

2. David Engel, "Away from a Definition of Antisemitism: An Essay in the Semantics of Historical Description," in *Rethinking European Jewish History*, ed. Jeremy Cohen and Moshe Rosman (Oxford: Littman Library of Jewish Civilization, 2009), 30–31.

3. Ibid., 53.

4. Ibid.

5. Ibid., 46.

6. Max S. Hering Torres, María Elena Martínez, and David Nirenberg, eds., *Race and Blood in the Iberian World* (Zürich: Lit, 2012), 3.

7. Max S. Hering Torres, "Purity of Blood: Problems of Interpretation," in ibid., 34.

8. Geraldine Heng, "The Invention of Race in the European Middle Ages II: Locations of Medieval Race," *Literature Compass* 8, no. 5 (2011): 338. Italics in the original.

9. Geraldine Heng, "The Invention of Race in the European Middle Ages I: Race Studies, Modernity, and the Middle Ages," *Literature Compass* 8, no. 5 (2011): 325. Italics in the original.

10. Christiane Stallaert, *Etnogénesis y etnicidad en España: Una approximación histórico-antropológica al casticismo* (Barcelona: Proyecto A, 1998).

11. Georg Bossong, *Die Sepharden: Geschichte und Kultur der spanischen Juden* (München: C. H. Beck, 2008), 65.

12. Bettina Voss, "Die zweite Reconquista? Spanische Identitätsentwürfe und Muslime nach 1975," in *Die drei Kulturen und spanische Identitäten. Geschichts- und literaturwissenschaftliche Beiträge zu einem Paradigma der iberischen Moderne*, ed. Anna Menny and Britta Voss (Freiburg: Fördergemeinschaft Wiss. Publ. von Frauen, 2011), 47.

13. Stefan Schreiner, "Das 'christliche Europa': Eine Fiktion," *Quantara.de*, August 7, 2012, https://de.quantara.de/node/1505.

14. Gil Anidjar, *Semites: Race, Religion, Literature* (Stanford, CA: Stanford University Press, 2008), 18.

15. See Benzion Netanyahu, *The Origins of the Inquisition in Fifteenth Century Spain* (New York: Random House, 1995); Yosef H. Yerushalmi, *Assimilation and Racial Anti-Semitism: The Iberian and the German Models* (New York: Leo Baeck Institute, 1982).

16. Edward W. Said, *Orientalism* (London: Routledge and Kegan Paul, 1978), 27–28.

17. James Pasto, "Islam's 'Strange Secret Sharer': Orientalism, Judaism, and the Jewish Question," *Comparative Studies in Society and History* 40, no. 3 (1998): 437–74.

18. Ivan D. Kalmar and Derek J. Penslar, eds., *Orientalism and the Jews* (Waltham, MA: Brandeis University Press, 2005).

19. It would be interesting to see how far this knowledge was preserved in the Jewish and Muslim communities in North Africa as well, where the majority of the refugees from Spain settled over the centuries.

20. Michael Ragussis, "Writing Spanish History in Nineteenth-Century Britain: The Inquisition and the 'Secret Race,'" in *Sephardism: Spanish Jewish History and the Modern Literary Imagination*, ed. Yael Halevi-Wise (Stanford, CA: Stanford University Press, 2012), 73.

21. John M. Efron, *German Jewry and the Allure of the Sephardic* (Princeton, NJ: Princeton University Press, 2016).

22. Carsten Schapkow, *Role Model and Countermodel: The Golden Age of Iberian Jewry and German Jewish Culture during the Era of Emancipation* (Lanham, MD: Lexington Books, 2015), 13.

23. See Florian Krobb, *Kollektivautobiographien, Wunschautobiographien: Marranen-schicksal im deutsch-jüdischen historischen Roman* (Würzburg: Königshausen & Neumann, 2002).

24. See Ragussis, "Writing Spanish History in Nineteenth-Century Britain."

25. See in general David Feldman, *Englishmen and Jews: Social Relations and Political Culture, 1840–1914* (New Haven, CT: Yale University Press, 1994).

26. David Feldman, "Evangelicals, Jews, and Anti-Catholicism in Britain, c. 1840–1900," *Jewish Historical Studies* 47, no. 1 (2015): 103.

27. See D. G. Paz, *Popular Anti-Catholicism in Mid-Victorian England* (Stanford, CA: Stanford University Press, 1992), 103–108; see also Feldman, *Englishmen and Jews*, 54.

28. Nadia Valman, *The Jewess in Nineteenth-Century British Literary Culture* (Cambridge: Cambridge University Press, 2007).

29. Ibid., 104.

30. Ibid., 10.

31. Diane Long Hoeveler, *The Gothic Ideology: Religious Hysteria and Anti-Catholicism in British Popular Fiction, 1780–1880* (Cardiff: University of Wales Press, 2014), 5.

32. Paz, *Popular Anti-Catholicism in Mid-Victorian England*, 299.

33. Feldman, "Evangelicals, Jews, and Anti-Catholicism in Britain," 88, 103.

34. Feldman, *Englishmen and Jews*, 56.

35. Ibid., 55.

36. See Paz, *Popular Anti-Catholicism in Mid-Victorian England*, 2, 131.

37. See also Stefanie Schüler-Springorum, "Von Mördern und Marranen: Antijudaismus und Antikatholizismus in Grace Aguilars *Vale of Cedars*," in *Bibel - Israel - Kirche: Studien zur jüdisch-christlichen Begegnung: Festschrift für Rainer Kampling*, ed. Sara Han, Anja Middelbeck-Varwick, and Markus Thurau (Münster: Aschendorff Verlag, 2018).

38. The following is part of my argument in my contribution to the roundtable debate in the *American Historical Review*: Stefanie Schüler-Springorum, "Gender and the Politics of Anti-Semitism," *American Historical Review* 123, no. 4 (October 2018): 1210–22.

39. See Ute Frevert, *Women in German History: From Bourgeois Emancipation to Sexual Liberation*, trans. Stuart McKinnon-Evans, Terry Bond, and Barbara Norden (Oxford: Berg, 1989); Shulamit Volkov, "Antisemitism and Anti-Feminism: Social Norm or Cultural Code?" [in Hebrew] *Zmanim: A Historical Quarterly*, nos. 46/47 (1993): 134–43; Angelika Schaser and Stefanie Schüler-Springorum, eds., *Liberalismus und Emanzipation: In- und Exklusionsprozesse im Kaiserreich und in der Weimarer Republik* (Stuttgart: Franz Steiner Verlag, 2010).

40. See Hannah Lotte Lund, *Der Berliner "jüdische Salon" um 1800: Emanzipation in der Debatte* (Berlin: De Gruyter, 2012).

41. Marion Schulte, *Über die bürgerlichen Verhältnisse der Juden in Preußen: Ziele und Motive der Reformzeit (1787–1812)* (Berlin: De Gruyter, 2014), 515.

42. Quoted in Michael Berger, *Eisernes Kreuz und Davidstern: die Geschichte jüdischer Soldaten in deutschen Armeen* (Berlin: Trafo, 2006), 137.

43. Sander L. Gilman, "The Jewish Foot: A Foot-Note to the Jewish Body," in *The Jew's Body* (New York: Routledge, 1991), 38–59.

44. See George L. Mosse, *Nationalism and Sexuality: Respectability and Abnormal Sexuality in Modern Europe* (New York: H. Fertig, 1985); Stefanie Schüler-Springorum, *Geschlecht und Differenz* (Paderborn: Schöningh, 2014).

45. See Gavin I. Langmuir, *Toward a Definition of Antisemitism* (Berkeley: University of California Press, 1990).

46. Jean Delumeau, *Sin and Fear: The Emergence of a Western Guilt Culture, 13th–18th Centuries* (New York: St. Martin's Press, 1990).

47. See Christian Begemann, *Furcht und Angst im Prozess der Aufklärung: zu Literatur und Bewusstseinsgeschichte des 18. Jahrhunderts* (Frankfurt am Main: Athenäum, 1987); Joanna Bourke, "Fear and Anxiety: Writing about Emotion in Modern History," *History Workshop Journal*, no. 55 (2003): 111–33.

48. Zygmunt Bauman, *Life in Fragments: Essays in Postmodern Morality* (Oxford: Blackwell, 1995), 208.

49. See Jonathan Judaken's highly instructive introduction to the *AHR* Roundtable on "Rethinking Anti-Semitism": Jonathan Judaken, "Rethinking Anti-Semitism: Introduction," *American Historical Review* 123, no. 4 (October 2018): 1122–38.

50. See Stefanie Schüler-Springorum, "Sex and Violence: Race Defilement in Nazi Germany," in *Contemporary Europe in the Historical Imagination*, ed. Darcy Buerkle and Skye Doney (Madison: University of Wisconsin Press, 2023), ch. 6.

III

PREMODERN CONTEXTUALIZATIONS

6

Separation, Judeophobia, and the Birth of the "Goy"
The Chicken and the Egg

ADI M. OPHIR *and* ISHAY ROSEN-ZVI

Antisemitism, Judeophobia, and Other Anachronisms: A Methodological Preface

Various scholars propose using terms like "Judeophobia" or "Jew-hatred" instead of "antisemitism" to signify a negative attitude toward Jews in antiquity, specifically in pre-Christian literatures. The new terms are no less fuzzy than "antisemitism," whose fluid usage David Engel identifies in his essay "Away from a Definition of Antisemitism."[1] However, in contrast to "antisemitism," the categories "Judeophobia," "Jew-hatred," and the like are meant to be *explicitly* and *avowedly* anachronistic. They entered use not to describe a distinct phenomenon, but to distinguish themselves from the transhistorical concept of antisemitism.[2]

It must be admitted, however, that the widespread use of the alternative terms is still a reification, flawed with all the same problems that Engel identifies with using the term "antisemitism." Together, they create a false impression of essential features and of historical continuity among different phenomena. To address this problem once and for all, Engel suggests getting rid of this broad categorization entirely and instead identifying each phenomenon separately. He thus presumes that it is possible to isolate and remove a problematic term like one would remove a weed or tumor, without impacting the system as a whole.

But is this really possible? Engel's compelling reconstruction of the evolution of the term "antisemitism" undermines his own thesis in that he describes how Jews and non-Jews participated in both using and problematizing the term "antisemitism." The term's vagueness enabled its application to phenomena that earlier speakers would not have associated with antisemitism. That is, when Engel studies the actual use of the term "antisemitism," he grasps it, notwithstanding his declarations to the contrary, as a completely discursive formation of which the term's vagueness is an integral part. Therefore, it is not sufficient to remove one concept in order to "fix" the historians' "mistake"; rather, it is necessary to scrutinize and deconstruct the discourse in its entirety. The scrutiny of a similar discursive formation occupies us when we turn our view to antiquity.

Separation as a Mirror Game: Between Judeophobia and Xenophobia

Holding stereotypical attitudes toward other peoples is not an extraordinary phenomenon in the ancient world, and Jews were not especially vilified in this regard.[3] Louis Feldman showed that most references to Jews in antiquity are not negative. Extreme expressions of Jew-hatred (which we will discuss in detail below) are the exceptions and do not attest to a general trend. Gideon Bohak compared Hellenistic writers' treatment of Jews to their treatment of Egyptians and concluded that not only was the attitude toward Jews no more negative than the attitude toward other peoples, but also that Jews did not especially interest Hellenistic writers.[4] Benjamin Isaac contended that the attitude toward Jews was even less severe in comparison to others, as no "natural" racial features were attributed to them.[5] The optics of special harassment of Jews in ancient writings, these scholars explained, stem both from how material was preserved and transmitted by Christian copyists (who were naturally more interested in stories about Jews than about Persians or Gauls) and from how descriptions of Jews are presented in modern scholarship (especially in the comprehensive work of Menahem Stern, on which much of the scholarship of recent decades is based), which isolates the treatment of Jews from its general ethnographic contexts.[6]

Yet even when taking all of this into consideration, one issue indeed remains extraordinary. Most writers who criticize Jews repeat, in various forms, the same claim: Jews are self-segregating, xenophobic, "misanthropes."[7] This motif appears from the beginning of the Hellenistic period (the first to mention it is Hecataeus of Abdera in ca. 300 BCE), and it recurs repeatedly from then on, even among writers who are not critical toward Jews, like Hecataeus and Strabo.[8] Individuals from various groups were occasionally slandered with the accusation of misanthropy, but it was directed against only one ethnic group: Jews.[9] Scholars disagree about whether Greece or Egypt was the birthplace of this motif,[10] but there is no disputing that from the moment of its birth, the motif was stable and migrated from writer to writer until reaching its fullest development in imperial Rome.[11]

For ancient writers, Jews were thus different from others in the ways they differentiated themselves from others. This is clearly expressed in Hellenistic writers' recurring emphasis on the main commandments that differentiate Jews: dietary laws, circumcision, and the Sabbath. Monotheism is also linked to Jewish difference because, in the eyes of Hellenistic writers, just as Jews seek to separate themselves, so too, their God refuses to associate with other Gods.[12] Note that for Hellenists, Jewish self-segregation is not the result of their strange conduct, but its cause. In the words of Diodorus Siculus, writing in the first century BCE, Jews "made hatred of mankind into a tradition, and on this account (*dia touto*) had introduced utterly outlandish laws: not to break bread with any other race, nor to show them any good will at all."[13]

Practices like circumcision, abstaining from eating pork, and making graven images, which on their own are inexplicable to these writers, are explained as means of self-segregation. Misanthropy is also the recurring motif in most Greek and Roman versions of the story of the Exodus from Egypt.[14] Various writers also emphasize the other side of the same coin: intra-ethnic fraternity (*symphonia*, *concordia*), which grants Jews, as a group, awesome political power.[15]

The most explicit formulation of these claims, which is also the most detailed and radical anti-Jewish depiction, appears as a sort of addendum to Book Five of Tacitus's *Histories*, prefacing a section devoted to Titus's suppression of the Jewish Revolt.[16] After Tacitus describes their origin (*origo*) and tells his version of the Exodus story, he turns to describing Jewish manners (*mores*) and identifying their characteristic self-separating practices.[17] He has no special sympathy for Jews—enemies who rebelled against the empire—but also does not use harsh expressions of hatred; it seems that the Jews do not cost him much sleep.[18] Several of his formulations have a patently negative tone, but there are also assertions that are nonjudgmental and matter-of-fact (for example, on worship and burial practices and the immortality of the soul) and even positive (for example, about compassion toward one another, shunning the abandonment of unwanted babies, and the absence of statues). For our purposes, it is significant that the negative attitude toward Jews is not the organizing motif of the entire tract; rather, it is discernible only in the description of Jewish separation,[19] where Tacitus, like other writers, expresses disdain and rejection.[20] Though the addendum was interpreted by scholars as an attempt to explain Jewish rebelliousness during the Jewish War in 66–73 CE, rebelliousness against the regime is not among the Jewish characteristics that the addendum itself addresses (at least not in the part that has reached us). Comparing Tacitus's descriptions, written in an imperial Roman context, with those of Hecataeus of Abdera, written over four centuries earlier in an Alexandrian Hellenistic context,[21] clarifies both the excessive radicalization vis-à-vis Jews and the stable motifs of this tradition, with self-separation and segregation foremost among them.[22] This stability warrants a structural analysis, which we will attempt to offer below.[23]

In Tacitus's description of Jews, four different planes of separation can be discerned: A) Their customs differ greatly from ours ("The Jews regard as profane all that we hold sacred"; "the other customs of the Jews are base and abominable"; and so forth). B) They devote special efforts to distinguishing themselves ("They sit apart at meals, and they sleep apart, [...] they abstain from intercourse with foreign women"). C) They exhibit solidarity within their community but "hate and enmity" for outsiders. D) They signify their separateness through circumcision "to distinguish themselves from other peoples by this difference." What impresses Tacitus is not just one custom or another but their accumulation, the way that Jews occupy themselves with and reinforce their own separateness.

Alongside emphasizing separation, various writers express fear about missionizing and Judaizing, fear that found clear expression in the legislation of Antoninus Pius in the second century CE, which permitted circumcision for Jews but forbade it for proselytization and conversion. The extant evidence does not permit us to decide the extent to which this was a real anxiety that emerged because of an actual Judaizing trend or mainly a rhetorical trope intended to serve other objectives.[24] Either way, fear of Judaization clearly did not contradict the view of Jews as separated. Tacitus states this explicitly:

> And the earliest habit [the converts] adopt is to despise the gods, to renounce their country, and to regard their parents, children, and brothers as of little consequence.

That is, Jewish separatism constitutes a problem not because Jews do not welcome outsiders into their communities, but because converts join the polarizing Jewish alignment of "us" versus everyone else.[25]

Things become more complicated once we discover that Jews too depicted Jewish separatism. To be sure, in various Jewish works "accusations" of misanthropy and separatism are placed in the mouths of non-Jews,[26] and writers like Philo and Josephus made efforts to counter these accusations by emphasizing Jewish philanthropy.[27] However, not all Jewish apologetic writers shy away from separatism. The Jewish Hellenistic *Letter of Aristeas* emphasizes Jewish separation, viewing the dietary laws as a barrier wall and segregation as their objective:

> Our Lawgiver being a wise man and specially endowed by God to understand all things, took a comprehensive view of each particular detail, and fenced us round (*periephraxen*) with impregnable ramparts and walls of iron, that we might not mingle at all with any of the other nations, but remain pure in body and soul, free from all vain imaginations ... Therefore lest we should be corrupted by any abomination, or our lives be perverted by evil communications, he fenced us round (*periephraxen*) on all sides by rules of purity.[28]

At the same time, Aristeas takes pains to explain that neither the

commandment to remain separate nor the practices it entails is exceptional, as every people has its own dietary customs.[29] The apologetics
of Aristeas does not minimize separation, but rather insists that self-
separation itself is something that Jews and others have in common.
However, the negative implies the positive; the claim to which Aristeas
responds is precisely the one articulated above, namely: Jews are different in the way they differentiate themselves from others.

The attempt to formulate the principles of Jewish separatism without turning these principles themselves into what differentiates Jews
from others is found in Philo and Josephus as well, for, alongside their
apologetics, they also emphasize the centrality of separation and difference to Jewish existence.[30] Josephus, whose *Contra Apion* is our
main source for documentation of anti-Jewish accusations,[31] responds
to them, first and foremost, with a claim of *intra*-Jewish solidarity.[32]
Additional Jewish writers use separation to explain the rationales for
various laws, primarily in matters of sexual ethics.[33] It is no wonder,
then, that several scholars maintain that the words attributed to Hecataeus above[34] are nothing but a Jewish forgery that purports to praise
and even celebrate Jewish exclusivity.[35] Whether we accept it or not, this
hypothesis is only possible because the claim of Jewish distinctiveness
sounds quite similar on both sides of the dividing line.

Indeed, Jews' awareness of the distinctiveness of their separateness
emerges from texts composed centuries apart: from the Book of Esther
through *Aristeas* and from 3 Maccabees to *Contra Apion*. Jews and non-
Jews alike portray everyday forms of Jewish separation and at the same
time imagine them as possibly leading to murderous behavior. Each
side, of course, imagines the murder as coming from the other. Thus,
on one side, there is Apion's notorious blood libel that the Jews have
an annual ritual in which they murder a Greek in their Temple (*Contra
Apion* 2:93–95), and on the other side are the royal decrees of genocide
as imagined in Esther and 3 Maccabees. Despite the clear differences, it
is important to note the shared aspects of the two forms of discourse.

An Amoraic midrash explicitly recognizes the link between Jewish
self-separation and Jew-hatred. The verse in Lamentations that articulates the hatred of gentiles for Israel is explained by the midrash as
the result of the God-given laws of separation:

"All my foes heard of my plight and exulted, for it is Your doing" (Lam. 1:21): It is You Who made it [that the nations would rejoice at my downfall]. They gave a parable: To what is this comparable? To a king who married a matron; he would command her and tell her: "Do not converse with your neighbors. Do not lend to them and do not borrow from them." One time, she mocked him, and [the king] tired of her and expelled her from his palace. She went from door to door among the neighbors, and not a single one accepted her.... She said to him, "My lord king, is it not you who did this? Did you not command me and say to me, 'Do not converse with your neighbors. Do not lend to them and do not borrow from them'?"... So too Israel said to the Holy One, blessed be He: "Sovereign of the universe, is it not You Who did this? Did You not write to us in the Torah, 'Do not marry among them; do not give your daughter to his son, and do not take his daughter for your son' (Deut. 7:3). Had we married among them or given [our daughters] to marry them, which of them would have seen a son or a daughter standing at the door and not have accepted them?" Thus: "for it is Your doing."[36]

But what is the nature of the connection between the image of Jews in the eyes of non-Jews, on one hand, and the ways that Jews distinguish themselves from non-Jews in their practices and self-perception, on the other? Is anti-Judaism just the mirror image of distinctive Jewish practices? Or perhaps the relationship is the reverse: Did Jews internalize an external image of them as self-segregating?

The question of the link between Jewish separateness and (pre-Christian) Jew-hatred is fraught with blatantly ideological and political dimensions.[37] Although most scholars acknowledge that Jewish separation formed, in one way or another, the real basis for Greek and Roman anti-Jewish sentiments,[38] and even though ancient sources—both Hellenistic and Jewish—connect Jewish separation with the attitudes toward them, scholars who consider the link between self-separation and Judeophobia focus mainly on the impact of "Jew-hatred" on Jews' self-image and their efforts to differentiate themselves from gentiles. The question of the impact of Jewish separation on Judeophobia, when it appears, is addressed only within local contexts: the links between specific events (like the Maccabean wars, the struggle of Alexandrian Jews for citizenship, or the strengthening of the Jewish community in Rome) and the emergence of anti-Jewish sentiments in certain communities.[39] There is no attempt to think about how Jewish separation feeds the discourse about Jews that appears in different places and at different times.[40] Perhaps the reason for this lacuna is a concern about a slippery slope that blurs the line between historical explanation and victim blaming, a matter that we cannot develop further here.[41]

An even deeper problem is the lack of attention to the motifs, metaphors, and discursive formations that serve both Jewish and non-Jewish descriptions and explanations of Jewish separation. This lack of attention reflects a schism in scholarship: The study of Jewish self-separation and the study of attitudes toward Jews are two branches of research, each productive on its own but rarely interacting with the other.[42]

How can the connection be made non-reductively? Obviously, there is some back-and-forth. Jewish self-separation is described in early texts, like Esther[43] and the beginning of Daniel, so the narrative cannot simply be of Jewish internalization of Hellenistic stereotypes.[44] On the other hand, writers like Philo and Josephus had already internalized Hellenistic accusations and reacted to them, as Katell Berthelot demonstrates in her study of the concept of "philanthropy" within Hellenistic Judaism.[45] The sources point to a shared discourse, part of which is a sort of mirror game. But the nature of the game is not clear, and the mirrors, each in its own way, distort.

Standing before the Drunk King: Jewish Extermination Fantasies

How do Jewish writers contend with the foreign gaze that regards their separateness? Side by side with attempts to normalize difference (like Aristeas regarding table customs or the apologetics of Philo and Josephus), we find profound anxiety over the meaning and implications of their exclusionary self-separation. This is already the case in the Book of Esther, and even more so in two proximate works: the additions to Esther in the Septuagint and 3 Maccabees.[46] While the texts that minimize separateness formulate and justify it politically as a familiar, normal phenomenon, the texts that express anxiety resort to miracles and thus divert the discussion to a blatantly theo-political plane: In Esther the miracle is still hidden, but it becomes explicit in the Septuagint's refashioning of the story and takes center stage in another version of the clash between the king and the Jews narrated in 3 Maccabees.

In the latter, the Egyptian pharaoh Ptolemy IV Philopator wants to force the Jews of Alexandria to participate in the worship of Dionysus. When most of them refuse, he orders that all the Jews of Egypt be rounded up into the hippodrome outside the walls of Alexandria and killed by drunken elephants. The Jews are saved through a series of surprising events, culminating in an overt miracle that causes the king to change his mind and blame the persecution on his wicked advisors. The story ends, like Esther, and apparently under its influence, with the Jews rejoicing and establishing a holiday in commemoration.

What makes 3 Maccabees a successful test case for our argument is its distinct theatrical dimension. The story creates a spectacle, vividly describing the detailed preparations for the destruction of Jewish life in Egypt, which include physical concentration and control of movement and involve the intricate organization of space and time. In doing so, the story sharpens the confrontation—and contrast—between God and the foreign king and displays the conditions of Jewish political existence. In the first act, the text clearly marks the Temple of Jerusalem as a place requiring the exclusion of strangers, in this case the foreign king himself, while bringing into sharp relief the danger involved in this exclusion. At the end of the plot, a solution allowing separation under the foreign ruler is formulated, and the threat associated with separation is eliminated. The anxiety produced in the first act thus finds its resolution through radicalization and catharsis. The Jewish obsession with their exclusionary difference is translated into anni-hilation anxiety that is created by a series of recurring scenes where the imminent catastrophe is narrated in detail. Shocked readers are led from the peak of anxiety through a comedy of suspense and errors to an ecstatic outlet and, finally, redemption. This detailed, theatrical unfolding of the plot allows us to identify the pattern of the relationship between separation, sovereign power, and violence.

Even if we assume 3 Maccabees has some real historical basis (itself a dubious proposition), it should obviously be viewed as a continuation and radicalization of biblical imaginings of annihilation.[47] The prayers that appear in 3 Maccabees explicitly invoke two scriptural models of mass annihilation—Sodom and Gomorrah (2:5) and the plagues of Egypt (2:6, 6:4).[48] The work is primarily in dialogue, however, with the Book of Esther. Both works revolve around practices—and accusations—of separation. In both, the Jews' insistence on separation provokes hatred and leads to a plan of total annihilation, but ultimately the plan is foiled, and the distinctive Jewish lifestyle of self-separation is allowed to continue under the aegis of a friendly foreign sovereign.

In this pattern, the external threat does not challenge the separation, but rather amplifies it—first, as the form of the disaster (the enslavement of and plan to gather and kill the Jews), next, as a response to the disaster (fasting and mourning), and, finally, as its solution (the holiday). The radicalization of separation ends in salvation, which reestablishes separatism. In both compositions, separation is the Jews' form of existence from beginning to end: the problem as well as the solution.

The narrative of annihilation is not solely a Jewish one, however. It appears also on the Hellenists' side. Diodorus Siculus recounts that the advisors of Antiochus VII Sidetes counseled him, during the siege of Jerusalem in 132 BCE, "to wipe out completely (*exelein*) the Jewish people, since they alone of all nations avoided dealings (*amixian*) with any other people and looked upon all men as their enemies."[49] Diodorus's narrative, like Esther and 3 Maccabees, focuses on a proposal of annihilation accompanied by a description of the Jews' strange customs, which is meant, just as when cited by Haman in the Book of Esther, as a sort of indictment. According to Diodorus, the king rejected the proposal and was content to ruin the city walls. Historians who view this narrative as reliable testimony connect the beginnings of Jew-hatred with the Hasmonean struggle.[50] But if we acknowledge that the story of Diodorus (or his source), just like those of Esther and 3 Maccabees, is likely to be imaginary, then we may leave aside historical speculations and acknowledge that the motif of a proposal to annihilate Jews—as well as its rejection—is entertained by Jews and non-Jews alike.

Nevertheless, as far as we can tell, Diodorus's story is singular, whereas the motif of a plot to annihilate Israel recurs time after time in the Jewish tradition—from Pharaoh in the Book of Exodus (1:22) and the eruptions of God's wrath in the wilderness, to the plots of Esther and 3 Maccabees, to later reworkings and Jewish liturgy. Diodorus's story is similar to those within the Jewish tradition in terms of both the motifs used and how they explain the relations between Jews and rulers. The connection between self-separation and annihilation, however, becomes a stable topos *only* in Jewish texts. For Hellenistic writers, Jewish separation is a marginal issue that emerges specifically at times of crisis (like with Apion and his colleagues concerning the disturbances in Alexandria), whereas for Jews it is constantly problematized.[51]

For Hellenistic writers, Jewish separation is a matter of lifestyle. Their versions of the Exodus story link it with mores and misanthropy, not rebelliousness. This is especially prominent in Tacitus, who, although interested in explaining Jewish might in their revolt during the first Roman–Jewish War,[52] is mainly occupied with Jewish separation in the context of everyday practices because, for him, it is these practices that are the key to understanding the Jewish character.[53] In contrast, Jewish writers see separation, first and foremost, as a political problem that emerges in times of crisis. In both Esther and 3 Maccabees, the grievance against Jewish distinctiveness is described as pertaining to citizenship (Esther 3:8: "their laws are different from those of any other people, and they do not obey the king's laws"; 3 Maccabees 3:7: "the foreigners [*allophules*] kept going on about the differences [*diastasis*] in doing obeisance and diet, claiming that these people...were hostile and vehemently opposed to affairs of state"; ibid., 3:19: "Unique amongst the nations in their haughtiness towards their kings").[54] The story in 3 Maccabees is resolved by demonstrating that the opposition is artificial. Rebelliousness is ascribed specifically to heretical Jews, while adherence to God and loyalty to the king are shown to be in line with one another (3 Maccabees 7:11).

The question of separation in 3 Maccabees, as in biblical and post-biblical texts before it, is considered in a concrete political context. Here, however, the separation is not seen as protection against the danger of annihilation, as it is presented in the Priestly or Deuteronomic layers of the Pentateuch, but as the source of the danger itself. The threat is transferred from God to the foreign ruler.[55] The relationship with the ruler, not God, is marked by the politics of separation, that is, the negotiation of difference that can be contained and accommodated. The success of the negotiations and the elimination of the threat depend on divine intervention, which must be renewed every time an external threat appears. However, divine intervention neither removes foreign rule nor claims to replace it. Rather than being predetermined, separation is an ongoing project for Jews that requires a sympathetic non-Jewish space. Jews can imagine such a space because they do not see the non-Jewish environment as homogenous; it includes friends as well as enemies, and the foreign rulers are fickle but not necessarily hostile.

Conclusion

To summarize, scholars of classical antiquity have avoided dealing with Jews' contribution to how they were perceived by others, and they therefore have not noticed that the idea of Jewish separateness was shared by Jews and non-Jews. Both sides recognized that Jews differ from other peoples in the manner and intensity of their separation. This insight recurs among Jews, Hellenists, and Romans alike, and it can be seen as a sign of a shared discourse, a common foundation for both Jewish xenophobia and Hellenistic Judeophobia. Moreover, in the corpus we examined, Jews always considered their separateness not only through their own eyes, but through those of outsiders as well. This perspective can be seen in Jewish descriptions of various reactions to their practices of separation (threats in Esther and 3 Maccabees; approval and acceptance in the *Letter of Aristeas*; discomfort and critique in *Contra Apion*).

But this is where the agreement ends. On the Hellenistic and Roman side, most stories of Jewish separation focus on lifestyle and do not have patently political contexts. Jews are tolerated despite their separation, even when it provokes criticism, and it alone cannot explain outbreaks of violence against them. In contrast, the Jewish texts we examined above consider separation primarily in imperial political contexts and through the eyes of the ruling power. Contemplating the foreign ruler's attitude to their separation leads simultaneously to two opposing results: On one hand, the dangers of a radicalized separation are exaggerated, and may even lead to total annihilation; on the other hand, the political contextualization of the threat ultimately allows them to imagine a situation in which the imperial regime includes Jewish separateness.

In both Esther and 3 Maccabees, Jews imagine their own annihilation, but this imagining is not a reaction to concrete events. (Scholarship has not found a set of circumstances that matches the stories of annihilation in the Persian, Hellenistic, or Roman eras.) In this context, "Judeophobia" is, in the first place, a Jewish phobia. But this phobia of being feared should be understood as a discursive element, not a psychological state. These representations express the self-consciousness of a minority culture subjected to an imperial regime as it projects biblical images of total annihilation, which God uses to intimidate his people, onto the alien regime. Imagining the threat and overcoming of annihilation offers writers a way to include the non-Jewish perspective in their representations of separation and, paradoxically, makes it possible to contend with the foreign threat.

The specific story of 3 Maccabees may be strange to us, but we can easily identify in it the template for the saying, "In every generation, they rise against us to destroy us." This particular formulation from the Passover Haggadah comes from a later period, but 3 Maccabees already freely uses motifs from the Exodus story and Esther to recount a "new incident." The myth, then, predates and shapes the history (logically and psychologically, of course, but in this case, chronologically as well), and its Jewish narrator actively fashions it. Yet at the same time, the texts examined here show that the effect, and perhaps even purpose, of the early appearances of the myth was not to posit a sharp contrast between the Jew and the world, but, on the contrary, to find a way to resolve the tension and enable loyalty to both the alien political power and to God. We propose to connect this complex way of thinking with the fact that when the works under discussion were composed, the "other" was still multifaceted, and there was not yet a ready-made mold of "gentiles" that incorporated this entire multiplicity.

Our contention, therefore, is that Jewish writers saw their relations with non-Jews as a double-edged sword. They looked primarily through a grandiose prism of cruel, malevolent rulers that contrasted sharply

with the more everyday perspective we identified in non-Jewish representations. On one hand, this prism caused these writers to imagine,
over and over, their own complete annihilation, but, on the other hand,
it enabled and in fact justified political negotiations with alien rulers,
and even proposed models for such negotiations.

This picture was fundamentally altered with the rise of the rabbinic
discourse regarding the "goy." This new discourse resolved internal
contradictions in the story of self-separation, gave it coherence, and
negated its dependence on the outsider perspective, while at the same
time it cut off possible *modi vivendi* with the other that had existed previously. This story, which we address elsewhere, lies beyond the scope
of the present study, whose aim is to discuss the early developments
of the theme of Jewish separation, Judeophobia, and the convoluted
connections between them.[56]

NOTES

1. David Engel, "Away from a Definition of Antisemitism: An Essay in the Semantics
of Historical Description," in *Rethinking European Jewish History*, ed. Jeremy Cohen
and Moshe Rosman (Oxford: Littman Library of Jewish Civilization, 2009), 30–53.

2. On the term "Judeophobia" and its history, see the preface to Peter Schäfer, *Judeophobia: Attitudes Toward the Jews in the Ancient World* (Cambridge, MA: Harvard
University Press, 1997). On the claim about the Christian origins of antisemitism,
see Rosemary Radford Ruether, *Faith and Fratricide: The Theological Roots of Anti-
Semitism* (New York: Seabury Press, 1974), and its critique in J. N. Sevenster, *The
Roots of Pagan Anti-Semitism in the Ancient World* (Leiden: Brill, 1975). See also the
studies addressed in nn. 4–6 below.

3. For a full statistical study, see Louis H. Feldman, *Jew and Gentile in the Ancient
World: Attitudes and Interactions from Alexander to Justinian* (Princeton, NJ: Princeton
University Press, 1993), 124.

4. Gideon Bohak, "The Ibis and the Jewish Question: Ancient 'Anti-Semitism' in
Historical Perspective," in *Jews and Gentiles in the Holy Land in the Days of the Second
Temple, the Mishnah and the Talmud*, ed. Menahem Mor (Jerusalem: Yad Ben Zvi,
2003), 23–24.

5. Benjamin H. Isaac, *The Invention of Racism in Classical Antiquity* (Princeton, NJ:
Princeton University Press, 2004). See his conclusion that even those traits of ancient
racism (or proto-racism, as he defines it on p. 446, namely, environmental deter-
minism and immutable, inherited characteristics), are not to be found with regard
to Jews. See also, Shaye J. D. Cohen, "Anti-Semitism in Antiquity: The Problem of
Definition," in *History and Hate: The Dimensions of Anti-Semitism*, ed. David Berger

(Philadelphia: Jewish Publication Society, 1986), 43–47; Zvi Yavetz, "Judeophobia in Classical Antiquity: A Different Approach," *Journal of Jewish Studies* 44, no. 1 (1993): 1–22; John G. Gager, *The Origins of Anti-Semitism: Attitudes toward Judaism in Pagan and Christian Antiquity* (New York: Oxford University Press, 1983); David Nirenberg, *Anti-Judaism: The Western Tradition* (New York: W. W. Norton, 2013).

6. Menahem Stern, ed. *Greek and Latin Authors on Jews and Judaism*, 3 vols. (Jerusalem: Israel Academy of Sciences and Humanities, 1974). On these biases, see Bohak, "Ibis," and Yavetz, "Judeophobia."

7. See Schäfer, *Judeophobia*, 19–20; Feldman, *Jew and Gentile*, 125; and Bezalel Bar-Kochva, *The Image of the Jews in Greek Literature: The Hellenistic Period* (Berkeley: University of California Press, 2010), 39, 108, 129–35.

8. Stern, *Greek and Latin*, vol. 1, no. 11, 26–35. See below, n. 23.

9. See Schäfer, *Judeophobia*, 170–1; Katell Berthelot, "Hecataeus of Abdera and Jewish 'Misanthropy,'" *Bulletin du Centre de Recherche Français à Jérusalem* 19 (November 30, 2008): 1, 5. See also Brent D. Shaw, "The Myth of the Neronian Persecution," *Journal of Roman Studies* 105 (2015): 73–100, 86; John Granger Cook, *Roman Attitudes toward the Christians: From Claudius to Hadrian* (Tübingen: Mohr Siebeck, 2010), 62–65. It is true that in the classical period, Egyptians were also accused of xenophobia (compare Genesis 43:32), but this accusation disappeared during the Hellenistic period with the transformation of Alexandria into a cosmopolis. See Bar-Kochva, *Jews in Greek Literature*, 130; Bohak, "Ibis," 35.

10. For the thesis of Egyptian origin, see John G. Gager, *Moses in Greco-Roman Paganism* (Nashville: Abingdon Press, 1972), 113; Bar-Kochva, *Jews in Greek Literature*, 116 and n. 70. The argument is based primarily on Manetho's account of the Exodus from Egypt and its traces among the Egyptian priests in the delegation against Philo, cited by Josephus in *Contra Apion*, 1.73–102; 227–253. Against this view, see Bar-Kochva, *Jews in Greek Literature*, 130; Schäfer, *Judeophobia*, 17; Berthelot, "Hecataeus," 1. The latter scholars contend that misanthropy is a distinctly Hellenistic accusation. Additional evidence of the Hellenistic source of the motif is that it first appears in Hecataeus, who was unfamiliar with the Egyptian exodus story of the lepers who took over the land. On this, see Berthelot, "Hecataeus," 4.

11. As shown by Isaac, the motif was especially developed by Roman writers such as Horace, Cicero, Seneca, Tacitus, Martial, Juvenal, and others. Isaac, *Invention of Racism*. The character of the recurring motifs is also distinctly Roman: accusations of contempt for Roman law and expressions and fears of secret worship, of repression of traditional customs, of collegiality, and of the takeover of Rome by the East. The writings of Tacitus are "the essence and climax of all the motifs which in antiquity are connected with the Jews." Schäfer, *Judeophobia*, 32. See Gager, *The Origins of Anti-Semitism*, 40, who maintains that we know very little about the attitudes of pagan writers prior to the Roman conquest of Judea.

12. Isaac, *Invention of Racism*, 469. As Isaac demonstrates, the adjective *akoinonetos* serves to describe the unsociability of both the Jewish people and their God. Compare

Josephus who cites Apollonius Molon on Jews who refuse "to share fellowship" (*koinonein*) with those who choose "a different way of life." *Contra Apion*, 2.258.

13. Diodorus Siculus, *Bibliotheca Historica*, 34–35.1.1. Stern, *Greek and Latin*, vol. 1, no. 63, 181–85. Translation based on Isaac, *Invention of Racism*, 451; see Schäfer, *Judeophobia*, 22.

14. See Feldman, *Jew and Gentile*, 128; Schäfer, *Judeophobia*, 32.

15. See Feldman, *Jew and Gentile*, 143, 173; Isaac, *Invention of Racism*, 454–55 (Cicero and Horace).

16. Tacitus, *Histories* 5.2–13; Stern, *Greek and Latin*, vol. 2, no. 281, 17–63. Translations based on Tacitus, *Histories: Books 4–5. Annals: Books 1–3*, trans. Clifford H. Moore and John Jackson (Cambridge, MA: Harvard University Press, 1931). Background material on this addendum can be found in the groundbreaking article by Yochanan Lewy, "Tacitus on the Origin and Manners of the Jews," [in Hebrew] *Zion* 8 (1942–43): 1–34, 61–84. On the article by Lewy and its context, see R. S. Bloch, *Antike Vorstellungen vom Judentum: der Judenexkurs des Tacitus im Rahmen der griechisch-römischen Ethnographie* (Stuttgart: Franz Steiner Verlag, 2002), 22–26.

17. Tacitus's narration of "the other customs of the Jews," which developed later and "are base and abominable," begins with practices of separation and then goes on to burial, theology, and worship. On the structure of the addendum, see Bloch, *Antike Vorstellungen vom Judentum*, 113–6.

18. "For a man who served as a governor of Asia his knowledge of Jews and Christians is woefully (and unnecessarily) confused." Ronald Mellor, *Tacitus* (New York: Routledge, 1993), 32.

19. We use "separation" to render the Hebrew term היבדלות (*hibadlut*) and maintain the double meaning of a state or a condition *and* a practice. When only the condition is meant, we use "separateness."

20. See Heinz Heubner, *Die Historien: Kommentar*, vol. 5 (Heidelberg: Carl Winter, 1982), 66–67.

21. "The sacrifices that he [Moses] established differ from those of other nations, as does their way of living, for as a result of their own expulsion (*ten idian xenelasian*) from Egypt he introduced a way of life which was somewhat unsocial and hostile to foreigners (*apanthrōpon tina kai misoxenon bion)*." Diodorus Siculus, *Bibliotheca Historica*, 40.3.4; Stern, *Greek and Latin*, vol. 1, no. 11; translation of Schäfer, *Judeophobia*, 16. See Bar-Kochva, *Jews in Greek Literature*, 99–135.

22. This is not self-evident. For the sake of comparison, in medieval Christian attacks, self-separation is taken as a given and is not the object of direct attacks. In the Paris disputation of 1240, the Talmud "stood trial" for its statements against gentiles and against Jesus, not for laws that separate Jews from gentiles, which Hellenistic writers attacked. See H. Merhavia, *The Talmud in the Eyes of Christianity: The View of Post-Biblical Jewish Literature in the Medieval Christian World, 500–1248* [in Hebrew] (Jerusalem: Bialik Institute, 1970), 258–62.

23. A comprehensive reading of Stern's three-volume work, which is ordered chronologically, does not reveal any substantive change. Stern, *Greek and Latin*. Similar claims of misanthropic practices and distinctiveness, which appear in Diodorus Siculus in the first century BCE and Tacitus in the first century CE, appear in Philostratus in the third century CE and in Synesius in the fifth. On the duplication of ethnic stereotypes of "barbarians" that disregard firsthand empirical knowledge, see Greg Woolf, "Enduring Fictions?," chap. 4 in *Tales of the Barbarians: Ethnography and Empire in the Roman West* (Chichester, West Sussex: Wiley-Blackwell, 2011).

24. On Tacitus and the fear of attraction to Judaism that characterized the senatorial class, see Isaac, *Invention of Racism*, 459; Gager, *The Origins of Anti-Semitism*, 64. On Judeophobia and the fear of Judaization more generally, see Feldman, *Jew and Gentile*.

25. See also Manetho in Schäfer, *Judeophobia*, 23: "have no connection with any save members of their own confederacy"; Juvenal in Stern, *Greek and Latin*, vol. 2, no. 301, 103: "conducting none but the circumcised to the desired fountain." Various scholars maintain that the possibility of conversion attests to openness and the lack of a sharp dichotomy. See, for example, Christine E. Hayes, *Gentile Impurities and Jewish Identities: Intermarriage and Conversion from the Bible to the Talmud* (Oxford: Oxford University Press, 2002). Clearly, however, for Tacitus, Juvenal, and their peers this was not the case.

26. For example, in the words of Haman in Greek Esther. See Samuel Abramski, "Antishemiyut kedam ideologit bemegilat esther," in *Sefer moshe goldstein: mehkarim bemikra uvemahshevet yisrael*, ed. B. Z. Luria and S. Z. Kahana (Jerusalem: Hahevrah leheker hamikra beyisrael, 1988), 1–23.

27. Katell Berthelot, *Philanthrôpia Judaica: Le débat autour de la "misanthropie" des lois juives dans l'Antiquité* (Leiden: Brill, 2003). On Jewish answers to these accusations, see Feldman, *Jew and Gentile*, 131–49. On the broader context of "apologia" of "Eastern" peoples to Hellenistic accusations, see Gideon Bohak, "Ethnic Stereotypes in the Greco-Roman World: Egyptians, Phoenicians, and Jews," in *Proceedings of the Twelfth World Congress of Jewish Studies B* (1997): 11–12.

28. *Letter of Aristeas*, 139, 142. Translation based on Moses Hadas, *Aristeas to Philocrates: Letter of Aristeas* (New York: Harper, 1951), 160–61. On this passage, see Ishay Rosen-Zvi, "What If We Got Rid of the Goy? Rereading Ancient Jewish Distinctions," *Journal for the Study of Judaism* 47, no. 2 (2016): 170–76. Compare this to 3 Maccabees 3:4: "They continued to revere God and live in accordance with his law and so kept themselves apart with respect to their diet, on account of which they appeared hateful to some." Translation from Cameron Boyd-Taylor, *A New English Translation of the Septuagint* (Oxford: Oxford University Press, 2009).

29. *Letter of Aristeas*, 182. For similar claims, see Philo, *Embassy to Gaius*, 362; Celsus, as cited in Origen, *Against Celsus*, 5.25.

30. See Yochanan Lewy's comparison of statements by Tacitus and Philo concerning converts and their disconnect from their past identities. Lewy, "Tacitus on the

Origin," n. 100. See also Josephus, who claims that Greek writers were not familiar with Jews, who did not intermingle with others, not because of any antipathy to Greeks (*Contra Apion*, 2.99; see ibid., 2.121), but due to their distinct lifestyle. *Contra Apion*, 1.60–61. Another comparison is relevant in this context. According to Juvenal (*Satire* 14): "[…] the Judaic code, as handed down by Moses in his mystic scroll… tells them not to show the way to anyone except a fellow worshipper […]." Juvenal, *Juvenal and Persius*, ed. and trans. Susanna Morton Braund (Cambridge, MA: Harvard University Press, 2004), 467. Yochanan Lewy writes, "Juvenal transformed the Torah of Moses into a mystical doctrine… not the Bible, but a secret book by Moses, preaching the idea of hatred for people, constitutes the true doctrine that members of his community are commanded to commit to memory." Lewy, "Tacitus on the Origin," 195. The idea of a secret, oral Torah that discriminates against gentiles is indeed found in early rabbinic literature. In the story of the two Roman officers sent to the study hall of Rabban Gamliel (*Sifre Devarim* §344 and parallels), the legal discrimination against the gentiles must be kept secret, and thus the officers promise not to tell it (in the *Sifre Devarim* version of the story) or forget it as soon as they leave (in the version of the Palestinian Talmud).

31. Bohak notes that because most of the writers cited in *Contra Apion* have not been preserved, we do not know the original context of their statements on Jews. Bohak, "Ibis," 28. When the context is known, as in the case of Cicero, for instance, we see that Jews are slandered, together with the peoples of the other claimants (Greeks and residents of Asia Minor), in the framework of a legal defense that enumerates the deficiencies of every people involved. On this, see Yochanan Lewy, "Cicero on the Jews in His Speech for the Defence of Flaccus," [in Hebrew] *Zion* 7, no. 3 (1941): 109–34.

32. Feldman, *Jew and Gentile*, 143–48. Other sources, however, view attitudes toward aliens and even enemies as an expression of philanthropy. See Ari Mermelstein, "Emotion, Gender, and Greco-Roman Virtue in Joseph and Aseneth," *Journal for the Study of Judaism* 48 (2017): 356, and the references in n. 96. See also N. Clayton Croy, *3 Maccabees* (Leiden: Brill, 2005), 68.

33. On these motifs, see John J. Collins, *Between Athens and Jerusalem: Jewish Identity in the Hellenistic Diaspora* (Grand Rapids, MI: Eerdmans, 2000).

34. See n. 21.

35. Daniel Schwartz, "Diodorus Siculus 40.3—Hecataeus or Pseudo-Hecataeus?," in *Jews and Gentiles in the Holy Land in the Days of the Second Temple, the Mishnah and the Talmud*, ed. Menahem Mor [in Hebrew] (Jerusalem: Yad Ben Zvi, 2003), 181–97. For the debate, see Bar-Kochva, *Jews in Greek Literature*, 106. This argument is based on the mostly positive descriptions, including a lengthy one of governance and the priestly order, that emphasize the wisdom and understanding of their founder Moses. See ibid., 135. There is a similar controversy regarding a possible Jewish source of Strabo's extraordinary addendum, where self-separation is described as praiseworthy religious piety. See Bezalel Bar-Kochva, "Antiochus the Pious and Hyrcanus the Tyrant: A Chapter in the Historiography of the Hasmonean State," [in Hebrew] *Zion* 61, no. 1 (1996): 36.

36. Bernard Mandelbaum, ed., *Pesikta derav kahana* 19:2 (New York: Jewish Theological Seminary of America, 1987), 302–3.

37. As Yavetz shows, there is a surprising coalition between Zionist historians and critics of Jews: "Zionist historians assume that even in antiquity, the alien character of the Jews is the central cause for antisemitism." Yavetz, "Judeophobia," 6. In contrast, historians critical of Jewish nationalism focus on the Maccabean wars as the beginning of anti-Judaism. Yavetz himself criticizes both approaches.

38. For a review, see Yavetz, "Judeophobia," and Croy, *3 Maccabees*.

39. Schäfer calls the first approach "substantialist," and the second, which locates the key within specific political contexts, "functionalist." Schäfer, *Judeophobia*.

40. Schäfer writes explicitly: "To what degree the Jews were separate *is not important.... [T]he only crucial question* is what the Greco-Egyptian and Greek authors made out of it." Schäfer, *Judeophobia*, 209–10. Emphasis added. See also Cynthia M. Baker, *Jew* (New Brunswick, NJ: Rutgers University Press, 2017), and Nirenberg, *Anti-Judaism*. For both authors, "Jew" became a marker of otherness through which the self, first and foremost the Christian self, was formed. The opposite binary marker, "gentile," is, however, ignored.

41. See Isaac, *Invention of Racism*, 445 and the references in n. 12 on p. 444. Compare to Yavetz, "Judeophobia"; Gager, *The Origins of Anti-Semitism*, 31; and Feldman, *Jew and Gentile*, 124, and more expansively in Louis H. Feldman, *"Remember Amalek": Vengeance, Zealotry, and Group Destruction in the Bible according to Philo, Pseudo-Philo, and Josephus* (Cincinnati: Hebrew Union College, 2004). Feldman is not exceptional in projecting later Jewish experience backward and reifying the Jew as victim.

42. We are not familiar with any studies in the context of the ancient world that devote specific attention to both sides of the phenomenon. There are attempts in other disciplines to undertake such an accounting. See, for instance, Howard F. Stein, "The Binding of the Son: Psychoanalytic Reflections on the Symbiosis of Anti-Semitism and Anti-Gentilism," *Psychoanalytic Quarterly* 46 (1977): 650–83. An obvious example from the modern era of scholarly and philosophical attention to both Jews' and gentiles' shared interest in Jewish distinctiveness is found in Hannah Arendt, *The Origins of Totalitarianism* (New York: Harcourt Brace Jovanovich, 1973), 3–133. See also Israel J. Yuval, *Two Nations in Your Womb: Perceptions of Jews and Christians in Late Antiquity and the Middle Ages*, trans. Barbara Harshav and Jonathan Chipman (Berkeley: University of California Press, 2006).

43. On the different views on dating the Book of Esther, see Lawrence M. Wills, *The Jewish Novel in the Ancient World* (Ithaca, NY: Cornell University Press, 1995), 99–100.

44. John J. Collins, *The Invention of Judaism: Torah and Jewish Identity from Deuteronomy to Paul* (Oakland: University of California Press, 2017), 76–79.

45. Berthelot, *Philanthrôpia*. Paul may be another example of such internalization by a Jewish writer. See James D. G. Dunn, "The New Perspective: Whence, What and Whither," in *The New Perspective on Paul: Collected Essays* (Tübingen: Mohr Siebeck, 2005), 1–97.

46. On the similarity between the Greek Esther and 3 Maccabees and the likely dependence of 3 Maccabees on Esther, see Carey A. Moore, "On the Origin of the LXX Additions to the Book of Esther," *Journal of Biblical Literature* 92 (1973): 384–85; Fausto Parente, "The Third Book of Maccabees as Ideological Document and Historical Source," *Henoch* 10 (1988): 175–76; Noah Hacham, "3 Maccabees and Esther: Parallels, Intertextuality, and Diaspora Identity," *Journal of Biblical Literature* 126 (2007): 765–68. This connection calls attempts to discover the historical kernel of the story into question. For the debates regarding the dating of 3 Maccabees, see Sara Raup Johnson, *Historical Fictions and Hellenistic Jewish Identity* (Berkeley: University of California Press, 2004), 129–41.

47. The linkage of both Esther and 3 Maccabees to the Exodus story is especially clear. On this, see D. S. Williams, "3 Maccabees: A Defence of Diaspora Judaism?," *Journal for the Study of Pseudepigrapha* 13 (1995): 17–29; Noah Hacham, "'The Letter of Aristeas': A New Exodus Story?," *Journal for the Study of Judaism* 36 (2005): 1–20. It is therefore the literary template that shapes a political portrayal, and not vice versa. Historians who view these texts as evidence of persecution reverse the proper order of things. See, for example, Sylvie Honigman, "Between History and Fiction: 3 Macc. and the Events of 38–41 CE in Alexandria," in *Tra politica e religione: I Giudei nel mondo greco-romano. Studi in onore di Lucio Troiani*, ed. Livia Capponi (Milano: Jouvence, 2019), 127–44.

48. See also verse 6:5, where Sennacherib's threat to destroy the land (2 Kings 18:25) appears.

49. Diodorus Siculus, *Bibliotheca Historica*. Various scholars contend that this story originates with Posidonius of Apameia, from which Josephus, *Antiquities* 13.245 also drew his similar but softened story. See Stern, *Greek and Latin*, 184; Bar-Kochva, "Antiochus the Pious," 24; Bar-Kochva, *Jews in Greek Literature*, 412 and the references in n. 35.

50. See Gager, *Moses*, 126, n. 32; Gager, *The Origins of Anti-Semitism*, 40; and Yavetz's criticism of this approach in Yavetz, "Judeophobia."

51. On the specific contexts of the disturbances, see John M. G. Barclay, *Jews in the Mediterranean Diaspora: From Alexander to Trajan (323 BCE–117 CE)* (Berkeley: University of California Press, 1996), 60–71. See there also Claudius's declaration of compromise, which restores limited rights to Jews.

52. See Bloch, *Antike Vorstellungen vom Judentum*, 129–42.

53. Tacitus similarly discusses the customs and daily life of German and Briton warriors. See Bloch, *Antike Vorstellungen vom Judentum*, chap. 4. What is particular to Jews is the negative attitude he expresses and, as mentioned, his emphasis on their self-separation. See Woolf, "Enduring Fictions?," 89–117.

54. This is even more prominent in the LXX additions to Esther. Addendum B emphasizes not only that Jews are different and distinct in their laws, but also that they are hostile (*antiparagôge*) to the rest of humanity and conspire (*dusnooun*) against the regime. See 3 Macc. 3:24. In Addendum E, the charge of rebellion is leveled by

Mordecai against Haman, who is presented as a Macedonian, alien to the Persians and working to undermine them. These claims are reworked extensively by Josephus in *Antiquities* 11. See Paul Spilsbury and Chris Seeman, *Flavius Josephus: Translation and Commentary* (Leiden: Brill, 2017), 53–58.

55. For example, Num. 14:11–20; 17:6–25, 25:1–11; Deut. 4:23–26, 28. See Adi M. Ophir, *In the Beginning Was the State: Divine Violence in the Hebrew Bible* (New York: Fordham University Press, 2022), 139–44, 160–78, 204–213.

56. This is the main contention of chapters 6 and 7, devoted to the goy in Tannatic literature, in Adi Ophir and Ishay Rosen-Zvi, *Goy: Israel's Multiple Others and the Birth of the Gentile* (Oxford: Oxford University Press, 2018).

7
Antisemitism and Islamophobia
A Medieval Comparison

YOUVAL ROTMAN

Aɴᴛɪsᴇᴍɪᴛɪsᴍ, Jew-hatred, and Islamophobia are modern terms signifying prejudices toward collectives that are defined in religious terms.[1] The historian working on the medieval period encounters many sources that attest to collective hostility toward various monotheistic religious groups. In a world where the term "orthodox" (the "right belief") served to define political entities and portray their conflicts as holy wars, it is only natural that political and cultural boundaries were defined according to religious features that helped establish hierarchical categorizations. The question is the degree to which the historian can use terms that were developed in the modern world in a medieval context without becoming anachronistic.[2] Are these terms specific to the modern contexts within which they were created, or can they reflect a much longer history of interreligious hostility?

To answer these questions, this article presents a comparative analysis of the treatment of Jews and Muslims during the early to mid-Byzantine era and examines whether the hatred of Jews in medieval thought, culture, and politics was characterized by unique features, especially in comparison to Muslims.[3] The period between the fifth and tenth centuries witnessed religiopolitical crises in the Eastern Mediterranean and therefore constitutes an ideal framework for examining what I will call the "Byzantine typology of religious hatred." A comparative analysis of how Jews and Muslims were portrayed throughout this period reveals the uniqueness of Byzantine political culture's treatment of these groups and offers new insights on the use of the terms in question.

Christian Byzantine culture approached Jews polemically from the outset with the explicit goal of their Christianization.[4] This made the Byzantine Christian perspective on Jews unique among other anti-Jewish views and actions in antiquity.[5] Conversion to Christianity was not meant for Jews only, of course; rather, it was an imperial Byzantine policy applied to other populations as well: pagans, non-Chalcedonian Christians, and, from the seventh and eighth centuries on, Muslims.[6] The Muslim conquests of the seventh century changed the map of the empire. In their wake, Byzantium found itself on both the political and the religious defensive against the Muslim caliphate. Muslim Arabs, called in Greek sources "Saracens," "Arabs," "Hagarenes," and "Mohammedans," became Byzantium's main rival on both religious and political fronts. Their success led to a crisis of Christian political culture and presented a political-cultural challenge of accounting for the religious rival's victory. Christian unity and solidarity, as well as religious self-justification of the Byzantine state, became a necessary policy both internally and externally.[7] Against this geopolitical background, Byzantium's iconoclastic policy seems to be an imperial reaction to the religiopolitical crisis precipitated by the Muslim threat—a policy meant to reform religion and produce unity around the image and icon of the emperor.[8] However, this policy, in both waves (726–787, 815–843), produced the opposite result. It threatened Byzantine unity and generated conflict between iconoclasts and supporters of the emperor, on one hand, and iconodules (Greek: *iconodouloi*), the "icon's slaves," on the other.

Religiopolitical crises accompanied the Byzantine Empire throughout its history and constituted an integral part of its political culture. These crises are therefore a suitable framework for examining the degree to which the Christian-Byzantine perspective on Jews and Muslims was unique, and what constitutes this uniqueness. In other words, to examine the basis of the terms "Jew-hatred," "antisemitism," and "Islamophobia," I propose scrutinizing them within Byzantine political culture's typology of religious hatred during the period in which religious rivalries played a political role and helped crystallize a Byzantine political culture.[9] A comparative analysis of the Byzantine perspective on Jews and Muslims within a range of Byzantine literary genres can contribute to our understanding of the uniqueness of the hatred of them as religious rivals. Byzantium considered both Judaism and Islam heretical.

This article will also include an analysis of Byzantine attitudes toward iconoclast Byzantines in order to expand the typology toward different types of internal religious rivals: Jews and iconoclasts. This comparison will shed new light on the use of the terms under discussion for the study of premodern societies. To analyze the role played by religious rivals in the consolidation of Byzantine political culture, I will focus on three Byzantine literary genres that shaped religiopolitical consciousness: historiography, hagiography, and liturgy. Analyzing images of religious rivals in these three genres will allow us to identify literary, historical, and political elements in the image of the religious rival and will reveal the role that they played in Byzantine political culture.

A general remark is needed regarding the methodology of the article's analysis of how Jews, Muslims, and iconoclasts were treated in Byzantium. There is an essential difference in Byzantine representations of Jews and Muslims in ecclesiastical writers. These sources use stereotypes to present Jews as internal enemies who collaborate with internal and external enemies of Christianity. By contrast, contemporaneous representations of Muslims and Islam are free of stereotypes. This comparison raises the question of whether the political success of the Muslim caliphate led Byzantine writers to treat it as an equal and worthy rival in contrast to Jews, who were seen as a despised, defeated rival. Comparing the treatment of iconoclasts in Byzantium will prove revelatory for this question as well. During the eighth and ninth centuries, Byzantine iconodules saw them as their main religious rival. In fact, we find that iconoclasts replace Jews as the main rivals and are indeed called "the new Jews." As internal religious rivals who had threatened the unity of belief and been subdued by the orthodox political culture, they were subject to the same vilification as Jews. In other words, precisely because they were weakened, defeated political rivals, they could be demonized.

The article will conclude with a comparison of how fundamental aspects of the Jewish and Muslim faiths are presented in the formulas of abjuration (anathemas) that the Byzantine church designed for conversion ceremonies. There and in contrast to Judaism, Islam is negatively stereotyped, as befits a situation of conversion. This typology of literary representations of different religious rivals shows that the religious rival can be demonized precisely when it is no longer really a threat. Although this article is centered on sources from the Middle Byzantine period (eighth to eleventh centuries), I will begin this investigation with pre-Islamic Byzantine sources in order to ascertain whether the Islamic conquests offered any change in how Jews were represented.

Religious Rivals in Byzantine Historiography

Historiography plays a major role in shaping the political narratives of states. Byzantine historiography both continued Greco-Roman historiography and adopted a new Christian type of historiography—"ecclesiastical history"—which imbued the chronicles of the Byzantine state with a religious, metahistorical dimension while integrating it with the Christian narrative that begins with the creation of the world.[10]

Inasmuch as it combines a Christian biblical narrative with a Byzantine political narrative, ecclesiastical history fashions a Christian religious perspective on the progression of history. Church historians frequently use the topoi of enemies of Christianity or of the Church, which originate in the ecclesiastical history of Eusebius.[11] These topoi reveal the religious agenda of constructing a historiographic narrative in Byzantium and fashioning a political culture in which religion plays a central role. As part of this process, the place of Jews, as a religious minority within the Byzantine political framework, is tailored to their relations with the Christian state.

Socrates Scholasticus of the fourth century (ca. 380–440) exemplifies how ecclesiastical historians of his era relate to Jews. He cites the letter of Constantine concerning the dissociation of Easter from the Jewish holiday of Passover: "And first of all, it appeared an unworthy thing that in the celebration of this most holy feast we should follow the practice of the Jews (*hoi ioudaioi*), who have impiously defiled their hands with enormous sin, and are, therefore, deservedly afflicted with blindness of soul.... Let us then have nothing in common with the detestable Jewish crowd.... Beloved brethren, let us with one consent adopt this course, and withdraw ourselves from all participation in their baseness."[12] In this case, Socrates Scholasticus presents Jews as disrupting the social and political order of the Christian state.[13] The author uses similarly negative descriptions of rival, nonorthodox Christian communities in mixed cities.[14] He singles out Jews, however, by linking them directly to the Crucifixion and portraying them as enthusiastic collaborators of the anti-Christian emperor Julian.[15]

His descriptions are similar to those of his contemporary Sozomenos (ca. 324–440), which rely on the church's perspective and present Jews as enemies of Christianity and the Christian state who collaborate with pagans within and the Persian enemy without.[16] Sozomenos thus locates Jews alongside both the religious enemy within and the political enemy without. Accordingly, he ascribes Julian's anti-Christian policy, which led to a wave of anti-Christian persecution in the Sasanian Empire, to Jews. They collaborated with the Persian magi and persuaded the government to persecute Christians and destroy churches throughout the empire.[17] The link between pagans, Jews, and Persians thus stands at the center of the religiopolitical logic that determined attitudes toward each of the enemies of Christianity and enabled the portrayal of Jews as enemies of the Christian state.[18] Hence, the descriptions of Jews in Christian historiography played an important role in constructing Christian Byzantine political culture. Moreover, such stereotypes draw on local rivalries and conflicts between Christians and Jews.[19]

In contrast to comments by Socrates and Sozomenos, there were only a few treatments of Jews in sixth-century historiography written outside the church. Especially prominent is the critical stance toward anti-Jewish hatred. John Malalas (ca. 491–578), for example, describes Emperor Zeno's (474–491) stereotypical hatred of Jews as ridiculous.[20] Although Procopius (ca. 500–565) continues the line of church historians when he presents Jews as supporters of the Goths in Italy and the Himyarite regime in its persecution of Christians,[21] his work *Secret History* presents the opposite perspective: Emperor Justinian (527–565) is portrayed as a scoundrel and the Jews are his victims.[22] Thus, while Byzantine historians of the sixth century continued the approach of church historiography from the fifth century that associated Jews with enemies of Christianity, later authors, like Malalas and Procopius, exhibited a more complex attitude that included awareness and criticism of earlier negative descriptions of Jews.

The historiographic perspective linking Jews to enemies of the Christian state continues in seventh-century historiography as well. Just as Socrates Scholasticus ties the Jews of Jerusalem to the anti-Christian policies of Julian the Apostate, and Sozomenos to the Persians, so the Armenian historian Sebeos links the Jerusalemite Jews to the Sasanian conquest of the city in 614.[23] The Crucifixion is the model Sebeos uses for the war between Jews and the Christian state: Jews are "God-killers" who aspire to torment Jesus again.[24] According to Sebeos, the Sasanian conquests are a Jewish initiative, as are the persecutions of the Christian population by proxy of the Sasanian government following the conquests.[25] Sebeos also links Jews to their Ishmaelite "cousins," whom they enlisted in their struggle against the Christian state.[26]

Sebeos's descriptions of Ishmaelites and their ties to Jews are well known.[27] Even though he describes Muhammad as the unifier of the "sons of Israel" under the army that conquered the land of their patriarch, Abraham, he does not denigrate Muslims. This is all the more surprising in view of the obvious religious threat they posed.[28] Here lies a significant difference in how Muslims and Jews are represented: The Muslim threat toward Christianity is represented as conversion while the Jewish threat is represented as destruction.[29] A century later, Theophanes the Confessor (758–817) repeats Sebeos's link between Jews and Muslims, writing that initially the Hebrews (*hoi hebraioi*) deemed Muhammad the long-awaited messiah and even abandoned the religion of Moses to join him. These Hebrews taught Muslims to oppose Christians and although disabused of his messiahship, they did not dare deny him and persuaded Umar to tear down the cross from atop the Mount of Olives.[30] Moreover, in his description of Jewish involvement in the iconoclastic policy of Caliph Yazid II (687–724), Theophanes borrows the early Byzantine topos of Jews as supporters of a foreign king persecuting Christians.[31]

This connection between Muslim iconoclasm and Judaism is completely abandoned when Theophanes begins to describe iconoclasm in

Byzantium.[32] Jews are not mentioned, while the Jewish wizard who persuades Yazid II in Sebeos's account is replaced with an apostate Christian captive who returns to Byzantium and influences the emperor.[33] From this point forward, it is iconoclast emperors and their supporters who function as representations of the despised religious rival.[34] Theophanes's references to Jews no longer include shameful descriptions, stereotypes, or their demonization as enemies.[35] His descriptions of Muslim Arabs also remain mundane; toxic language is reserved for iconoclasts.[36]

Unlike these accounts, the anti-Jewish attitude of ecclesiastical historians does not vary with the Muslim conquests. On the contrary, the conquests' harsh ramifications for Christianity in general and Byzantium specifically are partially attributed to Jews. Muslims, by contrast, are portrayed as an enemy that threatens the Christian state from the outside rather than an internal enemy that Christianity must subdue. It is only after the Byzantine iconoclasm of the eighth century (726–787) was over, in later narratives of the crisis, that we find evidence of change in the attitude toward Jews; the historical-literary role they played as persecutors of Christianity and murderers of God is now filled by the iconoclast emperors and their supporters. A similar shift can be found in Byzantine hagiography. An analysis of the figure of the religious rival in Christian hagiographic texts reveals a clear distinction between the way Jews are portrayed before the eighth century and after.

Religious Rivals in Byzantine Hagiography

Like historiography, hagiography played a major role in the construction and comprehension of past and present events within the Byzantine Christian religious framework. In the Early Middle Ages, it became the most prolific literary genre in Byzantium. Analyzing how the religious rival is presented in this literature reveals another aspect of the place occupied by this figure in Christian public opinion in Byzantium. An example of this place can already be found in early Christian martyrologies, which portray Jews as collaborators with Roman persecutors, and as archenemies who rejoice over every Christian martyr put to death.[37] By contrast, in the hagiographies of the fourth through sixth centuries, which focus on the lives of ascetic saints, there are few references to Jews.[38] Jews do not appear as stereotypes in these works, but do function as central elements of the plot.[39] This literature posits a different sort of feared enemy for the Christian Saint: demons.

As with historiography, the hagiography of the fourth through sixth centuries contains no reference to religious conversion. This changes in the seventh and eighth centuries. Three Byzantine texts of a hagiographic nature from this period addressing rivalries between Jewish and Christian communities within the Byzantine sphere conclude with the collective Christianization of a Jewish community: the conversion of the Jews of Carthage, the conversion of the Jews of Tomai (most likely Thmuis/el-Timai in the Nile Delta of Egypt), and the conversion of the Jews of Lentini in Sicily.[40] These three works were written against the backdrop of Emperor Heraclius's forced conversion of Jews in 630–631.[41] Regardless of whether or not these Jewish communities actually converted to Christianity, Christian writers built the legends of their Christianization on the basis of a polemical Christian, anti-Jewish archetype. By contrast, in hagiographic works written against the backdrop of rivalries between Christians and Muslims and Byzantium and the Caliphate, Jews are entirely absent. The issue of religious conversion dominates hagiographic narratives from the period after the Islamic conquests, but they no longer speak of converting Jews. Rather, they are concerned with the conversion of Christians to Islam, a central topic in literature composed in the regions of conflict between Byzantium and the Caliphate.[42]

It seems that the Muslim-Christian conflict replaces the traditional Jewish-Christian conflict in this period. However, the two rivalries are not portrayed on the same plane. The Jewish-Christian conflict is presented as an internal Byzantine religious issue that disrupts the potential consolidation of Byzantine society. The conversion of Jews offers a solution by transforming them into typical residents of Byzantium, that is, into Christians. The Muslims, by contrast, are portrayed as being entirely foreign, and ties between them and Christians are described as a political risk but not as a religious threat. That is, the internal rival is described as a religious threat, while the external rival is described as a political danger. The internal rivals, Jews, are portrayed stereotypically as anti-Christian, whereas the external rivals, Muslims, are not.

From Jew to Iconoclast

The demonization of Jews as "killers of God," which characterizes early Christian works, reappears in the new anti-iconoclast literature composed primarily in the ninth century. Written after the victory over the iconoclasts and the restoration of iconic worship, Byzantine hagiography focusing on the persecutions inflicted by the iconoclasts uses early Christian martyrology and its literary elements as a model. The iconoclasts are described as enemies of God who are trying to murder him again.[43] The destruction of Jesus's symbols is represented in Byzantine texts and their illuminations as a second Crucifixion.[44]

The connection between the Jewish prohibition against material representations of the divine and iconoclasm seems intuitive and is common to both Christians of heretic faiths and Jews in early descriptions.[45] The image of Jews as the traditional killers of God serves as a model for representing the internal political-religious crisis and describing God's new killers, the iconoclasts. As a rule, Jews are absent from texts that concern iconoclasm, and the iconoclast emperors themselves are represented as the Jews' successors. Thus, for example, Emperor Constantine V is described in the hagiography of Romanus the Neomartyr as "the true enemy of faith, the disciple of Satan... like a Jew in his faith and conduct."[46] In the *Life of Stephen the Younger*, the eponymous martyr is brought forth to be executed in the hippodrome before an inflamed iconoclast crowd "that was screaming, like the Jews of the past: 'Death! Crucify the son of God!'"[47] The Byzantine Christian hard line toward Judaism is now directed at the current internal religious enemy of orthodoxy: iconoclasm, which is termed a "Jewish sect."[48]

Iconoclasm replaces Judaism in hagiographic texts written by faithful iconodules, leaving Jews absent from these works. However, in manuscript illuminations from the period, iconoclasts are depicted alongside Jews. The meaning is clear: Iconoclasts are the new Jews.[49] Thus, Judaism acquires new meaning and anti-Jewish stereotypes are used to describe a phenomenon that has no real connection to Judaism.

Though Jews themselves are almost completely absent from the hagiography of the iconoclast period, stereotypes of them became useful for writers who needed familiar demonic representations to describe the internal religious rival.[50] In light of the fact that Caliph Yazid II's iconoclastic edict against Christian representations of the divine in 724 preceded Byzantine iconoclasm, we could expect to find comparisons of Byzantine iconoclasts with Muslims. But the question of whether the enemy actually threatened Christian faith is of secondary importance. The main objective was to portray the rival, especially after it had been defeated and subdued, as a threat to Christian unity. Islam never filled this position in Byzantium. Yet, in cases of Muslim captives who were encouraged to convert to Christianity, Islam did acquire demonic characteristics.

Heretics and Their Place in Byzantine Liturgy

Conversions occupied a central place in Byzantine political culture, and they are closely linked to Byzantine religious polemics against nonorthodox Christians as well as Jews and Muslims. In Byzantine political culture, Judaism and Islam were understood as heresies.[51] Jewish residents of the empire and captive Muslims were natural targets for conversion to Orthodox Christianity.[52] Conversely, Christian Byzantines had to oppose the threat of conversion to Islam if they were taken captive by the Caliphate.[53] A considerable part of the long Byzantine conversion process was the abjuration of the convert's old religious principles—the anathema. The ceremony was performed in church, before the community of the faithful, and it disclosed the principles of the rival religion in front of the Christian community that accepted the new believer into its ranks. The prayer book of the Great Church of Constantinople contains detailed descriptions of conversion processes for different types of heretics.[54]

The stages of the process are identical for all converts. For two weeks, the conversion candidate fasts and learns to pray. At the end of this period, the priest brings the candidate to be baptized, and the candidate publicly declares having reached the Christian faith out of free will and love for Christ. Then the candidate disavows their original faith and repudiates its fundamental principles, laws, and forms of worship, as detailed in the formulas of abjuration devised for each faith. The ceremony concludes with the candidate declaring the Orthodox creed, "I believe," to which the audience responds verbally. The formulas of abjuration listing the basic beliefs that the convert repudiates thus offer additional material on how Byzantine Christian culture represented its religious and political rivals. These lengthy descriptions detail the fundamentals of the Jewish and Muslim faiths as they were represented and perceived in Byzantium.[55]

A Jewish apostate had to repudiate Jewish ceremonies, holidays, prayers, and beliefs. These included the preparation of the Passover sacrifice, matzah, Sukkot, and other festivals and customs, including circumcision, the liturgy, purification rituals, sanctification rituals, fast days, and blowing the shofar. He (the text was written for male candidates but was also used for women) repudiated the lunar calendar, the Sabbath, synagogues, foods, drink, and various statutes. In some versions, the list of what was repudiated also included different Jewish faith groups: the Sadducees, Pharisees, and Essenes.[56] It even included a disavowal of the Mishnah (Greek: *deuterōseis*, that is, "the laws and statutes erroneously attributed to Moses"), as well as the laws of Rabbi Akiva and Rabbi Anan (ben David). In contrast to the stereotypical defamations that are common in historiography, hagiography, and manuscript illuminations, the formulas for abjuring Judaism do not include stereotypes in general or anti-Jewish polemics specifically. They consist entirely of a rather perfunctory description of the Jewish faith and lifestyle. These documents demonstrate that the Byzantine church was quite familiar with Jewish customs, statutes, and basic beliefs.

The anathema for Muslim converts reflected a much different approach.[57] A Muslim who converted to Christianity had to abjure Muhammad, his heirs, and his wives; the Qur'an; the writings and mysteries; the angels of the Qur'an; and the Qur'an's descriptions of biblical figures, Jesus, creation, and paradise. The convert also abjured predestination, jihad, and practices like the rite of purification in sand. These elements of the convert's repudiation were all real beliefs and practices of contemporary Islam.[58] Alongside these, the formula of repudiation also contained imaginary descriptions with no basis in reality. Thus, the convert's disavowal of the description of paradise included believers with forty-foot phalluses who ascend to the heavens and engage in adultery in the presence of the shameless God. The conversion candidate also had to repudiate other invented religious practices, such as stoning Christians and worshipping the morning star and Aphrodite. The description of Islam in Byzantine liturgy is thus comprised of authentic as well as imagined and even demonic elements.

Some of these latter elements are found in Nicetas of Byzantium's work refuting the Qur'an, *Anatropē*, which scholars date to the mid-ninth century.[59] The work addresses sections of the Qur'an and suggests unusual interpretations of certain verses. Thus, some of the fantasized descriptions in the formula for abjuring Islam, like that of the shameless God and the description of Muslims as worshippers of stars and constellations, seem to be based on the *Anatropē*, if it indeed predates the abjuration formula. At the same time, some of the descriptions do not appear in this work or other Byzantine works that describe Islam, Muslims, or Islamic practices.[60] Moreover, other contemporary texts demonstrate clearly that Christians were well acquainted with fundamental Muslim beliefs and practices.[61] How, then, can we account for the imagined elements in Byzantine depictions of Islam? And why do we find them specifically in a work on whose authenticity religious conversion depends, and one that should therefore hew as closely as possible to the principles of the original faith?

The description of Muslims as idolaters and adulterers demonizes them and casts the rival faith as a contemptible enemy. If we consider that these formulas were recited aloud and in public, we can understand them as Christian propaganda intended to be heard from the lips of Muslim apostates at the precise moment that they abandoned their faith, demonstrating to all that it had been vanquished. Although such imaginary descriptions do not appear in other Byzantine works vis-à-vis Muslims, they do appear in descriptions of Jews and iconoclasts in Byzantine hagiography, which depicts both as amoral fighters against the Christian truth. Thus, the demonization and ridicule of rival religions appear precisely when they do not constitute a danger or a worthy rival.

The Politics of Antisemitism and Islamophobia

Byzantine political culture expressed its attitudes toward Jews and Muslims in different ways and for different purposes. Islam was seen as a real threat to Byzantium, both politically and religiously, and the conversion of Byzantine Christian prisoners to Islam was a painful reality.[62] The Byzantine formula for the abjuration of Islam propagandistically demonizes a religious rival in a weakened, defeated state. This demonization contrasts with the absence of negative stereotyping in historiography and hagiography that represents Islam as a real threat. The representation of Jews follows the same model: They are presented as a danger even though they never posed a real threat to Christianity or the Byzantine state. Moreover, the hostile representation of Jews as dangerous heretics serves as a topos for any threat to Christian unity and is also used against iconoclasts and their supporters particularly in texts that postdate the iconoclastic crisis—in other words, when it no longer posed a threat. Thus, Jew-hatred serves as a model for constructing and solidifying a sociocultural hierarchy. Byzantium propaganda expressed hatred against religious rivals specifically when they did not constitute a threat. Can we call such a model "antisemitism"?

Today, the terms "antisemitism" and "Islamophobia" are used to identify and mark political and cultural phenomena. The terms themselves serve those who oppose expressions of hatred against Jews and Muslims as well as those who study them and claim that they are unique among all other expressions of hatred.[63] Indeed, in Byzantium too, Jew-hatred was distinct from any other hatred in the way that it was a cultural category with a political purpose. We are not dealing here with a "cultural code" that structured and redirected negative feelings within the Byzantine political sphere toward other rivals.[64] Negative representations of Jews did not substitute for other hatreds. On the contrary, the model of hostility toward Jews, it turns out, was used as a prototype for representing other weakened and vanquished religious rivals. For example, it helped construct political, religious, and historical representations for the iconoclasm crisis. The sources that model their representations of iconoclasm on Jew-hatred do not, however, express hate for Muslims or Islam. Islam is only presented as ridiculous when it is renounced in religious conversion and poses no threat.

To conclude, though Byzantium did not have the terms "Jew-hatred," "antisemitism," and "Islamophobia," their significance was not foreign to Byzantine political culture, which pitted the state religion against its two main monotheistic rivals: Judaism and Islam. Negative, menacing attitudes toward Islam do not appear when Islam constitutes a real threat, but only when it is no threat at all.[65] The same goes for Judaism: It is portrayed negatively precisely because it poses no threat. When another internal religious rival threatened the unity of belief and was subdued—like the case of the Christian iconoclast crisis—the "Jewish model" was replicated and applied to it even though Judaism and Jews had nothing to do with this particular crisis.

The Byzantine case shows that when religious hatred serves a political function it becomes different from other hatreds and can be used against any group. The terms themselves—"antisemitism," "Jew-hatred," and "Islamophobia"—help sharpen the unique characteristics of religious enmity and its causes in premodern eras. A comparative analysis of the different religious enmities reveals that hatred toward a weak, nonthreatening rival can be used as effective propaganda against it within the internal political sphere. Comparing how these concepts are applied in different eras is an important analytical tool for understanding their use today. Even societies that did not recognize the terms used antisemitism and Islamophobia as propagandist tools against internal rivals, specifically when they did not pose any danger. We can explain this paradox if we understand expressions of hatred as propaganda serving to justify and maintain a sociocultural hierarchy.

In "Race and History" (1952) and "Race and Culture" (1971), Claude Lévi-Strauss examined the social, cultural construction of race. A monotheistic society that needed a model for an inferior rival of a different faith could use this construction to justify its cultural hierarchy. The Byzantine typology of religious hostility shows that Jew-hatred was invented for precisely this purpose, whether it was directed against Jews or other groups. Moreover, if we accept Lévi-Strauss's theory, we can understand very different manifestations of antisemitism, Islamophobia, racism, and indeed chauvinism as moralistic justifications of a sense of superiority, a degrading attitude, and the attribution of social inferiority to anyone who is perceived as an inferior rival.

NOTES

1. Matti Bunzl, *Anti-Semitism and Islamophobia: Hatreds Old and New in Europe* (Chicago: Prickly Paradigm, 2007); Christine Achinger and Robert Fine, eds., *Antisemitism, Racism and Islamophobia: Distorted Faces of Modernity* (London: Routledge, 2015).

2. James Renton and Ben Gidley, eds., *Antisemitism and Islamophobia in Europe: A Shared Story?* (London: Palgrave Macmillan, 2016); David Engel, "Away from a Definition of Antisemitism: An Essay in the Semantics of Historical Description," in *Rethinking European Jewish History*, ed. Jeremy Cohen and Moshe Rosman (Oxford: Littman Library of Jewish Civilization, 2009), 30–53; Phyllis Goldstein, *A Convenient Hatred: The History of Antisemitism* (Brookline, MA: Facing History & Ourselves, 2012); Walter Laqueur, *The Changing Face of Antisemitism: From Ancient Times to the Present Day* (Oxford: Oxford University Press, 2006).

3. See David Nirenberg, *Anti-Judaism: The Western Tradition* (New York: W. W. Norton, 2013); Maurice Kriegel, "L'esprit tue aussi: Juifs 'textuels' et Juifs 'réels' dans l'histoire," *Annales: Histoire, Sciences sociales* 69, no. 4 (2014): 875–99; Anthony Bale, *The Jew in the Medieval Book: English Antisemitisms, 1350–1500* (Cambridge: Cambridge University Press, 2006); Jessica Boon, "Violence and the 'Virtual Jew' in Castilian Passion Narratives, 1490s–1510s," *Journal of Medieval Iberian Studies* 8, no. 1 (2016): 110–29.

4. Gilbert Dagron, "Judaïser," *Travaux et Mémoires*, no. 11 (1991): 359–80; Gilbert Dagron and Vincent Déroche, "Juifs et Chrétiens dans l'Orient du VIIe siècle," *Travaux et Mémoires*, no. 11 (1991): 17–46.

5. Benjamin H. Isaac, *The Invention of Racism in Classical Antiquity* (Princeton, NJ: Princeton University Press, 2004), 440–90; Zvi Yavetz, "Judeophobia in Classical Antiquity: A Different Approach," *Journal of Jewish Studies* 44, no. 1 (1993): 1–22; Peter Schäfer, *Judeophobia: Attitudes toward the Jews in the Ancient World* (Cambridge, MA: Harvard University Press, 1997); Averil Cameron, "Byzantines and Jews: Some Recent Work on Early Byzantium," *Byzantine and Modern Greek Studies* 20, no. 1 (1996): 249–74; Averil Cameron, "Blaming the Jews: The Seventh-Century Invasions of Palestine in Context," *Travaux et Mémoires*, no. 14 (2002): 57–78.

6. Paolo Eleuteri and Antonio Rigo, *Eretici, dissidenti, musulmani ed ebrei a Bisanzio: Una raccolta eresiologica del XII secolo* (Venice: Il cardo, 1993).

7. Youval Rotman, "Byzance face à l'Islam arabe VIIe-Xe siècles," *Annales Histoire, Sciences sociales* 60, no. 4 (2005): 767–88.

8. Averil Cameron, "Images of Authority: Elites and Icons in Late Sixth-Century Byzantium," pt. xviii, and "The Language of Images: The Rise of Icons and Christian Representation," pt. xii, in *Continuity and Change in Sixth-Century Byzantium*

(London: Variorum, 1981); M. T. G. Humphreys, *Law, Power, and Imperial Ideology in the Iconoclast Era, c. 680–850* (Oxford: Oxford University Press, 2015); Marie-France Auzépy, *L'histoire des iconoclastes* (Paris: Association des Amis du Centre d'Histoire et Civilisation de Byzance, 2007); Leslie Brubaker and John Haldon, *Byzantium in the Iconoclast Era, c. 680–850: The Sources, an Annotated Survey* (London: Ashgate, 2001); Leslie Brubaker and John Haldon, *Byzantium in the Iconoclast Era, c. 680–850: A History* (Cambridge: Cambridge University Press, 2011); Leslie Brubaker, *Inventing Byzantine Iconoclasm* (London: Bristol Classical Press, 2012).

9. Guy Stroumsa, "Barbarians or Heretics? Jews and Arabs in the Mind of Byzantium (Fourth to Eighth Centuries)," in *Jews in Byzantium: Dialectics of Minority and Majority Cultures*, ed. Robert Bonfil et al. (Leiden: Brill, 2012), 761–76; Vincent Déroche, "Polémique anti-judaïque et emergence de l'Islam (7e-8e s.)," *Revue des études byzantines* 57, no. 1 (1999): 141–62; Youval Rotman, "Converts in Byzantine Italy: Local Representation of Jewish-Christian Rivalry," in *Jews in Byzantium*, 893–922.

10. M. Amarise, "Eusebio fra storiografia e teologia politica: L'imperatore cristiano dalla Storia Ecclesiastica agli scritti costantiniani," *Adamantius* 16 (2010): 52–62.

11. Oded Irshai, "Jews and Judaism in Early Church Historiography: The Case of Eusebius of Caesarea (Preliminary Observations and Examples)," in *Jews in Byzantium*, 799–828, 801–806.

12. Socrates Scholasticus, *Histoire ecclésiastique*, vol. 1, ed. and trans. Pierre Périchon and Pierre Maraval (Paris: Cerf, 2004), 126–29. English translation based on Jacob R. Marcus, ed., *The Jew in the Medieval World: A Source Book, 315–1791* (Cincinnati, OH: Hebrew Union College, 1999), 105.

13. Socrates Scholasticus, *Histoire ecclésiastique*, vol. 1, 152; vol. 4, 48–55.

14. Ibid., vol. 1, 156–59; vol. 4, 28–35, 44–47.

15. Ibid., vol. 2, 322–27; vol. 4, 60–63. See Theophanes the Confessor, *Chronographia*, ed. Carl de Boor (Hildesheim: Georg Olms, 1963), A.M. 5908/A.D. 415/416.

16. Sozomenos, *Histoire ecclésiastique*, vol. 1, ed. Joseph Bidez, trans. André-Jean Festugière (Paris: Cerf, 1983–2008), 266–73; vol. 3, 214–24.

17. Ibid., vol. 1, 266–73. Cameron, "Blaming the Jews," 57–78.

18. See Theodoret of Cyrus, *Histoire ecclésiastique*, vol. 2, ed. and trans. Pierre Canivet (Paris: Cerf, 2006–2009), 156, 478.

19. Oded Irshai, "Christian Historiographers' Reflections on Jewish-Christian Violence in Fifth-Century Alexandria," in *Jews, Christians, and the Roman Empire: The Poetics of Power in Late Antiquity*, ed. Natalie B. Dohrmann and Annette Yoshiko Reed (Philadelphia: University of Pennsylvania Press, 2013), 137–53.

20. John Malalas, *Chronographia*, ed. Ioannes Thurn (Berlin: De Gruyter, 2000), 316–17.

21. Procopius, *De bello gothico*, ed. Gerhard Wirth (Leipzig: Teubner, 1963), 45, 53–54; Procopius, *De bello persico*, ed. Jakob Haury (Leipzig: Teubner, 1962), 107.

22. Procopius, *Anekdota*, ed. Jakob Haury (Leipzig: Teubner, 1963), 174.

23. Robert W. Thomson, trans., *The Armenian History Attributed to Sebeos*, vol. 1 (Liverpool: Liverpool University Press, 1999), 70.

24. Ibid., 71.

25. Cameron, "Blaming the Jews."

26. Thomson, *The Armenian History*, vol. 1, 95.

27. John Moorhead, "The Earliest Christian Theological Response to Islam," *Religion* 11, no. 3 (1981): 265–74. See Carl de Boor, ed., *Georgii monachi chronicon*, vol. 2 (Stuttgart: Teubner, 1978), 699–702.

28. Thomson, *The Armenian History*, vol. 1, 97, 103.

29. Ibid., 144–45.

30. Theophanes the Confessor, *Chronographia*, vol. 1, 333, 342.

31. Ibid., 402–403. See de Boor, *Georgii monachi chronicon*, vol. 2, 735.

32. Theophanes the Confessor, *Chronographia*, vol. 1, 404ff.

33. Ibid., 402–403. See de Boor, *Georgii monachi chronicon*, vol. 2, 735.

34. See, for a characteristic example, Theophanes the Confessor, *Chronographia*, vol. 1, 406.

35. Ibid., vol. 1, 446, 452.

36. However, see de Boor, *Georgii monachi chronicon*, vol. 2, 737–38; and Rivkah Fishman-Duker, "Images of Jews in Byzantine Chronicles: A General Survey," in *Jews in Byzantium*, 787–790.

37. Herbert Musurillo, ed. and trans., *The Acts of the Christian Martyrs* (Oxford: Clarendon Press, 2000), *passim*.

38. Athanasius of Alexandria, *Vie d'Antoine*, ed. and trans. G. J. M. Bartelink (Paris: Cerf, 1994); André-Jean Festugière, ed., *Historia monachorum in Aegypto* (Brussels: Société des Bollandistes, 1971); Jerome, *Trois Vies de moines (Paul, Malchus, Hilarion)*, ed. Edgardo M. Morales, trans. Pierre Leclerc (Paris: Cerf, 2007); Jean-Claude Guy, ed. and trans., *Les Apophtegmes des Pères* (Paris: Cerf, 1993–2005).

39. For example, in Jerome, "Life of Hilarion," in *Trois Vies de moines* (Paris: Cerf, 2007), chap. 38. See John Moschos, *Le Pré Spirituel*, ed. and trans. M.-J. Rouët de Journal (Paris: Cerf, 1946), chap. 15.

40. Dagron and Déroche, "Juifs et Chrétiens"; Robert Griveau, "Histoire de la conversion des juifs habitant la ville de Tomei en Egypte d'après d'anciens manuscrits arabes," *Revue de l'Orient Chrétien* 3 (1908): 298–313; *Vat. gr.* 1591, 165v ff., Latin trans. Papebroch in *Acta Sanctorum* Maii II, 537ff.; Mario Re, *Il codice lentinese dei santi Alfio, Filadelfo e Cirino: Studio paleografico e filologico* (Palermo: Istituto Siciliano di Studi Bizantini e Neoellenici, 2007); C. Gerbino, "Appunti per una edizione dell'agiografia di Lentini," *Byzantinische Zeitschrift* 84–85, no. 1 (1992): 26–36; Rotman, "Converts," in *Jews in Byzantium*.

41. Gilbert Dagron, "Le traité de Grégoire de Nicée sur le baptême des Juifs," *Travaux et Mémoires*, no. 11 (1991): 313–57; Dagron and Déroche, "Juifs et Chrétiens," 25–26.

42. François Halkin, "Passion inédite des quarante-deux martyrs d'Amorium," in *Hagiologie byzantine* (Brussels: Société des Bollandistes, 1986), 152–69; Paul Peeters, "S. Romain le néomartyr (1 mai 780) d'après un document géorgien," *Analecta Bollandiana* 30 (1911): 393–427; Youval Rotman, "Christians, Jews and Muslims in Byzantine Italy: Medieval Conflicts in Local Perspective," in *The Byzantine World*, ed. Paul Stephenson (London: Routledge, 2010), 223–34.

43. Ihor Ševčenko, "Hagiography of the Iconoclast Period," in *Iconoclasm: Papers Given at the Ninth Spring Symposium of Byzantine Studies, University of Birmingham, March 1975*, ed. Anothony Bryer and Judith Herrin (Birmingham, UK: University of Birmingham, 1977), 113–33.

44. Kathleen Corrigan, *Visual Polemics in the Ninth-Century Byzantine Psalters* (Cambridge: Cambridge University Press, 1992); Glenn Peers, *Sacred Shock: Framing Visual Experience in Byzantium* (University Park: Pennsylvania State University Press, 2004), chaps. 1–2.

45. Athanasius, *Orationes contra Arianos*, *Patrologia Graeca* 26: 11–526, e.g., 324–25.

46. Peeters, "S. Romain le néomartyr," 413.

47. Marie-France Auzépy, *La Vie d'Étienne le Jeune par Étienne le Diacre* (Farnham, UK: Ashgate Variorum, 1997), chaps. 15, 19.

48. Athanasios Markopoulos, "*Bios tēs autokrateiras Theodōras* (*BHG* 1731)," *Symmeikta* 5 (1983): 267.

49. Eleuteri and Rigo, *Eretici*, 109–23; Corrigan, *Visual Polemics*, 29–37, 164 n. 35.

50. For the return of this stereotype after iconoclasm, see Denis F. Sullivan et al., ed. and trans., *The Life of Saint Basil the Younger* (Washington, DC: Dumbarton Oaks Research Library and Collection, 2014), 344–62, 400–402; Albrecht Berger, *Life and Works of Saint Gregentios, Archbishop of Taphar* (Berlin: De Gruyter, 2006), 100–109, 796–98. See also *The Life of Constantine the Jew* (*Acta Sanctorum*), Nov. IV, 628–56.

51. Averil Cameron, "Jews and Heretics—A Category Error?," in *The Ways That Never Parted: Jews and Christians in Late Antiquity and the Early Middle Ages*, ed. Adam Becker and Annette Yoshiko Reed (Tübingen: Mohr Siebeck, 2003), 345–60; *Patrologia Graeca*, 94: 764–73; Armand Abel, "Le chaptire CI du livre des hérésies de Jean Damascène," *Studia Islamica*, no. 19 (1963): 5–25; Adel-Théodore Khoury, *Les théologiens byzantins et l'Islam: Textes et auteurs (VIIIe-XIIIe S.)* (Louvain: Nauwelaerts, 1969), 49–65.

52. Eleuteri and Rigo, *Eretici*; Marius Canard, *Histoire de la dynastie des H'amdanides de Jazîra et de Syrie* (Paris: Presses universitaires de France, 1953), 737–39; Marius Canard, "Quelques 'à-côtés' de l'histoire des relations entre Byzance et les Arabes," pt. xv in *Byzance et les musulmans du Proche Orient* (London: Variorum, 1973).

53. Rotman, "Byzance"; Rotman, *Byzantine Slavery and the Mediterranean World* (Cambridge, MA: Harvard University Press, 2009), 39–51.

54. Eleuteri and Rigo, *Eretici*; Miguel Arranz, "Les sacrements de l'ancient Euchologe constantinopolitain," *Orientalia Christiana Periodica* 48 (1982): 284–335; Miguel Arranz, "Les sacrements de l'ancient Euchologe constantinopolitain," *Orientalia Christiana Periodica* 49 (1983): 42–90; G. Ficker, "Eine Sammlung von Anschwörungsformeln," *Zeitschrift für Kirchengeschichte* 27 (1906): 443–64.

55. The following discussion is based on MS *Paris. Coisl.* 213 (copied in 1027), folios 140r–47r, which I consulted along with MSS *Escorial R-I-15*; *Athen.* 662; *Athen.* 714. *Patrologia Graeca*, 140: 123–36.

56. *Paris. Coisl.* 213, 140r–45r, in comparison to *Escorial R-I-15*, 74v–79v; *Athen.* 662, 242r–57v; *Athen.* 714, 40r–56v.

57. Daniel J. Sahas, "Ritual of Conversion from Islam to the Byzantine Church," *Greek Orthodox Theological Review* 36, no. 1 (1991): 57–69; E. L. Montet, "Un rituel d'abjuration des Musulmans dans l'église grecque," *Revue de l'histoire des religions* 53 (1906): 145–63.

58. *Paris. Coisl.* 213, ff. 140r–45v. See Antonio Rigo, "Una formula inedita d'abiura per i Musulmani (fine X–inizi XI secolo)," *Rivista di Studi Bizantini e Neoellenici* 39 (1992): 163–73.

59. *Patrologia Graeca*, 105: 670–842; Antonio Rigo, "Nicetas of Byzantium," in *Christian-Muslim Relations: A Bibliographical History*, vol. 1, ed. David Thomas and Barbara Roggema (Leiden: Brill, 2009), 751–56. Khoury, *Les théologiens*, 110–62; Astérios Argyriou, "Perception de l'Islam et traductions du Coran," *Byzantion* 75 (2005): 25–69; James M. Demetriades, "Nicetas of Byzantium and His Encounter with Islam: A Study of the 'Anatropē' and the two 'Epistles' to Islam" (PhD diss., Hartford Seminary Foundation, 1972).

60. Sahas, "Ritual of Conversion," 58–59.

61. Johannaes Damaskenos and Theodorus Abū Qurra, *Schriften zum Islam*, ed. and trans. Reinhold Glei and Adel-Théodore Khoury (Würzburg: Echter, 1995); Elizabeth Jeffreys, ed. and trans., *Digenis Akritis: The Grottaferrata and Escorial Versions* (Cambridge: Cambridge University Press, 1998), 26–30, 52.

62. See the formulas for apostates who converted back to Christianity in Elisabeth Schiffer, "Returning to the Fold: Observations on Prayers for Muslim Apostates in Byzantine Euchologia," in "Byzantine Prayer Books as Sources for Social History and Daily Life," Claudia Rapp et al., *Jahrbuch der österreichischen Byzantinistik* 67 (2017): 196–200.

63. See David Feldman's essay in this volume, "A Retreat from Universalism: Opposing and Defining Antisemitism and Islamophobia in Britain, ca.1990–2018," 251–77.

64. Shulamit Volkov, "Antisemitism as a Cultural Code: Reflections on the History and Historiography of Antisemitism in Imperial Germany," *The Leo Baeck Institute Year Book* 23, no. 1 (January 1978): 25–46. Volkov followed Clifford Geertz, "Ideology as a Cultural System," in *The Interpretation of Cultures* (New York: Basic Books, 1973), 193–233.

65. Christos Merantzas, "The Cultural Construction of the Byzantine Identity: The Case of 'Islamophobia,'" in *Proceedings of the International Symposium Byzantium and the Arab World Encounter of Civilizations (Thessaloniki, 16–18 December 2011)*, ed. A. Kralides and A. Gkoutzioukostas (Thessaloniki: Aristotle University of Thessaloniki, 2012), 325–38. This paper focuses on the late Byzantine period, with no comparative approach to either anti-Judaism or other religious hatreds.

8

The Term "Antisemitism" as a Category for the Study of Medieval Jewish History

TZAFRIR BARZILAY

D AVID ENGEL EMPHASIZES the fact that antisemitism is a scholarly category adopted by historians of Jewish history and claims that the use of this category obfuscates more than clarifies the discourse concerning relations between Jews and non-Jews.[1] It is hard to deny that antisemitism is a theoretical category and not a "simple" description, because the work of historians, as Engel himself notes, demands the constant use of such categories. When scholars declare that they are studying medieval European Jewish history, they are using a series of arbitrary categories based on the conventions accepted in their field. Each category raises questions. For instance, does the term "Jews" include converts? Does "Europe" include frontier regions that may not have belonged culturally to the continent during the Middle Ages? Does the "Middle Ages" refer to the period ending in 1348 (the beginning of the Black Death), 1492 (the European discovery of America and the expulsion of Jews from Spain), 1517 (the beginning of the Reformation), or a different year? These examples clarify the general principle: All terms, definitions, and periods used in scholarship and historical description are, in some sense, arbitrary, and they can be reexamined and redefined according to the nature of the topic. This includes the term "antisemitism."[2]

At the same time, the wheel of history cannot be reinvented for every single book and article. For example, a book describing some historical phenomenon that occurred between the fourteenth and sixteenth centuries might associate the cultural or social character of that phenomenon with the medieval era. Such a book would thus challenge the prevailing consensus, which demarcates the end of the Middle Ages around the turn of the fifteenth century. Perhaps the author would refrain from contending, in this book, with the consensus pertaining to the physical boundaries of Europe or with the names given to various groups within it. If a book tried to contend with all of these issues, it would become dictionary-like and would not be able to describe historical phenomena in depth; it would miss its primary purpose. Therefore, while it is sometimes necessary to question the accepted categories of a specific historical field, it should be remembered that the terms we use are all categories of this sort, and that an outdated term can only be replaced by another term that will have its own set of shortcomings.

Engel attempts to effect a profound change—a change that goes beyond the boundaries of semantics—in the discourse about violence, whether in thought or action, perpetrated against Jews by non-Jews. Had he merely proposed to replace the term "antisemitism" in the scholarly literature with another term—"anti-Judaism," for instance—the matter could be put to rest rather simply; every scholar would choose the most appropriate term and make that choice explicit.[3] Engel, however, wishes to effect a substantive change: At the end of his essay, he calls on "historians who are dissatisfied with the common practice of considering virtually the entire set of behaviors that Jews find threatening under a single analytical rubric" to "devise their own schemes for dividing the set in ways that best help them find answers to the questions that prompt their research."[4] This suggestion makes a great deal of sense because there is no reason to assume that the categories that served as the basis for past studies will effectively serve future studies. Nevertheless, Engel does not address the fundamental methodological disconnect that can emerge when scholars select different analytical categories to study the same historical events. Different categories prompt different research questions that can only be answered with different sources and methods. This issue will be clarified through several examples below and then expanded upon further at the end of the essay.

The central question about historians' use of the terms "antisemitism" or "anti-Judaism" to describe the violent ideas or actions of Christians against Jews in the Middle Ages is not whether this use is proper, but, rather, whether or not it is productive. In other words, we must clarify what historians gain by using these terms and categories as well as the structural failures resulting from each particular choice. This article seeks to do just that. A comprehensive survey of the extant literature on this topic would be too lengthy and not helpful to scholars in other fields. Therefore, I identify central historiographic trends, mainly over the past three decades, as efforts aimed at reconsidering the terms "antisemitism" or "anti-Judaism," or that proposed a different thematic framework for discussing Jewish-Christian relations in the period. I have selected a few examples of each critical approach, that, in my eyes, present novel perspectives on the question before us. The survey of these critical approaches will be accompanied by a discussion of the possibilities that each approach offers for reanalyzing medieval Jewish-Christian relations and their relationship with the extant historiography. I will conclude the article with some general thoughts on the state of this field and a proposal for future avenues of study.

Before examining the central problems connected with using the terms "antisemitism" and "anti-Judaism" to describe Jewish-Christian relations in the medieval era, I will discuss the history that these terms played in the historical narratives used by the different scholars addressing this subject, starting from the beginning of the academic study of Jewish history. Even though he did not explicitly employ the term "antisemitism," Heinrich Graetz, in his late nineteenth-century history of the Jewish people, used Christian violence against Jews as a central narrative axis. Graetz's work characterizes periods of Jewish history based on the effects of major intellectual currents or waves of persecution.[5] Thus, if Judah Halevi, Maimonides, and the emergence of Kabbalah characterize, according to Graetz, specific periods within medieval Jewish history, then the persecution of Jews during the First Crusade, the Black Death, and the expulsion from Spain represent other periods. This narrative emphasizes the great accomplishments of medieval Jewish culture in the face of Christian attempts to suppress, limit, and even annihilate that culture. The story of the Jews in Europe during this era, according to Graetz, is the story of the survival and flourishing of a small, tenacious minority in the face of a hostile Christian majority.

Many scholars subsequently adopted some or all of Graetz's perspective, but this is not the place to enumerate them. The crystallization of Zionist ideology at the end of the nineteenth century and during the twentieth century reinforced the narrative that emphasized the unfortunate state of the Jews in exile, including in medieval Europe. Prominent Zionist historians sought to justify the Jewish national project, and they did so by portraying Jewish existence in Christian society as an unending struggle to preserve Jewish identity and even to defend Jewish lives.[6] It should be emphasized that Zionist historians saw not only the ideological but also the clear historiographic advantages of this narrative: The Jews were a distinct minority within Christian society in the Middle Ages, various elements in this society openly sought their conversion, and the Jews occasionally suffered persecutions, expulsions, and the abrogation of their rights. Hence, using these facts as a central narrative axis to delineate European Jewish history seemed quite reasonable.

After World War II and the Holocaust, this historiographic trend was strengthened by the study of antisemitism as a distinct academic discipline. Léon Poliakov, in his comprehensive study of the history of antisemitism, devotes special attention to medieval Jewish history.[7] In his view, the development of antisemitic thinking was tied mainly not to theological disputes, but rather to incidents where Christians perpetrated violence against Jews and wished to justify their actions after the fact. According to this idea, large-scale violence by Christians against Jews, primarily during the First Crusade, led to the development of anti-Jewish ideas and to the gradual deterioration of the condition of the Jews—a deterioration that reached its peak with the wave of persecutions in the fourteenth century. Violent incidents in Spain throughout the fourteenth century, especially the wave of attacks in 1391, created the problem of forced converts and their descendants (conversos) that, in turn, led to the establishment of the Inquisition and ultimately to the expulsion of the Jews in 1492. In this sequence of events, it was violence that led to institutional expressions of anti-Jewish sentiment, and not the other way around. According to Poliakov, this process was characteristic of the Middle Ages but not of antiquity, which, though filled with theological disputes, was not characterized by large-scale waves of violence by non-Jews against a Jewish minority. Therefore, the roots of antisemitism, according to Poliakov, are to be located specifically in the Middle Ages.

Gavin Langmuir concurs with this view, and it is the theoretical framework proposed in his book *Toward a Definition of Antisemitism* that Engel critiques in his essay.[8] Without addressing Engel's fundamental critique, it should be noted that the parts of Langmuir's book that are devoted to the historical analysis of the roots of antisemitism focus entirely on the Middle Ages. According to Langmuir, during this period there was a transition from "anti-Jewish" patterns of thought, which were widespread in antiquity, to "antisemitic" patterns of thought, which characterized later periods. The new, "antisemitic" patterns of thought viewed Jews as a real threat to the existence of Christian society, protested their protected legal status, and cultivated "irrational fantasies" against them. These fantasies included ritual murder and cannibalism libels, which were used against Jews starting in the twelfth century, as well as accusations of host desecration and poisoning wells, which developed later. Christian hatred of Jews was thus justified not due to their actual behavior—like their refusal to convert in 1096—but to fantasies and libels ascribed to them.[9]

It is, of course, possible to broaden and sharpen this overview, but the general picture is clear: Prominent scholars of medieval Jewish history viewed the conflicts between the Christian majority and the Jewish minority as a major characteristic—perhaps the defining characteristic—of the era. Additionally, major scholars of the history of antisemitism identified the Middle Ages as the period when the roots of this phenomenon developed.[10] This attitude often dictated the framing narrative for Jewish historiography concerning this era, a narrative in which persecution, expulsion, and deterioration of Jews' legal and political status played a major role. Presumably, even during periods of calm, the threat of Christian persecution loomed menacingly over Jewish existence and profoundly affected the development of local Jewish culture.

The historian Salo Baron critiqued the approach of Graetz and his successors throughout his lengthy career. In 1928, he labeled the narrative that focused on the persecution of the Jews as the "lachrymose conception of Jewish history," and objected to the narrative's neglect of other historical developments.[11] Baron sought to present a more balanced portrait of Jewish history that would also emphasize the Jews' integration into their surroundings and the collaborations they devised with non-Jews. In 1937, he began to publish his massive and influential *A Social and Religious History of the Jews*, a project that he expanded over the years.[12] Despite his criticism of Graetz, Baron did not forgo writing Jewish history from a broad perspective that presumed the existence of fundamental characteristics that could be identified across long periods and vast geographic expanses. Yet, as Baron's enormous study progressed and developed, the vaguer it became about those general characteristics of Jewish history. It is difficult, for example, to understand what exactly late modern Chinese Jews have in common with Palestinian Jews of the Second Temple era without reverting to the two factors that Graetz identified: halakhic Jewish culture and the hostility of the non-Jewish environment.[13]

Other historians also consciously chose to forgo the framing narrative proposed by Graetz, even though various versions of this narrative served as the basis for many other studies. As Baron claimed, focus on conflict with Christians, on one hand, and on Jewish intellectual history, on the other, produced a narrative that ignored many questions about the lives of Jews in medieval Europe. This narrative, for example, barely addresses changes in family structure, economic activity, the education of children, or living conditions. Sometimes historians discussed these subjects as part of a treatment of halakhic or intellectual sources, or as details in a description of interreligious tensions between Jews and Christians, but they were rarely the objects of study in themselves.

In recent decades, studies focusing on the social history of the daily lives of medieval European Jews have been written with the goal of challenging the dominant narrative.[14] Many of these studies assert that Jewish society should be examined as part of the Christian majority society within which it existed. In contrast to the traditional narrative, which portrayed the Jews as a self-segregating minority with an almost entirely separate culture, the new studies identify similarities and moments of influence between the groups. Some scholars propose discussing a "shared culture" for medieval Christians and Jews, a culture that developed out of the reality of a shared existence between the two groups within the small cities that characterize medieval Europe. This narrative does not ignore the fact that Christians sometimes expressed hostility and even acted violently against Jews, but it considers these facts as part of a broader picture. It also considers the long years of Jewish-Christian coexistence, which included economic cooperation and cultural dialogue. For the scholars who adopt this approach, the discourse about the development of antisemitism in the Middle Ages, though not necessarily mistaken, distracts attention from the central task of studying the Jewish history of this era: describing the everyday reality of Jewish life as it was normally, not just during periods of crisis.

In addition, during recent decades various scholars have offered other perspectives on the relations between majority and minority groups, including non-Jewish minorities, in medieval Europe. Robert I. Moore devoted many years to the study of heretical Christian groups of this era, and his first two books attempt to map and link these groups.[15] However, Moore gradually found himself grappling with questions similar to the ones that Engel raises in his essay (though on a different subject): What is the fundamental connection between the various historical phenomena and movements cataloged under the term "heresy"? Is there an essential definition of heresy that determines which movements were deemed heretical and which were accepted as legitimate? Why did the struggle against heresy appear as a central motif of European culture from the eleventh to thirteenth centuries?

In attempting to answer these questions, Moore came to realize that all heretical movements promoted reforms that met with institutional opposition as they sought to bring the medieval church closer to the model of the church presented in the New Testament. The difference between heretical movements and legitimate reform movements, many of which flourished in the High Middle Ages, did not stem from clear ideological differences, but rather from how the church establishment and secular institutions reacted to the movements' demands for reform. Movements that obtained official approval became an important part of the church, and those that were rejected, for whatever reason, were branded heretical. Once a particular movement was branded hereti-cal, church officials quickly attributed to it negative imagery and wanton acts to justify the actions of secular institutions against it. These images and accusations form the bulk of the information that has reached us concerning medieval heretical movements (or rather, reform movements), and most of the extant sources were produced by church personnel who wanted to undermine the legitimacy of these new movements. Therefore, they tarred them with the same brush.[16]

In his 1987 book *The Formation of a Persecuting Society*, Moore pres-ents and expands this claim.[17] He begins his book by describing the persecution of three main minority groups in medieval Europe: heretics, lepers, and Jews. The portrayal of these groups as a danger to the public, the development of negative rhetoric about them, and their organized persecution by church and secular institutions occurred simultane-ously from the eleventh century to the mid-fourteenth century. Moore shows that much of the negative imagery used to describe members of these groups was similar, and that similar social mechanisms were applied against them. Thus, he claims, the negative approach to these minority groups stemmed from the comprehensive reform that the church underwent during the High Middle Ages—a reform that sought to redefine Christian orthodoxy, to preserve "pure" Christian society, and to defend it from external enemies. The minority groups were perceived as threats to the hegemony of the church establishment, and so this establishment worked to incite Christian society against them, mainly through accusations and the cultivation of negative images.

Moore's conclusions require a rethinking of the history of Christian violence against the Jewish minority in medieval Europe. If we accept his claims, the main explanatory narrative of this violence should not be based on the unique relations between Jews and Christians or on the religious and cultural tensions associated with them, but on the fact that the Jews constituted one of several potentially threatening minori-ties. According to this theory, attacks against Jews during the First Cru-sade were not substantively different from the execution of "heretics" in eleventh-century France and the Rhineland. Both were members of minority groups that were perceived as threats against Christian orthodoxy and were thus treated harshly. Therefore, to understand the characteristics of the violence that the majority perpetrated against the minorities, one must turn to the central institutions of the persecuting society and accept the idea that the unique characteristics of the persecuted groups are less relevant.[18]

In this context, Sara Lipton's 2014 book *Dark Mirror* should also be mentioned. It deals with the development of imagery representing Jews in medieval Christian visual art. Lipton claims that this imagery was not originally created out of a desire to portray Jews antagonistically, and that such meanings were only attributed to it gradually. Many of the changes to the imagery stemmed from theological trends in Christian society and the role played by Jews within the Christian theological narrative and had relatively little connection to practical relations with actual Jews. Lipton proposes that the starkly anti-Jewish understanding of these images stemmed primarily from some observers' lack of proficiency with the theological ideas that shaped them. Like Moore, she emphasizes the importance of broad Christian religious currents in shaping attitudes toward Jews. However, she differs from him in claiming that the exacerbation of this attitude was oftentimes unplanned.[19]

David Nirenberg, in his 1996 book *Communities of Violence*, presents a completely different approach to understanding the violence that erupted between groups and individuals within medieval society.[20] This society, Nirenberg claims, was inherently violent and this violence could be used to express religious feelings, protest royal policy, obtain economic goals, express gendered power relations, or manage conflicts between neighbors. He demonstrates the violent nature of this society through a meticulous examination of various types of violent incidents that occurred in and around the Kingdom of Aragon in the first half of the fourteenth century. This society included different minority groups, most prominently lepers, Jews, and also Muslims, who did not live elsewhere in Europe during the Late Middle Ages. Nirenberg claims that the tendency of scholars to view every violent incident involving minority groups, and Jews in particular, as an instance of "interreligious" violence often kept them from attaining a deeper understanding of the social dynamic that produced the violence. When Christians attacked Jews in Aragon, it was generally due to local political, economic, or social circumstances, rather than to the negative images of Jews that were common in Christian European society or to an enduring historical enmity. The attackers often sought to strengthen a local political group, destroy evidence of debt to Jews, or solve family disputes by force.

Therefore, to understand the reasons for any violent incident, one must examine the status of the attackers and victims within the society in which the incident occurred and not turn to discussions of larger cultural, religious, or historical factors. For example, examining a violent incident against the Jews of Mainz during the First Crusade cannot, according to Nirenberg, offer insight into the factors that led Christians to attack Jews in fourteenth-century Gerona. To understand these factors, it is preferable, in his view, to investigate the political, economic, and social situation in Gerona and locate the incident within the context of other violent incidents that occurred at that time, even if the victims in these other cases were Muslims or Christians and not Jews.[21]

Nirenberg's approach does not present violence as a marginal phenomenon in medieval society, nor does it claim that violence against minorities had a uniform character. Rather, it emphasizes precisely that violence was widespread in this society and played a part in a variety of distinct social processes. According to Nirenberg's interpretation in this book, the treatment of "antisemitism" or "anti-Judaism" as a distinct phenomenon and the scholarly tendency to link different incidents as expressions of this phenomenon misses the mark when it comes to the historical analysis and understanding of each incident. The primary sources, Nirenberg claims, often emphasize specifically the local causes of violence, even if it erupted between members of different religious groups. Scholarly attempts to isolate the particular details within these sources that justify understanding the violence as part of an essentially religious conflict are distortions that should be avoided in favor of addressing each incident in its immediate historical context. Thus, it seems that Nirenberg would agree with Engel's claim that there is little reason to use "antisemitism" as a scholarly category because it is hard to identify a common historical denominator between different incidents that are likely to be thus classified. However, in his second book, *Anti-Judaism: The Western Tradition*, from 2013, Nirenberg takes an entirely different approach and analyzes negative attitudes toward

Judaism as an intellectual and cultural phenomenon that passes from one society to the next throughout history.[22] He thus forgoes, in fact, treatment of specific violent incidents within their immediate historical context and instead addresses how anti-Jewish ideas developed. This approach is somewhat similar to Lipton's, which emphasizes that the history of anti-Jewish ideas can have significance apart from actual relations with Jews.

Nirenberg's change of direction notwithstanding, his call to focus on local history at the expense of the traditional broad narratives of Jewish history has gained interest among scholars of the Middle Ages.[23] Mark Meyerson, in his 2004 book *A Jewish Renaissance in Fifteenth-Century Spain*, focuses on the Jewish community of Morvedre, near Valencia.[24] Meyerson's study examines the economic situation of the town's Jews and traces the relations between them and local Christians, conversos, and Jews in other places. He demonstrates that the situation of the Jews in Morvedre was, contrary to the commonly accepted view, quite secure during the period between the wave of persecution in 1391 and the Expulsion of 1492. They prospered economically, enjoyed a stable political status, and did not suffer from harsh attacks. In stark opposition to traditional historiography, which views the last century of Jewish existence in Spain as a period of ongoing deterioration culminating with the Expulsion, Meyerson calls this period a "renaissance."

Meyerson demonstrates that focusing on one community over a relatively brief time period reveals a picture that differs greatly from the impression produced by discussions of larger waves of persecution and expulsion. In this sense, his approach is something of a synthesis between Nirenberg's first book and the approach of scholars who focus on the quotidian lives of Jews. Meyerson examines local political and social incidents in addition to the Jews' daily routine to address how they affected one another. This perspective also influences his explanation of the Expulsion—an explanation that shines the spotlight on daily interactions between Jews and conversos. There were extensive ties between the two groups after the wave of forced conversions in 1391 and throughout the fifteenth century. Christian society perceived these ties as part of a Jewish attempt to reconvert the conversos back to Judaism. According to Meyerson, the Expulsion was conceived as a solution to this problem and did not necessarily stem from increased anti-Jewish sentiment in Spain. Thus, the model that views the history of Spanish Jewry in the fourteenth and fifteenth centuries as hinging on changes in patterns of antisemitism within Christian society is presented in Meyerson's book as being irrelevant, if not misleading.

The most comprehensive attempt to reject antisemitism or anti-Judaism as a major characteristic of medieval European society is Jonathan Elukin's 2007 book *Living Together, Living Apart*.[25] In this book, Elukin extends the approach of scholars who focus on everyday Jewish life in Europe and points to the normal relations that prevailed between Jews and their Christian neighbors. According to Elukin, not only do these historians favor the primary issue (tranquil daily life) over the secondary one (infrequent violent incidents), but they also present a broader and far more accurate portrait of European Jewish history than the traditional historiography. Elukin maintains, following Baron, that Graetz and his successors viewed the concept of Jewish exile (*Galut*) as an enduring tragedy, an idea that stemmed from traditional Jewish sources. Despite their desire to write Jewish history based on academic research, they did not abandon the traditional framing narrative and therefore tended to describe the relationship between Jews and their Christian environment as a series of persecutions and attacks. In fact, these scholars presented the entirety of medieval European Jewish history as a gradual deterioration culminating inevitably in expulsion. Elukin questions this perspective and claims that shining the spotlight on violent incidents—which indeed occurred—obscures the essential reality of medieval European Jewish history: Jews survived and even thrived. Even if Jews occasionally suffered the attacks of Christians, they generally chose to continue living where they already were. According to Elukin, Jews viewed themselves as an inextricable part of European society and were linked to their Christian neighbors in myriad ways—economically, culturally, and politically.[26] Thus, studies that focus on daily connections between Jews and Christians present a fuller, more convincing historical portrait of their relations.

This approach does not view the study of antisemitism merely as a distraction preventing the focus on more important topics of Jewish history, but also as the source of a historical narrative that is mistaken and ultimately distorts scholarly descriptions of medieval European Jewish life. Christian society was not a "persecuting society," as Moore suggests, nor did it seek opportunities to harm or expel Jews, as scholars of antisemitism often propose. It was, instead, a relatively tolerant society by premodern standards, one that enabled a secure existence and even prosperity for the Jewish minority living within it. This new narrative rejects vast portions of the traditional historiography and gives center stage to studies that focus on fruitful contacts between Jews and Christians.

It was, in fact, Nirenberg who sharply criticized Elukin's approach, accused him of a selective reading of the sources, and sparked a pointed historiographical debate.[27] Yet Nirenberg did not reject out of hand the challenge to the traditional framing narrative that presents medieval Jewish history as a series of misfortunes; rather, he attacked what he deemed to be Elukin's recklessness in presenting his new narrative framework. Hence, the possibility of presenting such a framework convincingly remains high on the scholarly agenda.

We have seen that in recent decades, several scholarly approaches have reformulated or even outright rejected the central role granted to antisemitism or anti-Judaism in traditional historiography. Each of these approaches sparked reaction and debate that lie beyond the scope of this essay. Nonetheless, I have shown that many historians of medieval Jews have adopted, and even expanded on, reservations similar to those proposed by Engel. These studies not only reject older scholarly models but also offer new narrative frameworks to describe relations between Jews and Christians in the medieval period. Each of these narratives demands that historians pose new research questions and adopt different assumptions. Thus, for instance, a scholar who accepts Moore's view of the link between the patterns of persecution of different medieval minorities would want to undertake a comparative study of the types of violence directed against these groups. However, such a broad study will not be very useful to a historian who accepts Nirenberg's earlier claims regarding the importance of analyzing violence at the local level. Scholars who adopt Elukin's critique would reject both of these approaches outright, claiming that they emphasize violent incidents instead of engaging with the central historical phenomena that are referred to far more frequently in the sources. All of them would find the traditional historiography that focuses on antisemitism or anti-Judaism as a central theme in medieval Jewish history to be irrelevant at best and misleading at worst. Thus, abandoning the traditional framing narrative about the central role played by antisemitic or anti-Jewish attitudes in shaping medieval Jewish history can divide the discipline into a number of different scholarly subfields.

Given the many examples and critiques presented above, how should we study Christian-Jewish relations in medieval Europe? In my view, new studies that seek to address this issue will need to include several main characteristics, in particular an extensive analysis of the local level. As Nirenberg, Meyerson, and others have shown, social incidents in the medieval era, including violence against Jews, were influenced by a set of local factors and cannot be understood without analyzing all of these factors. This does not invalidate reaching larger, more general conclusions about Christian attitudes toward Jews, but such conclusions need to be based on a survey of local case studies (or of all instances, if the phenomenon is sufficiently narrow) and a discussion of the insights that emerge from this data set.

The second characteristic of this scholarly approach is the need to examine other developments in Christian society even if they lack a direct connection to Jews. As Moore and Lipton have shown, sometimes Jews were victims of historical processes that characterized Christian society in general and did not stem from relations with or attitudes toward the Jewish minority. Focusing on violent incidents themselves or on related propaganda without looking at larger processes can result in a partial, flawed understanding of what led to the violence. In other words, it is impossible to understand the minority society without understanding the majority society.

The third characteristic of new studies should be a broadening of the scope beyond political and intellectual history in their narrow sense. As Baron and Elukin claim, and as other historians who examine the daily life of medieval Jews have shown, Jewish existence did not revolve solely around interreligious violence. Jews had a series of routine relations with Christians, formed economic ventures with them, shared the same urban space, spoke the same languages, and even resembled them in certain aspects of religious and communal culture. Even when studying the negative imagery of Jews within Christian society or the violence that developed as a result of these images, we cannot ignore these more common, everyday connections. Many of the studies presented above lay the groundwork for this type of historical research, but much room remains for progress. Terms like "antisemitism" and "anti-Judaism" can, in my view, remain in use within scholarly discourse as long as it is understood that they do not represent the full dynamic of Jewish-Christian relations in medieval European society and if the guidelines that I have enumerated above are adopted and expanded upon.

NOTES

This article was written with the support of the research group "Beyond the Elite: Jewish Daily Life in Medieval Europe," led by Elisheva Baumgarten and funded by the European Research Council, ERC (grant agreement ID 681507). I thank Elisheva Baumgarten, Eyal Levinson, and Aviya Doron for their help in the preparation of this article.

1. David Engel, "Away from a Definition of Antisemitism: An Essay in the Semantics of Historical Description," in *Rethinking European Jewish History*, ed. Jeremy Cohen and Moshe Rosman (Oxford: Littman Library of Jewish Civilization, 2009), 30–53.

2. See the discussion in Moshe Rosman, *How Jewish Is Jewish History?* (Oxford: Littman Library of Jewish Civilization, 2007), 1–55.

3. The term "antisemitism" implies certain attitudes toward ideas of race. Several historians claim that these ideas are not relevant to the Middle Ages, while others claim that they were shaped during this period and therefore are applicable only to parts of it. See Miriam Eliav-Feldon, Benjamin Isaac, and Joseph Ziegler, eds., *The Origins of Racism in the West* (Cambridge: Cambridge University Press, 2009). Other scholars prefer terms like "anti-Judaism" to describe negative ideas and actions by Christians against Jews in the Middle Ages, as the term locates the enmity within an interreligious context, not an interracial one. In this article I have chosen not to examine this debate, though it is worthy of a discussion. The debate was recently rekindled in reaction to Geraldine Heng, *The Invention of Race in the European Middle Ages* (Cambridge: Cambridge University Press, 2018).

4. Engel, "Away from a Definition of Antisemitism," 51.

5. Heinrich Graetz, *Geschichte der Juden von den ältesten Zeiten bis auf die Gegenwart* (Leipzig: O. Leiner, 1860–1866), 5–8.

6. For an examination of these developments, see David N. Myers, *Re-Inventing the Jewish Past: European Jewish Intellectuals and the Zionist Return to History* (Oxford: Oxford University Press, 1995); Amnon Raz-Krakotzkin, "The National Narration

of Exile: Zionist Historiography and Medieval Jewry" [in Hebrew] (PhD diss., Tel Aviv University, 1996). See also Rosman, *How Jewish Is Jewish History?*, 24–27, 38–43.

7. Léon Poliakov, *Histoire de l'antisémitsme: Du Christ aux Juifs de Cour* (Paris: Calmann-Lévy, 1955), 42–192; Léon Poliakov, *Histoire de l'antisémitsme: De Mahomet aux Marranes* (Paris: Calmann-Lévy, 1961), 85–203.

8. Gavin Langmuir, *Toward a Definition of Antisemitism* (Berkeley: University of California Press, 1990); Engel, "Away from a Definition of Antisemitism," 51–53.

9. Trachtenberg proposed a similar line of thinking in works written during the Second World War. See Joshua Trachtenberg, *The Devil and the Jews: The Medieval Conception of the Jews and Its Relation to Modern Anti-Semitism* (New Haven, CT: Yale University Press, 1943).

10. This approach remains relevant. See Robert Chazan, *From Anti-Judaism to Anti-Semitism: Ancient and Medieval Christian Constructions of Jewish History* (Cambridge: Cambridge University Press, 2017), 109–248.

11. For an overview of this debate, see Robert Liberles, *Salo Wittmayer Baron: Architect of Jewish History* (New York: New York University Press, 1995), 116–19, 295–97, 340–45; Rosman, *How Jewish Is Jewish History?*, 40.

12. Salo W. Baron, *A Social and Religious History of the Jews*, vols. 1–3 (New York: Columbia University Press, 1937). Volumes of the second (greatly) expanded edition were published until 1983.

13. See Rosman, *How Jewish Is Jewish History?*, 20–34.

14. This trend was presaged by Israel Abrahams, *Jewish Life in the Middle Ages* (London: Macmillan, 1896). Several other prominent examples include Thérèse Metzger and Mendel Metzger, *Jewish Life in the Middle Ages: Illuminated Hebrew Manuscripts of the Thirteenth to the Sixteenth Centuries* (New York: Alpine Fine Arts Collection, 1982); Ivan Marcus, *Rituals of Childhood: Jewish Acculturation in Medieval Europe* (New Haven, CT: Yale University Press, 1996); Avraham Grossman, *Pious and Rebellious: Jewish Women in Medieval Europe* (Waltham, MA: Brandeis University Press, 2004); Elisheva Baumgarten, *Mothers and Children: Jewish Family Life in Medieval Europe* (Princeton, NJ: Princeton University Press, 2007); Ephraim Shoham-Steiner, *On the Margins of a Minority: Leprosy, Madness, and Disability among the Jews of Medieval Europe* (Detroit, MI: Wayne State University Press, 2014).

15. Robert Moore, *The Birth of Popular Heresy* (Toronto: University of Toronto Press, 1995); Robert Moore, *The Origins of European Dissent* (New York: St. Martin's Press, 1977).

16. This explanation is developed more fully in Moore's latest book, *The War on Heresy: Faith and Power in Medieval Europe* (London: Profile, 2012).

17. Robert Moore, *The Formation of a Persecuting Society: Power and Deviance in Western Europe, 950–1250* (Oxford: Basil Blackwell, 1987). In the 2007 edition, Moore sharpens his ideas and clearly presents the mechanisms of persecution developed within European society during the High Middle Ages.

18. In the second edition of his book (see the previous note), Moore qualifies his view and addresses with greater precision the differences in the perception of different minorities.

19. Sara Lipton, *Dark Mirror: The Medieval Origins of Anti-Jewish Iconography* (New York: Metropolitan Books, 2014).

20. David Nirenberg, *Communities of Violence: Persecution of Minorities in the Middle Ages* (Princeton, NJ: Princeton University Press, 1996).

21. This problem is presented differently in Rosman, *How Jewish Is Jewish History?*, 34–38.

22. David Nirenberg, *Anti-Judaism: The Western Tradition* (New York: W. W. Norton, 2013).

23. Engel cites Nirenberg's approach as a possible solution for writing Jewish history without the term "antisemitism." See Engel, "Away from a Definition of Antisemitism," 53, n. 60.

24. Mark Meyerson, *A Jewish Renaissance in Fifteenth-Century Spain* (Princeton, NJ: Princeton University Press, 2004).

25. Jonathan Elukin, *Living Together, Living Apart: Rethinking Jewish-Christian Relations in the Middle Ages* (Princeton, NJ: Princeton University Press, 2007).

26. Elukin was not the first to question Moore's view that intolerance was a major characteristic of medieval European society. See John Christian Laursen and Cary J. Nederman, eds., *Beyond the Persecuting Society: Religious Toleration before the Enlightenment* (Philadelphia: University of Pennsylvania Press, 1998), 1–93.

27. David Nirenberg, "Hope's Mistakes," *The New Republic*, February 13, 2008, https://newrepublic.com/article/62288/hopes-mistakes.

IV

MODERN
CONTESTATIONS

9

"Feverish Preference"
Philosemitism, Anti-antisemitism, and Their Critics

OFRI ILANY

Can there be love between collectives? Is there such a thing as "political love"? Or is love exclusive to private relationships between people? Surprisingly, there is almost no theoretical writing on love as a phenomenon in the history of peoples. It seems that in human life, love occupies a place no less central than hate; accordingly, it constitutes a major subject for works of art, literature, and cinema. But this is not the case when it comes to history. While a notable portion of historiography is devoted to phenomena like hostility, enmity, and discrimination against the "other," public displays of love suffer from historiographic neglect. This asymmetry is especially prominent in historiography about the relations between Jews and non-Jews. On the spectrum of possible feelings toward Jews, it seems that the pole of hatred and resentment is overemphasized.

The existence of philosemitism—the love of Jews—as a significant phenomenon is far from self-evident. Philosemitism is often portrayed as a fabrication or a secondary effect of antisemitism. This view requires explanation: Why is the ontological status of philosemitism so unstable, while antisemitism is almost never suspected of being fabricated? Indeed, the excessive prominence of antisemitism compared to philosemitism reflects historical reality. Even the scholar of Judaism Hans-Joachim Schoeps, who is occasionally described in the historiography of philosemitism as exaggerating the historical dimensions of the phenomenon, claims that philosemitism "represents a mere sluggish trickle compared with a wide river" of antisemitism.[1] Nevertheless, the importance of historical phenomena is not measured only qualitatively. Philosemitism is an important layer of major phenomena in Jewish history beginning with the status enjoyed by Jews (unlike Muslims and numerous Christian factions) of a tolerated minority in parts of medieval Europe and culminating with the support of European powers like Great Britain for the Zionist movement. Moreover, dealing with philosemitism is essential for the reflexive examination of the field of Jewish studies itself, and especially of the study of antisemitism. This is because quite a few Jewish studies articles (those not written by Jews) could not have been motivated by anything but philosemitism.

In recent years, several comprehensive works have dealt with and examined various aspects of philosemitism. This scholarly attention contrasts with the meager engagement with philosemitism in the decades after World War II, certainly when compared to research on antisemitism. Scholarly treatment of philosemitism is growing and diversifying along with the recognition of the existence of philosemitism as a serious phenomenon whose different manifestations, with their positive and negative facets, ought to be examined. The awakening of the study of philosemitism can be ascribed to two factors. The first is the receding of the Holocaust into remote history, which gradually detracts from the exclusivity of antisemitism in Jewish historical memory. The second is the strengthening of contemporary political and cultural trends that admire the State of Israel and the Jewish people. These trends include "Christian Zionist" evangelical movements from the United States to Korea, but also a variety of other new philosemitic manifestations, for example, soccer fans of the Dutch team Ajax and the British team Tottenham who wave Israeli flags and call themselves "super Jews," and people who search for "Jewish roots" in Spain, Poland, and elsewhere. That is, philosemitism is currently emerging as an undeniable phenomenon—a development that is familiar even to official institutions like the World Zionist Organization.[2] This contemporary trend offers new perspectives on historical manifestations of philosemitism.[3]

In this essay, I present methodological questions that have emerged within recent scholarship concerning philosemitism as a historical phenomenon. The first part of the essay will examine the genealogy of the term "philosemitism," emphasizing its German contexts, and characterize how this term has been used since it was coined in the late nineteenth century. I will show how the term "philosemitism" was developed by anti-Jewish writers in Germany and adopted as a positive concept after World War II by Jewish and Christian intellectuals who hoped to advance interreligious dialogue. This essay will also discuss criticisms of philosemitism that appeared in the decades after the war, mainly by liberal and Marxist thinkers and intellectuals.

In the second part of the essay, I remap the forms of philosemitic discourse. Various distinctions have been outlined in the history of the study of philosemitism—for instance, between religious and secular, elitist and popular, and authentic and fabricated philosemitism. These are all important, but I wish to propose a more substantive distinction that cuts across several of the earlier distinctions. I mean to distinguish philosemitism—special love or adoration for Jews in particular—and anti-antisemitism—the opposition to antisemitism and anti-Jewish discrimination that stems from a universalist, humanitarian view. I will explain this distinction with two forms of positive relations toward Jews that appear in the writings of the German philosopher Gotthold Ephraim Lessing. Ultimately, this essay presents three main claims. First, I claim that philosemitism is a real phenomenon that should be examined on its own instead of seeing it as a derivative of antisemitism. Second, I show that the critique of philosemitic discourse generally hinges on setting Jews apart as a unique group with a special impact on history. Third, I argue that approaches that claim to relate to Jews with "neutrality" should be regarded with critical suspicion and attention to their ideological foundations.

From Antagonism to Esteem

As a basis for a critical discussion of the category of philosemitism, it is necessary to undertake a genealogical examination of the term itself and its underlying motives. The term "philosemitism" came into use in the context of the antisemitism controversy that broke out in Berlin in the 1880s. In the circles around the historian Heinrich von Treitschke

(1834–1896), who was considered the leader of mainstream antisemites, liberal defenders of Jews were called "philosemites." It seems that Treitschke himself coined the term in an article from December 1880 in which he attacked the "philosemitic zealotry" of the left-wing liberal party (*Fortschrittspartei*).[4] The term was later adopted by various groups and individuals from the left as well. For example, Germany's socialist leader Franz Mehring (1846–1919) wrote an essay called "Anti- und Philosemitisches," and the Socialist International issued a notice in 1891 decrying both "antisemitic and philosemitic incitement."[5]

The term "philosemitism," then, initially served as a polemical, negative, nonscientific concept and was primarily used this way from the late nineteenth until the mid-twentieth century. It was coined in direct contrast to the term "antisemitism," and, as in the case of antisemitism, it refers only to Jews and not to any other "Semitic" peoples.[6] However, the choice of the prefix "philo," meaning "love" (instead of "pro" to form "prosemitism," the true opposite of "antisemitism"), paints a picture of something emotional and irrational. It is therefore not surprising that opponents of antisemitism, like members of the liberal Society for the Defense against Antisemitism (*Verein zur Abwehr des Antisemitismus*), tried to avoid the term.[7]

Until after World War II, the term "philosemitism" was used negatively in a large majority of cases.[8] Only after the Holocaust did the term begin to fill a different function. We can thus distinguish two ways of using the term: "pro-philosemitic" and "anti-philosemitic." Though both were born in the early 1950s, they are still in use today, to one degree or another.

Positive use of the term "philosemitism" flourished within interreligious dialogue in the post-Holocaust period. Schoeps, in his 1952 book *Philosemitismus im Barock*, was the first scholar to invest the term with positive meaning while ignoring its anti-Jewish roots. As Marc Grimm has claimed, Schoeps's works on the subject are a milestone in the development of scholarly engagement with philosemitism.[9] Schoeps, a German-Jewish scholar of Judaism, focused on early modern pro-Jewish Hebraists and millenarians, including Isaac La Peyrère (1596–1676) and Johann Peter Spaeth (1642–1701). Spaeth converted to Judaism and was known as "Moses Germanus." In this context, Schoeps outlined a typological division of the different types of philosemitism:

A. Missionary philosemitism: based on the hope that Jews will convert
B. Biblical (or chiliastic) philosemitism: based on the significant role played by Jews in the history of the redemption
C. Utilitarian philosemitism: based on the material boon brought by Jews
D. Liberal philosemitism: based on humanitarian claims
E. Religious philosemitism: based on an attraction to Jewish texts that leads to conversion to Judaism

This typology is derived from Schoeps's focus on manifestations of Christian religious enthusiasm, and it therefore emphasizes different types of Christian philosemitism.[10] His differs in this way from later typologies, which narrowed all forms of Christian philosemitism into one class and added other types. These new forms of philosemitism included philosemitism as the extension of adoration for a particular Jewish person; love for Jews out of a yearning for the exotic; Zionist philosemitism; and philosemitism that stems from guilty feelings about the Holocaust.[11] In any case, Schoeps's typology of philosemitism suits his general conception of history, which emphasizes the close connection between Judaism and Christianity; Schoeps himself equated the organizers of the "Week of Brotherhood" between Christians and Jews, established in Germany in 1952, with seventeenth-century philosemites.[12] It is worth noting that Schoeps was one of the only scholars of Judaism who held conservative-monarchist views and returned to Germany immediately after the war.

From then on, the positive conception of philosemitism began to appear primarily in the works of historians and conservative intellectuals who sought to illuminate the positive aspects of Christian-Jewish relations. Examples include the historian Gertrude Himmelfarb's book that sketches an enduring philosemitic tradition in England from Cromwell to Churchill and the book by William and Hilary Rubinstein that emphasizes the connection between the philosemitic tradition and liberal or conservative circles.[13] Their book also argues for a close connection between the Marxist left and antisemitic views.[14] Other works, like that of Adam Edelstein, present the philosemitic strains of Christianity, humanism, and nationalism as enabling Jews to exist in Europe despite persecution, expulsion, and forced conversion.[15]

The Critique of Setting Jews Apart

After the war, a critical characterization appeared alongside the use of philosemitism as a positive concept, generally from a leftist or liberal point of view. This critical view examined expressions of philosemitism with suspicion and often linked them with antisemitism. In the expansive Part One of her 1951 book *The Origins of Totalitarianism*, which is devoted to antisemitism, the political philosopher Hannah Arendt characterizes the social function assigned to Jews who were admitted to European elite circles of the late nineteenth century. She argues that the characterization of Jews as a "race of traitors" actually granted individual Jews social prestige and cultivated a form of philosemitism. Society discriminated against unenlightened "ordinary Jews," but at the same time, "it was generally easier for an educated Jew to be admitted to fashionable circles than for a non-Jew of similar condition."[16] That "feverish preference" is what opened the doors of society to some Jews—primarily famous Jews whose portraits grace history books. Nevertheless, philosemitism still played a role in marking Jews and setting them apart—thus "adding to political antisemitism that mysterious fanaticism without which antisemitism could hardly have become the best slogan for organizing the masses."[17] According to Arendt, it was precisely the admirers of Jews who ultimately became their murderers: "These 'philosemites' felt as though they had to purge themselves of secret viciousness, to cleanse themselves of a stigma which they had mysteriously and wickedly loved."[18] As Gabriel Motzkin explains, "A philo-Semitic society can desire Jews or be repelled by them, but it cannot accept them, because it always has the possibility of being anti-Semitic."[19]

Other scholars also claimed that philosemitism has no real connection to its alleged object; rather, it creates an imaginary construction of the Jew as the consummate other. On this basis, the Marxist philosopher Ernst Bloch argued in 1963 that philosemitism is inherently tied to antisemitism—a claim that has since become a hackneyed cliché.[20] Christopher Clark articulated this when he said, "a philosemite is an antisemite who loves Jews."[21]

A critical examination of philosemitism was formulated most comprehensively by Frank Stern in his book on the postwar discourse about Jews in Germany, *Im Anfang war Auschwitz*.[22] Here, Stern claims that philosemitism expresses the absence of an authentic processing of antisemitic sentiments, because it preserves the conception of Jews as a distinct group. Thus, churches changed the narrative about Jews being the crucifiers of Jesus when they posited that Jews are the new Jesus.[23] The German discourse about "Jewish cultural contributions" produces, in Stern's view, a distinction between Jews and the rest of the German population—thus distancing them from German history. It should be noted that the critiques of philosemitism by Stern and those like him are completely different from the criticisms of antisemites in Treitschke's milieu: The main claim against philosemites does not pertain to any flaws in Jews, but only to the lack of authenticity on the part of the philosemites. The critique places philosemitism in quotation marks as a sort of sleight of hand, behind which stands the same old antisemitism.

Even scholars who do not question philosemitic sentiment itself have generally criticized the essentialist assumptions underlying it—namely, that it treats Jews as a distinct, homogeneous group. For example, the historian Shmuel Almog wrote that to understand relations between Jews and gentiles, "one must examine unique attitudes toward Jews, even if they contain no animosity." According to Almog, philosemitism must also be included in the discussion, "for it too views the Jews as a group that is naturally distinct from other people. Excessive love also has a distortive effect and sometimes leads to disappointment and animosity."[24]

At its core, criticism of philosemitic discourse protests the separation of Jews from other human beings. The sociologist Zygmunt Bauman popularized the term "allosemitism," (from the Greek *allos*, meaning "other"), which he defined as "the practice of setting Jews

apart as a people radically different from all the others, needing separate concepts to describe and comprehend them."[25] Bauman claims
that most types of antisemitism and philosemitism are ramifications
of a broader sociopsychological phenomenon, allosemitism. According
to Bauman's definition, allosemitism indicates neither a positive nor a
negative view of Jews, but it contains the seeds of both. Because allosemitic discourse sets Jews apart, it ensures a radical attitude toward
Jews that views them as a group with fateful significance. According
to Bauman, Christian tradition first transformed "the Jew" into an
ahistorical abstraction disconnected from concrete experience. Other
forms of ambivalence about social and cultural conflicts surfaced during
the modern era and were cast into this theological mold.

Critiquing the Critique

The critical attitude toward philosemitism describes it as stereotyping
and, ultimately, fetishizing the Jew. Michael Brenner wrote, in an article
on philosemitism during the Second Reich, that "it cannot be said of
any of the philosemites in the Reich that they had familiarity with Jews
as Jews; rather, they all created an ideal counter-image of the Jew as an
imaginary dialogue partner."[26] Critics of philosemitism would contend
that this sentiment did not actually help Jews and may have caused
more harm than good, as it differentiated them as "others" vis-à-vis
the Christian, European, or national "self." However, it must be noted
that there are cases in which defenders of Jews were motivated by a
conception of the Jewish people as God's people, and not necessarily by
universal humanitarian motives. For example, several German pietistic
movements of the last third of the nineteenth century anticipated the
conversion of Jews to Christianity at the end of days, but on the social
and political front supported rights of Jews.[27]

To a large extent, the critique of philosemitism is equivalent to critiques of other essentializing discourses, for example, Edward Said's
critique of Orientalism, which condemns all discursive subjugation of
"the East," even if its contents are ostensibly positive.[28] Irving Massey
articulated a similar critical approach in his work, *Philo-Semitism in
Nineteenth-Century German Literature*. There, he claims that it is hard

to accept the philosemitic stance because it singles out Jews and gives them special prominence—an attitude that is itself a form of discrimination: "To be made to stand out is to put in an exposed position, and so, once again, to be made to feel threatened." He adds: "One simply wants to be accepted and not noticed too much."[29]

But is this last assertion really self-evident? Is it true in general, and is it true in the Jewish case specifically? It seems to negate a significant element of modern Jewish self-conception, which emphasizes the uniqueness or special mission of the Jews. "The Jewish mission" is one of the main metanarratives of Jewish modernity, and it has been articulated in various ways since the end of the eighteenth century. Moreover, the idea of the "chosen people" enjoys the enduring support of many Jews.[30]

In this context, it is worth noting another historical critique of philosemitism, which is aimed specifically at the liberal defender of the Jews. Several early twentieth-century Zionist thinkers criticized liberal philosemites specifically for their denial of a difference between Jews and non-Jews. For instance, the philosopher and publicist Jakob Klatzkin claimed that he prefers antisemites to philosemites because the former at least concede that there is a "separate Jewish essence" whereas the latter deny it.[31] Revisionist Zionist thinker Abba Ahimeir went even further in his denunciation of liberal philosemitism: "Philosemitic thinking is facile, philanthropic. In contrast, antisemitic thinking is profound, penetrating, interesting. What is Nathan the Wise compared to Shylock? Could it be that on the Jewish question as well, the wicked is wiser than the righteous?"[32] Even if the views of Klatzkin and Ahimeir are eccentric and contrarian, they delineate the opposition that any attempt to "flatten" Jewish difference is likely to provoke.

In any case, we have seen that many critics of philosemitism oppose the essentializing differentiation of Jews from non-Jews—the same differentiation that Zygmunt Bauman defined as "allosemitism." However, the preceding discussion emphasizes the problems raised by this opposition. The very characterization of the allosemitic attitude as a setting apart of Jews presumes the possibility of a "normal state" of relations between Jews and non-Jews, one in which Jews would be considered "normal human beings." However, it may be that the theological and historical baggage weighing down relations between Judaism and Christianity makes the expectation of an "unbiased" attitude toward Jews and Judaism unreasonable. As the historian Dan Diner claimed with regard to the memory of the Holocaust, because Christian self-conceptions position Jews as exceptional, giving them metaphysical, ahistorical importance, "the features of religious narrative have strongly stamped an unfolding, ostensibly secular historical discussion," and the attempt to escape the vortex of ancient narratives pertaining to Jews is thus futile.[33] Because the connection between the people of Israel and Christendom was historically based on chosenness, it is impossible to understand attitudes toward Jews without this theological layer.

That said, the same scholars who criticize philosemitism do not disqualify expressions of opposition to antisemitism, nor do they oppose tolerant and even supportive attitudes toward Jews. Arendt, Bloch, and their successors generally praised anti-antisemitic attitudes even while criticizing philosemitic attitudes. As the intellectual historian Jonathan Judaken notes, anti-antisemitism is "opposition to prejudices and stereotypes related to Jews, Judaism, and Jewishness."[34] Tolerance toward Jews should thus stem from a generally tolerant attitude and from opposition to discrimination of any kind.

But in many cases, the neutral, "unconditional" approach is itself clearly ideological. Thus, Bloch opposed the philosemitic stance but championed the attitude of socialist intellectuals who, he claimed, did not distinguish Jews from non-Jews. Yet not only is this claim imprecise, but, as Alan Levenson notes, "blindness" concerning the Jewish issue (which Bloch promoted) means, in many cases, ignoring a social conflict that is actually present and that cannot be swept under the rug.[35] Furthermore, the liberal effort to diminish or overlook the difference between Jews and non-Jews is a sort of symbolic erasure of the Jewish other. It is no coincidence that anti-antisemites themselves sometimes used anti-Jewish stereotypes in their polemics against antisemites.

New approaches, which differ from the camps that emerged in the postwar decades, can be discerned in several recent studies. Especially noteworthy is the anthology *Philosemitism in History*, edited by Jonathan Karp and Adam Sutcliffe, which surveys a variety of phenomena, including medieval papal protection of the Jews, early modern Christian Hebraism, and Christian Zionism in Britain.[36] In their introductory essay, the editors present a fresh approach to the phenomenon of philosemitism that neither invalidates the philosemitic stance nor approaches the phenomenon uncritically. Sutcliffe and Karp seek to dissociate philosemitism from antisemitism and, instead of presenting it as "the reverse side of the antisemitic coin," describe it as an independent phenomenon with motives and rhetorical features of its own. A similar stance is taken by Georg Braungart and Philipp Theisohn in an anthology that focuses mainly on philosemitism within German culture.[37] Unlike many earlier works that addressed the subject, this collection strives to avoid the question of the "hidden motives of the philosemite" and instead explores the motifs, metaphors, and modes of philosemitic discourse.[38] Likewise, it emphasizes the impact of philosemitism on Jewish self-consciousness; after all, philosemitic discourse shapes as well as describes its Jewish object. Like the phenomenon of "Jewish self-hatred" that, as Theodor Lessing described in 1930, emerged under the influence of antisemitism, today it is possible to speak of "Jewish self-love" that was produced under the influence of philosemitism.

Gotthold Ephraim Lessing as a Test Case

As with the term "antisemitism," the fact that the term "philosemitism" was coined by anti-Jewish circles did not prevent it from taking hold as a legitimate term within political, academic, and popular discourse. In his essay "Away from a Definition of Antisemitism," David Engel argues against using the term "antisemitism" as a theoretical scholarly category. According to Engel, antisemitism is a social-semantic convention invented in the late nineteenth century that has been used ever since "for political needs, not for scholarly needs."[39] Similarly, albeit with somewhat different motives, some have claimed that the concept of philosemitism should be abandoned and viewed as a misleading category. Lars Fischer convincingly argues that in the antisemitic/philosemitic distinction devised by German Jew-haters, "there could be no neutral ground, no nonexceptionalist discourse on this issue: one could only be the Jews' foe or their 'friend.'" The very use of these categories presumes that Jews can only be loved or hated.[40] But instead of completely repudiating the concept of philosemitism, perhaps it is better to sharpen its meaning as a particularly admiring or adoring attitude toward Jews. To that end, one should take care to distinguish between philosemitism and anti-antisemitism, while acknowledging that each of these phenomena—philosemitism and anti-antisemitism—entails its own problems and dangers.

On this point, I wish to turn to a test case: the writings of Gotthold Ephraim Lessing. This playwright, theologian, critic, and man of the Enlightenment can indeed be considered the most significant philosemitic German thinker of the eighteenth century, or perhaps ever. Indeed, he had virtually no competitors in terms of the admiration he garnered among the enlightened Jewish bourgeoisie of western and central Europe.[41] In the history of relations between Jews and non-Jews, Lessing is remembered favorably due primarily to his special relationship with Moses Mendelssohn and his plays *The Jews* (*Die Juden*, 1748) and *Nathan the Wise* (*Nathan der Weise*, 1779). The comedy *The Jews*, which Lessing composed at the age of nineteen, tells of a generous and upright traveler who saves a baron from scoundrels who seek to rob him. Because the robbers are bearded, the baron thinks they are Jews. But at the end of the play, when the baron wants to marry his daughter to the traveler, it turns out that it is the traveler who is a Jew, while the would-be robber was the baron's own Christian servant who disguised himself as a Jew by putting on a fake beard. The central message of the play is thus the absurdity of prejudices. "How worthy of respect Jews would be, if only they were all like you," the baron says in the play. Indeed, the main criticism raised against the play after its release was that the figure of the noble Jew could only exist on stage.[42]

The Jew in *The Jews* has no specifically Jewish characteristics: He is admirable only because he looks and acts exactly like a Christian. Likewise, Nathan, the protagonist of *Nathan the Wise*, has no distinguishing Jewish features. He does not perform any Jewish religious practices and refuses to identify with any Jewish collective. He is worthy of esteem only because of his spotless humanistic conduct.[43]

The Jews and *Nathan the Wise* embody a type of enlightened philosemitism derived from general Christian-humanist tolerance toward religious difference. From this perspective, they are more anti-antisemitic than philosemitic works. However, a different form of engagement with Jews finds expression in Lessing's most significant philosophical work, *The Education of the Human Race* (*Die Erziehung des Menschengeschlechts*).[44] In this work, Lessing reinterprets the concept of revelation, describing it as the gradual development of human intelligence from savagery to reason and refinement. "That which education is to the individual, revelation is to the race," he asserts in the opening sentence. This philosophical idea is articulated concretely as a new, philosophical version of the history of Christian redemption. God chose to reveal himself to a single people so that he could begin his education of the human race from the very beginning. He chose the Jewish people (*das Israelitische Volk*) in order to cultivate from within them the educators of the rest of the human race. Lessing explains this choice accordingly:

> But, it will be asked, to what purpose was this education of so rude a people, a people with whom God had to begin so entirely from the beginning? I reply, in order that in the process of time He might employ particular members of this nation as the teachers of other people. He was bringing up in them the future teachers of the human race. It was the Jews who became their teachers, none but Jews; only men out of a people so brought up, could be their teachers.

Later in his work, Lessing describes the following revelatory educational processes: the appearance of Jesus, the first teacher of the idea of the immortality of the soul, and, ultimately, a third covenant, a "new eternal gospel" that will replace the New Testament. This is a clear example of Christian "replacement theology" in an Enlightenment-style, rationalist guise. Nevertheless, the processes express the great importance ascribed to the ancient Israelites in the Enlightenment portrayal of history. The Jewish people signify the original encounter between revelation and enlightenment, between election and universal mission. From this perspective, Lessing's work differentiates the Jewish people from other peoples, a blatantly allosemitic move.

In Lessing's thought we can thus identify two approaches to Jews: one that emphasizes the *sameness* of Jews and all humans, and another that emphasizes Jews' *uniqueness*. Though sometimes interwoven, there is an essential conflict between these two approaches—no less essential than the conflict between philosemitism and antisemitism. These two approaches coexisted within Enlightenment thought and later in the modern era. The first approach is anti-antisemitic, and the second is philosemitic. The first approach is consistent with liberal and socialist thought that opposes discrimination against Jews and sometimes sees them as a litmus test for human rights in general. The second approach attributes fateful significance to the role of the Jewish people in history and even has a messianic character—although in certain cases the messianism was secularized.

While the allosemitic approach engages with mythical Jews and occasionally recoils from real Jews, the anti-antisemitic approach rushes to the defense of real Jews and has reservations about the mythic dimension. But this is a double-edged sword; in many cases, the anti-antisemitic approach aspires to assimilate Jews and eliminate any defining differences. This leads to the blurring of the distinctions between Jews and non-Jews, which are based on prejudice and oppose reason and enlightenment. A tolerant approach to Jews is strongly linked to their assimilation. In the context of eighteenth-century Germany, it suits the prevailing mood of enlightened bourgeois circles in Prussia, as embodied, for example, in the plans of Prussian reformer Christian Wilhelm von Dohm (1751–1820). In his book *On the Civil Improvement of the Jews*, Dohm calls for granting Jews full equality, which will lead to their "assimilation in the larger harmony of the state" so that ultimately, "they will, in fact, cease to be Jews."[45] Dohm offers Jews integration into the state but demands that they give up the idea of chosenness. According to him, the primary obstacle Jews face on the path to integration during the Enlightenment is their own prejudice, according to which they were chosen by God and distinguished from other peoples.[46]

But many Jews were not happy about giving up this idea. Accordingly, the special place granted to Jews within the history of revelation, such as in *The Education of the Human Race*, was quite significant for individual and collective Jewish self-perception in the modern era. Indeed, it was specifically enlightened Jews who in many cases adopted the inclusive image of the Jewish people as the teacher of the human race. They sought to respond to historical and metaphysical narratives that emerged in that period and, in the guise of enlightenment and liberalism, negated the Jewish right to exist in the modern world.[47] A similar attitude was expressed by Immanuel Kant, who demanded that Judaism "self-euthanize" and integrate into moral religion by abandoning old doctrines.[48] However, in contrast to Kant, who reduced Judaism to a particularist law and completely denied its role in the development of reason, Lessing granted Jews the role of redeeming humanity and signifying the continuity between themselves, Christians, and the future universal religion.[49]

It can be said that each type of philosemitism is related to a different vision concerning the place of Jews within society. The anti-antisemitic approach aims for emancipation and the removal of social and constitutional distinctions between Jews and other citizens. In contrast, particularistic philosemitism ascribes to the Jewish people collectively a fateful, occasionally messianic, role in human history. This insight is also important for understanding the background of contemporary debates about philosemitism—whether they address historical eras or the present day.

From many perspectives, the present can be described as a new philosemitic moment in the history of Christianity.[50] In 1945, manifestations of philosemitism were overshadowed by manifestations of antisemitism, but in the postwar era, philosemitism is of much greater importance. In the contemporary world—after the Holocaust and the establishment of the State of Israel—two different phenomena must be distinguished, even as they occasionally overlap: first, attempts to atone for the West's antisemitic past, that is, an anti-antisemitic approach, and second, admiration for the Jewish people and the State of Israel, which mainly rests on the religious idea of the chosen people. These two forms of positive attitudes toward Jews will impact the perspectives from which philosemitism is examined as a historical phenomenon.

NOTES

1. Hans-Joachim Schoeps, "Philosemitism in the Baroque Period," *Jewish Quarterly Review* 47 (1956): 139.

2. Noa Landau and Chaim Levinson, "Israeli Ministry Sets Sights on Millions of 'Potential Jews' to Improve Country's Image and Fight BDS," *Haaretz* (English edition), March 27, 2018, www.haaretz.com/israel-news/2018-03-27/ty-article-magazine /israeli-ministry-sets-sights-on-millions-of-potential-jews/0000017f-e018-d75c-a7ff -fc9d1a530000.

3. On this issue, see David S. Katz, "The Phenomenon of Philo-Semitism," *Studies in Church History* 29 (1992): 327–61.

4. Heinrich von Treitschke, "Zur inneren Lage am Jahresabschlusse," *Preussische Jahrbücher* (December 1880), reprinted in Walter Boehlich, ed., *Der Berliner Antisemitismusstreit* (Frankfurt am Main: Insel-Verlag, 1965), 227–29.

5. Franz Mehring, "Anti- und Philosemitisches," *Die Neue Zeit* 9, no. 45 (July 1891): 587.

6. It is nevertheless interesting to note that the classic philologist Ulrich von Wilamowitz-Moellendorff used the term in 1895 when discussing the adoration of certain scholars of antiquity for ancient Semitic peoples, particularly the Phoenicians, whom he calls "the darlings of modern philosemitism" ("Schoßkinder des modernen Philosemitismus"). See Ulrich von Wilamowitz-Moellendorff, *Herakles* (Berlin: Weidmann, 1895), 4.

7. See, for example, Lars Fischer, "Anti-'Philosemitism' and Anti-Antisemitism in Imperial Germany," in *Philosemitism in History*, ed. Jonathan Karp and Adam Sutcliffe (Cambridge: Cambridge University Press, 2011), 41.

8. Exceptional in this regard is the periodical published in Prague in 1931 and 1932, *Der Philosemit: Ein Weltbild des Judentums in Monatsheften.*

9. Marc Grimm, "Die Begriffsgeschichte des Philosemitismus," *Jahrbuch für Antisemitismusforschung* 22 (2013): 244–66.

10. It is interesting to note that Schoeps apparently adopted this typology from the work of the Nazi scholar Wilhelm Grau. On this, see Wolfram Kinzig, "Philosemitismus—was ist das? Eine kritische Begriffsanalyse," in *Geliebter Feind, gehasster Freund: Antisemitismus und Philosemitismus in Geschichte und Gegenwart*, ed. Irene A. Diekmann and Elke-Vera Kotowski (Berlin: Verlag für Berlin-Brandenburg, 2009), 29.

11. See, for example, the itemization in Wolfram Kinzig, "Neuere Typologien von 'Philosemitismus,'" in *Geliebter Feind, Gehasster Freund*, ed. Irene A. Diekmann and Elke-Vera Kotowski, 679–80.

12. On this subject, see Richard Faber, *Deutschbewußtes Judentum und jüdischbewußtes Deutschtum: der historische und politische Theologe Hans-Joachim Schoeps* (Würzburg: Königshausen und Neumann, 2008).

13. Gertrude Himmelfarb, *The People of the Book: Philosemitism in England, from Cromwell to Churchill* (New York: Encounter Books, 2011); William D. Rubinstein and

Hilary L. Rubinstein, *Philosemitism: Admiration and Support in the English-Speaking World for Jews, 1840–1939* (London: Palgrave Macmillan, 1999).

14. Rubinstein and Rubinstein, *Philosemitism*, 123–24.

15. Alan Edelstein, *An Unacknowledged Harmony: Philo-Semitism and the Survival of European Jewry* (Westport, CT: Greenwood Press, 1982).

16. Hannah Arendt, *The Origins of Totalitarianism* (New York: Harcourt Brace Jovanovich, 1973), 65.

17. Ibid., 87.

18. Ibid., 86.

19. Gabriel Motzkin, "Love and *Bildung* for Hannah Arendt," in *Hannah Arendt in Jerusalem*, ed. Steven Aschheim (Berkeley: University of California Press, 2001), 291.

20. Ernst Bloch, "Die sogenannte Judenfrage [1963]," in *Literarische Aufsätze. Gesamtausgabe* 9 (Frankfurt am Main.: Suhrkamp, 1965), 533.

21. Christopher Clark, *The Politics of Conversion: Missionary Protestantism and the Jews in Prussia, 1728–1941* (Oxford: Oxford University Press, 1995), 281.

22. Frank Stern, *Im Anfang war Auschwitz: Antisemitismus und Philosemitismus im deutschen Nachkrieg* (Gerlingen: Bleicher, 1991).

23. On this, see also Ulrike Zander, "Christlicher Philosemitismus in Deutschland nach der Schoa," in *Geliebter Feind, Gehasster Freund*, ed. Irene A. Diekmann and Elke-Vera Kotowski, 487–509.

24. Shmuel Almog, "The Development of the Jewish Question in England at the End of World War I," [in Hebrew] *Zion* 50 (1985): 397–431, esp. 399.

25. The term was coined by the Polish-Jewish literary scholar Artur Sandauer. Zygmunt Bauman, "Allosemitism: Premodern, Modern, Postmodern," in *Modernity, Culture, and 'the Jew,'* ed. Bryan Cheyette and Laura Marcus (Cambridge: Polity, 1998), 143–56. Also see Artur Sandauer, *On the Situation of the Polish Writer of Jewish Descent in the Twentieth Century: It Is Not I Who Should Have Written This Study...*, trans. Abe Shenitzer, ed. Scott Ury (Jerusalem: Hebrew University-Magnes Press, 2005).

26. Michael Brenner, "'Gott schütze uns vor unseren Freunden'—Zur Ambivalenz des Philosemitismus im Kaiserreich," *Jahrbuch für Antisemitismusforschung* 2 (1993): 175.

27. Alan Levenson, "Missionary Protestants as Defenders and Detractors of Judaism: Franz Delitzsch and Hermann Strack," *Jewish Quarterly Review* 92 (2002): 383–420.

28. Edward Said, *Orientalism* (New York: Pantheon, 1978).

29. Irving Massey, *Philo-Semitism in Nineteenth-Century German Literature* (Tübingen: Niemeyer, 2000), 31–32.

30. S. Leyla Gürkan, *The Jews as a Chosen People: Tradition and Transformation* (New York: Routledge, 2009).

31. Jakob Klatzkin, *Krisis und Entscheidung im Judentum* (Berlin: Jüdischer Verlag, 1921), 89–92.

32. Abba Ahimeir, *Yuda'ikah* (Tel Aviv: Ankor, 1960), 276.

33. Dan Diner, *Cataclysms: A History of the Twentieth Century from Europe's Edge* (Madison: University of Wisconsin Press, 2008), 197–98.

34. Jonathan Judaken, "Between Philosemitism and Antisemitism: The Frankfurt School's Anti-Antisemitism," in *Antisemitism and Philosemitism in the Twentieth and Twenty-First Centuries*, ed. Phyllis Lassner and Lara Trubowitz (Newark: University of Delaware Press, 2008), 29–30.

35. Alan T. Levenson, *Between Philosemitism and Antisemitism: Defenses of Jews and Judaism in Germany, 1871–1932* (Lincoln: University of Nebraska Press, 2013), 147.

36. Adam Sutcliffe and Jonathan Karp, "A Brief History of Philosemitism," in *Philosemitism in History*, ed. Karp and Sutcliffe, 1–26.

37. Georg Braungart and Philipp Theisohn, eds., *Philosemitismus: Rhetorik, Poetik, Diskursgeschichte* (Paderborn: Fink, 2017), 10. See also Tony Kushner and Nadia Valman, eds., *Philosemitism, Antisemitism, and 'the Jews': Perspectives from the Middle Ages to the Twentieth Century* (Burlington, VT: Ashgate, 2004).

38. Braungart and Theisohn, *Philosemitismus: Rhetorik, Poetik, Diskursgeschichte*, 10.

39. Engel, "Away from a Definition of Antisemitism: An Essay in the Semantics of Historical Description," in *Rethinking European Jewish History*, ed. Jeremy Cohen and Moshe Rosman (Oxford: Littman Library of Jewish Civilization, 2009), 28.

40. Fischer, "Anti-'Philosemitism' and Anti-Antisemitism," 174.

41. See Ritchie Robertson, *The "Jewish Question" in German Literature, 1749–1939: Emancipation and Its Discontents* (Oxford: Oxford University Press, 2001), 34.

42. Gotthold Ephraim Lessing, "Über das Lustspiel 'Die Juden' (1754)," in *Werke* (Köln: Kiepenheuer & Witsch, 1962), 731. Translation from Gotthold Lessing, *Two Jewish Plays*, trans. Noel Clark (London: Oberon, 2002), 53.

43. See Robertson, *The "Jewish Question,"* 39–40.

44. Gotthold Ephraim Lessing, *Die Erziehung des Menschengeschlechts* (Berlin: Voss, 1780). Translation by F. W. Robertson (1910), available at https://sourcebooks.fordham.edu/mod/1778lessing-education.asp.

45. Christian Wilhelm Dohm, *Über die bürgerliche Verbesserung der Juden* (Berlin: Nicolai, 1781).

46. Ibid., 19.

47. On this, see Michael Graetz, "'Die Erziehung des Menschengeschlechts' und jüdisches Selbstbewusstsein im 19. Jahrhundert," *Wolfenbütteler Studien zur Aufklärung* 4 (1977): 273–95.

48. Immanuel Kant, "Der Streit der Fakultäten," in *Werkausgabe in 12 Bänden*, ed. Wilhelm Weischedel, vol. 11 (Frankfurt am Main: Suhrkamp, 1977), 321.

49. Bettina Stangneth, "Antisemitische und Antijudaistische Motive bei Immanuel Kant? Tatsachen, Meinungen, Ursachen," in *Antisemitismus bei Kant und anderen*

Denkern der Aufklärung, ed. Horst Gronke, Thomas Meyer, and Barbara Neisser (Würzburg: Königshausen & Neumann, 2001), 27–29.

50. Rubinstein and Rubinstein, *Philosemitism*, 195–200.

10

Cautious Use of the Term "Antisemitism"—for Lack of an Alternative
Interwar Poland as a Test Case

GERSHON BACON

It was well known that the village of Chelm was ruled by the head of the community council and the six Elders, all fools. The name of the head was Gronam the Ox....The elders met in Gronam's house. The subject under discussion was the upcoming Shavuot festival, a holiday when a lot of sour cream is needed to eat with blintzes. That year there was a scarcity of sour cream. It had been a dry spring and the cows gave little milk. The Elders pulled at their beards and rubbed their foreheads, signs that their brains were hard at work....Suddenly, Gronam pounded on the table with his fist and called out: "I have it!...Let us make a law that water is to be called sour cream and sour cream is to be called water. Since there is plenty of water in the wells of Chelm, each housewife will have a full barrel of sour cream."...That Shavuot, there was no shortage of "sour cream," but some housewives complained there was a lack of "water"...Gronam the Ox became famous all over the world as the sage who—by passing a law—gave Chelm a whole river and many wells full of sour cream.[1]

IN HIS ESSAY "Away from a Definition of Antisemitism: An Essay in the Semantics of Historical Description,"[2] David Engel presents a fresh approach to a complex historiographic issue. In addition to historiographic studies, Engel has written a long list of books and articles that deal with both broadly and narrowly defined historical subjects, especially concerning the history of Polish Jewry. My response to Engel's essay draws examples mainly from this shared area of research.

In "Away from a Definition of Antisemitism," an essay of relatively limited scope, Engel presents an exemplary study in the discipline of conceptual history (*Begriffsgeschichte*). In it, he traces the sources and immediate historical context of the term "antisemitism" to the 1870s and 1880s. Engel demonstrates convincingly that within a short amount of time, the term was "adopted" by both opponents and defenders of Jews, and each side broadened the usage and meaning of the term for their own political and personal purposes. Engel further claims that antisemitism's lack of a clear definition impairs historical research, as the debate about the definition of the term places the cart before the horse: Historians reify a concept and are drawn into fruitless debates about semantics. What should serve as an aid to constructing a historical narrative became a burden and an obstacle. Engel solves this conundrum by completely avoiding the term "antisemitism," and, as his work over many years attests, this eschewal has not impeded his scholarship.

Engel's hesitation to use the term "antisemitism" because of the "supercharged" nature of the term that obscures more than it illuminates is entirely understandable. Nevertheless, I think that while it is impossible to avoid using it, the term "antisemitism" ought to be used with the proper precautions. Firstly, why must we assert that the original meaning of "antisemitism" is its real meaning? Moreover, people—not just scholars and publicists—shape the process by which the meaning and understanding of concepts like "democracy," "family," "childhood," and "antisemitism" evolve over the course of hundreds of years. Yehuda Bauer similarly describes the use of the term "antisemitism":

> There are other difficulties with the term "antisemitism." One is the conflation of periods and the ignoring of historical contexts by academics and laymen alike.... Another problem is that people tend to apply the word broadly to all negative relationships to Jews....

Still, having said all that, there is little point in fighting battles that cannot be won. Semantic struggles are bound to fail; and there is little choice but to follow the popular trend and to use the unscientific, inaccurate, confusing, and misleading term "antisemitism" as a catch-all, and to consider "Jew-hatred" and "Judeophobia" its synonyms.[3]

I share both Bauer's resignation and Engel's uncertainties and try to achieve a middle position: logical, cautious use of the term "antisemitism" coupled with an insistence that each specific instance is anchored in its immediate historical context. Historical sources and discourse among historians are riven by numerous invocations of the term, such that it seems impossible to liberate ourselves from it completely. Below I will attempt to clarify my points of agreement as well as disagreement with Engel.

Antisemitism: An Unmistakably Modern Phenomenon

If we use the model that Engel proposes, that organizing information into "files" is an integral part of the scholar's work, it becomes clear that too many concepts and phenomena are assigned to the "file" called "antisemitism." However, in my view we cannot simply eschew the term or redistribute the information in a single file to many others. Antisemitism is an inseparable part of the process that historians over generations have viewed as the basic narrative of modern Jewish life— emancipation, a process that encompassed political, cultural, religious, and social components. These works describe the efforts, and the reactions to these efforts, of governments, societies, and Jews themselves to integrate Jews as citizens and partners into the surrounding society. Antisemitism, as an ideology and a political phenomenon, is part of this process. Amos Funkenstein's description of the difference between antisemitism and medieval Jew-hatred is succinct and on the mark. According to him, in the eyes of an antisemite:

Being Jewish is a *character indelebilis*, unchangeable by baptism or other external signs of changed identity. Therefore, the first political aim of the anti-Semite is to undo the original sin of nineteenth-century Europe: to revoke legal emancipation granted to Jews, and, by discrimination, make them recognizable again...Such, in rough outline, is the phenomenology of anti-Semitic utterances. They presuppose emancipation and are directed against it, which makes them *a new phenomenon altogether in Jewish history*.[4]

Modern antisemitism also includes a racial element that was absent from the Jew-hatred of earlier eras. Engel argues that the commonalities shared by the different manifestations and movements identified as antisemitic are ultimately very small. Nevertheless, these movements share a cluster of characteristic features that, though they may appear in different measures and with different emphases, make it possible and even desirable to include them in the same "file," the file of "antisemitism."

I accept Engel's view concerning one major point: Using the term "antisemitism" to describe Jew-hatred or anti-Jewish hostility in antiquity or the medieval era is anachronistic and misleading.[5] Let us take, for instance, the idea propagated by antisemites that there is a Jewish conspiracy to take control of the world through economics and culture—an idea that would have seemed delusional to both Christians and Jews in medieval Europe. In the modern world, by contrast, the relative success of Jews collectively, in adapting to the new conditions of capitalist, industrialized Europe, as well as the economic prosperity of prominent Jews, like the Rothschilds, lends this claim a certain "logic." For example, in the public debate in mid-seventeenth-century England about readmitting Jews 350 years after their expulsion, rumors were spread that given the proven economic abilities of Jews in other places, the Jews who would settle in England were liable to buy St. Paul's Cathedral, entire English towns, or the libraries of Oxford and Cambridge.[6]

In the case of nineteenth-century Polish lands, the pronounced demographic heft of Jews (they comprised close to ten percent of the total and a much higher percentage of the urban population) and the leading role of Jews (and converted Jews) in Polish financial development and industrial entrepreneurship contributed to the Polish nightmare of a Jewish "takeover" of Poland. Already in 1817, Polish author Julian Ursyn Niemcewicz penned a dystopian work titled *Rok 3333* (*Year 3333*), which was published posthumously only in 1858. The novella describes Warsaw of the future as a Jewish city renamed Moszkopolis.[7]

The best-known example of this foreboding vision is *The Protocols of the Elders of Zion*, a forgery apparently produced in the early twentieth century by the intelligence services of tsarist Russia, and which achieved broad international circulation after the Bolshevik Revolution. Despite overwhelming evidence that its contents are false, this document continues to appear, even today, in different forms and in various languages; it has become an almost permanent feature of anti-Jewish discourse.[8] Another nightmare scenario, based largely on the notion in *The Protocols* of a Jewish conspiracy, attributed the Bolshevik Revolution and Communist rule, as well as Communist activities in other countries from Poland and Hungary to the United States and Argentina, to "Jewish Bolshevism." Right-wing forces viewed this "alliance" as a threat to the world political order and Western culture as a whole. Thus, *żydokomuna*, a Polish portmanteau of Judaism and Communism, became part of the political discourse of interwar (and postwar) Poland, symbolizing the alleged Jewish hostility to traditional religious, political, and social values that must be fought by any means necessary.[9]

Engel demonstrates that those who used the term "antisemitism" to examine earlier periods did so out of convenience as well as to produce an imagined historical continuum of hatred spanning different empires, nations, and religions across thousands of years. We can add that these writers were likely to admit that the term "antisemitism" is modern but would claim that the phenomenon is ancient, even if it went by different names throughout history.

One final point about historical continuity emerges from another of Engel's studies. In his 2010 book *Historians of the Jews and the Holocaust*, Engel sharply criticizes Jewish historians of the modern era who have failed in the vital task of incorporating the Holocaust within the continuous narrative of Jewish history.[10] In my view, if we wish to integrate the Holocaust within longer narratives and not treat it as a chapter that is disconnected from earlier periods, then it is incumbent upon us to use one of the most significant potential "bridges" between eras—the tradition of antisemitic rhetoric, symbolism, ideology, and political activism of the nineteenth and early twentieth centuries.

Antisemitism: The Crucial Importance of Historical Context

In an article on antisemitism in Poland, the historian Raphael Mahler establishes clear rules for a scholar who wishes to address the phenomenon:

> The character of antisemitism in a given country can be explained only in terms of the specific social, economic and political forces operating within that country. Racial, religious or mystical theories of antisemitism are inadequate to explain the peculiar developments in individual countries. An analysis of the special character of Polish antisemitism, therefore, must be related to the social and economic evolution of the country and to the special role of Jews in Polish history.[11]

True to his historiographic method, which emphasizes the role of economics in history, Mahler poses a challenge to the historian seeking to describe manifestations of antisemitism in a particular country. However, he also offers a way to escape, at least partially, the semantic trap that concerns Engel. Indeed, a focused discussion of antisemitism in Poland demands the utmost caution from the historian. Intelligent use of the term "antisemitism" concerning Poland (and other countries) requires a sober view of the social environment, government policy and legislation, and bureaucratic procedures.

In the case of interwar Poland, the 1922 elections law, passed in advance of the first regular elections to the Polish parliament, had a clear agenda: limiting the parliamentary representation of national minorities in general, not just of Jews. Minority representatives, including Jews, consolidated into a Minorities Bloc with agreed-upon candidates to resist this agenda and prevent the loss of votes that would result from competition between the minorities. Thus, they foiled, in part, the plans of the large Polish parties and attained something unprecedented (and never to be repeated): almost 90 of the 444 seats in the Sejm, the lower house of the Polish parliament, were representatives of different minority communities.[12] In this case, the law was intended to curtail the Jews, albeit among other minorities, out of a desire to prevent the minorities from being the deciding factor on matters of the Polish state. However, a specifically Jewish aspect was not absent from the discourse, and after a few weeks, when Gabriel Narutowicz was elected Poland's first president with the support of the minority parliamentarians, right-wing factions began denigrating the "Jewish" (not the "minority") president. A few days later, Narutowicz was murdered by a right-wing assassin.[13]

Regarding economic policy, the picture is no less complicated. The regime gave control of major industries, banking, and credit to the state. Several industries that were important to the average citizen (matches, salt, the lottery, tobacco, and the manufacture of alcohol) became government monopolies. The declared objective was to grant concessions in these industries to military veterans, and especially to the war-wounded.[14] Coincidentally or not, many factories in these industries had been established by Jewish entrepreneurs and employed Jewish labor. This policy placed these factories at risk of nationalization and the employees in fear of unemployment. In certain cases, Jewish owners installed a non-Jewish Pole as the titular "president" of the company while continuing to run the businesses themselves.[15]

Both within the economic realm and in professional opportunities, we must examine whether Polish policy was directed specifically against Jews, against minorities in general, or merely affected Jews disproportionately due to their economic and demographic profile. Poland implemented mandatory military conscription, but the higher echelons of the officer corps (considered a national elite) were generally closed to members of minorities. Most candidates for the higher ranks had attained university degrees, so this policy disproportionally harmed Jews as a minority group with a relatively large number of members with higher education.[16] Government policies that favored the rural over the urban population also disproportionally harmed Jews, seventy-five percent of whom were urban and only twenty-five percent rural, the opposite of the proportion among the non-Jewish population. One can, of course, claim that this policy discriminated against non-Jewish urbanites to the same degree; however, contemporary sources show that Jews complained of discriminatory enforcement of these policies, for example in the realm of taxation.

Concerning public service and the extension of credit, we again witness an unwritten policy of discrimination against Jews. Data from the 1921 and 1931 population censuses attest to the almost complete absence of Jews in public service. Moreover, most of the Jews who worked in a ministry had already served in the Austro-Hungarian bureaucracy before World War I and continued in that capacity after Polish independence. A clear policy of early retirement was applied to these Jews.[17] Jewish contractors had no chance of winning large tenders put out by the government—for instance, for the construction of a new port in the city of Gdynia. And, during the Great Depression of the late 1920s, unemployment payments were made only to laborers at plants with more than fifty employees; most Jewish-owned plants employed a smaller number.

The almost complete lack of any anti-Jewish legislation is a prominent feature of Polish policy. Scholarly literature and contemporary sources generally mention only two laws: the Sunday Rest Law of 1919 and the 1936 law concerning kosher slaughter. The first law, which purported to ensure a day of rest for laborers, did not provide any exception for citizens who observed a different day of rest. The intensified enforcement of this law posed a dilemma for Sabbath-observant Jews: to forgo Sabbath observance or shut down their businesses two days every week. Only food stores were permitted to open for a few hours on Sunday.[18] The second law, concerning the slaughter of animals for food, was intended to limit kosher slaughter (*shehitah*) to the needs of Jews alone. At first glance, the motive was humanitarian. However, like a similar law passed a few years earlier in Nazi Germany, this law, too, was meant to restrict Jews and, in the case of Poland, to break Jewish dominance over the beef market.[19]

Finally, when we address the status of Poland's Jews between World Wars I and II, the question of physical violence against Jews inevitably arises. Anti-Jewish pogroms, especially at the beginning and end of this period, caused property damage, injury, and loss of life. There were several hundred victims during the years immediately before and after Polish independence. Polish elements denied the accusations that were made and complained that even if the number of victims were correct, it paled in comparison to the thousands of Jewish victims of the adjacent Russian Civil War. The controversy that began then about the scope or denial of anti-Jewish violence continues in contemporary scholarly literature.[20]

During the 1930s, especially after the 1935 death of Polish leader Józef Piłsudski, the number of violent incidents against Jews rose in towns, on university campuses, and in city streets.[21] Additionally, from the 1920s on, the phenomenon of *numerus clausus* expanded in university departments. "Ghetto benches" were also instituted in lecture halls, limiting where Jewish students could sit. Given the toxic environment, the violence, the discrimination, and the quotas, the number of Jewish students declined not only in relative but also in absolute terms.[22] The Polish government officially denounced the violence, but it did very little to quell it. It encouraged the economic fight against Jews and even spoke at international forums on the need for a considerable migration of "excess" Jews from Poland, even as states were increasingly closing their borders to migrants and refugees.[23]

The purpose of this brief survey is to demonstrate how complex it is to determine clearly whether the Polish state of that period was "antisemitic," as Ezra Mendelsohn discussed in a classic article.[24] The trap of a semantic debate can be avoided by presenting the complex situation of events and manifestations in their historical context. Thus, David Engel is correct that using the term "antisemitism" does not necessarily contribute to historical analysis and understanding, but, as we have seen, it also does not necessarily detract from it. It seems to me that the willy-nilly appearance of the term "antisemitism" in historical discussions and sources from the period is inevitable. However, this does not turn the term itself into the focus of discussion.

Perceptions and Awareness of Antisemitism during the Interwar Period

The field of research regarding the feelings of people during the interwar period also involves the term "antisemitism." Both Jewish political leaders and the Jewish rank and file perceived much of what happened to them as manifestations of antisemitism. In the memoir literature, we occasionally encounter a certain degree of shame and regret over this perception, for instance, vis-à-vis Polish authorities' meticulous standards of hygiene in bakeries and butcher shops. Thus, in her memoir about her hometown of Michałowo, Zipora Lyvne wonders why local Jews had such a hard time adapting to modern hygienic conditions and why they interpreted every requirement to meet these regulations as punishment or harassment. Every new regulation or ordinance—for instance, the ban on workers sleeping in bakeries—was interpreted as antisemitic harassment. She recalls the curses that Jews heaped on the heads of the Polish state following the directive that every store and business must install a sink with running water and place a bar of soap and a towel next to it.[25] In his memoir, Ben-Zion Gold describes the frustration of his father, an observant Jew and member of the municipal council of Radom, who warned bakery owners that health ministry officials would be visiting them, but discovered that on the appointed day the owners had not cleaned out their bakeries because they relied on him to protect them from the government.[26]

Perhaps Polish Jews exaggerated when they asserted that almost every government initiative that negatively impacted them stemmed from antisemitic motives. This assertion gave the term "antisemitism" an elastic meaning that included anything that bothered Jews. Nevertheless, their feelings and repeated allegations of antisemitism were part of their existence and thus have a place in the historical narrative.

Yet, the feeling among many Jews that they experienced antisemitism in their encounters with the Polish regime or Polish society is only the starting point for discussion. Despite this feeling, many Polish Jews remained loyal to Poland and had an emotional connection to the land of their birth—a connection that was expressed in both word and deed. In *Relations between Jews and Poles during the Holocaust*, Havi Dreifuss (Ben-Sasson) discerns three stages of how Polish Jews explained the antisemitic behavior of Poles at the outbreak of World War II and during the period of ghettoization. Dreifuss calls the first one the "comforting explanation" stage in which Jews described the antisemitic activities of Poles as exceptions that did not represent the Polish collective.

Even in the later stages, when Jewish attitudes toward Poles became more negative, the sense of connection with Poland remained.[27] When Polish Jewish refugees in eastern regions, then under Soviet rule, were given the option of renouncing their Polish citizenship and adopting Soviet citizenship, the vast majority refused. Their loyalty to Poland and refusal to give up the hope of eventually returning to their homeland and their families led to the exile of many to Siberia and other eastern areas of the Soviet Union—an exile that many did not survive.[28]

Antisemitism in interwar Poland thus did not alter the deep connection between Jews and Poland. Even the ghetto walls, the betrayals that the Jews sustained during the Holocaust, and exile to Siberia could not sever this connection. Yet at the same time, in the interwar period these perceptions of antisemitism in Poland and the frequent appearance of the term "antisemitism" in contemporary sources, even if seemingly erroneous to us, affected how people thought and behaved. Analysis of the events and the atmosphere indeed poses methodological difficulties, but it is hard to envision how eschewing a term that is so prevalent in the sources will improve our efforts or make our scholarship more precise.

The same applies when we turn to Polish society and politics. We encounter the term "antisemitism" almost every step of the way, both in contemporary sources and in scholarly literature. Engel contends that the commonality among antisemites was relatively low. It was, however, sufficient to contribute to the consolidation of the Polish right-wing camp. As I noted above regarding Jewish feelings about antisemitism, Polish politicians also felt that they were part of a broader Polish and even international movement of opposition to Jews; this feeling, too, is worthy of historians' attention.

An important recent book contends that the changes to Poland and Jewish politics in the wake of the 1905 revolution were crucial to the development of antisemitism in Poland as a political movement. Their ideological and organizational stances influenced each other.[29] Other studies emphasize the unique features of antisemitism in Polish society as well as aspects it shared with antisemitism in central and western Europe in the period leading up to World War I. Right-wing antisemitism had a pivotal effect on the consolidation of Polish politics, which also had long-term ramifications.

Past political discourse and today's academic discourse are so intertwined with the term "antisemitism" that it seems difficult and inefficient to avoid the use of this term. This contention can be demonstrated by an important, fascinating document published by Engel himself: the full version of the preliminary report of Jan Karski, who served during World War II as an emissary of the Polish government-in-exile.[30] In his report to the Polish government-in-exile, Karski described strong antisemitic feelings among the Polish population, which many attributed to the alleged Jewish cooperation with the Soviet regime in the eastern regions of Poland, then under Russian occupation. Karski considered the possibility of forming a joint front against Poland's occupiers but added that any attempt to establish a unified front including Jews would encounter many difficulties due to the antisemitism among vast sectors of the Polish population.[31] The question arises again: How can we judge, analyze, and historically contextualize manifestations of antisemitism without explicitly mentioning it by name, but instead by resorting to a series of "files" and circuitous formulations?

Even if we manage to identify a particular figure or political party as antisemitic, the discussion is not over. People in every generation were complicated and inconsistent. Even blatantly antisemitic Poles extended aid to Jews who were placed in danger by the Nazi occupation. The best-known example of this is Zofia Kossak-Szczucka, a renowned author and devout Catholic who was a founder and active member of Żegota, a Polish organization that aided Jews in hiding after the liquidation of the ghettos. She penned a manifesto calling on Poles to speak out and protest the murder of Jews. Yet in the same manifesto in which she objected to the persecution of Jews she also used classic antisemitic imagery and spoke of Jews as enemies of Poland, enemies she said Poles must help now, but with whom they would someday have to settle accounts.[32] The apparent contradiction of the antisemite who saved Jews can be seen in others as well, like the anatomy professor who was an avowed antisemite who tormented his Jewish students, yet aided them during the Holocaust,[33] or antisemitic relatives of Jewish converts to Christianity who gave their Jewish relatives in the ghetto hiding places on the "Aryan" side.[34]

It is not necessary to delve into a fruitless semantic debate about ascribing some abstract definition of antisemitism to a person or movement. It is more justified and effective to examine their views and deeds, ascertain how they perceived themselves, and examine them against the background of their time.

Historical Research and Debates about Antisemitism and Jewish-Polish Relations

In recent years, there has been a vocal public debate regarding the Polish law that at first threatened criminal sanctions and was later amended to allow civil suits against anyone who accuses the Polish nation or state of any responsibility for the Holocaust. This law is an unhealthy mix of politics and historical research.[35] Right-wing Polish websites and radio stations spread conspiracy theories about an organized "Jewish" effort to sully the name of Poland. The historian Jan Tomasz Gross has also been the target of invective-filled attacks following the publication of his books, which, beginning with *Neighbors* (published in Polish in 2000 and translated into many languages), document the actions of local Poles who killed Jews with their own hands and looted their property.[36] Many Poles refuse to accept such claims about Polish participation in the murder of Jews despite the extraordinarily well-documented studies by Gross, Jan Grabowski,[37] Barbara Engelking,[38] and others. Instead of confronting these difficult findings, Polish politicians prefer to try to rewrite the historical narrative by threatening legal suits and presenting an alternate narrative that emphasizes Polish suffering under the Nazis and exaggerates the scope of actions taken by Poles to rescue Jews.

The debate about the definition of antisemitism also continues, but nowadays the primary arena is not scholarly literature but many political struggles around the world, especially concerning the Israeli-Palestinian conflict.[39] A variety of prominent figures participate in discussions about the definition of antisemitism and related topics, including author J. K. Rowling,[40] Nobel Prize-winning economist and columnist Paul Krugman,[41] former Labour Party chairman Jeremy Corbyn,[42] and former prime minister of Malaysia Mahathir Mohamad.[43]

The case of Corbyn has engaged British and global politics and journalism for many years and carried significant political implications when Corbyn was the leader of the Opposition and a potential candidate for prime minister. The debate about him and the other figures mentioned illustrates the concerns raised by Engel because it does not analyze their words or deeds, but instead asks an essentially semantic question: Do they or don't they meet some abstract definition of antisemitism? The Labour Party debated which definition to adopt with the clear agenda of excluding people and groups that Corbyn favored from the category of antisemites.[44] Political agendas and semantic hairsplitting overcame relevant historical discussion.

It is hard to dissociate the discussion of antisemitism's definition from the debate about equating anti-Israelism or anti-Zionism with antisemitism. Defenders of Israel appeal to the concept of a "new antisemitism" in efforts to taint opposition to Israeli policy, and opponents deny their accusations. I find it fascinating that all the participants in this polemic (except for Mahathir Mohamad, who publicly took pride in being an antisemite) presume that antisemitism is completely negative, a view that was not accepted in earlier periods.

Efforts to gain temporary political advantages can disregard historical precision and the importance of placing things in their proper contexts, and there is a danger that these flaws will trickle into academic discourse. Nevertheless, we historians must not completely abandon the battlefield and leave it to rival forces. We must continue to offer measured, topical historical discussion, even if our conclusions are not readily available to the broader public.

Conclusion: Antisemitism—Historical Reality and Historical Narrative

We can view Engel's essay as a sort of *Mahnruf*, to use the subtitle of Yehudah Leib Pinsker's *Autoemancipation*, a warning call to his fellow historians to become aware of what they do and say and of how widespread discourse fosters the use and misuse of terminology, thus harboring dangers for measured historical discussion. If we do our job properly, we can avoid the twin dangers to which Engel alerts us: We will not allow words to control us, and we will take care not to be reckless with our ability to control them. It seems to me that the middle path is to continue using terms that are not exactly clear—like "anti-semitism" and "race"—but to try always to place them in the proper historical context.

As in the story of Gronam the Ox with which we began this essay, any change in terminology has its costs and its benefits. The approach proposed by Engel, to eschew using the term "antisemitism" and to focus on specific events in specific contexts, has clear advantages, and here I adopt it at least in part. Yet abandoning the aspiration toward a relatively broad narrative has a cost. Despite the differences between phenomena that are conventionally inserted into the historian's "anti-semitism file," there are grounds to create a long-term narrative, at least concerning the modern era, of "opponents of the Jews" (*Judengegner*) and various types of antisemites. This is indeed a low threshold of commonality, but it was enough to contribute to the feeling of both antisemites and their rivals that there is something beyond the local events that, prima facie, have no connection with one another—that is, there is a broad phenomenon with a history and a historical context worthy of study. When describing the general approach underlying his treatment of anti-Jewish thought, David Nirenberg articulates well the dilemmas facing the historian:

> There is no metaphor, no model, no formula that can securely relate to one another all the moments in this long history that I have produced, or for that matter in any other history. Does this mean that we historians should sever all the more severely, isolating each moment from all others?...To me it seems that—at least in terms of the work that figures of Judaism do in our thinking about the world—the risks of hyper-sectioning the history of thought are once again as real as those of overdetermining it.[45]

At the end of his essay, Engel invites his colleagues to join him in the search for new frameworks for analyzing the traditional components of antisemitism. In the present essay, I eagerly responded to his invitation. We owe him a debt of gratitude for his fruitful, challenging essay and hope for discussions, conversations, exchanges of opinion, and even debates in the future.

NOTES

1. Isaac Bashevis Singer, "The Elders of Chelm and Genendel's Key," in *When Shlemiel Went to Warsaw and Other Stories* (New York: Farrar, Straus & Giroux, 1968), 45–46, 49, 51. I am grateful to Prof. Monika Adamczyk-Garbowska for bringing this story to my attention.

2. David Engel, "Away from a Definition of Antisemitism: An Essay in the Semantics of Historical Description," in *Rethinking European Jewish History*, ed. Jeremy Cohen and Moshe Rosman (Oxford: Littman Library of Jewish Civilization, 2009), 30–53.

3. Yehuda Bauer, "In Search of a Definition of Antisemitism," in *Approaches to Antisemitism: Context and Curriculum*, ed. Michael Brown (New York: American Jewish Committee, 1994), 11–12.

4. Amos Funkenstein, *Perceptions of Jewish History* (Berkeley: University of California Press, 1993), 324. Emphasis added. On Funkenstein's approach, see David Engel, "The Concept of Antisemitism in the Historical Scholarship of Amos Funkenstein," *Jewish Social Studies* 6, no. 1 (1999): 111–29.

5. For various approaches to the continuity or discontinuity between the hatred of Jews or Judaism in the medieval era and modern antisemitism, see the recent work by Jonathan Adams and Cordelia Hess, eds., *The Medieval Roots of Antisemitism: Continuities and Discontinuities from the Middle Ages to the Present Day* (New York: Routledge, 2018).

6. Todd M. Endelman, *The Jews of Britain, 1656–2000* (Berkeley: University of California Press, 2002), 25.

7. Harold B. Segel, ed., *Stranger in Our Midst: Images of the Jew in Polish Literature* (Ithaca, NY: Cornell University Press, 1996), 12–13. On Niemcewicz, see Jacob Goldberg, "Julian Ursyn Niemcewicz on Polish Jewry," *Polin* 18 (2005): 323–35.

8. See Norman Cohn, *Warrant for Genocide: The Myth of the Jewish World Conspiracy and the Protocols of the Elders of Zion* (New York: Harper & Row, 1966).

9. On these ideas, see Paul Hanebrink, *A Specter Haunting Europe: The Myth of Judeo-Bolshevism* (Cambridge, MA: Harvard University Press, 2018); Joanna Beata Michlic, *Poland's Threatening Other: The Image of the Jew from 1880 to the Present* (Lincoln: University of Nebraska Press, 2006), 88–93, 174–80.

10. David Engel, *Historians of the Jews and the Holocaust* (Stanford, CA: Stanford University Press, 2010).

11. Raphael Mahler, "Antisemitism in Poland," in *Essays on Antisemitism*, ed. Koppel S. Pinson (New York: Conference on Jewish Relations, 1946), 145. It is worth noting that Mahler begins his discussion with the medieval era.

12. On the election law, its agenda, and the struggles of the minority representatives, see Shlomo Netzer, *The Struggle of Polish Jewry for Civil and National Minority Rights (1918–1922)* [in Hebrew] (Tel Aviv: Tel Aviv University Press, 1980), 282–315.

13. On the assassination and the major role of antisemitic incitement in the events, see

Paul Brykczynski, *Primed for Violence: Murder, Antisemitism, and Democratic Politics in Interwar Poland* (Madison: University of Wisconsin Press, 2018).

14. There were many complaints by Jewish organizations and individuals with respect to benefits for the war-wounded as well. Jewish veterans' organizations and the Jewish press reported on discrimination against Jewish war invalids in employment opportunities, including the very concessions for selling monopoly products, supposedly set up for the benefit of veterans. See the recent work by Oksana Vynnyk, "The Welfare State and National Minorities: Disabled Veterans in Interwar Lviv," ASN World Convention, Columbia University, 2016, www.academia.edu/24607510.

15. Simon Segal, *The New Poland and the Jews* (New York: Lee Furman, 1938), 130–31.

16. Jerzy Ogonowski, *Sytuacja prawna Żydów w Rzeczyspospolitej Polskiej 1918–1939* (Warsaw: Żydowski Instytut Historyczny, 2012), 60–61.

17. Raphael Mahler, "Jews in Public Service and the Liberal Professions in Poland, 1918–1939," *Jewish Social Studies* 6, no. 4 (1944): 291–350.

18. Frank Golczewski, "The Problem of Sunday Rest in Interwar Poland," in *The Jews of Poland Between Two World Wars*, ed. Yisrael Gutman et al. (Hanover, NH: University Press of New England, 1989), 158–72.

19. On the law and its implications for the Jewish public in Poland, see Eva Plach, "Ritual Slaughter and Animal Welfare in Interwar Poland," *East European Jewish Affairs* 45, no. 1 (2015): 1–25.

20. David Engel, "Lwów, 1918: The Transmutation of a Symbol and Its Legacy in the Holocaust," in *Contested Memories: Poles and Jews during the Holocaust and Its Aftermath*, ed. Joshua Zimmerman (New Brunswick, NJ: Rutgers University Press, 2003), 32–44.

21. On violence against Jews in the 1930s, see Emanuel Melzer, *No Way Out: The Politics of Polish Jewry, 1935–1939* (Cincinnati: Hebrew Union College Press, 1997), 53–70; Jolanta Żyndul, *Zajścia antyżydowskie w Polsce w latach 1935–1937* (Warsaw: Fundacja im. K. Kelles-Krauza, 1994).

22. Natalia Aleksiun, "Jewish Students and Christian Corpses in Interwar Poland: Playing with the Language of Blood Libel," *Jewish History* 26 (2012): 327–42; Zofia Trębacz, "'Ghetto Benches' at Polish Universities: Ideology and Practice," in *Alma mater antisemitica: Akademisches Milieu, Juden und Antisemitismus an den Universitäten Europas zwischen 1918 und 1939*, ed. Regina Fritz, Grzegorz Rossolinski-Liebe, and Jana Starek (Vienna: New Academic Press, 2016), 113–35; Melzer, *No Way Out*, 71–80.

23. Edward Wynot, "A Necessary Cruelty: The Emergence of Official Anti-Semitism in Poland, 1936–39," *American Historical Review* 76 (1971): 1035–37.

24. Ezra Mendelsohn, "Interwar Poland: Good for the Jews or Bad for the Jews?," in *The Jews in Poland*, ed. Chimen Abramsky, Maciej Jachimczyk, and Antony Polonsky (Oxford: Blackwell, 1986), 130–39.

25. Zipora Lyvne, *Ayarati mikhaelovah: pirke havai behaye ayarah yehudit* (Tel Aviv: Am hasefer, 1975), 31–32.

26. Ben-Zion Gold, *The Life of Jews in Poland Before the Holocaust: A Memoir* (Lincoln: University of Nebraska Press, 2007), 11.

27. Havi Dreifuss (Ben-Sasson), *Relations between Jews and Poles during the Holocaust: The Jewish Perspective*, trans. Ora Cummings (Jerusalem: Yad Vashem, 2017), 101, 166, 203.

28. Timothy Snyder, *Bloodlands: Europe between Hitler and Stalin* (New York: Basic Books, 2010), 141.

29. Scott Ury, *Barricades and Banners: The Revolution of 1905 and the Transformation of Warsaw Jewry* (Stanford, CA: Stanford University Press, 2012), chaps. 4–6.

30. On Karski's activities during the war, see Jan Karski, *Story of a Secret State* (Boston: Houghton Mifflin, 1944); E. Thomas Wood and Stanisław Jankowski, *Karski: How One Man Tried to Stop the Holocaust* (Lubbock: Texas Tech University Press, 2014); Claude Lanzmann, director, *The Karski Report*, 2010, available at www.youtube.com /watch?v=JQ7Y1dc6sbQ.

31. David Engel, "An Early Account of Polish Jewry under Nazi and Soviet Occupation Presented to the Polish Government-in-Exile, February 1940," *Jewish Social Studies* 45, no. 1 (1983): 13. It is worth noting that Karski prepared a "softer" version of the report, in which he emended or omitted several passages with harsh expressions against the Jews. See ibid., 14.

32. See Antony Polonsky, *The Jews in Poland and Russia: Volume III: 1914 to 2008* (Oxford: Littman Library of Jewish Civilization, 2012), 445–46. For an example of the ongoing debate regarding Kossak-Szczucka, see also "Zofia Kossak-Szczucka: An 'anti-semite' who saved Jews," February 2018, https://poland.pl/culture-and-art /literature/zofia-kossak-szczucka-anti-semite-who-saved-jews. It is worth noting that in 1982, Kossak-Szczucka was recognized by Yad Vashem as a Righteous Gentile.

33. Natalia Aleksiun, "Christian Corpses for Christians! Dissecting the Anti-Semitism behind the Cadaver Affair of the Second Polish Republic," *East European Politics and Societies* 25, no. 3 (2011): 403.

34. Emmanuel [*sic*] Ringelblum, *Polish–Jewish Relations during the Second World War* (Jerusalem: Yad Vashem, 1974), 211.

35. Marc Santora, "Poland's Holocaust Law Weakened After 'Storm and Consternation,'" *New York Times*, June 27, 2018, www.nytimes.com/2018/06/27/world/eu rope/poland-holocaust-law.html; Mateusz Morawiecki, "Poland's Misunderstood Holocaust Law," *Foreign Policy* (blog), March 19, 2018, https://foreignpolicy.com /2018/03/19/polands-misunderstood-holocaust-law; Manuela Tobias, "Understanding Poland's 'Holocaust Law,'" *PolitiFact*, March 9, 2018, https://www.politifact.com /article/2018/mar/09/understanding-polish-holocaust-law.

36. Jan Tomasz Gross, *Neighbors: The Destruction of the Jewish Community in Jedwabne, Poland* (Princeton, NJ: Princeton University Press, 2001); Jan Tomasz Gross, *Fear: Anti-Semitism in Poland after Auschwitz: An Essay in Historical Interpretation* (Princeton, NJ: Princeton University Press, 2006); Jan Tomasz Gross with Irena

Grudzińska Gross, *Golden Harvest: Events at the Periphery of the Holocaust* (Oxford: Oxford University Press, 2012).

37. Jan Grabowski, *Hunt for the Jews: Betrayal and Murder in German-Occupied Poland* (Bloomington: Indiana University Press, 2013). For a personal diary from the period that documents Polish collaboration in the murder of their Jewish neighbors, see Zygmunt Klukowski, *Diary from the Years of Occupation, 1939–44* (Urbana–Chicago: University of Illinois Press, 1993).

38. Barbara Engelking, *Such a Beautiful Sunny Day...: Jews Seeking Refuge in the Polish Countryside, 1942–1945* (Jerusalem: Yad Vashem, 2016); Barbara Engelking and Jan Grabowski, eds., *Night Without End: The Fate of Jews in German-Occupied Poland* (Bloomington: Indiana University Press, 2022). One chapter of this book served as grounds for a libel suit against the editors, who were found guilty in a lower court but exonerated on appeal. See Anna Wlodarczak-Semczuk and Alan Charlish, "Polish Appeals Court Dismisses Claims against Holocaust Book Historians," *Reuters*, August 16, 2021, www.reuters.com/world/europe/polish-appeals-court-dismisses -claims-against-holocaust-book-historians-2021-08-16.

39. See Deborah E. Lipstadt, *Antisemitism: Here and Now* (New York: Schocken Books, 2019), 11–21.

40. Ron Kampeas, "J. K. Rowling Schools Twitter After Non-Jew 'Explains' Anti-Semitism," *Haaretz*, April 19, 2018, www.haaretz.com/jewish/2018-04-19/ty-article/j-k-rowling-schools-twitter-after-non-jew-explains-anti-semitism/0000017f-e9cb-df5f-a17f-fbdfd71f0000.

41. Paul Krugman, "Opinion: Return of the Blood Libel," *New York Times*, June 21, 2018, www.nytimes.com/2018/06/21/opinion/blood-libel-trump-immigrants.html.

42. "Jeremy Corbyn's Anti-Semitism Problem," *Economist*, March 31, 2018, www.econo mist.com/britain/2018/03/31/jeremy-corbyns-anti-semitism-problem; "Corbyn's 'anti-Semitism' Could Drive Jews from UK, Jewish Leader Says," *Times of Israel*, May 31, 2018, www.timesofisrael.com/corbyns-anti-semitism-could-drive-jews-from-uk-jewish -leader-says.

43. "Malaysia's new 92-year-old prime minister is a proud anti-Semite," *Times of Israel*, May 10, 2018, www.timesofisrael.com/malaysias-new-92-year-old-prime-minister-is -a-proud-anti-semite; "Mahathir unfazed by anti-semite tag," *Al Jazeera*, October 22, 2003, www.aljazeera.com/news/2003/10/22/mahathir-unfazed-by-anti-semite-tag.

44. Sam Knight, "Jeremy Corbyn's Anti-Semitism Crisis," *New Yorker*, August 12, 2018, www.newyorker.com/news/letter-from-the-uk/jeremy-corbyns-anti-semitism -crisis; Bret Stephens, "Opinion | Jeremy Corbyn, Accidental Anti-Semite," *New York Times*, March 29, 2018, www.nytimes.com/2018/03/29/opinion/jeremy-corbyn -anti-semite.html; Dave Rich, *The Left's Jewish Problem: Jeremy Corbyn, Israel and Anti-Semitism* (London: Biteback, 2018).

45. David Nirenberg, *Anti-Judaism: The Western Tradition* (New York: W. W. Norton, 2013), 471. In his book, Nirenberg declares that, like Engel, he too will not use the term

"antisemitism," but for almost the opposite reason: not because antisemitism has no stable meaning, but because the term's meaning is too narrow and cannot serve the purposes of his research. It is ironic that despite Nirenberg's explicit declaration, the catalogers of the Library of Congress in Washington saw fit to catalog his book under the topic "Antisemitism, History." Ibid., 3.

11
America and the Keyword Battle Over "Antisemitism"

ELI LEDERHENDLER

Oᴜɢʜᴛ ᴡᴇ ᴛᴏ ʀᴇʟʏ any longer on the term "antisemitism," given its use as a generic callout for virtually any real or perceived affront to either some or many Jews? That is the semantic question that the historian David Engel raised in a discussion that goes well beyond semantics. Engel pointed to basic problems of methodology as well as terminology, arguing how difficult it is to prove the accuracy of conceptual models based on affirmed (but not necessarily confirmed) causal linkages between events. He further suggested how much more credible it is when one works without the ballast of overdetermined concepts. "Antisemitism," he argued, is a Jewish historian's albatross. Its clumsiness at the cognitive level leads to diminished credibility at the rhetorical and analytical levels.[1]

In the wake of much discussion among scholars in response to his original challenge, Engel has revisited his critique. He offers examples from his own published work, spanning several decades, in which he found it possible—and appropriate—to dissect historical events in all their particulars without cataloging them under the rubric of "antisemitism."[2] Spurred by his example, I have reexamined my own practice in this regard and found that, though I have not categorically dispensed with them, I have made rather sparing use of the term "antisemitism" and its derivatives.

· In discussing particular events, I have defined specific outcomes of attitudes and behavior that have harmed Jews, their human rights, or their interests, without supplying them with a generalized epithet (hence, my use of "anti-Jewish violence," "discrimination in employment," "animosity toward Jews," "Jew baiting," and the like); I have at times applied concepts derived from social science, such as "social distance," to describe a habitus characterized by adverse relations dividing Jews from their gentile peers; and I have described Jews' subjective feelings and perceptions (being marginalized, vulnerable).[3] However, in compiling indexes for my books, I have grouped those specific references under the single generic entry, "antisemitism," having in mind my readers' possible interest in locating discussions of antisemitism's various permutations within my text. Generalizations do help, I believe, in conceptualizing ideas for a larger historical canvas.

· I have used "antisemitism" for empirical documentation when another word simply will not suffice. Thus, when, making a point about Bolshevik policies in the years after 1917, I wrote that "the Soviets ruled out antisemitism as a matter of policy," meaning that official regulations explicitly referred to antisemitic acts as counterrevolutionary and illegal. Similarly, when citing studies whose stated objective was to examine "antisemitism" as such, or when paraphrasing or quoting verbatim statements, I have found it best to mention the term explicitly.[4]

Thus, I could say that in practice I have adopted Engel's critical point of view, though I have applied it selectively, not in an all-or-nothing way. I regard antisemitism as a challenging and significant topic for research. However, as an American-educated academic who came of age in the 1960s, my personal research concerns were honed amidst an atmosphere of identity politics, which left a huge impression on cultural and social studies of history. Having undertaken the study of Jewish ethnicity, I was led to migration studies and back again, because migrants often develop into ethnic groups in the context of their new homes. By contrast, the subject of "antisemitism" seemed to me a secondary matter, an almost extraneous irritant, apart from the ways in which it might inhibit the social integration of Jews in American society. I was aware of ways in which Jews might be conscious of gentiles' attitudes toward them (what is known as "the gentile gaze"), and that

Jews may be said to have internalized or sublimated it as part of their own identity, but this issue, treated by other scholars, was not my primary concern. To my way of thinking at the time, the issue of "antisemitism" was liable to distract me from focusing on group processes that really interested me. True, culture is deeply influenced by political processes and vice versa. This insight lay at the heart of my first book, *The Road to Modern Jewish Politics*.[5] In recent years, however, as the salience of "antisemitism" has risen in public discourse, periodically spiking in the wake of harassment and life-threatening and murderous acts against Jews, I have begun initiating and accepting invitations to explore its impact.

Nevertheless, despite the moral and cognitive provocation caused by recent events, it is not antisemitism's most extreme or lethal dimension (which so often is associated with post-Holocaust history and memory) that draws my interest. Rather, I hold that a new perspective on the relevance of "antisemitism" requires some conceptual separation from older historical models in which anti-Jewish hatred and violence are associated with totalitarian and genocidal ideologies. What seems most urgent today is the foregrounding of contemporary democratic societies, not a retreat to Holocaust-based paradigms. Democracies are among the chief settings in which racialized and politicized antagonisms are acted out, and Jews, among others, are experiencing this firsthand. The present essay has been written in that context.

IF I TAKE ISSUE with Engel's thought-provoking argument, it is mainly because of the hard, categorical edge of his methodological critique. But I also demur on a secondary matter that has influenced the entire discussion—namely, the political manipulation of "antisemitism" in public discourse. Let us dispense with the latter point at the outset: I am not persuaded that the term "antisemitism" should be disqualified on the grounds of its blurry tendentiousness any more than I believe that sort of fastidiousness to be required for other such "-isms" and their ilk: racism, sexism, genderism, misogyny, fascism, Orientalism. Those words, too, are liable to be overpoliticized, subject to conflicting interpretations, loosely bandied about, and deployed for special agendas. None of them, in fact, is devoid of essentialism, yet no one seems particularly bothered by this.

Every field, as we know, has a jargon that practitioners deploy not just for special, personal quests but also to carry on conversations across and beyond their individual projects. We are on shaky ground unless we take a stance against all such constructs and demand of historians in the field of Jewish history what we do not require in any other context. Other observers have similarly argued the case against attempts to dislodge "antisemitism" from academic and intellectual parlance.[6]

The importance of the "a-word" for scholars does not depend on its precision, accuracy, or immaculate objectivity, but rather on the way in which it is entwined—and yes, encumbered—with the inflammatory freight that it carries in public parlance. By extension, historians need to be cognizant of the explicit use of "antisemitism" and its synonyms in the ways that past events were recorded and remembered.[7] It is that very freight that has lent the term its expressive power in modern media, and this, in turn, warrants its documentation and its discussion. The term was never "neutral." It was, after all, a fighting word that was coined in the second half of the nineteenth century by people who made a public issue of their own Jew-hatred (hating not just "a Jew" but the supposedly baleful "essence" of Jews as a class) and sought to lend it the veneer of civil discourse.[8]

My brief in favor of retaining "antisemitism" as an analytical category—and not just as documentation—is based partly on its form: The word does not have a correspondingly neutral or positive category (shorn of the prefix "anti-")—that is, there is no "semitism" that is not actually a projection of "antisemitism," a roster of "Jewish characteristics" proposed by antisemites. It differs from a case such as "communism," which is still comprehensible without its negative analog, anti-communism. "Antisemitism" is not a secondary conceptual formulation that merely reflects its binary opposite, but a primary site of meaning. Hence it is proper to write it in English as one, unhyphenated word. (Please note that it is not hyphenated in German, French, Hebrew, or Russian.) Tainted as the term may be by its origins, or—to quote Engel—by the fact that it was a "socio-semantic convention created in the nineteenth century and sustained throughout the twentieth for communal and political ends,"[9] it is still useful to us, not because of (or despite) its unpalatable foundations, but because it is a keyword with a great deal of contextual and historical significance.

My approach to the problem, therefore, is not semantic but dialectical. I do not argue that we "need" the term for want of a better one (as some would have it),[10] or because we are—in Engel's terms—behaving unreflectively as the "servants" of the word instead of asserting mastership over our language. No: I say that we "need" it for its textured and layered character that prompts us (in our better moments) to search for and weigh its connection to larger issues. That being said, I would not presume to prescribe this approach in every single case or, of course, for every scholar. I agree with Engel and others that the term should not be fetishized or abused for political or other polemical purposes.

In the pages that follow, I propose to conduct a thought experiment in order to test my "defense" of antisemitism terminology by arguing from an ostensibly weak case—the American one—in order to support stronger cases. Specifically, let us ask whether the American case of "antisemitism," in which Jews (or "the Jews") have been tagged with negative associations, targeted by hate groups, or discriminated against, can be analyzed fruitfully without recourse to the term "antisemitism." Would this case—the most amenable one from which to support Engel's proposal—tell us something about the methodological and semantic questions at stake?

The point about engaging with "antisemitism" in the United States is that it appears weak on two counts: weak when compared to other instances of Jew-hatred (across both time and space), and also because it is a "minor" variant (in some imaginary quotient of relative victimhood) of racist or xenophobic behavior aimed against other groups in American society, both past and present.[11]

I will argue that even in this "best-case" scenario (for Engel's argument), American Jewish history presents sufficient grounds for using "antisemitism" dialectically and for empirical documentation. Implied, as well, is that American Jewish history is not so anomalous (with due respect to the oft-buried "American exceptionalism") as to permit no comparison to the history of Jews in other lands.[12] If the alleged inaptness or inutility of "antisemitism" as a documentary category or as an analytical hypothesis is unwarranted in this case, then by extension the term should in principle apply much more to other, much stronger cases.

As I have already remarked, the uptick in the debate over epistemic issues surrounding "antisemitism" reflects the times in which we live. It would be either naive or disingenuous to maintain that a prestigious academic intervention such as the special roundtable issue on "antisemitism," published in the *American Historical Review* (*AHR*) in 2018, was not correlated in some way with the arc of contemporary events and the public clamor about them.[13]

To be sure, the participants in that discussion underscored the need, on academic grounds per se, to reexamine theories of "antisemitism" in light of current intellectual agendas and in particular to engage more closely with what is being learned and written about racism, gender, class, and the problematic histories of subaltern groups living under colonial rule. But the discussion among scholars, as some have made explicit, is willy-nilly connected to the public dimension of the issue. Jonathan Judaken, in introducing the *AHR* roundtable, raised the specter of the Israel-Palestine conflict as a factor that has encumbered the academic discussion to a frustrating degree. Faced by the polarization of that debate, he suggested that the way out lay with challenging the boundaries of "antisemitism" via a new and more sophisticated level of theorization, including far more attention to interactions between Jews and other minorities (including Muslims).[14] A similar concern with the hyperpoliticization of "antisemitism," in connection with anxieties over Zionism and anti-Zionism, is tagged by Scott Ury in the *AHR* roundtable, and by him together with Guy Miron in their joint introduction to this volume, as well as by Amos Goldberg and Raz Segal in their contribution.[15]

Yet, the question is far from resolved by placing the "blame" on the politics of Israel-bashing. A glance at contemporary history, particularly in Europe and the United States, reveals many instances of barefaced, debasing expressions of antagonism toward Jewish people per se. They are part of a "turn" that has in recent decades eroded some of the momentous gains achieved by and for Jews, including their security and safety. That reality is far more disturbing than would be suggested solely by the contention among intellectuals over how best to define "antisemitism" and whether one should or should not exclude from it hostile references to the collective Jewish society in Israel. More troubling than these debates, I believe, is how social and political discourse "bends" toward antisemitic tropes at both the hard-core right- and left-wing ends of the spectrum, as well as the actuality of sporadic assaults against Jews and Jewish institutions. And yes, in more than just a few instances of verbal intimidation and physical violence directed at Jews, a connection has been drawn between the Jew as "Jew" and the "Jew" as proxy for Israel.[16]

There was, of course, a whole branch of specifically "anti-Zionist" discourse that was inherently related to anti-Jewish propaganda, images, and actions, and which exploited the word "Zionist" euphemistically and cynically. I refer to the now-defunct communist regimes in Europe, which foreswore "antisemitism" but freely used "anti-Zionism" when they carried out domestic purges that targeted Jews specifically. More-over, there is reason to ask whether such communist-era phenomena have not acquired an afterlife in post-communist societies.[17] These con-siderations ought to give pause to those who propose cordoning off "anti-Zionism" from the discursive field of "antisemitism." The quest for a dissenting voice on issues related to Israel and Palestine is always legitimate, but it ought not be pursued in ways that block significant avenues of research. The attempt to do so caters solely to hegemonic Western liberal sensibilities while marginalizing the east European scene. There are also similar issues related to the Muslim world that present comparable questions. That, however, is not at issue in this essay.

What is at issue is how best to proceed, on intellectual, method-ological, and semantic grounds, in light of the real-life background of contemporary events. It will not do to simply hark back to previously conceived paradigms, as if the early twenty-first century were an omi-nous reiteration of the 1930s. Not every anti-Jewish epithet hurled on the internet is the beginning of the road to Auschwitz. David Engel's essay is instructive in pointing to the large cache of knowledge that has been accumulated about the history of Jewish-gentile relations and showing that what we mean by "antisemitism" includes a broad spectrum of exhibited behaviors and attitudes. To glean some useful insight from that approach, we ought to consider the significance of nonlethal forms of antagonism toward Jews and their symbolic projection, "the Jews."

That brings us to the American case, which, as already stated, is relevant precisely because of its "low wattage." This "low wattage" does not make it a mere appendage, an afterthought to the discourse about allegedly more serious hate-mongering. Rather, it signifies how these behaviors *coexist* with countervailing social and political factors in a generally democratic setting and therefore offers an opportunity for reassessing the reality around us. For the crux of the matter is that expressions of bias, resentment, delegitimating invective, and even acts of violence directed against Jews have been occurring with alarming repetitiveness in post-millennial societies, all of them self-described democracies, and nearly all of them governed by states that eschew (or even prosecute) antisemitism.

IN THE MID-1960S, the American historian John Higham confidently asserted that the antisemitic urges that he had documented for the preceding century of American life were largely related to the period of mass immigration and, hence, were already spent—a thing of the past. Historians, he proposed, would do better to take greater interest in bigotry, race hatred, and discrimination with reference to groups other than the Jews.[18]

The United States (including its antecedent colonial past) lacks a history of anti-Jewish expulsions, blood libels, pogroms, and the like. Jews' experiences with antagonism and discrimination on American soil seem to pale in comparison with what certain other descent groups have had to contend with. That is to say, although Americans have certainly exhibited a capacity, historically, to legalize forms of intolerance or to burst out in violent and sometimes lethal forms of aggression, the force of such actions has nearly always been vented upon people other than Jews. The seismograph of American antisemitism, ever since the colonies and the early republic, has registered minor tremors and even a few mid-level quakes and aftershocks (particularly during the 1920s and 1930s), but no tectonic cataclysms or tsunamis.[19]

To this negative formulation (i.e., the general absence of lethal antisemitism) one must add the positive factor of American society's relative receptivity—especially since the 1950s—to the social integration of Jews. Through applying the updated lens of contemporary American social studies, that positive receptivity ought to be critically evaluated and problematized under the rubric of "whiteness" or "white privilege."[20] In principle, that proposed critique does not differ altogether from Hannah Arendt's insistence that modern, political antisemitism emerged in late nineteenth-century French and German public life at a time when bourgeois, affluent Jews enjoyed a privileged station and yet failed to correctly comprehend their particular vulnerability. By the time of the First World War and its aftermath, she argued, Jews "became an object of universal hatred because of [their] useless wealth, and of contempt because of [their] lack of power."[21] The Arendtian notion of Jews' coresponsibility, along with all of their fellow citizens, for the societies in which they flourished (and their peculiar, fatally blind political ignorance) is now being reapplied within the "white privilege" critique—the only distinction lying in the fact that her thesis is now read against the specific background of Americans' racial problems in a way that Arendt never anticipated nor even entertained.[22]

"Racism" (as a variant of "racialism") is a term of modern vintage, with its earliest documented use around the turn of the twentieth century, from the French *racisme*, and as the years progressed it was applied to the racial ideologies and policies implemented in Nazi Germany against Jews. One could conceivably suggest, today, that we simply subsume the discussion of anti-Jewish forms of bigotry under the more universal rubric of "racism" (as is semantically conceivable and practiced in France), and thus neatly avoid the terminology of "antisemitism" and its attendant problems of Jewish particularism. Perhaps so, but such an idea would misfire in American parlance, where "race" has been indelibly defined by the essentializing and imprecise division of people according to "skin color" and other such visible personal characteristics. Jews, who had been racialized in the American filing system of "races and peoples" around the turn of the twentieth century, are no longer considered a so-called "race," or so it seems as of late.[23]

Some latter-day residue of Jewish racialization is worthy of mention, though. I cite as an example an incident that occurred in 1970, a year after the first human step was taken on the moon. The events took place in Money, Mississippi, not far from the town of Greenwood. A Jewish woman named Barbara Lipman arrived in the area to work as a schoolteacher, in the company of her husband David, an attorney active in civil rights litigation. Barbara Lipman took up a teaching assignment at a school for African American children (the school district was not yet desegregated). Lipman recalled the following about her time there:

> When I taught at the Money School, there was an ongoing school desegregation [court] case. The case listed the number of white teachers and black teachers and then—one "other." I could not figure it out; I thought maybe it was an Indian or Asian. It was me. I was the Jewish teacher.[24]

Was the racialization of Lipman as "other" a residual form of anti-semitism? That is a potentially fascinating question with much ambiguity at its core. Judaken's introductory remarks in the *AHR* roundtable highlighted the point, previously made by Matthew Frye Jacobson, about that ambiguity: namely, that the Jews' experience in America is "neither wholly divisible from nor wholly dependent upon the history of whiteness" in America's racialized society.[25] I dare say that one could avoid discussing this as "antisemitism" and instead, with some reliability, state that Lipman's case was evidence of a deeply embedded racial hierarchy. Someone who was nonindigenous to the local area and did not match the culturally encoded criteria of "whiteness" (namely, she could not blend completely into the local dominant group) could well end up being deemed "other." However, one ought to follow up on that presumption and ask whether the same "othering" was applied to other Jews in the Deep South. The answer to that question, too, may be ambiguous, but Jews were indeed specifically targeted in acts of violence.

Less than one hundred miles from Greenwood, over in Jackson, Mississippi, Perry Nussbaum, a rabbi originally from Canada, led a congregation called Beth Israel. Nussbaum, as it happened, was an active supporter of the civil rights movement. In 1964, he, together with local pastors and ministers, organized a fund for the reconstruction of firebombed African American churches. In 1967, his friends and colleagues in the Black community attended the celebratory opening of Beth Israel's freshly constructed building, whereupon the synagogue and its members were subjected to a wave of vicious antisemitic leafletting (no scare quotes required). The synagogue was dynamited on the night of September 18 of that year, apparently by members of a group called "Americans for the Preservation of the White Race." A month later, Nussbaum's home was also attacked (the Nussbaums were not at home at the time and thus remained unharmed).[26]

Clearly, such episodes (there were numerous similar cases during the 1950s and 1960s[27]) have to be understood against the background of American racism and the conflict over racial politics. At the same time, however, "racism" is insufficient to the task of fathoming the anti-Jewish angle. To my knowledge, "white" churches were not firebombed in retaliation for the "collaboration" of white Christian leaders with the civil rights movement nor—had they been—would their religion as such have been subjected to hate speech. Thus, the universalizing or neutralizing impulse to subsume "antisemitism" under the "racism" rubric would seem to have certain natural limits. Race politics may not be antisemitic per se, but there are types of racialized Jew baiting, sometimes combined with physical violence, that do fit the meaning of the word "antisemitic."

We stand to learn about American antisemitism—and about its academic treatment—not by a simplistic segue into abstract theories of race and color, but rather through taking concrete cases into greater account. Eric Goldstein, a historian with a special expertise in contextualizing the history of American Jews within white America's "race question," points out that despite the supposed privilege that their "whiteness" afforded Jews and that led to their eventually successful integration around the turn of the twentieth century, there is sufficient reason not to minimize anti-Jewish rhetoric as something essentially marginal or irrelevant. Looking back to that era, he reminds us that there are simply too many documented examples of socially institutionalized barriers, "of real social consequences that Jews of this period faced as a result of the place they held in the American imagination.... Jews faced discrimination in obtaining credit and loans;...they were refused employment in certain trades, industries, and professions;... they were prevented—sometimes by written covenants and sometimes by custom—from living in many neighborhoods; [and] many colleges and universities had anti-Jewish quotas."[28]

Some historians have been prepared to see "antisemitism" per se as an issue and to probe its relevance to the resilience of American democracy. John Higham's analysis, cited earlier, is instructive in that connection. Higham portrayed the post-1945 wave of scholarly interest in American antisemitism, up through the 1960s and beyond, as reflecting two different approaches, that of social scientists—for whom Jew-hatred served predominantly as an archetype for understanding universal psychological and asocial pathologies in complex, modern societies—and that of historians, who were less apt to theorize all hatreds into one.[29] It is not entirely coincidental that the better-known social scientists, several of whose studies were supported and published by the American Jewish Committee, wrote ideologically scripted reports aimed to boost postwar Jewish morale and Jewish integration. Antisemitism in America, they argued, was not a "thing" in itself but a psychosocial symptom of social alienation in urban mass society and, as the victims of that prejudice were in effect interchangeable with other victims, prejudice against Jews had no palpable distinctiveness.[30]

At the same time, however, historians—schooled to inquire into events and not just concepts—took anxious note of anti-Jewish aspects that surfaced in populist movements in America during the late nineteenth and early twentieth centuries. Such groups had flourished, particularly but not exclusively in agrarian parts of the country, at a time when the United States was contending with large-scale urbanization, immigration, and commercialization. Higham explained those studies of populism in the context of Cold War–era fears about the erosion of American democracy from within, at the hands of demagogic right-wing radicals.[31] Several liberal historians had raised the specter of American populism's generic resemblance to proto-*völkisch* ideas, ominously akin to those in prewar Germany, but they failed, in Higham's view (and in the view of others), to make the analogy stick.[32]

This line of analysis might support David Engel's larger argument in the sense that overdetermined comparisons and generalizations do not succeed as good historical method. I would, however, draw a different lesson here. The way in which nativist and populist brands of social protest deployed antisemitic tropes about "the Jews"—which was an expression of local, regional, and national class tensions and not a proxy for, or harbinger of, proto-fascism—concretizes what I mean by the *coexistence* of active strains of anti-Jewish rhetoric and behavior alongside and within democratic and even liberal aspects of the American social regime.

THE MOST PERSUASIVE CONSIDERATION, in my opinion, in favor of retaining "antisemitism" in our research and writing is that its use allows us to relate empirically to Jewish perceptions, thus lending substance and due representation to the subaltern voice. Even in the "weak" American case, which raises all sorts of caveats and ambiguities, the conventional terminology is more adequate for accessing the feedback loop by which Jews themselves have monitored and processed their experiences.

Admittedly, there is something circular about the argument from perception, because the term "antisemitism" is routinized in the public square via opinion polls, the publication of annual statistics about the number and trends of reported incidents, and statements released by government officials at various levels. Nonetheless, when we take account of Jewish perceptions, we are also able to consider the various ways in which Jews choose to respond to (real or perceived) threats to their interests or well-being. Engel is right in saying that the term "antisemitism" has been used by Jews to further a range of communal purposes. It was the perceived threat of "antisemitism" that motivated some of them to embrace political action in defense of inclusion, toleration, nondiscrimination, and other liberal causes, just as it persuaded other Jews to endure difficulties and practice reticence or employ tactics of protective camouflage (such as changing their surnames or—among women in particular—wearing a cross when going to a job interview[33]). Yet, these behavioral responses by Jews are empirical data of some significance. Rather than seeing them as proof that Jews "use" antisemitism to justify some course of action, and thereby tend to amplify the term out of all proportion—as Engel's argument would have it— these behaviors and their motivations deserve the proper attention and analysis of the historian.

Hence, it is viable to argue that Shakespeare's *The Merchant of Venice* is (or is not) "antisemitic," but it is undeniable that it was called out by some Jews on the grounds that it harmed the fight against anti-Jewish prejudice. The Anti-Defamation League of B'nai B'rith (ADL), established after the First World War, initiated a campaign to have the Shylock play eliminated from public school assignments, and by 1920 no less than forty-one school districts had agreed to do so. The ADL acted on their belief that in the political atmosphere of that time—rife with nativist, anti-immigration fears about renegade, unassimilable, and subversive foreigners—the play was liable to evoke and possibly feed antisemitic stigmas (connecting "the Jew" with traits such as avarice, vengefulness, and a thirst for Christian blood), and detract from the acceptance of ethnic and cultural diversity.[34] The question of Shakespeare's own penchant for generic tropes was not at stake, nor was the question of his personal "antisemitism." What was at stake was the fact that Shylock's character "traded" in certain images, and, in turn, these supplied a recognizable face and name to prejudices about Jews that were alive in the public imagination. It would be remiss, from a historical point of view, not to look at the ADL's efforts against the background of antisemitic discourse both at home and abroad—and that is just one example.

Taking account of perceptions, as in the case described, also means that we might ask whether American Jews were "overreacting" or hypersensitive (in this or similar cases). We would find that hyperbolic responses were not generally part of the American Jewish institutional playbook. Even had they had the term in those days, it is nearly impossible to picture the ADL labeling *The Merchant* as a tool of "cultural genocide." Perhaps that would have been incommensurate with the undoubted freedoms that Jews enjoyed in an America that was relatively benign toward them. Be that as it may, their sensitivity was directly proportionate to the ways that antisemitism surged in the "Jazz Age," when (in the words of the historian Michael Alexander) "the Ku Klux Klan rode strongly for the first time in fifty years and Henry Ford appealed to a burgeoning popular spirit of antisemitism in the *Dearborn Independent*...," when exclusionary attitudes were given free rein, "typical of an age some have described as tribal and others have recognized as systemically antisemitic, anti-Catholic, and anti-immigrant."[35]

As a historian, I am bound to take "antisemitism" seriously—specifically in all its cloudy, metaconceptual, and propagandistic imperfection—in order to grasp the worldview of historical actors who took that word seriously and acted accordingly. Louis Marshall, leader of the American Jewish Committee, took up the public and legal cudgels at his command to wage war on Henry Ford's flagrant promotion of texts and narratives that drew extensively on the *Protocols of the Elders of Zion* because he saw this as something linked to a larger, more dangerous issue. He feared that the publication in the United States of pamphlets and newspapers with calumnious intent might exacerbate the problem of anti-Jewish hatred in Europe.[36] In *his* mind—and in Henry Ford's and that of his admirer, Adolf Hitler—these two realms were interconnected. Therefore, in interrogating their world, we need to talk about transnational linkages in terms that are authentically rooted in their history.

Conclusion

A wide-angle conceptual lens, such as is provided by touchstone words—large, general, aggregate terms—helps us engage in vital research tasks, including analysis and interpretation. Indeed, we do this all the time, using pliable, oft-debated, general constructs that are never satisfactorily pegged to a single, agreed-upon definition ("class," "culture," "identity"). They are useful to different scholars applying different methodologies, who are apt to refine such concepts in particular ways. Even though we may run some degree of semantic risk, it is up to us to make the conceptual terminology work for us in a judicious manner—quite in keeping with the spirit of David Engel's plea for a scholar's sovereignty in matters of choosing rhetorical tools.

"Antisemitism," both as a social phenomenon and as a dialectically robust part of our verbal tool kit, is significantly present in the history and historiography of American Jewry. How much more relevant does this term seem when examining modern Jewish history more globally? Today's scholars' attention to the use and abuse of the term has become ubiquitous, and future historians might well seek to explain the sheer volume of material being published on the topic in the context of contemporary events. If they do, I wonder whether they will shrink from the "a-word" or apply it in an appropriate and credible fashion.

NOTES

1. David Engel, "Away from a Definition of Antisemitism: An Essay in the Semantics of Historical Description," *Rethinking European Jewish History*, ed. Jeremy Cohen and Moshe Rosman (Oxford: Littman Library of Jewish Civilization, 2009), 30–53, esp. 53.

2. Ibid.

3. Eli Lederhendler, *New York Jews and the Decline of Urban Ethnicity, 1950–1970* (Syracuse, NY: Syracuse University Press, 2001), 130–31, 61; Eli Lederhendler, *Jewish Immigrants and American Capitalism, 1880–1920* (New York: Cambridge University Press, 2009), 3, 6; Eli Lederhendler, *American Jewry: A New History* (New York: Cambridge University Press, 2017), 65, 144, 148, 169, 288.

4. Lederhendler, *New York Jews*, 41; Lederhendler, *Jewish Immigrants and American Capitalism*, 113, 117; Lederhendler, *American Jewry*, 172.

5. Eli Lederhendler, *The Road to Modern Jewish Politics: Political Tradition and Political Reconstruction in the Jewish Community of Tsarist Russia* (New York: Oxford University Press, 1989).

6. For instance, David Berger, "Anti-Semitism: An Overview," *History and Hate: The Dimensions of Anti-Semitism*, ed. David Berger (Philadelphia: Jewish Publication Society, 1997), 3; see David Berger, *"Gilgulei hamusag 'antishemiyut': teguva lema'amaro shel David Engel," Zion* 85, nos. 1–4 (2020): 363–73.

7. Ben Halpern, "What Is Antisemitism?," *Modern Judaism* 1, no. 3 (1981): 251.

8. Dan Michman, *"Shimush be 'antishemiyut' kekategoriya bamehkar: teshuva ledavid engel," Zion* 85, nos. 1–4 (2020): 391–408.

9. Engel, "Away from a Definition of Antisemitism," 53.

10. Yehuda Bauer, "Problems of Contemporary Antisemitism," *Varieties of Anti-semitism: History, Ideology, Discourse*, ed. Murray Baumgarten, Peter Kenez, and Bruce Thompson (Newark: University of Delaware Press, 2009), 315.

11. Elsewhere I summarize the idea of a pallid American version of antisemitism while developing an argument about Jews' sensitized awareness to it: Eli Lederhendler, "American Antisemitism in Its Historical and Social Background," Institute for National Security Studies (INSS) Special Publication (online), August 1, 2021, www.inss.org.il/publication/american-antisemitism-historical. On the amelioration of antisemitism in the United States, see Jeffrey E. Cohen, "From Antisemitism to Philosemitism? Trends in American Attitudes toward Jews from 1964 to 2016," *Religions* 9, no. 4 (2018): 107.

12. Edward S. Shapiro's, *A Unique People in a Unique Land: Essays on American Jewish History* (Brookline, MA: Academic Studies Press, 2022), owes its title to exceptionalist narratives; still, of the book's five topical sections, the section on "Antisemitism" is the longest, with nearly twice the number of essays as he chose to include in either his section on "Religion" or the one on "Identity," which seems to prompt the question, "Is America different?"

13. Jonathan Judaken, guest ed., "*AHR* Roundtable: Rethinking Anti-Semitism," *American Historical Review* 123, no. 4 (October 2018).

14. Jonathan Judaken, "Rethinking Anti-Semitism: Introduction," *American Historical Review* 123, no. 4 (October 2018): 1122–24.

15. Scott Ury, "Strange Bedfellows? Anti-Semitism, Zionism, and the 'Fate of the Jews,'" *American Historical Review* 123, no. 4 (October 2018): 1151–72; Scott Ury and Guy Miron, "Antisemitism: On the Meanings and Uses of a Contested Term," 1–32; Amos Goldberg and Raz Segal, "'Antisemitism' as a Question in Holocaust Studies," 299–318. See Brian Klug, "The Collective Jew: Israel and the New Antisemitism," *Patterns of Prejudice* 37, no. 2 (2003): 117–38.

16. See the discussion in Alan Partington, "The Changing Discourses on Antisemitism in the UK Press from 1993–2009," *Journal of Language and Politics* 11, no. 1 (2012): 51–76.

17. The matter is treated by several essays in *Studies in Contemporary Jewry*, vol. 33, *Becoming Post-Communist: Jews and the New Political Cultures of Russia and Eastern Europe*, ed. Eli Lederhendler (New York: Oxford University Press, 2023); see Ildikó Barna and Anikó Félix, eds., *Modern Antisemitism in the Visegrád Countries* (Budapest: Tom Lantos Institute, 2017).

18. John Higham, "American Anti-Semitism Historically Reconsidered," in *Jews in the Mind of America*, ed. Charles H. Stember et al. (New York: Basic Books, 1966), 237–38, 243, 252–53.

19. For example, Jonathan D. Sarna, "American Anti-Semitism," in *History and Hate*, ed. David Berger, 115–28; Lloyd Gartner, "The Two Continuities of Antisemitism in the United States," in *Antisemitism Through the Ages*, ed. Shmuel Almog, trans. Nathan Reisner (Oxford: Pergamon, 1988), 311–20; Frederic Cople Jaher, *A Scapegoat*

in the Wilderness: The Origins and Rise of Anti-Semitism in America (Cambridge, MA: Harvard University Press, 1994).

20. Michael Rogin, *Blackface, White Noise: Jewish Immigrants in the Hollywood Melting Pot* (Berkeley: University of California Press, 1996); Matthew Frye Jacobson, *Whiteness of a Different Color: European Immigrants and the Alchemy of Race* (Cambridge, MA: Harvard University Press, 1998); Matthew Frye Jacobson, *Roots Too: White Ethnic Revival in Post-Civil Rights America* (Cambridge, MA: Harvard University Press, 2006); David R. Roediger, *Working Toward Whiteness: How America's Immigrants Became White* (New York: Basic Books, 2005); Eric Goldstein, *The Price of Whiteness: Jews, Race, and American Identity* (Princeton, NJ: Princeton University Press, 2006).

21. Hannah Arendt, *The Origins of Totalitarianism* (Cleveland: Meridian Books, 1958), 8, 9, 25, 51, 54, 67, quotation on 15.

22. Arendt commented that Jews, "alone among all other [American] groups, have... within their history and their religion, expressed a well-known principle of separation," and therefore, should "social discrimination" ever become the focus of an American political movement, Jews would be far more politically vulnerable to attack than "the Negroes and Chinese [who lack such cultural baggage], who are... less endangered politically, even though they may differ more from the majority than the Jews." Arendt, *Origins*, 55 n. 1.

23. Joel Perlmann, *America Classifies the Immigrants: From Ellis Island to the 2020 Census* (Cambridge MA: Harvard University Press, 2018); see David A. Hollinger, "Haley's Choice and the Ethno-Racial Pentagon," chap. 2 in *Postethnic America: Beyond Multiculturalism* (New York: Basic Books, 1995).

24. Kent Spriggs, ed., *Voices of Civil Rights Lawyers: Reflections from the Deep South, 1964–1980* (Gainesville: University of Florida Press, 2017), 127.

25. Matthew Frye Jacobson, "Looking Jewish, Seeing Jews," in *Theories of Race and Racism, A Reader*, ed. Les Back and John Solomos (London: Routledge, 2009), 303–304, cited by Judaken, "Introduction," 1123; see Howard N. Rabinowitz, "Nativism, Bigotry and Anti-Semitism in the South," *American Jewish History* 77, no. 3 (1988): 437–51.

26. "Encyclopedia of Southern Jewish Communities—Jackson, Mississippi," Goldring/Woldenberg Institute of Southern Jewish Life, last updated November 2021, www.isjl.org/mississippi-jackson-encyclopedia.html; see Gary Phillip Zola, "What Price Amos? Perry Nussbaum's Career in Jackson Mississippi," in *The Quiet Voices: Southern Rabbis and Black Civil Rights, 1880s to 1990s*, ed. Mark Bauman and Berkley Kalin (Tuscaloosa: University of Alabama Press, 2014), 251–56; Allen P. Krause, *To Stand Aside or Stand Alone: Reform Rabbis and the Civil Rights Movement* (Tuscaloosa: University of Alabama Press, 2016); Clive Webb, *Fight Against Fear: Southern Jews and Black Civil Rights* (Athens: University of Georgia Press, 2001), 169–216; *Rabbi Perry Nussbaum and Wife after Bombing of Their Home*, November 1967, photograph, Jewish Women's Archive, https://jwa.org/media/rabbi-perry-nussbaum-and-wife-after-bombing-of-their-home.

27. Between 1957 and 1967, dynamite, incendiary, and other attacks on southern US synagogues took place in Charlotte and Gastonia, NC; Birmingham and Gadsen, AL; Nashville, TN; Miami and Jacksonville, FL; and Atlanta, GA. On the Atlanta synagogue bombing of October 12, 1958, see Melissa Fay Greene, *The Temple Bombing* (Cambridge, MA: Da Capo Press, 2006); Claude Sitton, "Temple Bombing Stirs Wide Hunt," *New York Times*, October 14, 1958, 46.

28. Response by Eric Goldstein, in "Roundtable on Anti-Semitism in the Gilded Age and Progressive Era," *Journal of the Gilded Age and Progressive Era* 19 (2020): 477.

29. Higham, "American Anti-Semitism," 237–38.

30. See the series of studies, collectively entitled *Studies in Prejudice*, alluded to in this book's introduction, and authored by Max Horkheimer, Theodor Adorno, and Bruno Bettelheim, among others.

31. For example, Richard Hofstadter, *The Age of Reform: From Bryan to F.D.R.* (New York: Alfred A. Knopf, 1955); Richard Hofstadter, *The Paranoid Style in American Politics and Other Essays* (New York: Alfred A. Knopf, 1965); Richard Hofstadter, "The Pseudo-Conservative Revolt—1955," in *The Radical Right* (rev. ed. of *The New American Right*), ed. Daniel Bell (Freeport, NY: Books for Libraries Press, 1971), 8–79; Oscar Handlin, "American Views of the Jew at the Opening of the Twentieth Century," *Publications of the American Jewish Historical Society* 40 (1951): 323–44; John Higham, "Anti-Semitism in the Gilded Age: A Reinterpretation," *Mississippi Valley Historical Review* 43 (1957): 559–78; Leonard Dinnerstein, *The Leo Frank Case* (New York: Columbia University Press, 1968); Glen Jeansonne, "Combating Anti-Semitism: The Case of Gerald L. K. Smith," in *Anti-Semitism in American History*, ed. David A. Gerber (Urbana: University of Illinois Press, 1986), 152–66.

32. Higham, "American Anti-Semitism," 237; Michael Kazin, *The Populist Persuasion: An American History* (Ithaca, NY: Cornell University Press, 2017); Edward S. Shapiro, "John Higham and American Anti-Semitism," *American Jewish History* 76, no. 2 (1986): 208–9.

33. Higham, "American Anti-Semitism," 246, after J. X. Cohen, *Jews, Jobs, and Discrimination: A Report on Jewish Non-Employment* (New York: American Jewish Congress, 1944), 11, 16–17.

34. Leonard Dinnerstein, *Anti-Semitism in America* (New York: Oxford University Press, 1994), 102.

35. Michael S. Alexander, *Jazz Age Jews* (Princeton, NJ: Princeton University Press, 2001), 8.

36. Neil Baldwin, *Henry Ford and the Jews: The Mass Production of Hate* (New York: Public Affairs, 2003); Naomi W. Cohen, *Not Free to Desist: The American Jewish Committee, 1906–1966* (Philadelphia: Jewish Publication Society, 1972), 127–35; John Higham, *Strangers in the Land: Patterns of American Nativism, 1860–1925* (New York: Atheneum, 1973), 277–86; Dinnerstein, *Anti-Semitism in America*, 80–102; Matthew Silver, *Louis Marshall and the Rise of Jewish Ethnicity in America: A Biography* (Syracuse, NY: Syracuse University Press, 2013), 381–401.

12

"Fog in Channel— Continent Cut Off?" Remarks on Antisemitism, Pride, and Prejudice in Britain

ARIE M. DUBNOV

"Although I loathe anti-semitism, I do dislike Jews."
HAROLD NICOLSON

LET US NOT beat around the bush but get straight to the crux of the matter. At the heart of this article stands the following claim: that overuse of the term "antisemitism" in general, and its sloppy applications to the post-1945 British sphere in particular, result in a double if not even triple problem. First, by marking events, verbal pronouncements, or ideas as "antisemitic," we fail to explain the disparity in post-Holocaust Anglo-American culture between expressions of prejudice and even hostility toward Jews, on one hand, and Jews' actual legal status and social standing in British society, where the absence of legal or institutional discrimination is the prevailing norm, on the other. Second, as a concept, antisemitism leaves us with very limited room to discuss how various conceptions of Jewish metaphysical difference have been internalized and appropriated by Jewish thinkers and writers, who transformed claims about Jews' "otherness" into tools serving their own hermeneutic and ideological agendas. Third, the unbearable ease with which accusations of antisemitism are made nowadays exposes a stubborn attempt to blur the essential difference between critiques of Zionism and the idea of a Jewish nation-state, on one hand, and anti-Jewish sentiments and policies, on the other.

The broad ramifications of the present discussion are relevant beyond Britain, of course. As David Engel shows in the essay that triggered this collection, the list of analytic problems from which most contemporary definitions of antisemitism suffer is fairly long. In the following pages, I will illustrate some of these problems, focusing primarily on those stemming from the search for "generic" antisemitism that ignores the particular features of British history, and the complicated relationship between Britain and the Zionist movement before and after statehood. The objective of my article is not to provide a conceptual alternative to the concept of antisemitism, nor shall I weigh in on the tempestuous debate about the use or nonuse of the hyphen when writing the term anti(-)semitism in English. One of the criticisms leveled at Engel's programmatic essay was that he refrains from proposing such an alternative ("Jew-hatred," "Judeophobia," "anti-Judaism," and "anti-Jewishness" are several of the candidates mentioned).[1] This criticism also applies to me. Yet my desire is not to alter the scholarly agenda and cut off altogether the branch of research called the study of antisemitism. I am merely a guest for the night, joining the conversation from a particular, self-serving angle, as a historian who moves along the seam between Jewish history and British imperial history. This perspective dictates my approach to the subject, leading me to ask: What can I learn from the contemporary study of antisemitism? Does it offer only a list of prohibitions and obstacles or also new insights that could add nuance and enrich one's understanding of the manifold, complicated, and never straightforward encounter among Jews, Britain, and the British Empire?

In other words, I would like to supplement our discussion by asking, first and foremost, to what extent does the branch of research dedicated to the study of antisemitism offer fresh perceptions and understandings that might support the work of historians who observe its controversies from the margins? Does the contemporary controversy concerning definitions of antisemitism help historians for whom these questions are of secondary importance or historians who do not study eastern Europe or the German-speaking sphere—the locus classicus of the study of antisemitism?

To this list, I would like to add two additional types of questions.

A second group of questions, moored more specifically in the history of Britain, would be this: Is it possible to understand the sources or manifestations of hostility toward Jews apart from broader discussions concerning the place of other religious or ethnic minorities in modern Britain? Can our discussion about Jews and Britain continue in its present form, tightly anchored to a communal perspective but detached from broader discussions concerning the links between Great Britain, the imperial sphere, and the colonial dynamics that shaped British history? I am concerned by the possibility that we shall continue reading Jewish history in Britain as a unique test case, examining it as distinct and separate from broader questions concerning xenophobic attitudes toward migrants and foreigners in modern British history. If we continue to insist that antisemitism qualifies as a distinct, isolated, *sui generis* phenomenon, then the term loses its power as an analytic, illuminating concept when applied to the British context.

The absence of open, institutional, and violent antisemitism on the part of state apparatuses or political parties is indeed a prominent feature of British history. However, the absence of this species of antisemitism can easily be used as evidence reinforcing a fabled and epic view of Britain and its history, as a society and culture immune to hatred, a special polity that was always enlightened, progressive, distinctly anti-nationalist, separate from "Continental" Europe. This leads to my third type of question, alluded to in the title of this article and shamelessly plagiarized from Jane Austen: How can we assess manifestations of hostility toward and prejudice against Jews in Britain without lapsing into coarse generalizations and self-congratulatory narratives about Britain's admirable exceptionalism? How should we write histories of antisemitism in Britain without ignoring the laudable, unique features of twentieth-century Britain, on the one hand, but without adopting the mythic view of Britain as different, in a positive sense, from all its neighbors, on the other hand? A mini-*Begriffsgeschichte* exercise is useful here: As I will argue, a meticulous examination of the use of the word "antisemitism" in the English language in the first years after its appearance attests to the British tendency to regard antisemitism as the by-product of "Continental" nationalism, which never found fertile soil in which it could grow on the British Isles. The way

English journalists and writers began to use the concept illustrated the exceptionalist self-perception expressed in the famous saying, "Fog in Channel—Continent Cut Off." A classic error of positivistic historians is to duplicate the language of their primary sources without scrutiny or interpretation. Contrary to that echoing impulse, we need to understand from where such views and sentiments sprang without assuming that they straightforwardly reflect a given historical situation or reality. Sentiments, phrases, and idioms open windows into the past. They help us comprehend it, but they are never the past—*"wie es eigentlich gewesen"*—as it actually was.

Contemporary definitions of antisemitism do not offer tools to answer these questions, in part because the underlying core concept that they rely upon lacks clarity and specificity. Debates concerning British antisemitism illustrate the fact that formal definitions of antisemitism fail to provide a precise or reliable index for examining attitudes toward Jews. As Colin Holmes argued many years ago, if social and economic discrimination, government policy (overt or covert), and open violence provide our indices of antisemitism, then, without a doubt, antisemitism suffered a crushing political defeat in Britain.[2] According to that logic, antisemitism in Britain is defined by its absence: acerbic, exclusionary discourses of *Völkism*, whether theologically inspired or, in its twentieth-century manifestations, neopagan; ethnonationalism; a deep-seated yearning to return to an organicist, premodern *gemeinschaft* (community) have clearly had a hard time taking root under the auspices of the Church of England; and by defining itself as the union of the Welsh, English, Scottish, and Irish, the United Kingdom remained, at the core, a liberal, "supranational" conglomerate.

From this perspective, despite Anthony Julius's efforts to present Jew-hatred as part of the English cultural DNA—in his voluminous survey of discrimination against Jews in England—it is hard to claim that antisemitism served the same nationalist coagulating function in twentieth-century British society and politics as in the German-speaking world, where it was at the center of ideological radicalization.[3] In other words, discrimination and manifestations of hostility toward Jews were not absent from Britain, and they regrettably still exist to some degree or another, yet antisemitism never reached the status of a "cultural code," as Shulamit Volkov called it, on the British Isles.[4] This conceptualization, like the somewhat mythic image of the "singular path" of Britain vis-à-vis the Continent, ultimately dismisses Oswald Mosley's British Union of Fascists in the 1930s and the neo-Nazi Greater Britain Movement that sprang up in 1964 as weak and historically unimportant phenomena. Even worse, it minimizes and even conceals the central role played by thinkers like Houston Stewart Chamberlain and a long list of British social Darwinists and anthropologists in the science of eugenics and race theories that were crucial steps toward the Final Solution.[5] The challenge facing contemporary scholars of Britain and its Jews is thus linked, in my opinion, to the difficulty of finding a way to treat British difference from the Continent without lapsing into ahistorical mythologizing.

I will proceed from here in four steps. First, I will examine the earliest pre-1930s appearances of the term "antisemitism" in English. Second, I will address the loaded English phrase "the Jewish question" and argue that it filled a completely different role in Britain than did the *Judenfrage* in Germany. Third, I will briefly address the crucial context of the complicated relationship between Zionism and the British Empire, highlighting in particular how political arguments, rationales, and justifications developed in this context were often linked to anti-Jewish conceptions alongside philosemitic discourse. Ultimately, I will claim that in the short but dramatic postwar phase between 1945 and 1948, there was a far-reaching transformation in the meaning and understanding of the concept of antisemitism.

How to Do Things with Words

I am neither a linguist nor a semiotics expert. However, at the outset of our discussion, we must distinguish between two types of usage and two diametrically opposed functions of the word "antisemitism." I will call the first form "vernacular usage," that is, use of the word in spoken, everyday language. In the second form of usage, which I call "theoretical" or "academic," a word is elevated to a concept meant to serve an analytic function: to define and elucidate a complex phenomenon.

The distinction can be defined as follows: A vernacular usage of almost any word assumes some direct relationship between referent and sign, or, in the context of the present discussion, when making such utterances we assume a direct relation between the social or historical *phenomenon* and the *name* given to it. Such usage is the product of social consensus. In vernacular usage, adherence to a formal (or specialized) definition of the term is of secondary importance. Instead, the word's impact is measured according to its effectiveness and imprint on the agora (literally, the marketplace), the public space in which the word circulates. The vernacular word exists as long as a given group of people (usually speakers of the same language) uses the word and because, for these lay users, this word best describes a particular phenomenon or a certain reality they wish to discuss.

By contrast, the theoretical-academic or analytic usage of words has a completely different goal. The objective of a theoretical concept is to elucidate and illuminate a multidimensional phenomenon. The value of a theoretical concept is not dependent on nor determined by the uses of the same words in the public sphere. It serves as a heuristic tool and captures a given phenomenon regardless of whether that very same word is being used in everyday language or is part of the vocabulary of the human subjects under study. When dealing with historical research, in which questions of continuity and change are central, these concepts become double-edged swords. Not infrequently, the purpose of a historical concept is to attempt to capture a moving target, a phenomenon whose contours and forms of expressions vary over time. It seeks to identify a common thread, a recurring pattern.

But most historical phenomena elude such definitions. We can take Friedrich Nietzsche's famous warning—only that which has no history can be defined—and turn it on its head:[6] While words do a fine job helping us navigate in the present, the constant change wrought by the passing of time and the sensitivity of historians who wish to avoid anachronisms that project present feelings, conceptions, and thoughts on a radically different past society make the attempt to form a rigid definition impossible if not futile. History revolts against all too rigid definitions. The critical element is this: A theoretical concept is not a simple sign whose purpose is to describe or identify a static object, and it does not sustain a simple sign/referent relationship. Its validity and effectiveness are measured by its ability to reveal and interpret a complex relationship or explain the source of a particular phenomenon. A concept is meaningless unless accompanied by a full, formal definition.

This distinction is fundamental for two reasons. First, because the everyday, colloquial, or vernacular use of the word "antisemitism" cannot be measured using the same yardstick we use in professional, academic settings. These are different vocabularies. A categorical error is committed once one attempts to measure the analytical value of a charged word like "antisemitism" when it is used by the lay public using the same criteria with which we examine our academic lexicon and the viability of its concepts. Vernacular usages of words presume that the objects they describe have a closed, absolute meaning. The routine usage and everyday reliance on such words is not based on our need as academics to discuss the word's significance and the source of the types of phenomena it seeks to capture. Naturally, David Engel's criticism was directed, first and foremost, at academic usage of the concept "antisemitism." A conceptual history (*Begriffsgeschichte*), however, must relate to both a word's vernacular and theoretical usage. Second, it would be a mistake to assume that the vernacular usage of a word is immune to change. The questions of what and how we do things with words should not keep only analytic philosophers up at night. Understanding the sense or meaning of a word is linked, inter alia, to the historical context within which it is used.

One of the problems implicit in the concept "antisemitism" within the British context is tightly linked to these everyday nonacademic usages. The word, with all its derivations ("antisemite," "antisemitic"), entered the English language as early as the 1880s, precisely when the root *antisemit* entered broad usage in Germany. But a careful examination of these vernacular usages attests to the somewhat mythological self-perception of Britain as positively and fundamentally different from the Continent. Thus, for example, the *Oxford English Dictionary* details common usages of the word during the first decades of its existence that describe German hostility and prejudice against Jews and, most significantly, deprecate such practices without any attempt to describe or conceptualize the attitudes of Britain's Christian citizens toward their Jewish neighbors. It was a word to describe events taking place "elsewhere," not to reflect upon oneself. Locating and mapping these usages does not help us understand the phenomenon that historians call "antisemitism," but it captures a certain self-perception—it hints at how British writers perceived their own identities, usually as diametrically opposed to Europe's zealous nationalists. It is worth remembering that in the first years after the term's appearance in English, the local Jewish community was still relatively small, a situation that changed radically after the great migrations of east European Jews. Moreover, these initial appearances of the term did not come from within the Jewish community.

The historian David Feldman, who sketched the path of the term and the way its meaning changed over the years, used a short encyclopedia entry penned by Lucien Wolf in 1910 for *Encyclopædia Britannica* as his point of departure.[7] As Feldman shows, from Wolf's perspective, the concept of antisemitism was meant to describe a new phenomenon, an unfortunate by-product of industrialization and modernization, in historical terms. Wolf's theoretical move identified Britain as differing, in a positive sense, from the Continent and sought to distinguish antisemitism from the old Jew-hatred. Moreover, this theoretical analysis also mapped antisemitism spatially as a "Western" phenomenon. As such, antisemitism was not a term he applied to discrimination or persecution of Jews outside Europe, nor even in tsarist Russia, which was considered non-European.

The Minority Treaties, signed at the end of World War I, marked a new phase in the definition of antisemitism. After 1918, the earlier socioeconomic analysis gave way to the identification of antisemitism with intolerance toward national minorities in Europe. This conceptual shift involves a slight geographical transition, as alongside Germany, the establishment of an independent Polish Republic in the aftermath of the First World War drew the most attention at that moment in history. Feldman shows that during the 1920s, English writers began using the concept of antisemitism to describe the Polish arena. This stage in the development of the concept "antisemitism" in the English language is critical for our discussion: The meaning of the term shifted due to an emergence of a new understanding of the term "minority," which, after 1918, began to describe ethnonational and religious groups. The term "minoritization" referred to the new way that beleaguered, persecuted, and uprooted groups were subordinated yet tolerated enough by a majority population to demand political rights. Minoritization was relevant in the new eastern and central European contexts, where the new political order was focused on transitioning from empire to nation-state, but it remained irrelevant to Britain and its empire. Not surprisingly, Britain viewed the "minorities question," like antisemitism, as a foreign problem.

This claim is important for our discussion. The use of the adjective "antisemitic" to describe an English play like Shakespeare's *Merchant of Venice* or a novel like Dickens's *Oliver Twist* is a later development. Indeed, it is hard to find examples of writers who make use of the word in this sense, at least within the Anglophone world before World War II. Take for example the Anglican theologian James Parkes: When he began to search for premodern Christian roots of antisemitism in the 1930s, he identified a new line of discussion. His intention was to enable interfaith dialogue and religious tolerance—unsurprisingly, against the background of the rise of the Nazi Party in Germany and the strengthening of anti-Jewish voices in Britain.[8] Earlier English writers did not refrain from expressing hostility and negative prejudices against Jews in Britain, insisting that such negative characterizations should not be identified with antisemitism. The diplomat Harold Nicolson's famous quote (which serves as the epigraph for this article)—"[a]lthough I loathe anti-semitism, I do dislike Jews"—succinctly and sharply expresses this contradiction.[9]

The British Version of "the Jewish Question"

We thus see that attempting to outline a conceptual history of the term "antisemitism" in the English language offers one way to address the absence of institutional antisemitism together with the presence of prejudice against Jews in modern Britain. Precisely because British authors habitually used the word to refer to the non-British sphere, the history of the concept of antisemitism is probably not a good indicator of the way in which Jewish-British relations were conceived within Britain. A much more productive line of inquiry, I would suggest, is investigating how the phrase "the Jewish question" entered the English-speaking world.

Famously, Left-Hegelian thinkers like Bruno Bauer and the young Karl Marx authored the key texts discussing the German term "*Juden-frage*," which became widespread after 1843. The German-born Israeli historian Jacob Toury (1915–2004) argued that the term's appearance indicated, without a doubt, a new phase in the development of discrimination against Europe's Jews.[10] And yet, once we move away from the German-speaking sphere we see that the first appearance of the phrase "the Jewish question" appears in English, and can be traced back to circa 1830, long before the word "antisemitism" entered the English language.[11] The appearance of the phrase is linked to a specific campaign triggered by Sir Robert Grant, who proposed on April 15, 1830, a new bill that would rescind older legislation that discriminated against Jewish residents of the kingdom. Even though the attempt to pass the Jews' Civil Disabilities Bill failed that year, the stormy debates about it in Parliament moved the discussion about the legal discrimination against British Jews from the margins of political discourse to its center. The phrase, "the Jewish question"—a shorthand for "the question of Jewish emancipation" or the "question of Jewish disabilities"—began to appear frequently in newspaper reports.[12]

It was a crucial moment in the struggle for civil emancipation of Britain's Jews. The term emancipation must not mislead us: Unlike in France or many other European countries, where granting citizenship rights or civic equality to Jews was an act of legislation passed through edicts or decrees, in Britain, Jewish emancipation was not experienced as a onetime event as much as a slow, piecemeal process. Legally and politically, it commenced in 1830, in the wake of Catholic emancipation, but the campaign continued well into the 1840s and 1850s. Furthermore, the call to emancipate Jews emerged against the backdrop of the Roman Catholic Relief Act of 1829 rather than that of rising ethnic or race-based hatred.

The deep scars left by religious violence—including the English Civil War—made hostility toward Catholicism in England far more powerful than anti-Jewish sentiment. The Catholic emancipation was the real watershed moment. It had little to do with Jews, but it inspired the

Board of Deputies of British Jews and the Jewish community's oligarchic leadership to launch their own campaign, hoping that Jews would be next in line and would join other non-Anglican groups relieved from legal restrictions of their movement and occupations. The protracted emancipation process provided the discursive framework and political momentum that led to discussions concerning the so-called Jewish question in Britain. This is a very different backdrop than the radically dissimilar environment in which the German *Judenfrage* entered wide circulation. The use of this linguistic pattern itself—"the X question"—indicates that "the Jewish question" was seen, from the outset, as tied to other "questions." Indeed, it is evident that in the 1830s and 1840s "the Jewish question" was not only tightly linked to "the Catholic question," but even viewed as its derivative.[13] Furthermore, in the vast majority of cases, the phrase "the Jewish question" is seen as an internal British matter, not a European matter.[14]

Yet the phrase "the Jewish question" did not continue to indicate an internal British matter for long. As the historian Abigail Green has shown, a new identification of "the Jew" with revolutionary forces began to appear around 1848. At the time, the language of race began to infiltrate anti-Jewish discourse in Britain, which until then had emphasized Jewish difference as being grounded in religion. This mid-nineteenth-century "internationalization" of "the Jewish question" was largely due to the combination of political radicalization in Europe and the rise of Jewish notables like Moses Montefiore, who began speaking a new political language. This political language emphasized the unity and shared fate of Jews everywhere.[15]

Green advances Jonathan Frankel's thesis and disentangles it from several axiomatic premises of Zionist master narratives. According to Green, this mid-nineteenth-century discursive development did not come out of the blue but was tied to the blossoming of a new type of Jewish politics centered around modern Jewish diplomacy and based on delegations, lobbying, and international philanthropic organizations.[16] New expressions of hostility emerged in response to this Jewish political action. In the British case, we cannot disconnect this pre–World War I "internationalization" from the imperial and colonial context in which these new political strategies and institutions developed.

Zionism and Empire

Thus far, I have shown the contours of a narrative highlighting Britain's magnificent difference, its separateness and immunity from a European pandemic of racial acrimony. This, to evoke the title of Herbert Butterfield's famous tract, is a very Whiggish reading of history.[17] We can now turn our attention to the problematic consequences of this narrative and castigate it.

One of the problems inherent in the "Whig" perception of Britain as a liberal bastion, free of "Continental" Jew-hatred, is how it collapses, paradoxically as it may sound, into a Germanocentric narrative about the path toward the Final Solution. No serious, honest history of racism can be written by focusing on German authors alone, while marginalizing the theories of social Darwinism and eugenics that were developed and perfected on the British Isles. In the framework of this essay, I will not be able to survey the various links between the rise of social Darwinism and the growth of what historians often refer to as the "New Imperialism" of the last third of the nineteenth century.[18] Nor will I be able to provide a detailed account of how Victorian authors' fascination with Celtic folklore, archeology, and philology quickly lent itself to tracts that introduce crude racist taxonomies into glorifying origin stories of the English nation.[19] I will merely note that this issue becomes especially complicated once we acknowledge the Jewish doctors, anthropologists, and scholars of race who worked within the discursive boundaries set by their Welsh and English colleagues and did not reject categorically the suggestion that there is a biological basis to Jewish difference.[20] Thus, for instance, the Jewish-Australian folklorist Joseph Jacobs (1854–1916)—who was not only among the first to write the history of English Jewry and to defend the Jews of Russia but also a pioneering Jewish race theorist—highlighted that only a small percentage of "Aryan blood" had been infused into Jews and, at the same time, pushed against the inclination of Beddoe and others to read any sociocultural divergence as a symptom of racial difference.[21] Noteworthy in the context of our present discussion, Jacobs's series of articles on the persecution of Russian Jews helped turn the phrase "the Jewish question" into a general label, applicable to cases beyond

Britain of the 1830s.[22] As I show elsewhere, the author and playwright Israel Zangwill, Herzl's greatest supporter among British Jews and the founder of the Jewish Territorialist movement, was close with Jacobs and adopted many of his operating assumptions when developing the idea of "reverse racism," which viewed Jews as a racial subgroup different and separate but also superior in character to the non-Jewish groups around it.[23]

Another baffling issue stems from contemporary attempts to identify antisemitism with anti-Zionist and anti-Israeli attitudes. These attempts all too often hinder our appreciation of the cumbersome British-Zionist nexus. The definition offered by the International Holocaust Remembrance Alliance (IHRA), tailored to address contemporary concerns rather than past processes, prevents us from acknowledging the extent to which, historically, imagery and discourse about Jews that could be easily described as "antisemitic" occupied a surprisingly central place in the complex web of relations between the British Empire and the Zionist movement.

This seemingly implausible phenomenon of evoking anti-Jewish stereotypes to support and justify Jewish nationalism is discernible, for example, in Winston Churchill's 1920 essay, "Zionism Versus Bolshevism." Composed about six months before the granting of the British Mandate over Palestine, the essay responded to growing alarm in British conservative circles over the leftward drift among second-generation Jewish immigrants in London. An ostensibly "sociological" discussion of the Jewish mentality lays the groundwork for the heart of Churchill's essay: a tripartite typology that distinguishes between three categories of Jews: "National Jews" (that is, patriotic Jews loyal to the state they reside in and in the British case, Churchill explains, this category consists of those declaring "I am an Englishman practising the Jewish faith"), "International Jews" (including a subset of "Terrorist Jews"), and Zionists. Karl Marx, Rosa Luxemburg, and Leon Trotsky are listed among the International Jews and described as dangerous radicals who abandoned the faith of their ancestors and adopted gross materialism and a strong desire to overthrow the existing European order as part, according to Churchill, of a "world-wide conspiracy for the overthrow of civilisation and for the reconstitution of society on the basis of arrested development, of envious malevolence, and impossible equality." National Jews, who "regard themselves as citizens in the fullest sense of the State which has received them," and especially Zionists like Chaim Weizmann, provided Churchill with a counterbalance to prevent Jews from streaming toward Bolshevism. The role of the British government, Churchill concluded, is to create "by the banks of the Jordan a Jewish State under the protection of the British Crown," which would not only promote the interests of the British Empire but also prevent the slide toward Bolshevism and play a central role in the "struggle for the soul of the Jewish people."[24]

Is Churchill's essay antisemitic or pro-Zionist? In my view, the question is essentially groundless precisely because the essay blatantly contains both elements. Its very manner of endorsing Zionism rests on crude anti-Jewish prejudice and stereotypes, associating Jews with an innate radical tendency that threatens the existing political order. Zionist historiography preferred to ignore such texts. Non-Jewish supporters of Jewish nationalism were labeled "philosemites" or "gentile Zionists" without questioning their motives or analyzing their underlying assumptions. From today's vantage point, it seems clearer that this labeling helped minimize the weight of other—colonialist and racist—impulses and motivations, which were translated into support of the Zionist movement.

The Uniqueness of the Postwar Moment: 1945–1948

As I have argued thus far, precisely because the term "antisemitism" encompasses such a broad range of behaviors, ideas, policies, and institutions, it offers a flawed general analytic category. Evoking the term makes it difficult to detect changes in forms and expressions of "anti-Jewishness" in Britain, which were remarkably unstable during World War II and the immediate postwar period. During the war, and particularly after Oswald Mosley's British Union of Fascists was declared illegal (1940), due to fear of a "fifth column" of Nazi supporters, antisemitic sentiments declined significantly, at least according to reports from the time, including by Jewish journalists and organizations.[25] In an essay he penned in February 1945, George Orwell also suggested that antisemitism had been almost eradicated in Britain: Jokes, expressions of derision, and other manifestations of banal, everyday anti-Jewish sentiment that had been common in Orwell's social and intellectual circles, the author declared, became so much more restrained upon the Nazi Party's ascendance to power that it seemed as though such expressions had disappeared entirely.[26]

The critical postwar years between 1945 and 1948 are a brief but dramatic historical moment that requires our attention precisely because it was rich in contradictions. On one hand, the triumph over Nazi Germany was the apogee of the myth of liberal, tolerant British exceptionalism. It was easy to present antisemitism as one of the toxic expressions of the foreign fascist regime that had just been annihilated. Furthermore, as G. Daniel Cohen has recently shown, the rise in popularity of the concept of "philosemitism" and the beginning of its use to signify "anti-antisemitism" are inextricably linked to this foundational moment.[27] On the other hand, this moment also witnessed increasing antisemitic publications and even violent incidents against Jews in Britain. What was the source of this hostility? A hint can be found in a speech delivered at the House of Lords by the Archbishop of York, Cyril Forster Garbett, in December 1945:

I dread anything like Anti-Semitism. I believe Anti-Semitism is un-Christian and irrational, but I notice with anxiety some signs of it—not yet very serious, but quite unmistakable—in this country. I cannot say too strongly that it is the duty of every Christian and of every freedom-loving citizen to do all in his power to resist and rebuke Anti-Semitism where-ever it shows itself. But the leaders of Jewish opinion have also a great responsibility. They can do much to restrain the persistent attacks against this country made by Jewish speakers and writers and by the Jewish Press on both sides of the Atlantic. Great Britain is being vehemently accused day by day of bad faith, of breaking its promises, of callous indifference to the sufferings of the Jews, and even of responsibility for the deaths of many thousands of them. These charges are not true, and are causing the greatest resentment among many who are conscious that this country has done more than any other to help the Jews. This resentment may very easily turn into indignant hostility. I dread what the result would be on public opinion at home if many of our soldiers in Palestine lose their lives at the hands of Jews. It is because I hate Anti-Semitism—we have seen sufficiently what it has meant on the Continent—that I appeal to Jewish leaders on both sides of the Atlantic to check this violent, and sometimes almost hysterical, anti-British propaganda which may easily lead to a most dangerous reaction.[28]

The archbishop's gloomy forecast was realized in the early days of August 1947, when a series of anti-Jewish incidents erupted around the country. It peaked with a wave of vandalism, looting, and violence directed against Jews—primarily shopkeepers and small business owners—in Liverpool, Manchester, and Glasgow. This wave of disturbances broke out against a backdrop of economic recession and severe austerity measures. The immediate trigger, however, was the anti-British terrorism of Jewish underground groups in Palestine, and the harsh public response to the kidnapping of two British sergeants by the underground Jewish group, the Irgun. Rioters went out to the streets shortly after the *Daily Express* published gruesome photos of the soldiers' hanged bodies.

Despite their magnitude, the anti-Jewish riots of the summer of 1947 almost completely vanished from the collective British and Anglo-Jewish memory. Similarly forgotten are the group defamations and slurs that led to a libel trial against James Caunt, a journalist in a local newspaper in Morecambe, Lancashire, who published a hate-filled editorial accusing British Jews of defending Jewish extremists with "face-saving propaganda" and urging American Jews to stop funding the terrorist activities of "Jewish scum" with their "ill-gotten wealth."[29] The historian Tony Kushner argues that the marginalization of these anti-Jewish incidents was made possible, inter alia, by presenting the wave of riots as a gut reaction to an overseas drama, thus dissociating the violence from its local context. Blaming Jews for the financial hardships of their non-Jewish neighbors, however, demonstrated the stubborn power of the "Shylock stereotype." All too briskly, the faraway terror of Jewish underground groups in a colonial struggle ignited a familiar pattern of hatred for the simple Jewish shopkeeper in a provincial town.[30]

I suggest that the friction between the domestic context and the broader imperial-political context animated much of the relationship between non-Jewish Britons and Jews during the twentieth century. A considerable tension can also be discerned in George Orwell's significant but not problem-free analysis of antisemitism in Britain. From a historical perspective, it seems clear that his essay evinces a post-Holocaust moment of spiritual reckoning and introspection, an attempt to reveal "banal," everyday antisemitism in order to uproot it. Orwell was acutely aware of the difficulty of the task he set for himself. He understood the naivete of presuming that the struggle against Nazi Germany would cause Britons to repudiate their anti-Jewish prejudice overnight. Still, one had to admit that the war forced them to temper their modes of expression, or at least to be ashamed of antisemitic statements. In Orwell's provocative formulation:

> Thanks to Hitler, therefore, you had a situation in which the press was in effect censored in favour of the Jews while in private antisemitism was on the up-grade, even, to some extent, among sensitive and intelligent people.[31]

In other words, antisemitism did not vanish from Britain as much as it went underground, turning into a discreet opinion kept hidden in the private sphere. It did not disappear but was tagged, particularly among members of the middle class, as dishonorable, disrespectful.

Orwell's interpretation of antisemitism is connected to his personal growth as an independent thinker of the Left, a process that required him to eschew the colonialist, conservative, and paternalistic worldviews of his youth. His commitment to progressive values notwithstanding, it is hard to ignore how an attempt to protect, at all costs, the image of the pure English working class sneaks into Orwell's analysis, making it seem that he was convinced that—unlike the "lower-upper-middle class" he was born into, as he memorably put it in *The Road to Wigan Pier*—authentic workers were free of any and all hatred of others. It is also possible to discern, between the lines, his firm disavowal of the clearly pro-Zionist stance that guided the Labour Party's position on the Palestine issue until 1939. Indeed, in his essay's conclusion, Orwell refused to view antisemitism as a unique phenomenon, insisting instead that it was one of the uglier manifestations of "the disease loosely called nationalism." And because this disease, he claimed, manifests everywhere with different symptoms, even Jews are not immune to it:

> A Jew, for example, would not be antisemitic: but then many Zionist Jews seem to me to be merely antisemites turned upside-down, just as many Indians and Negroes display the normal colour prejudices in an inverted form. The point is that something, some psychological vitamin, is lacking in modern civilization, and as a result we are all more or less subject to this lunacy of believing that whole races or nations are mysteriously good or mysteriously evil.[32]

Within a few months, Orwell's scrutiny of nationalism became starker.[33] Despite his criticism of British colonialism, he dismissed out-of-hand claims of mitigating circumstances for the armed Jewish resistance against British authorities in Palestine. He did not hide his agitation about the anti-British violence and inserted into his essay a fetid hint in the form of a rhetorical question: Perhaps, unlike the working class, members of the middle class were not so easily shocked by the image of British soldiers whose bodies had been dismembered by the bombs of Jewish terrorists?[34] The nasty comment aimed to upset his bourgeois readers. Later, New Left critiques sought to solve the problem Orwell confronted by offering a categorical identification of Jews with white imperialists. The new formula provided a solution to those who sought to "square the circle," that is, to adhere to anti-colonialist worldviews while simultaneously denigrating the anti-colonialist turn of the Zionist movement after World War II.

Clearly, the desire to reconceptualize antisemitism after 1945 was not unique to Orwell. It was part of the general postwar "realignment," a process that had at least three significant political and discursive ramifications. First, it required that a new kind of a "cultural code" and a new general category for Jews be designed, a category that now branded as "white settlers" those who, a few years earlier, had not been sufficiently "white." This process of cultural reimagining was not free of ethno-racial assumptions.

Second, the shift in emphasis that tied debates about attitudes toward Jews to colonialism and anti-colonial struggles helped divert the question of antisemitism from the domestic arena, away from the British Jewish community itself, and turn them into debates about overseas policies and diplomacy. With this act of "displacement," the local British Jewish community ceased to be the main object of discussions about antisemitism. Instead, they almost exclusively focused on British attitudes toward Israel. New tensions and contradictions emerged as a result. It is clear that pro-Palestinian organizations and lobbies established after 1967, like the Council for the Advancement of Arab-British Understanding and the Labour Middle East Council, adopted and improved models of discourse that mark Zionism as the undertaking of white colonists. They never called for discrimination against Jews residing in Britain. Nonetheless, in response Jewish organizations rushed to label this type of political activity as antisemitic.[35] This new dynamic had little to do with older forms of anti-Jewish behaviors or policies. It was shaped in a new context, as part of a struggle between pro-Israel and anti-Israel political lobbies. And precisely because the term was evoked so often in these debates, they can be described as marking a new chapter in the history of the term "antisemitism."

Third, the reconceptualization of antisemitism after 1945 dissociated discussions concerning the place of Jews in Britain from the discussion of a core question of British society at that time: the question of attitudes toward migrants and minorities. The legislation that exists in Britain today, meant to prevent racist discrimination, incitement to ethnic violence, and hate speech against nonwhite minorities, emerged not against the backdrop of the turbulent anti-Jewish events of the summer of 1947, but instead after later violent disturbances, such as the 1958 Notting Hill riots against Black immigrants from the Caribbean and defamatory speeches against nonwhite immigrants in the 1950s and 1960s.[36]

The attempt, in recent years, to promote legislation forbidding expressions of antisemitism separate from the existing legislation

designed to outlaw slurs against other ethnic groups in Britain continues the trend we see emerging after 1945, divorcing discussions about
antisemitism and anti-Jewish prejudices from a broader conversation
about intolerance, xenophobia, and hatred of minority communities.
The yearning to exceptionalize antisemitism and set it apart from other
patterns of prejudice can be seen as one of the products of the post-1945
cultural imagination. Differentiating Jews from other minority ethnic
or religious groups was one of its dominant features. Contemporary
populism confronts us with a challenge. The tendency to explain the
emergence of today's xenophobia as an expression of an identity crisis
of the "new," post-imperial white Brit makes it hard to discern the clear
continuity in the hostile behavioral patterns against those perceived
as foreign or other.

Coda

In this essay, I sketched a preliminary outline of the conceptual history of the terms "antisemitism" and "the Jewish question" in Britain.
I believe that we can reach several tentative conclusions from this exercise. First, the widespread, vernacular uses of the word "antisemitism"
and the adjective "antisemitic," and even the early theoretical, academic
usages of the concept, attest to a sense of uniqueness and positive
British exceptionalism in the use of these expressions. This attitude is
anchored in a historic and mythic worldview, a British version of the
Sonderweg thesis, which claimed that the course of German history was
radically different from that of its neighbors. Many historians adopted
this "Whig" conception uncritically, by osmosis. Part of the challenge
facing us today relates to the paradoxical fact that locating usages of the
term "antisemitism" in the English language will not necessarily help us
understand the patterns of discrimination and expressions of enmity
against Jews because the term actually represents self-glorifying,
exceptionalist British sentiments. This exceptionalism flows into the
populist surge that threatens to drown contemporary British politics
in the era of Brexit.

Second, I believe that David Engel's call for historians to demonstrate greater awareness of the problems inherent in the concept of

"antisemitism" and its limitations as an analytic or hermeneutic concept would find an attentive audience in historians focused on modern Britain. I do not believe that the tenacity of the adjective "antisemitic" proves its worth in helping us decipher the particular cultural and political codes of nineteenth-century Britain or the far-reaching changes in attitudes toward Jews and the shifting meanings of the very term "antisemitism" that we recognize as taking place in interwar and postwar Britain. As an analytic concept, "antisemitism" is quite limited. As I have tried to show, it does not help us illuminate an essential ambivalence that is ingrained in British discussions of "the Jewish question" at one end of the spectrum or attitudes toward Zionism and the State of Israel at the other end. The term antisemitism does not enable us to apprehend how the Jews of England and the British Empire contended with discourse about race and class.

Finally, the term does not help us distinguish the new models of discourse, generated after 1945 against the backdrop of decolonization and the Holocaust, from earlier discursive conventions, patterns of representation and cultural practices that shaped the attitude toward Jews in British public discourse. Indeed, much of the power of the vernacular usage of the word "antisemitism" lies in its ability to obscure this fundamental change over time and place and assume a persistent, perverse continuity. The case of modern Britain thus exemplifies Engel's claim well: Here the concept "antisemitism" has not proven itself to be a useful analytic category or a reliable yardstick.

Ultimately, the overuse of the word "antisemitism" in contemporary debates blurs the distinction between the vernacular term and the theoretical concept, thus impairing our ability to grasp the phenomenon historically. To clarify, I am not calling for the cancellation of the field of research about antisemitism, nor am I sticking my head in the sand, declaring that prejudice against Jews is a thing of the past. My suggestion is entirely different: The time has come to eliminate the artificial dichotomy between contemporary antisemitism and contemporary models of prejudice and xenophobia. My second suggestion is to pay greater attention to questions of agency: When we examine the cultural construction and language of "race," nation, color, and national origin, we must not assume that Jews were only objects of hatred but also identify the cases where Jews played an active role as theoreticians, writers, and scientists contributing to the discourse about Jews from the inside.

The recent, excessively politicized debate concerning the concept "antisemitism" has not helped us connect Jewish history to the core areas of twentieth-century British history, which is centered around questions of decolonization, migration, and class tensions. A dialectical stance toward "Continental" Europe and refugees and other migrants continues to shape British society and politics today. The link between this dialectical attitude and the ambivalent status of the Jew in British culture awaits the attention of historians.

NOTES

1. David Nirenberg, *Anti-Judaism: The Western Tradition* (New York: W. W. Norton, 2013); Jonathan Judaken, guest ed., "*AHR* Roundtable: Rethinking Antisemitism," *American Historical Review* 123, no. 4 (October 2018): 1122–38.

2. Colin Holmes, *Anti-Semitism in British Society, 1876–1939* (London: Arnold, 1979).

3. Anthony Julius, *Trials of the Diaspora: A History of Anti-Semitism in England* (Oxford: Oxford University Press, 2010).

4. Shulamit Volkov, *Germans, Jews, and Antisemites: Trials in Emancipation* (Cambridge: Cambridge University Press, 2006).

5. George L. Mosse, *Toward the Final Solution: A History of European Racism* (New York: H. Fertig, 1978).

6. Friedrich Wilhelm Nietzsche, *On the Genealogy of Morality*, trans. Carol Diethe (New York: Cambridge University Press, 1994), 53.

7. David Feldman, "Toward a History of the Term 'Anti-Semitism,'" *American Historical Review* 123, no. 4 (October 2018): 1139–50.

8. James Parkes, *The Jewish Problem in the Modern World* (London: T. Butterworth, 1939).

9. Harold Nicolson, *Diaries and Letters*, vol. 2, ed. Nigel Nicolson (New York: Atheneum, 1967), 469.

10. Jacob Toury, "'The Jewish Question': A Semantic Approach," *The Leo Baeck Institute Year Book* 11, no. 1 (1966): 85–106.

11. Holly Case, *The Age of Questions: Or, a First Attempt at an Aggregate History of the Eastern, Social, Woman, American, Jewish, Polish, Bullion, Tuberculosis, and Many Other Questions over the Nineteenth Century, and Beyond* (Princeton, NJ: Princeton University Press, 2018), 154–57.

12. See, for example, "General Gascoyne and the Representation of Liverpool," *Liverpool Mercury*, May 28, 1830 (issue 995); "Two Lectures upon Jewish Claims," *Freeman's Journal and Daily Commercial Advertiser* (Dublin), August 4, 1841; "Society for Promoting Christianity amongst the Jews," *The Essex Standard, and General Advertiser for the Eastern Counties* (Colchester), August 6, 1841 (issue 553).

13. Todd Endelman, *The Jews of Georgian England, 1714–1830: Tradition and Change in a Liberal Society* (Ann Arbor: University of Michigan, 1999).

14. The sole exception that I have found is from an 1840 article that refers to "the Jewish question" in the context of a report about the Damascus "Blood Libel": "Egypt and Syria," *The Bury and Norwich Post, and East Anglian* (Bury Saint Edmunds), September 16, 1840 (issue 3038).

15. Abigail Green, *Moses Montefiore: Jewish Liberator, Imperial Hero* (Cambridge, MA: Belknap Press, 2010), see especially chap. 12.

16. Ibid.; Abigail Green, "Old Networks, New Connections: The Emergence of the Jewish International," in *Religious Internationals in the Modern World: Globalization and Faith Communities since 1750*, ed. Abigail Green and Vincent Viaene (London: Palgrave Macmillan, 2012), 53–81.

17. Herbert Butterfield, *The Whig Interpretation of History* (London: G. Bell and Sons, 1931).

18. Paul Crook, "Social Darwinism and British 'New Imperialism': Second Thoughts," *European Legacy* 3, no. 1 (1998): 1–16.

19. John Rhys, *Celtic Britain* (London: Society for Promoting Christian Knowledge, 1882); John Beddoe, *The Races of Britain: A Contribution to the Anthropology of Western Europe* (Bristol: J. W. Arrowsmith, 1885). Rhys was appointed the inaugural chair of Celtic at Oxford University after Matthew Arnold publicly lamented the lack of such a position. Beddoe was the founding president of the Anthropological Society of London and president of the Anthropological Institute of Great Britain and Ireland.

20. John M. Efron, *Defenders of the Race: Jewish Doctors and Race Science in Fin-de-Siècle Europe* (New Haven, CT: Yale University Press, 1994).

21. Joseph Jacobs, "On the Racial Characteristics of Modern Jews," *Journal of the Anthropological Institute of Great Britain and Ireland* 15 (1886): 23–62; Joseph Jacobs, "The Comparative Distribution of Jewish Ability," *Journal of the Anthropological Institute of Great Britain and Ireland* 15 (1886): 351–79.

22. Joseph Jacobs, *The Jewish Question, 1875–1884, Bibliographical Hand-List* (London: Trübner, 1885).

23. Arie M. Dubnov, "'True Art Makes for the Integration of the Race': Israel Zangwill and the Varieties of the Jewish Normalization Discourse in Fin-de-Siècle Britain," in *New Directions in Anglo-Jewish History*, ed. Geoffrey Alderman (Boston: Academic Studies Press, 2010), 101–34.

24. Winston S. Churchill, "Zionism Versus Bolshevism: A Struggle for the Soul of the Jewish People," *Illustrated Sunday Herald*, February 8, 1920, 5.

25. Jewish Central Information Office, *Organised Antisemitism in Great Britain, 1942–1946* (London: Jewish Central Information Office, 1946).

26. George Orwell, "Antisemitism in Britain," *Contemporary Jewish Record*, April 1945. Reprinted in *The Collected Essays, Journalism, and Letters of George Orwell* (New York: Harcourt, 1968), 332–41.

27. G. Daniel Cohen, "Between Pity and Solidarity: 'Philosemitism' in Western Europe, 1945–1950," paper presented in the international workshop "1948: The Jewish Quest for Rights and Justice in the Postwar Moment" (Brandeis University: The Tauber Institute for the Study of European Jewry, April 2018).

28. Cyril Garbett, the Lord Archbishop of York, "The Jewish Problem," *Hansard*, HL Deb, December 10, 1945, vol. 138, cc. 506–10.

29. The original article, published on August 6, 1947, was reprinted in a volume published by Caunt shortly after he was acquitted of seditious libel. The volume also included the transcript of the trial and a second, even more tenacious article, in which Caunt reiterated his earlier statements and celebrated his acquittal as a triumph of free speech. The matter was briefly discussed in the House of Commons, following a suggestion made by Henry ("Harry") Hynd, Labour MP for Central Hackney, that the Home Department should "seek further legislative powers to enable anti-semitism to be dealt with." To the best of my knowledge, the discussion did not advance beyond that point. See James Caunt, *An Editor on Trial. Rex v. Caunt: Alleged Seditious Libel* (Morecambe and Heysham: Morecambe Press, 1948); H. Hynd, James Ede, and John Platts-Mills, "Anti-Semitism (Legal Proceedings)," *Hansard* HC, December 1, 1947, vol. 445, cc. 32. For further discussion, see Thomas D. Jones, "Group Defamation under British, Canadian, Indian and Nigerian Law," *International Journal on Minority and Group Rights* 5, no. 3 (1997): 281–335; Christopher Hilliard, "Words That Disturb the State: Hate Speech and the Lessons of Fascism in Britain, 1930s–1960s," *Journal of Modern History* 88, no. 4 (2016): 764–96.

30. Tony Kushner, "Anti-Semitism and Austerity: The August 1947 Riots in Britain," in *Racial Violence in Britain in the Nineteenth and Twentieth Centuries*, ed. Panikos Panayi (Leicester: Leicester University Press, 1996), 149–68.

31. Orwell, "Antisemitism."

32. Ibid.

33. George Orwell, "Notes on Nationalism," in *England Your England and Other Essays* (London: Secker & Warburg, 1953), 41–67.

34. Giora Goodman, "George Orwell and the Palestine Question," *The European Legacy* 20, no. 4 (2015): 321–33.

35. James R. Vaughan, "'Mayhew's Outcasts': Anti-Zionism and the Arab Lobby in Harold Wilson's Labour Party," *Israel Affairs* 21, no. 1 (2015): 27–47.

36. Kennetta Hammond Perry, "'Little Rock' in Britain: Jim Crow's Transatlantic Topographies," *Journal of British Studies* 51, no. 1 (2012): 155–77.

13

A Retreat from Universalism
Opposing and Defining Antisemitism and Islamophobia in Britain, ca. 1990–2018

DAVID FELDMAN

1

Antisemitism is a socially constructed category, David Engel observes in his essay "Away from a Definition of Antisemitism." When we call something or someone "antisemitic," he points out, we exercise our judgment and align that case with others that we think it resembles. Engel also reminds us that the category "antisemitism" has a history. The stem *antisemit* first achieved currency in a particular place and moment, and its meaning has changed over time. When it came into usage in Germany in the early 1880s, *antisemit* referred specifically to individuals and groups who believed it had been a great mistake to allow Jews civil and political equality in the new German Reich. Yet by the mid-1890s, Engel argues, the meaning of *antisemit* had expanded to encompass "a broad range of utterances and actions by non-Jews that had opposed Jewish interests or threatened Jews throughout the ages." This enlarged concept of antisemitism, he suggests, became fixed and has shaped what historians have written on the subject ever since, leading them to assume a relationship across time and space between "particular instances of violence, hostile depiction, agitation, discrimination, and private unfriendly feeling" directed at Jews. This practice, Engel argues, has been sustained for communal and political reasons, but among historians it has become a barrier to understanding. By revealing the contingent origins of the category of antisemitism, Engel's purpose is to expose and criticize the unreflective way in which historians have employed the term.[1] He advises scholars to develop new frameworks with which to better analyze the elements conventionally brought together beneath the umbrella term "antisemitism." In short, Engel begins with an analysis and a brief history of a category—antisemitism—and ends up advising us to return to the social and political history that the concept "antisemitism" purports to grasp, but to do so armed with finer tools.

In an essay published in 2018, I developed Engel's insights in two directions. First, I argued that the meanings invested in "antisemitism" did not freeze in 1890 but continued to change thereafter.[2] This history is longer and more diverse than Engel allows. Second, I suggested that this history unfolded as Jews claimed new rights in the nineteenth and twentieth centuries—equal civil rights, minority rights, human rights, national rights. New rights and norms extended the sorts of discrimination, activity, and speech that Jews and their allies were able to regard as illegitimate and, hence, label antisemitic. It follows from this second argument that although Engel is correct when he tells us that antisemitism is a socially constructed category, it is also more than this. In describing actions as antisemitic, Jews have not only classified those actions, they have also declared them to be unjust and unacceptable. Actors employing the term "antisemitism" not only describe the world, but they also seek to change it.[3]

The present essay extends this argument in new ways. It highlights changes in the concept of antisemitism in the last decade of the twentieth century and in the early twenty-first century. It considers this history alongside parallel changes in how racism more broadly and Islamophobia in particular have been conceived. In doing so it suggests that these changes in the concept of antisemitism are an episode not only in Jewish history but also in the history of anti-racist movements. The core of the essay examines attempts in the present century to persuade governments and other bodies to adopt and promote particular definitions of antisemitism and Islamophobia. It asks how the concepts of antisemitism and Islamophobia changed in these years and what difference in the world these changes were intended to make.

The events narrated and analyzed here spill over geographical and temporal boundaries. I focus on events in Britain but, as we shall see, these developments interacted with initiatives in Europe and the United States. This essay ends in 2018 with the publication of a new definition of Islamophobia. However, the debates with which it deals remain unresolved.[4]

2

In 1994 the Runnymede Trust, a think tank and campaign organization, convened a commission on "the persistence and dangers of antisemitism." The commission's report, entitled *A Very Light Sleeper*, included a hope that the Trust would set up a similar body "to study prejudice against Muslims and Islam."[5] The term Islamophobia had begun to figure in public debate from the early 1990s.[6] In the twenty-first century, some scholars—notably anthropologists and sociologists—began to argue that Islamophobia and antisemitism should be conceived within a single frame of analysis. They emphasized the common roots of antisemitism and Islamophobia in a conception of Europe that has been essentially Christian.[7] Their attempts to highlight the shared origins of antisemitism and Islamophobia also addressed a political context in which many others—politicians, policy makers, and pundits—construed Islamism and antisemitism as twin and connected enemies of the West.[8] The contemporary articulation of this idea can be traced to the Gulf War of 1991 but still more to the attacks on the World Trade Center and the Pentagon on September 11, 2001. In the years that followed, Muslim populations globally, and not least in Britain, were identified both as a security threat and as a source of antisemitism.[9] In the face of this focus on Islam and Muslims as sources of enmity to the West and to Jews, the decisions of scholars to highlight the similarities or connections between antisemitism and Islamophobia motioned toward the possibility of a countervailing Muslim-Jewish alliance.

Yet in contrast to the common sources of antisemitism and Islamophobia emphasized by academics and policy experts, the conditions shaping the lives of Jews and Muslims in Britain have been moving in opposite directions. Jews comprise a shrinking population in Britain and Europe. By contrast, the Muslim population is growing. Despite the toll taken by the Nazis and their allies, European Jewry numbered just below 4 million in 1945, and the question of how to integrate a religious minority in Europe remained, in the first instance, a question of how to integrate Jews.[10] Nearly eight decades later this is no longer the case. Today there are approximately 1.4 million Jews in Europe and more than 25 million Muslims in the twenty-eight countries of the European Union. In 2010 the number of Jews in the United Kingdom had fallen below 300,000, a reduction of twenty-five percent over the previous fifty years, whereas the Muslim population had grown by a factor of ten and stood at 3.4 million.[11]

There are also substantial economic and social differences between Muslims and Jews in Europe. In Britain, Muslims are the religious population most likely to live in poverty, whereas Jews are the least likely. At the other end of the social scale, Muslims are the religious group least represented in "top professions" in proportion to their total number, and Jews are the most highly represented. These different experiences create spatial as well as social distance: Whereas forty-six percent of the Muslim population lives in the top ten percent of the most deprived areas in England, the figure for Jews is just three percent.[12]

Divergences in social class between Jews and Muslims are supplemented by political and attitudinal differences. Jews and Muslims tend to have contrary allegiances in the conflicts between Israel and Palestine.[13] In the domestic political arena, there are also striking dissimilarities. In the United Kingdom over the last fifty years the political allegiance of Jews has shifted from left to right, away from the Labour Party and toward the Conservative Party. Muslims, however, continue to vote for the Labour Party in disproportionate numbers.[14]

If we turn from these allegiances to the ways in which Jews and Muslims figure in public debate, we find another divergence. Jews have been portrayed by political leaders in the United Kingdom as a model minority—law-abiding, aspiring, and having a strong sense of collective identity that dovetails with patriotism. Muslims, by contrast, are presented as a group that places itself and others in jeopardy—inhabiting a culture of poverty, insufficiently integrated into Western society, and harboring sympathy for terrorism.[15]

This pattern of separation and divergence between Jews and Muslims is modified but also extended by experiences of racism. Both Jews and Muslims suffer hostile commentary, negative stereotyping, physical abuse, and are the targets of hate crime. However, the racism experienced by Muslims reaches into economic and social life, and notably into the labor market, to a degree that it does not for Jews.[16]

Racism also shapes relations between Jews and Muslims. Antisemitic attitudes are more extensively present among Muslims than within the population as a whole. An extensive survey of antisemitism in Britain, published in September 2017, discovered that most Muslims do not respond positively to antisemitic statements but, at the same time, it found that antisemitic statements are between two and four times more likely to receive assent within the Muslim population in Great Britain than among the population as a whole. For example, whereas twenty-seven percent of Muslims agreed with the statement that Jews have too much power in Britain, the figure among the total population is just eight percent.[17] We cannot say whether Islamophobia among Jews is above or below average because the necessary research has never been undertaken. We can say, nevertheless, that some Jews regard the growing Muslim population as an existential threat. In autumn 2017 the plan to convert a theater, located in a part of London with a large Jewish population, into an Islamic center and mosque was met with a petition of opposition that gathered 5,676 signatures. Comments on the Facebook page of "Golders Green together" illustrate that Jews were one source of hostility to Muslims and Islam in this protest. The local council hid from public view residents' responses to the planning application, so bitter had the controversy become. One person wrote as follows:

> We don't want a mosque and who can blame us? Those Muslims purposely picked Golders Green because it is a Jewish area. They want to stamp us out.... It's one of the only Jewish areas left in London and we don't want it polluted and destroyed by a bunch of Jew-hating Muslim terrorists.[18]

In the face of these social and political influences separating Jews and Muslims, an ethical commitment to anti-racism conceived in universalist terms generated the idea that the struggle against antisemitism and Islamophobia should be conjoined. In the 1990s the Runnymede Trust was one influential source of this type of anti-racist engagement. In *A Very Light Sleeper*, the Runnymede Trust Commission on Antisemitism highlighted similarities and overlaps between antisemitism and Islamophobia: Both sorts of prejudice perceived Jews and Muslims as foreigners and intruders in European society; both contained a strong religious component dating back to medieval Christianity; both required similar educational, legal, and political measures as remedies; and both were connected to the global politics of the Middle East.[19] However, beyond these historical and contemporary connections, Runnymede linked its work countering antisemitism to its "holistic and indivisible" struggle against racism.[20] From this standpoint it became possible to think of antisemitism and Islamophobia within a single framework.

In 1997 in *Islamophobia: A Challenge for Us All*, the Runnymede Trust anatomized and analyzed Islamophobia in the context of the same liberal, social democratic, and pluralist values that it had brought to bear on antisemitism three years earlier. "The term Islamophobia," the report stated, "refers to unfounded hostility towards Islam." This hostility had malign consequences: unfair discrimination against Muslim individuals and communities and the exclusion of Muslims from mainstream political and social affairs. The roots of the problem, the report claimed, lay in prejudice and faulty cognition. The solution would be found in respect for empirical variation (in order to undermine any negative generalization about Islam or Muslims) and rational debate. The goal of policy should be to promote equal opportunities and harmonious relations between members of different communities. The report's key recommendation was to extend antidiscrimination legislation to cover religious as well as ethnic minorities.[21]

This alliance against antisemitism and Islamophobia based on a commitment to equal opportunities, cultural pluralism, and the repudiation of prejudice was a fragile construction. In the mid-1990s, British Jewry continued to provide significant support for a liberal and universalist anti-racism. The eleven Runnymede Trust Commissioners responsible for *A Very Light Sleeper* included five Jews: Neville Nagler, the chief executive of the Board of Deputies of British Jews; Geoffrey Alderman, an eminent historian with a connection to the strictly Orthodox Federation of Synagogues; Julia Neuberger, a leading Reform rabbi and a senior member of the Liberal Democrats; Ivor Crewe, a leading political scientist; and Antony Lerman, director of the Institute of Jewish Affairs. However, a symposium on antisemitism published in 1991 had already revealed misgivings among Jews who were conservative politically. The historian and peer Max Beloff expressed his concern at the rapid growth of the Muslim population and questioned whether "multiculturalism" is "good for the Jews." Julius Gould, a sociologist connected to right-wing think tanks, resisted anti-racism—which he derided as "a form of social bullying"—and multiculturalism.[22] Both conservatives and progressives were keenly aware of the capacity of Zionism to divide Muslims and Jews. Lord Jakobovits, the chief rabbi and an ally of the Conservative prime minister Margaret Thatcher, believed that antisemitism in the 1990s was fostered by and manifested in anti-Zionism. "The emergence of Islamic fundamentalism is therefore of critical importance," he added.[23]

These apprehensions contributed to the difficulty of translating opposition to antisemitism and Islamophobia into an alliance between Jews and Muslims. The Runnymede Trust Commission on Antisemitism observed regretfully that the Arab-Israeli conflict is seen frequently as a Jewish-Muslim conflict and for this reason it could be "very difficult" for Jewish and Muslim organizations "to establish sufficient mutual trust to be able to work together on anti-racist projects to combat antisemitism and Islamophobia together."[24] It expressed unease about the prevalence of antisemitic conspiracy theories among Muslims and the content of sermons in mosques after Friday prayers when "Palestine is often taken as the subject" and "Muslim anti-Zionism does sometimes use, or appear to use, antisemitic ideas or references."[25] The report conveys a sense of the friability of the anti-racist alliance it aimed to construct.

The political divisions that made it hard for Jews and Muslims to ally against Islamophobia and antisemitism became more marked in the twenty-first century. The year 2000 witnessed an upswing in antisemitic incidents. This rise, in turn, reflected heightened tension and violence in Israel/Palestine following the failure of the Camp David peace talks in July 2000 and the outbreak of the Second Intifada in September of that year.[26] At the same time, Jewish and non-Jewish targets across the globe were subject to murderous attacks in the name of jihad. Mainstream Jewish organizations were now more likely to see Britain's Muslim population as a problem and less as a potential ally against antisemitism.[27] These fears and suspicions appeared to be confirmed in 2006, when an opinion poll published in *The Times* found that thirty-seven percent of Muslims questioned agreed that the Jewish community was a legitimate target in the struggle for justice in the Middle East.[28] Later that year, the All-Party Parliamentary Inquiry into Antisemitism (APPIA) published a report that dedicated just two pages each to antisemitism on the Far Right, on the Left, in the media, and on the internet but devoted six full pages to Muslims and antisemitism.

3

At the same time as sections of the Jewish community felt growing perturbation in the face of the Muslim population, they began to formulate an alternative to the liberal and universalist formulation of anti-antisemitism as it had been expressed, for example, in *A Very Light Sleeper*. This can be seen clearly in the September 2006 report from the APPIA, which was conceived by the All-Party Parliamentary Group Against Antisemitism. Chaired by a former minister, the Labour MP Denis MacShane, and undertaken by thirteen other members of Parliament, the inquiry received oral and written evidence from more than a hundred witnesses, including the Board of Deputies of British Jews and the Community Security Trust (CST), a charitable organization whose role had been and continues to be providing protection and advice to the Jewish community.[29] The report that ensued called for a change in the way antisemitism was conceived, both in public debate and in policy making. This shift had two components. The first concerned who had the right to define antisemitism. The second element was substantive and concerned what the definition of antisemitism should be. Both changes were promoted forcefully by Jewish leaders in Britain, Europe, and the United States.

The 2006 report insisted that Jews themselves or, in effect, their representatives in mainstream communal organizations and NGOs, had the prerogative to identify and define antisemitism. It derived this doctrine from *The Stephen Lawrence Inquiry*, a report arising from the murder of Stephen Lawrence—a Black teenager stabbed to death in April 1993 in South East London—that was published in 1999. Written by Sir William Macpherson, a retired high court judge, the inquiry aimed "to identify the lessons to be learned from the investigation and prosecution of racially motivated crimes." The 2006 APPIA report stated, "We support the view expressed in the Macpherson report that a racist act is defined by its victim."[30] However, this was not at all what Macpherson had written. His report had proposed that "a racist incident" (not act) should be defined "as any incident which is perceived to be racist by the victim or any other person." Macpherson explained that all racist incidents should be reported, recorded, and investigated by the police.[31] In other words, Macpherson was not engaged in defining *a racist act* but *a racist incident*, and in his mind, *a racist incident* was an event that required investigation; it was something yet to be categorized definitively as *a racist act*. In short, the APPIA's attribution of its doctrine to Macpherson was an invention.

Although false, the APPIA's claim—that a racist act is defined by its victim—has been repeated on countless occasions, not least by Jewish communal leaders as well as by campaigners for a legal definition of Islamophobia.[32] The APPIA's misreading of Macpherson gained traction because it drew on a rising current of law and opinion that placed emphasis on the experiences and perceptions of the victims of discrimination and hate crimes. This current can be traced to the interpretaion of harassment under the 1976 Race Relations Act, which held that "any remark, insult or act the purpose or effect of which is to violate another person's dignity or create an intimidating, hostile, degrading, humiliating or offensive environment for him is [*sic*] antisemitic."[33] The 2006 report provides an example of a widespread shift away from definitions of racism based on general principles—exemplified by the two Runnymede Trust reports on antisemitism and Islamophobia published in

1994 and 1997—toward a greater emphasis on the lived experience and self-understanding of minority groups.[34]

Having established to its own satisfaction that Jewish representatives should define antisemitism, the APPIA moved on to promote its preferred definition. Its first and main recommendation was that the British government and law enforcement agencies should adopt and promote the working definition of antisemitism drawn up the previous year by Jewish NGOs and academics at the request of the director of the European Union Monitoring Commission on Racism and Xenophobia (EUMC), Beate Winkler.[35] More than a decade later, in 2016, this would provide the foundation for the working definition of antisemitism promoted by the International Holocaust Remembrance Alliance (IHRA) and subsequently adopted by thirty-eight states, as well as numerous other governmental and intergovernmental institutions and civil society organizations. In short, it has been central to the reconceptualization of antisemitism in the early twenty-first century.

The EUMC was established in 1997 by the European Union to provide data for policies to counter racism. Its remit required it to develop "common indicators, working definitions and methodologies" for data collection by itself and by other organizations.[36] The EUMC had originally addressed antisemitism in a way that was similar to the approach taken by the Runnymede Trust in the 1990s. In its report *Manifestation of Antisemitism in the EU, 2002–2003*, it had focused on representations of the stereotypical "Jew": for instance, on depictions of Jews as greedy, deceptive, or conspiratorial. This way of identifying antisemitism as a collection of timeworn stereotypes held significant implications for how the EUMC categorized the hostility directed at Jews in Europe when they were attacked as proxies of Israel. According to the EUMC, these attacks were not to be classified as antisemitic when they did not correspond to one of their acknowledged stereotypes of "the Jew": Instead, they were branded "a serious threat to basic European values and democracy."[37]

The EUMC's position did not satisfy key Jewish NGOs, including the American Jewish Committee (AJC), the European Jewish Congress, the Community Security Trust (CST), and the Israeli academics with whom they worked—notably, Professor Dina Porat, who was then director of Tel Aviv University's Stephen Roth Institute for the Study of Contemporary Antisemitism and Racism. Kenneth Stern, director of the division on antisemitism and extremism at the AJC, argued that what mattered was the selection of a victim because they were a Jew, not the cause or justification for the attack.[38] His case was dramatized in April 2004, shortly before Winkler was due to address the annual meeting of the AJC, when a Jewish school in Montreal was firebombed in retaliation for the killing of a Hamas leader by the Israeli army. Stern and his AJC colleagues seized on the event to persuade Winkler to consider a different approach. In the months that followed, a group drawn from Jewish NGOs and academics worked to produce a new working definition of antisemitism, which was then further modified in discussion with the EUMC.[39]

The new working definition had a twofold function. In part, it was an attempt to ensure that criticism and violence directed at Jews living outside Israel that took them as proxies for the State of Israel would be regarded, recorded, and condemned as antisemitism. In part, however, it was also an attempt to revise the prevailing and conventional meaning of antisemitism so that it would encompass criticisms of Israel that seemed to the architects of the EUMC working definition to be unfair or unhinged.[40] Notoriously, this kind of criticism had surfaced at the United Nations World Conference Against Racism, Racial Discrimination, Xenophobia and Racial Intolerance, held in Durban, South Africa, in August and September 2001, and especially at the NGO forum that preceded the conference. Here, the charge that Zionism is racism had been revived, representatives of Jewish NGOs were shocked by the antisemitism they encountered, and the United States and Israel delegations withdrew from the conference itself. As Kenneth Marcus and Antony Lerman have demonstrated, these events led to a series of initiatives that aimed to shift the meaning of antisemitism so that it would more clearly encompass some forms of anti-Zionism and severe criticism of Israel. The EUMC working definition was one element in this larger project.[41]

The document that became known as the EUMC working definition of antisemitism began vaguely: "Antisemitism is a certain perception of Jews, which may be expressed as hatred of Jews." However, the key point was precisely expressed next: namely, that manifestations of anti-semitism "could also target the state of Israel, conceived as a Jewish collectivity." The largest part of the document was taken up by examples that, "taking into account the overall context," could be instances of antisemitism. These examples were presented in two lists; the first list dealt with antisemitism as it had been conventionally conceived. The second list dealt with manifestations of antisemitism that arose in the context of debate and protest over Israel. The latter included "denying the Jewish people their right to self-determination, e.g., by claiming that the existence of the state of Israel is a racist endeavour"; "applying double standards by requiring of it behaviour not expected or demanded of any other democratic nation"; and "holding Jews collectively responsible for the actions of the state of Israel."[42] This last example directly addressed the predicament of Jews living outside of Israel who faced attack because they were taken as proxies for Israel. However, taken as a whole, the list went further than this. As we can see from the other examples above, it also encompassed anti-Zionism and some sorts of criticism of Israel.

The Board of Deputies of British Jews and the 2006 report promoted the EUMC working definition of antisemitism. Just as the working definition not only pointed to moments when Jews were held collectively responsible for Israel's actions (either through physical attack or the use of antisemitic stereotypes) but also set out to categorize some anti-Zionist and anti-Israel rhetoric and arguments as antisemitic, so too the Board of Deputies and the Community Security Trust (CST) highlighted these twin dimensions in their written testimony to the APPIA. Using an argument similar to the one set out by Stern, the CST explained that "Jewish people and property have been attacked for their Jewishness...This is a basic building block of antisemitism and should not be obscured by the fact that events in the Middle East appear to be a catalyst for attacks."[43] The board emphasized the way in which "the language of Jew-hate" was brought to bear on Israel, and it commended the working definition as "an important step forward" in allowing police forces and other bodies "to identify discrimination in their midst."[44] However, both organizations also complained that antisemitism "now has a national focus on the collective identity of

Jews, the state of Israel" and protested that Israel is "singled out for extraordinary criticism" as a result of which British Jews who feel connected to Israel "become political pariahs."[45] In short, their analysis of antisemitism was a response to two developments: first, the elements in anti-Zionist and anti-Israel politics that employed antisemitic stereotypes or that targeted Jewish bodies and property and, second, the ways in which the attack on Israel as a rogue state were renewed at Durban.

Unlike previous efforts, the EUMC working definition did not situate its expanded definition of antisemitism within a universalist anti-racist framework that aimed to promote human rights and safeguard the rights of minorities more broadly.[46] In view of Israel's sustained dominion beyond its internationally recognized boundaries, its denial there of rights and freedoms to Palestinians, and in the face of global criticism of Israel on universalist grounds as a racist state, it is easy to understand why universalist rhetoric did not come readily to those who drafted the working definition and others who supported it.[47] Yet the abandonment of universalism was only partial. Jewish leaders in Britain were caught between their support for Israel, which as we have seen drew them away from universalist anti-racism, and their defense of Jewish interests as a minority in Britain, which led them to depend on legal protections cast in universalist terms. Universalism still offered rewards to Jewish NGOs when it provided an apparatus with which to combat discrimination and antisemitism. For instance, the APPIA report in 2006 placed its recommendations in the context of existing race-relations legislation and the work of the government's Commission on Racial Equality. In 2015, when the All-Party Parliamentary Group Against Antisemitism carried out a follow-up inquiry, the Board of Deputies fully endorsed the 2010 Equality Act: The legal framework it had established "made it clearer what constitutes antisemitism and antisemitic discrimination."[48]

The retreat from universalism was piecemeal and driven by the politics of Israel/Palestine. Leading Anglo-Jewish communal organizations were now suspicious of the anti-racist political movement. In part this was because they believed the movement's universalism did not extend to Jews: that its sympathy for the Palestinians led it to be indifferent (or worse) to antisemitism.[49] The 2006 report recommended that the

Foreign and Commonwealth Office give full support to the work against antisemitism being undertaken in Europe by the Organization for Security and Co-operation in Europe (OSCE), the European Union, and the Council of Europe but counseled them tartly to "avoid the temptation to bury the specific problem of antisemitism in a wider context of anti-racism."[50] This tendency was even more marked in 2015.[51] In its report that year, the APPGAA raised the issue of racism only to highlight the specificity of antisemitism.[52] It placed renewed emphasis on the impact of conflict in Israel/Palestine on Jews' feelings of fear and anxiety. This perspective was underpinned by findings from a survey into Jews' perceptions and experiences of antisemitism. Both the survey itself and the use made of it in the 2015 report emphasized the shift toward experience as a yardstick to measure racism.[53] This was some distance from the standpoint of the Runnymede reports of the 1990s.

Finally, having been sidelined by the Fundamental Rights Agency (the successor to the EUMC), the working definition of antisemitism reemerged in 2016, slightly amended but clearly recognizable, in the form of a document, adopted by the International Holocaust Remembrance Alliance (IHRA) at a conference held in Bucharest in May 2016.[54] In 2012 the IHRA developed from the Task Force for International Cooperation on Holocaust Education, Remembrance and Research created in 1998 on the initiative of the Swedish prime minister Göran Persson with the support of Bill Clinton and Tony Blair. The use of this international NGO to bring the working definition back to life was a coup and an opportunity for its supporters. In December that year the British government was the first to adopt the IHRA working definition as a non-legally binding definition of antisemitism. This decisively codified the retreat of anti-antisemitism from universalist anti-racism.[55]

4

We have seen how the campaign against antisemitism in the United Kingdom responded not only to developments that affected Jewish people but also to changes in anti-racist thinking and policy. The latter can be seen, for example, in the role played by the Runnymede Trust and the (mis)use of the Macpherson report. The influence of changing anti-racist ideas and politics was evident, not least in the retreat from universalism and the move to address antisemitism independently of racism more broadly. The black-white binary that had characterized anti-racist politics in the 1970s and 1980s had begun to fragment by the last decade of the twentieth century, as activists and scholars observed. Some of them, such as the British Muslim social scientist and political theorist Tariq Modood, welcomed the emergence of a plurality of identities and the use of those identities in the formation of pressure groups. In the same spirit, in 2000 Runnymede's major report, *The Future of Multi-Ethnic Britain*, projected a view of the country as a "community of communities."[56] However, others to the left, such as the cultural studies scholar Paul Gilroy, and the Sri Lankan Marxist scholar-activist Ambalavaner Sivanandan, deplored the "sudden flowering of a thousand ethnic groups.... Irish, Italians, Rastas, Sikhs, Chinese, Jews, Bengalis, Gypsies ... politicking for ethnic power."[57] In this light, the retreat of mainstream Jewish organizations from universal anti-racism was just one aspect of the development of a pluralist anti-racist politics. One feature of these new forms of politics was their concern with particular ethnic or religious identities and interests and with specific types of racism. A significant dimension of this new politics was the emergence of political organization on the basis of Muslim identity and interests.[58]

Almost a year after the British government's endorsement of the IHRA working definition of antisemitism, Baroness Sayeeda Warsi, the chair of the All-Party Parliamentary Group on British Muslims (APPGBM), questioned Lord Bourne, the Parliamentary undersecretary of state for Communities and Local Government, about the absence of a government-endorsed definition of Islamophobia. She asked "whether he agrees it is high time to have a definition of Islamophobia, and that to fundamentally challenge the hate that underpins hate crime, we need to define what that hate is."[59] This provides one moment of origin for the campaign to arrive at a definition of Islamophobia that could be adopted by the British government, as well as by statutory agencies and civil society organizations. The steps taken by supporters of the IHRA definition of antisemitism provided a model. Muslim activists and their allies in the campaign for a definition of

Islamophobia concentrated their activity on an inquiry by the All-Party Parliamentary Group on British Muslims that lasted two years; took written and oral evidence; held community consultation events in London, Sheffield, and Manchester; and issued questionnaires. In 2018 the APPGBM published its report, *Islamophobia Defined*. The findings were supported by 750 Muslim organizations, including the Muslim Council of Britain, and were adopted by the Labour Party, Liberal Democrats, and Plaid Cymru.[60]

Islamophobia Defined asserted that Islamophobia and antisemitism "cannot be separated." Both sorts of racism, it stated, focus on racial features, ethnic appearances, and cultural practices, and both Muslims and Jews, it pointed out, are viewed by the majority as "external dangers and threatening." Because the government had by this time adopted the IHRA working definition of antisemitism, these analytical connections drawn by the APPGBM carried an implication for policy. If the two forms of racism were similar, and the government had decided to combat one using a definition, then why should it not do the same for the other?[61]

Paradoxically, this claim that antisemitism and Islamophobia are similar distinguishes supporters of a definition of Islamophobia from advocates for a definition of antisemitism. As we have seen, Jewish representatives have been keen to underline the singularity of antisemitism, not its comparability to any other form of racism. The campaign for a definition of Islamophobia not only drew parallels with Jews' experiences of antisemitism but also identified their own campaign as a form of anti-racism.[62] In contrast to mainstream Jewish leaders in the early twenty-first century who did not regard the anti-racist movement as their natural partner, some Muslims and their representatives did just that.[63]

Nevertheless, there was a tension between advocates of a definition of Islamophobia who maintained that Islamophobia is a form of racism and others who held that religion is at the heart of their identity as Muslims and also at the core of Islamophobia.[64] The APPGBM rejected the austere, secular definition devised in 2017 by the Runnymede Trust, which stated simply that Islamophobia is "anti-Muslim racism."[65] Instead, *Islamophobia Defined* adopted advice provided by the academics Salman Sayyid and AbdoolKarim Vakil, which combined secular and religious perspectives: "Islamophobia is rooted in racism and is a type of racism that targets expressions of Muslimness or perceived Muslimness."[66]

As one friendly observer noted, the term "Muslimness" was "open to wide interpretation."[67] In the course of its seventy-two pages, *Islamophobia Defined* provided at least three different interpretations of what was meant by "Muslimness" and "perceived Muslimness." First, the APPGBM targeted forms of racism that promote stereotypes and essentialize Muslims. Its report summed up this discussion of Islamophobia by stating that "in short ... [it] essentialises Muslims, locating them in a homogenous group defined by one, single essence that is continually depicted and perceived as incompatible or unassimilable to western societies."[68] A second interpretation developed this idea so that it addressed not only discursive racism but also how racism demeans Muslim identity.[69] However, the APPGBM report also provided a third interpretation that highlighted the evidence of witnesses who used the concept of "Muslimness" to bind the concept of anti-Muslim racism tightly to criticism and disparagement of Islam and who argued for the inseparability of the two.[70] One academic suggested that "criticism directed at Muslims often entails (at least implicitly) criticism against Islam." Others claimed that Islamophobia identified Muslims on the basis of their "visible Islamic identity."[71]

The APPGBM was aware that by focusing on depictions of Muslimness it was likely to provoke opposition on the grounds that it was seeking to protect Islam from scrutiny and critique. It was not its aim, the APPGBM insisted, to limit criticism of Islam as a religion or to curtail freedom of speech.[72] Tariq Modood prescribed a path through this minefield. He acknowledged that if all critical or disparaging remarks about Islam or Muslims can be called Islamophobia, then there would be no space for any criticism. Accordingly, he proposed a series of five questions that could help distinguish "reasonable criticism" from Islamophobia.[73] Nevertheless, Southall Black Sisters, a secular and feminist organization for Asian and African Caribbean women, was apprehensive that a definition of Islamophobia would conflate "any criticism of Islam with discrimination and hate crimes against Muslims."[74] Taking a position against "racism, inequality and oppression" on the basis of the "application of universal equality and human rights–based norms," the Southall Black Sisters argued that a definition of Islamophobia could be used to protect "fundamentalism and religious intolerance":

> Would the following be considered Islamophobic: a condemnation of political Islam; criticism of patriarchal and heterosexual structures inherent in Islam; criticism of "sharia laws" and gender segregation; criticism of prominent Muslim leaders; promotion of atheism and secularism? We would argue that these are all legitimate expressions of free speech that should be protected by [the European Convention on Human Rights] ... but may be caught by a definition of Islamophobia.[75]

The APPGBM report declared Modood's five tests "helpful." However, when it came to addressing "the appropriate limits to free speech," the report declared that it had been guided by the "harm principle": John Stuart Mill's dictum that "the only purpose for which power can be rightfully exercised over any member of a civilized community, against his will, is to prevent harm to others." Yet Mill infamously failed to specify what counts as harm. Invoking the harm principle, therefore, did not in itself help determine the limits of legitimate speech.[76] Modood's five tests are compatible with the harm principle, but the APPGBM also embraced other, more capacious, interpretations of harm. There was broad agreement among witnesses that harm encompasses negative stereotypes and forms of "othering," which essentialize and demonize Muslims.

However, some aspects of the APPGBM report pointed to a more expansive understanding of harm. The report approvingly cited the Crown Prosecution Service's definition of an Islamophobic incident as one perceived to be such "by the victim or any other person" and in doing so repeated the APPIA's misunderstanding of Macpherson's distinction between a racist incident and a racist act.[77] On similar lines, Tell MAMA, an NGO that addresses anti-Muslim hate crimes, advised that a definition "should primarily centre the voices and experiences of Muslims," and Sariya Cheruvallil-Contractor, a sociologist at the University of Coventry, advised that the right to freedom of speech was qualified by the need "to protect the dignity and rights of everyday Muslims."[78]

Some witnesses to the inquiry undertaken by the APPGBM suggested that Muslim sensibilities should be decisive. Nadya Ali and Ben Whitham, respectively at that time academics at the University of Sussex and De Montfort University, were most sweeping of all, and invoked the concept of harm to argue that "there is no 'good faith' criticism of Islam" and to declare "the supposed right to criticise Islam," in effect, was nothing more than "a form of anti-Muslim racism, whereby the criticism humiliates, marginalises and stigmatises Muslims."[79] Salman Sayyid has argued that "an understanding of Islamophobia in absence of an understanding of the way in which there has been a global reassertion of Muslim identity is difficult to sustain."[80] Elements of *Islamophobia Defined* provide powerful evidence for his argument. In doing so, however, these assertions of "Muslimness" leave no space for the secularism and the defiance of sex and gender hierarchies that the Southall Black Sisters, among others, articulate and advocate.

5

In retreating from universalism, both Jewish and Muslim leaders have aimed to protect what they perceived to be their own community's interests, but they have not done so with equal success. Following the 2006 report on antisemitism, the All-Party Parliamentary Group Against Antisemitism received four official responses: two from the Labour government in power until 2010 and two from the Conservative-Liberal Democrat coalition government that followed. The report led to the creation of a Whitehall Government Working Group, which has gathered together communal representatives with civil servants from different departments, including the Home Office, the Department of Communities and Local Government (DCLG), the Foreign Office, and the Ministry of Justices. It also helped promote a working relationship between the Community Security Trust, the police, the Home Office, and the DCLG.[81] Today the government provides financial support for security at synagogues and schools and, as we have noted, in 2016 Britain was the first country to adopt the International Holocaust Remembrance Alliance (IHRA) working definition of antisemitism.

The picture for Muslims and others concerned with Islamophobia is less auspicious. To be sure, there is a Cross-Government Working Group on Anti-Muslim Hate Crime, established in 2012, and mosques and Muslim schools are eligible to apply for state funds to help protect their premises.[82] However, the Cross-Government Working Group has been criticized as feeble by one member who resigned in frustration.[83] The British government's counterterrorism strategy continues to be charged with having a discriminatory impact on Muslims. The 2018 report *Islamophobia Defined* complained that at the same time as steps had been taken to adopt a definition of antisemitism, "commensurate efforts on Islamophobia has been [*sic*] lacklustre."[84] The report's definition was adopted by opposition political parties and parts of local government but was rejected by a Conservative government that, at the same time, failed to provide an alternative of its own.

These divergent outcomes reflect the different social composition of the Jewish and Muslim populations in Britain today as well as different levels of consensus, organization, and effective lobbying among Jews and Muslims. For example, the Federation of Student Islamic Societies rejected the definition produced by the APPGBM because its emphasis on Islamophobia as a form of racism, in its view, failed to acknowledge that Muslims are primarily targeted because of their religion.[85] The success of British Jewish leaders in achieving their goals and influencing policy is a significant outcome, but one that reflects not only their own agency but also the willingness of successive governments in the present century to identify antisemitism as a fundamental evil.

Nevertheless, in the early twenty-first century there is a new commonality between many Jews and Muslims. This lies in the ways organizations and individuals invoke the concepts of antisemitism and Islamophobia. Some opponents of anti-Jewish and anti-Muslim racism have maintained universalism when it has suited them to do so, but overall they have retreated from it and have adopted instead a politics that promotes the experiences, perceptions, and interests of a particular group. Moreover, they have tried to extend the meanings of antisemitism and Islamophobia so that they can protect practices that would normally run afoul of a universalist politics that promotes equal rights for individuals and minorities. In these ways both Jews and Muslims confirm that the definitions of antisemitism and Islamophobia function not only to understand the world but also to change it.

NOTES

I am grateful to the editors and Julie Kalman, Brendan McGeever, and Tariq Modood for comments on an earlier draft of this essay.

1. David Engel, "Away from a Definition of Antisemitism: An Essay in the Semantics of Historical Description," in *Rethinking European Jewish History*, ed. Jeremy Cohen and Moshe Rosman (Oxford: Littman Library of Jewish Civilization, 2009), 30–53.

2. David Feldman, "Towards a History of the Term 'Anti-Semitism,'" *American Historical Review* 123, no. 4 (October 2018): 1139–50.

3. This is an approach widely associated with the work of Quentin Skinner. See, for example, the essays in *Visions of Politics*, vol. 1 (Cambridge: Cambridge University Press, 2002), esp. chaps. 4–7.

4. The year 2020 saw the publication of the Jerusalem Declaration on Antisemitism; in the following year the Muslim Council of Britain published a new report titled *Defining Islamophobia*. "The Jerusalem Declaration on Antisemitism," https://jerusalemdeclaration.org; *Defining Islamophobia: A Contemporary Understanding of How Expressions of Muslimness Are Targeted* (London: Muslim Council of Britain, 2021), https://mcb.org.uk/report/defining-islamophobia-a-contemporary-understanding-of-how-expressions-of-muslimness-are-targeted.

5. Runnymede Trust Commission on Antisemitism, *A Very Light Sleeper: The Persistence and Dangers of Antisemitism* (London: Runnymede Trust, 1994), 15. The origins of the commission are more complex than this, not least in that they followed from interaction between Runnymede staff and Muslim groups and individuals. See Robin Richardson, "The Runnymede Commission on British Muslims and Islamophobia: A History," in *Islamophobia: Still a Challenge for Us All*, ed. Farah Elahi and Omar Khan (London: Runnymede Trust, 2017), 82–85.

6. Chris Allen, *Islamophobia* (Farnham, UK: Ashgate, 2010), 5–9; All-Party Parliamentary Group on British Muslims, *Islamophobia Defined: Report on the Inquiry into a Working Definition of Islamophobia/anti-Muslim Hatred* (n.p.: All-Party Parliamentary Group on British Muslims, [2018?]), 27, accessed January 26, 2023, https://appgbritishmuslims.org/publications.

7. See, for example, Matti Bunzl, *Anti-Semitism and Islamophobia: Hatreds Old and New in Europe* (Chicago: Prickly Paradigm, 2007); Nasar Meer, "Racialization and

Religion: Race, Culture and Difference in Antisemitism and Islamophobia," *Ethnic and Racial Studies* 36, no. 3 (March 2013): 385–98; James Renton and Ben Gidley, "Introduction: The Shared Story of Europe's Idea of the Muslim and the Jews: A Diachronic Framework," in *Antisemitism and Islamophobia in Europe: A Shared Story*, ed. James Renton and Ben Gidley (London: Palgrave Macmillan, 2017).

8. Renton and Gidley, "Introduction," 1–4; Samuel P. Huntington, *The Clash of Civilizations and the Remaking of the World Order* (New York: Simon and Schuster, 1996); Douglas Murray, *The Strange Death of Europe: Immigration, Identity, Islam* (London: Bloomsbury Continuum, 2017); Jared Ahmad, *The BBC, the "War on Terror" and the Discursive Construction of Terrorism* (Cham, Switzerland: Palgrave Macmillan, 2018).

9. Therese O'Toole et. al., "Governing Through Prevent? Regulation and Contested Practice in State-Muslim Engagement," *Sociology* 50, no. 1 (2016): 160–77.

10. Bernard Wasserstein, *Vanishing Diaspora: The Jews in Europe since 1945* (London: Penguin Books, 1997), viii.

11. Sergio DellaPergola and L. Daniel Staetsky, *Jews in Europe at the Turn of the Millennium: Population Trends and Estimates* (London: Institute for Jewish Policy Research, 2020), 18, www.jpr.org.uk/reports/jews-europe-turn-millennium-popula tion-trends-and-estimates?id=17623; Bichara Khader, "Muslims in Europe: The Construction of a Problem," in *The Search for Europe: Contrasting Approaches* (n.p.: Open Mind BBVA, 2016), 303, https://www.bbvaopenmind.com/en/books/the -search-for-europe-contraising-approaches. Also see the 2018 report *Muslim Population in the UK* by the UK Office for National Statistics, www.ons.gov.uk/aboutus /transparencyandgovernance/freedomofinformationfoi/muslimpopulationintheuk.

12. Anthony Heath and Yaojun Li, *Review of the Relationship Between Religion and Poverty: Analysis for the Joseph Rowntree Foundation* (Oxford: Nuffield College, 2014); David Graham, Marlena Schmool, and Stanley Waterman, *Jews in Britain: A Snapshot from the 2001 Census* (London: Institute for Jewish Policy Research, 2007); Muslim Council of Great Britain, *British Muslims in Numbers* (London: Muslim Council of Britain, 2015); Louis Reynolds and Jonathan Birdwell, *Rising to the Top* (London: Demos, 2015).

13. See, for example, Nasim Ahmed, "UK Survey on British Muslims Cites Palestine as Major Issue," *Middle East Monitor*, February 24, 2016, www.middleeastmonitor .com/20160224-uk-survey-on-british-muslims-cites-palestine-as-major-issue; Daniel Staetsky, *Antisemitism in Contemporary Britain: Key Findings from the JPR Survey of Attitudes Towards Jews and Israel* (London: Institute for Jewish Policy Research, 2017).

14. Andrew Barclay, Maria Sobolewska, and Robert Ford, "Political Realignment of British Jews: Testing Competing Explanations," *Electoral Studies* 61 (October 2019), https://www.sciencedirect.com/science/article/pii/S0261379419300721; Nicole Martin and Omar Khan, *Ethnic Minorities at the 2017 British General Election* (London: Runnymede Trust, 2019), www.runnymedetrust.org/publications /ethnic-minorities-at-the-2017-british-general-election.

15. See David Cameron, "Extremism" (speech, Birmingham, UK, July 20, 2015), www

.gov.uk/government/speeches/extremism-pm-speech; David Cameron, "Community Security Trust" (speech, London, March 19, 2015), www.gov.uk/government/speeches/community-security-trust-cst-prime-ministers-speech.

16. Valentina Di Stasio et al., "Muslim by Default or Religious Discrimination? Results from a Cross-National Field Experiment on Hiring Discrimination," *Journal of Ethnic and Migration Studies* 47, no. 6 (2021): 1305–26; Elahi and Khan, eds., *Islamophobia: Still a Challenge for Us All*.

17. Staetsky, *Antisemitism in Contemporary Britain*, 57. In fact, despite the greater concentration of anti-Jewish attitudes among Muslims, the Muslim population is too small for it to be responsible for more than a fraction of hate crime and for those antisemitic attitudes in the population as a whole revealed by survey data.

18. Adam Lusher, "Plan for Islamic Centre in Largely Jewish London Area Sparks Anger and Islamophobia Allegations," *Independent*, October 17, 2007, www.independent.co.uk/news/uk/home-news/islamic-centre-golders-green-jewish-north-london-area-islamophobia-racism-muslim-anti-semitism-a8005486.html.

19. Runnymede Trust Commission on Antisemitism, *A Very Light Sleeper*, 55.

20. Ibid., 12.

21. Elahi and Khan, eds., *Islamophobia: A Challenge for Us All*.

22. Lord Beloff et al., "Antisemitism in the 1990s: A Symposium," *Patterns of Prejudice* 25, no. 2 (1991): 5, 34–35.

23. Ibid., 36.

24. Runnymede Trust Commission on Antisemitism, *A Very Light Sleeper*, 55.

25. Ibid., 56.

26. All-Party Parliamentary Group Against Antisemitism, *Report of the All-Party Parliamentary Inquiry into Antisemitism* (London: Stationery Office, 2006), 4, 7, https://antisemitism.org.uk/wp-content/uploads/2020/06/all-parliamentary-group-against-antisemitism-2006.pdf.

27. These attacks were reflected in evidence to the APPG inquiry. See APPGAA, *All-Party Parliamentary Inquiry into Antisemitism: Selection of Written Evidence* (n.p.: All-Party Parliamentary Group Against Antisemitism, 2006), 29, 31, https://antisemitism.org.uk/wp-content/uploads/2020/06/writtenevidence-2.pdf.

28. APPGAA, *Report of the All-Party Parliamentary Inquiry into Antisemitism*, 30.

29. MPs involved in the inquiry included Iain Duncan Smith, who had been leader of the Conservative Party, and Chris Huhne, who stood for election as leader of the Liberal Democrats that year.

30. APPGAA, *Report of the All-Party Parliamentary Inquiry into Antisemitism*, 1.

31. William Macpherson of Cluny, *The Stephen Lawrence Inquiry: Report of an Inquiry by Sir William Macpherson of Cluny* (London: Stationery Office, 1999), chap. 47, recommendations 12–13.

32. See Adam Langleben, "UCU Is Actively Alienating Its Jewish Members," *Left Foot Forward*, June 4, 2011, https://leftfootforward.org/2011/06/university-and-college-union-ucu-actively-alienating-jewish-members; Mike Katz, "Labour Must Listen to Jews and Adopt IHRA. Properly," *Medium* (blog), July 17, 2018, https://mikekatz.medium.com/labour-must-listen-to-jews-and-adopt-ihra-properly-c4eb82dbc13c.

33. APPGAA, *Report of the All-Party Inquiry into Antisemitism*, 1.

34. Tariq Modood, "Islamophobia, Antisemitism and the Struggle for Recognition: The Politics of Definition," in *Antisemitism, Islamophobia and the Politics of Definition*, ed. David Feldman and Marc Volovici (Cham, Switzerland: Palgrave Macmillan, 2023) 235–58.

35. APPGAA, *Report of the All-Party Parliamentary Inquiry into Antisemitism*, 52. Both Antony Lerman, *Whatever Happened to Antisemitism?: Redefinition and the Myth of the Collective Jew* (London: Pluto Press, 2022), 126–29, and Kenneth Marcus, *The Definition of Anti-Semitism* (New York: Oxford University Press, 2015), 151–62, provide helpful accounts of the interaction between the EUMC and Jewish NGOs and academics.

36. Lerman, *Whatever Happened*, 126.

37. European Monitoring Centre on Racism and Xenophobia (EUMC), *Manifestations of Antisemitism in the EU 2002–2003* (Vienna: EUMC, 2004), 12, 14.

38. Kenneth S. Stern, *The Conflict Over the Conflict: The Israel/Palestine Campus Debate* (Toronto: University of Toronto Press, 2020), 151; Lerman, *Whatever Happened*, 126.

39. Stern, *The Conflict*, 151; Lerman, *Whatever Happened*, 126–27.

40. Supporters of the definition were very clear that criticism of Israel should not in itself be regarded as antisemitic. APPGAA, *Report of the All-Party Parliamentary Inquiry into Antisemitism*, 17.

41. For a mainstream Jewish view of Durban, see Harris O. Schoenberg, "Demonization in Durban: The World Conference Against Racism," *The American Jewish Yearbook* 102 (2002): 85–111. On the Jewish response, see Marcus, *The Definition*, 151–62; Stern, *The Conflict*, 149–55; Lerman, *Whatever Happened*, 110–36.

42. The text was reproduced in the APPIA. See APPGAA, *Report of the All-Party Parliamentary Inquiry into Antisemitism*, 6.

43. APPGAA, *Selection of Written Evidence*, 28.

44. Ibid., 5, 9.

45. Ibid., 5, 31.

46. On the history of Zionism's preceding engagement with universalism, see James Loeffler, *Rooted Cosmopolitans: Jews and Human Rights in the Twentieth Century* (New Haven, CT: Yale University Press, 2018); Nathan Kurz, *Jewish Internationalism and Human Rights after the Holocaust* (Cambridge: Cambridge University Press, 2021).

47. "Military Occupation of Palestine by Israel," *RULAC-Geneva Academy of International Humanitarian Law and Human Rights*, www.rulac.org/browse/conflicts

/military-occupation-of-palestine-by-israel. On the status of Palestinians within Israel's green line see, Ilan Peleg and Dov Waxman, *Israel's Palestinians: The Conflict Within* (Cambridge: Cambridge University Press, 2011), 19–46.

48. APPGAA, *Report of the All-Party Parliamentary Inquiry into Antisemitism*, 33.

49. Ibid., 70.

50. APPGAA, *Report of the All-Party Parliamentary Inquiry into Antisemitism*, 51.

51. Nevertheless, the APPG report published in January 2015 did not press its support for the EUMC working definition. This had been abandoned by the Fundamental Rights Agency (FRA) (the successor to the EUMC) and appeared to have lost essential support. Instead, at that time the APPGAA promoted a more universalist approach to identifying antisemitism, which had been recommended in a report commissioned from the present author.

52. APPGAA, *Report of the All-Party Parliamentary Inquiry into Antisemitism* (London: Stationery Office, 2015), 10.

53. Ibid., 18–19.

54. International Holocaust Remembrance Alliance Plenary in Budapest, May 26, 2016, www.holocaustremembrance.com/sites/default/files/press_release_document _antisemitism.pdf.

55. David Torrance, "UK Government's Adoption of the IHRA Definition of Antisemitism," *House of Commons Library*, October 4, 2018, https://commonslibrary .parliament.uk/uk-governments-adoption-of-the-ihra-definition-of-antisemitism.

56. Tariq Modood, "The Changing Context of 'Race' in Britain," *Patterns of Prejudice* 30, no. 1 (January 1996): 3–13; Commission on the Future of Multi-Ethnic Britain, *The Future of Multi-Ethnic Britain* (London: Runnymede Trust, 2000).

57. Ambalavaner Sivanandan, *Communities of Resistance* (London: Verso, 1990), 147–48; Paul Gilroy, "The End of Anti-Racism," in *"Race," Culture and Difference*, ed. James Donald and Ali Rattansi (London: Sage Publications, 1992), 49–61.

58. On the beginnings of these mobilizations, see Helen Carr, "'I think you have ignored the relevant provisions of the 1944 Education Act': Muslims, the State and Education in England c. 1966–c. 1985," *Contemporary British History* 35 (2021): 52–71; Tariq Modood, *Not Easy Being British: Colour, Culture and Citizenship* (Stoke-on-Trent: Runnymede Trust and Trentham, 1992).

59. Baroness Warsi's words are cited in Pragna Patel, "The APPG, Islamophobia and Anti-Muslim Racism," *Feminist Dissent* 6 (2022): 205–29, 207.

60. Jessica Elgot, "Government Criticised for Rejecting Definition of Islamophobia," *Guardian*, May 15, 2019, www.theguardian.com/news/2019/may/15/uk-ministers -criticised-rejecting-new-definition-islamophobia; Chris Allen, "Fact Sheet: Defining Islamophobia," Religion Media Centre, June 13, 2019.

61. All-Party Parliamentary Group on British Muslims, *Islamophobia Defined: The*

Inquiry into a Working Definition of Islamophobia/anti-Muslim Hatred (London: APPGBM, 2018), 24, 32, 42–43, 56–57.

62. Ibid., 7, 22, 50.

63. Ibid., 10, 34, 45.

64. Tariq Modood, "Islamophobia, Antisemitism and the Struggle for Recognition"; Federation of Student Islamic Societies, "FOSIS' Position on the APPG definition of Islamophobia," November 17, 2020, https://www.fosis.org.uk/news/fosis-position -on-the-appg-definition-of-islamophobia; Yahya Birt, "Why This New Definition of Islamophobia Is Bittersweet," *Medium* (blog), December 5, 2018, https://yahyabirt .medium.com/why-this-new-definition-of-islamophobia-is-bittersweet-99b7f9993d73.

65. APPGBM, *Islamophobia Defined*, 25.

66. Ibid., 50; S. Sayyid and AbdoolKarim Vakil, "Defining Islamophobia," *Critical Muslim Studies*, December 5, 2018, https://criticalmuslimstudies.co.uk/project/de fining-islamophobia.

67. Birt, "Why This New Definition of Islamophobia Is Bittersweet."

68. APPGBM, *Islamophobia Defined*, 48.

69. APPGBM, *Islamophobia Defined*, 24, 43; the Muslim Council of Britain emphasized this dimension of Muslimness in its lengthy and detailed report published in 2021.

70. Ibid., 29, 31.

71. Ibid. This claim is true in many instances, but empirically the statement is too sweeping. For example, it is difficult to see how the racist stereotypes that represent Muslims as terrorists are immediately connected to depictions of Islam. We can draw a parallel to the way in which ideas concerning a global Jewish conspiracy derive ultimately from Christian anti-Judaism, but in themselves, in their present articulations, are received as attacks on Jews, not Judaism.

72. Ibid., 11.

73. Ibid., 36. The five questions were the following: "Does it stereotype Muslims by assuming all think the same? Is it about Muslims or a dialogue with Muslims which they would wish to join? Is the language civil, and contextually appropriate? Is it insincere criticism for ulterior motives?" It is doubtful, however, whether Southall Black Sisters would have found all these criteria reassuring or appropriate. If the answer to any of the five tests is a "yes," Modood suggests, then we may be dealing with Islamophobia or anti-Muslim racism.

74. Patel, "The APPG," 213.

75. Patel, "The APPG," 220.

76. APPGBM, *Islamophobia Defined*, 11; John Stuart Mill, *On Liberty* (London: 1859), 22; Piers Norris Turner, "'Harm' and Mill's Harm Principle," *Ethics* 124 (January 2014): 299–326.

77. APPGBM, *Islamophobia Defined*, 25.

78. Ibid., 25, 35, 50.

79. Ibid., 35–36.

80. Salman Sayyid, "Out of the Devil's Dictionary," in *Thinking Through Islamophobia: Global Perspectives*, ed. S. Sayyid and AbdoolKarim Vakil (New York: Columbia University Press, 2010), 11. See also Allen, *Islamophobia*, 77–79, 196.

81. APPGAA, *Report of the All-Party Parliamentary Inquiry into Antisemitism* (2015), 22–25.

82. "Govt Encourages Mosques and Muslim Schools to Apply for Security Funding," *5Pillars*, May 24, 2022, https://5pillarsuk.com/2022/05/24/govt-encourages-mosques -and-muslim-schools-to-apply-for-security-funding.

83. Chris Allen, "Why I Quit the Government's Anti-Muslim Hatred Working Group," *Huffington Post*, October 30, 2014, www.huffingtonpost.co.uk/dr-chris-allen /anti-muslim-hatred-working-group_b_6064866.html.

84. APPGBM, *Islamophobia Defined*, 10.

85. Federation of Student Islamic Societies, "FOSIS' Position on the APPG definition of Islamophobia."

V

POST-HOLOCAUST
RUMINATIONS

14

In Defense of
the Concept of "Antisemitism"
in Holocaust Studies

HAVI DREIFUSS

DAVID ENGEL'S ESSAY deals with a central concept in the study of modern Jewish history (antisemitism), criticizes how it is used in scholarship, and in fact objects to its use as a scholarly category altogether. According to Engel, the changes that the concept underwent over time, the impact of public discourse on it, and the broad conceptual framework that has solidified cause far-reaching distortions within the scholarship. These distortions include ignoring major aspects of the history of relations between Jews and non-Jews and an excessive focus on peripheral issues. Engel raises fundamental questions not only about antisemitism and its manifestations but also about the conceptualizations that serve historians.[1]

Language, Conceptualization, and History

I cannot address here the questions raised by Engel about the function of conceptualization in the work of the historian, nor can I delve into his first claim about changes related to the concept of antisemitism over time. Yet I will claim that as long as human language is a primary mode of communication and historical research studies a variety of human societies, historical concepts will be derived from public discourse and continue to undergo fundamental changes. For example, if we were to apply Engel's claim to other disciplines, it would be impossible to apply the term "slavery" to a phenomenon in antiquity and in the United

States; one who studied the enslavement of African Americans in the United States would have to avoid discussing the status of a slave, the slave trade, and the daily life of slaves, and instead invent new conceptual categories.

A close study of the changes undergone by concepts associated with Jewish studies poses similar challenges. For instance, although Jewish nationalism was linked to various non-Jewish national movements, the meaning of the term was different in each of these societies. Likewise, recent studies have shown that the concept "ghetto" changed its meaning not only in regard to the different contexts of the medieval ghetto, but also among Nazi policy makers in Germany in the 1930s. Ignoring these concepts, which were—each in its era—part of the broader public discourse and entered academic treatments, will result, in the best-case scenario, in convoluting historical discourse, and in other scenarios, in impairing the ability to understand and address them. The fact that any concept, be it "slavery," "nationalism," or "ghetto," changes its meaning or exists in nonacademic discourse does not render its use superfluous. Rather, it demands, as Engel argues clearly, that scholars clarify precisely the concepts they refer to within the discrete contexts of their deployment. Furthermore, adopting Engel's call to avoid using basic categories might also destabilize the ability to deeply engage with concepts like "enlightenment," "socialism," "liberalism," and so forth. In fact, it can undermine any comparative historical analysis.

Antisemitism and the Holocaust

Throughout this article, I wish to delve deeper into a different aspect of Engel's essay: his questioning of the extent to which there is any common denominator in the various instances of violence against Jews over the years—a commonality that should be called "antisemitism." The study of modern Jewish history shows that Jews were victims of a broad variety of negative feelings and acts in different places and across vast time periods. Engel asks whether the attempt to trace some commonality among them—an attempt that might attest to similar and different patterns of action, to a variety of motives on the part of the perpetrators, or to similarities in the different experiences of the victims—contributes to the discussion or inhibits it. According to him, the bundling of such disparate events within one concept, antisemitism, created a situation in which the concept does more harm than good. Therefore, use of this concept, which impairs the scholar's ability to analyze these human phenomena in a real way, should be avoided.

This claim is closely connected to the study of the Holocaust and the role of antisemitism in this realm. The truth is that the debate between intentionalism and functionalism died down some time ago, and the paradigm accepted today synthesizes the two schools of thought that emerged out of German historiography beginning in the late 1960s. Most scholars agree that the decision to murder all of European Jewry was made in the second half of the year 1941, was influenced both by grassroots factors and by the highest echelons of the Nazi regime, and stemmed both from Nazi ideology and from how Nazi Germany perceived the actual developments of the war. That is, today's scholarly discourse does not adopt simplistic views of complex events; within the discrete context of antisemitism, it maintains that Nazi antisemitism played an important role in the formulation of anti-Jewish policy, but that the actual development of this policy hinged on a variety of other factors.[2]

Additionally, anti-Jewish policy throughout Europe is presented in all its vicissitudes and addressed as something that was shaped by Nazi ideology—toward Jews and non-Jews alike—and by a variety of local factors.[3] As a rule, these local factors are incorporated within the complex relations between Jews and the communities in which they lived during and prior to the Nazi occupation. Most scholarship maintains that, alongside ethnic and national tensions as well as the personal baggage of envy and rivalry, antisemitism among the local population—traditional religious hatred or local incarnations of modern antisemitism—had an impact on the fate of the Jews.[4]

However, several studies that deal with the Holocaust, mainly within the broader context of mass violence and genocide, and recently also colonialism, maintain that antisemitism did not play a prominent role in the murder of Jews. They ascribe the annihilation of Jewish communities to a different array of circumstances, primarily ethnic tensions that prevailed throughout Europe. Although some of these scholars make this claim without reference to Engel's essay, some take it as a basis for making much sharper claims than he did. Engel draws critical attention to the concept of antisemitism and calls for discussion about how to conceptualize negative feelings toward Jews and the motivation to do them harm. These scholars claim that negative feelings toward Jews (if they existed) had no connection to "antisemitism"—however defined—and that they did not motivate their murder. According to this interpretation, the killing of Jews stemmed from a mixture of attitudes and considerations that are not specific to Jews. There are those, then, who interpret Engel's call to renounce the use of "antisemitism" as an analytic category as a denial of the very existence of a specific hatred of Jews as a motive for harming them and of the role that this hatred played in the Holocaust.

This claim can be linked to another trend that has emerged in Holocaust studies in recent years. Various scholars, including leading scholars who author comprehensive studies, avoid addressing certain concepts within academic discourse: Engel comes out strongly against the concept of "antisemitism," Blatman opposes all use of the concept of "uniqueness," even for the sake of comparison, and Bloxham maintains that the concept of "Holocaust" itself has a problematic charge that impairs the study of genocide.[5]

In addition, other studies question not only one concept or another, but also the accepted periodization and geographical borders of the Holocaust. These studies shape an emerging trend that calls for the revision of Holocaust research, sometimes questioning the very legitimacy of such a field. They claim that rather than "the Holocaust"—however defined—there was a series of events that occurred in a certain geographic space, during a specific period. The victims included, but were not exclusively, Jews, and were murdered for a variety of local reasons.[6] These claims reveal that Engel's question about the price we pay for grouping various events under one definition is also quite relevant to the discourse about the Holocaust of European Jewry.

In light of these developments, I would like to use the discussion about how the concept of "antisemitism" causes distortions in scholarship as the basis for a study of similar issues regarding the concept of "the Holocaust." It is true that "the Holocaust" is a much narrower term—chronologically, geographically, and thematically—than "antisemitism," but precisely for that reason it can serve as a test case for the basic methodological question of how terms gather disparate phenomena together. In other words, the concept "the Holocaust" also demands a basic clarification: To what extent can different and disparate historical events be included within a single historical category, and what price do scholars pay for including or excluding them from this category?

It is important to note that the question of what to include within the framework of "the Holocaust" arises not only with respect to events that took place at the chronological or geographical margins of the Holocaust period, such as the anti-Jewish policy of the Italian regime in Libya or the outbreaks of violence against Jews that proliferated in Europe after the war's conclusion. It also arises with respect to events that occurred under the control and influence of Nazi Germany in Europe between 1933 and 1945. The question arises, in all its severity, in light of the massive differences between the manifold events that fall within the framework of "the Holocaust." For example, how can the situation in 1933 be compared to that in 1943? What differentiates the fate of the Jews of France (both Occupied and Vichy France) from that of Lithuanian Jewry? What does a Jewish man who joined the underground Slovakian resistance have in common with an Italian Jewish woman held in a labor camp? The enormous range of human experiences during the Holocaust era raises difficult questions about the price paid by scholarship that binds them under the single conceptual category of "the Holocaust." Let us examine—as does Engel regarding the concept of antisemitism—the extent to which the persecution toward the middle of the twentieth century of Jews by Nazi Germany, assisted by many others, can be bundled into the single conceptual category of "the Holocaust."

The Use of "the Holocaust" as a General Category

Another study by Engel can help us chart a path for a preliminary discussion of this broader question. In his article, "Patterns of Anti-Jewish Violence in Poland, 1944–1946," Engel addresses a similar issue of narrower scope.[7] Engel examines the patterns of the murder of hundreds of Jews in Poland after the conclusion of the war, during a period of civil war that cost thousands of Poles their lives. In this meticulous study, Engel identifies the different character of the violence against Jews and shows that the murder of Jews was perpetrated in different places, at different times, and with different characteristics than the violence against the non-Jewish population. In his words:

> Comparing the most easily identifiable and quantifiable features of attacks upon Jews and upon Polish government supporters appears to suggest, then, that each set of aggressive acts displayed its own characteristic fingerprint, as it were, and that the two fingerprints deviated from one another far more than they coincided. Jews were more at risk of being killed at different times and in different places than were government supporters, and Jewish women and children were in considerably greater danger than were Poles of the same sex and age.[8]

In other words, over and above analyzing murders of Jews for being Jews, Engel examines these murders in the context of the murder of non-Jews, thus identifying the unique aspects of the violence against Jews. According to him, among ethnic Poles, only those who perpetrated very specific "crimes" were marked for execution, while the fate of the Jews was sealed regardless of their actions (or, in this case, their supposed attitudes toward Communism). Thus, according to Engel, the murder of Jews cannot be removed from the context in which it occurred. His examination of this specific context shows, furthermore, that these murders differed from other murders in Poland in the same period. Engel concludes that these acts of murder were motivated by a variety of concrete reasons but still had something in common. This tension between the actual motives leading to the persecution of Jews and the commonality of all instances of violence against Jews is precisely what must be examined, in my view, vis-à-vis various conceptual categories, including "the Holocaust" and "antisemitism."

There is no doubt that the incidents and human interactions that took place during the Holocaust varied enormously. The victims of the Holocaust did not have a common identity, they did not speak the same language, and their lives never intersected before or during the Holocaust. They did not have the same allies and enemies, nor were the direct reasons for their persecution the same.

I wish to demonstrate these fundamental differences by examining the fate of a handful of Jews during the Holocaust: an anarchist Jew in a German concentration camp in the 1930s, two young women murdered by Poles in their hiding place in 1943, a former athlete murdered during his labor service in Hungary, and a French and a Greek child murdered in extermination camps.

Erich Mühsam (1878–1934), a Jewish poet and anarchist, was among thousands of Germans—mostly non-Jews—arrested during the hours and days after the burning of the Reichstag in 1933. He was not arrested as a Jew, but as a dissident with a close associate in Communist circles. While imprisoned in Nazi concentration camps, Mühsam was subject to terrible physical and psychological abuse. According to a German report, Mühsam committed suicide while in custody of the Oranienburg concentration camp on July 11, 1934; other evidence indicates that he was tortured to death.[9]

Miriam and Hannah Lerner, aged twenty-two and twenty, respectively, never reached a camp. Their murderers were not Germans, but Polish family friends from the town of Komorowo who helped them, their mother, and their three brothers hide in occupied Poland. The relative wealth of the Lerner family was its undoing. On April 30, 1943, when the Lerner family had nothing left after several months of extortion, the Polish friends raped Miriam and Hannah and then killed them along with the rest of their family, dividing their remaining property among themselves.[10]

Attila Petschauer (1904–1943), a Hungarian Olympian in fencing, also seems to have known his murderer. However, the direct motive for killing him was not greed, but rather the opportunity to settle a personal score. Thanks to his athletic accomplishments that included winning several Olympic medals (in 1928 and 1932), Petschauer was exempted from conscription into the homicidal labor service to which young Jewish Hungarian men were sent even before the German occupation. It was only after he struck a Hungarian officer who identified him and called him a "dirty" Jew that Petschauer was sent to a labor battalion.

In the labor camp, he was identified by a fellow member of the 1928 Hungarian Olympic team, who began to torment him mercilessly. On the eve of the Red Army invasion, Petschauer was tied naked to a tree. He froze to death after his Hungarian tormenters poured water on him in the minus-35-degree weather.[11]

Yitzhak Mallach and Colette Allouche never met each other or any of the individuals discussed above. Both were born in 1938, and both perished before reaching the age of five. Yitzhak was born to Avraham and Metouka (Mazal-Tov) in Thessaloniki, Greece. According to the testimony filled out by his brother, Yitzhak was murdered at Auschwitz-Birkenau on March 21, 1943.[12] Colette was born in Paris to Alfred (Fredi) and Rose. She was imprisoned on October 10, 1942, and, on March 25, 1943, after five months in the Drancy internment camp, was deported on Transport 53 with about a thousand other Jews. According to the information recorded by her half-sister, Colette was murdered at Sobibor on March 30, 1943.[13]

Is there some commonality between these two instances of (Jewish) five-year-old children—one from Greece and the other from France—who were transported around the same time to two different murder sites in occupied Poland where they were murdered? Do their deaths have anything to do with the deaths of the Lerner sisters, the fencer Petschauer, or the poet and anarchist Mühsam? This group includes men and women, children and adults, intellectuals and laypersons. Moreover, their murderers were Germans, Poles, and Hungarians, and a long list of accomplices transported them in trains, guarded the camps, and abetted the killings in a host of other ways. The direct motives for the murders were also different: political persecution, greed, personal vengeance, and Nazi ideology.

Studying additional geographical regions as well as the identities and fates of other Jews will only amplify—appreciably—the differences presented here. The six million Jews who lost their lives during the period of the Holocaust were of different nationalities, characterized by a range of demographic features, and murdered by many means and in many different places—although mainly on European soil. Moreover, their murderers hailed from a variety of nations in addition to Germany. Only in some instances can Nazi ideology (or antisemitism) be identified as the actual motive for the Jews' murder. Not infrequently, the direct causes of the killing were political views, past actions, national aspirations, ethnic tensions, personal enmity, profit, and even bad luck.

This being the case, how—if at all—can these different incidents be included within the single conceptual category of "the Holocaust"? Do they share any common features? According to Engel's own methodology in his study regarding the patterns of anti-Jewish violence in Poland at the end of the war, the problem should be formulated differently: One should not ask about the similarities among different incidents, but instead about how distinct each incident is in relation to its own context. In other words, one should ask whether the killing of a Jew in Poland was more similar to the killing of a Pole in Poland or to the killing of a Dutch Jew in the Netherlands.

The cases mentioned above enable us to examine this dilemma rather concretely: It is true that Mühsam was imprisoned as a Communist, but from the moment he was identified as a Jew his fate was different from that of his Communist comrades. The fate of Jewish prisoners was determined by their Jewishness rather than their communism. His difference from his comrades becomes sharper in light of the fact that in this period, at the beginning of the Nazi regime in Germany, Jews did not yet constitute the majority of camp inmates. Thus, even when Jews were not yet arrested for being Jews and constituted a minority within the Nazi concentration camps, they became, like Mühsam, the preferred victims of their persecutors.

Likewise, the crime perpetrated against Miriam and Hannah Lerner cannot be explained simply as wartime violence against women. The context within which they were raped and murdered shows that even if their abuse stemmed from them being young women, it happened, first and foremost, because of their Jewishness. The Lerner family went into hiding because of German murderousness, but they died at the hands of people who knew them and lived as their neighbors for decades before their murder. Greed and deviant impulses, even if they were present, did not lead to similar actions before the war. However, under German occupation and against the backdrop of the extermination of the Jews in Poland, Miriam and Hannah Lerner were cruelly raped and murdered by acquaintances. There is no doubt that the fate of the Lerner women is firmly embedded in the draconian occupation of Polish rural regions. Still, according to Engel's methods, we must examine whether their fate is more similar to that of young, non-Jewish Polish women or to that of other Jewish women in the same period.

And Attila Petschauer? Young, non-Jewish Hungarians were not murdered during their years of hard labor; they were not even conscripted. There were, of course, young Hungarians killed on World War II battlefields fighting alongside the German military and others who died under different circumstances. Were the circumstances and motives of their deaths at all similar to those of Petschauer's?

It must be emphasized that this is not a moral question. Death is death, regardless of the identities of the victims and perpetrators. As scholars, we do not evaluate the suffering of the victims or their families, but only the processes that produced it, the circumstances that enabled it, and the people involved in it. We compare dissimilar incidents to understand their similarities and differences. This is especially true when addressing the death of children. Alongside approximately 1.5 million Jewish children, tens of thousands of non-Jewish children were also murdered during World War II. True, many of the non-Jewish children were casualties of war and died as the result of military operations, starvation, and expulsions, but some were also murdered. The murder of dozens of children from the Czech village of Lidice, hundreds of children from Oradour-sur-Glane in France, and thousands of children from the Zamość district of Poland are but a few examples of the atrocities against non-Jewish children committed by Nazi Germany. Are the deaths of Jewish children more similar to the deaths of other Jews across Europe or to the deaths of non-Jewish children in this period?

One should note that this question does not assess the suffering of the children or the terrible grief of their parents, but only the circumstances of their death. It interrogates the reasons that so many Jewish children—of French, Greek, and many other nationalities—were transported across half a continent so that they could be murdered in a (more or less) clean, modern fashion in the heart of Europe, even though they had no real conflict with the Germans. Does that "commonality" among these children have any connection with the various ways and situations in which other Jews were murdered during the war?

Without a doubt, examining the specific situations in which Jews lived and died yields important perspectives regarding the study of the Holocaust. Mühsam's death cannot be understood without being familiar with the world of the concentration camps; the Lerner women's deaths cannot be studied absent familiarity with the cruel, menacing oppression in Poland; it is impossible to analyze Petschauer's death without addressing the fate of Hungary and its Jews during the 1930s and 1940s; and, the deaths of the children Yitzhak Mallach and Colette Allouche are closely tied not only to the history of the Holocaust but also to the lives of Jews in France and Greece before and during the war.

However, examining the fate of Jews only in light of their specific circumstances can also lead to distortions. Thus, just as it is difficult, if not impossible, to address the fate of Jews during the Holocaust without addressing the specific context within which they lived and died, it is similarly difficult, if not impossible, to address their persecution without addressing the wider context of the Holocaust. Both similarities and differences are crucial to gaining a better understanding of the fate of Jews and non-Jews during this period.

Studying the divergent fates of Jews during the Holocaust brings out clear differences among the specific circumstances of their murders and the motives that led to their deaths. And yet, such comparisons also yield important similarities—for instance, that Jews were the preferred victims in Europe during this period and their murder often involved unnecessary violence and more humiliation than "required."

Even though some societies were more liberal and progressive, Jews were more vulnerable than others in western and eastern Europe regardless of both their actions and their proportion within different societies. Jews were murdered for a wide range of concrete reasons, but these murders also definitely had something in common. To paraphrase Engel: Comparing the attacks upon Jews and non-Jews demonstrates that each set of aggressive acts displayed its own characteristic fingerprint and that the sets deviated more than they coincided. Jews were more at risk of being killed than any other European citizens; Jewish women and children were in considerably greater danger—in fact, ten times greater—than non-Jewish European women and children. Even though the murder of Europe's Jews during the Holocaust was perpetrated for a variety of reasons, these murders also had something in common. The willful disregard of this commonality, a commonality conceptualized with the aid of the word "Holocaust," yields a local, artificial demarcation of the events and can cause fundamental distortions in our understanding of the events and the period.

A "Commonality" and Antisemitism

But what is that "commonality"? What is the basis of the common fate of Jews throughout Europe despite their different circumstances and experiences? Was it how Nazi ideology defined the Jews? Was it the barbarity of warfare against a background of preexisting religious, ethnic, or national tensions? Did the foreignness of the Jews, despite their integration, make them preferred victims? Did antisemitism play a role in their common fate?

Any response that is presented as the unequivocal answer to the question of "commonality" will necessarily be a simplistic response that has already been dismissed by Holocaust scholars: Jews were not always murdered specifically because of Nazi ideology; there were not preexisting tensions everywhere Jews were murdered; not infrequently, Jews with an impressive record of integration were murdered alongside those seen as "foreigners"; and, given the large number of other motives, antisemitism cannot fully answer the question of why Jews were murdered. And yet, alongside these additional explanations, was the hatred of Jews as Jews—that is, antisemitism—also part of that "commonality" that made Jews preferred victims?

Here we must emphasize that even if during the early years of Holocaust studies there were those who presented antisemitism as the primary—and sometimes even exclusive—reason for persecuting Jews, for many years now Holocaust scholars have adopted far more complex attitudes. They are well aware of the role played by grassroots elements and bureaucrats, in addition to senior Nazi officials, in formulating anti-Jewish policy; they do not view the murder of the Jews as the action of the SS or of Nazi Germany alone, and the involvement of many other Europeans—soldiers, police officers, and common citizens—has been and continues to be studied. In addition, Holocaust scholars study the assistance given to Jews not only by the noble "Righteous Among the Nations" but also by antisemites, "paid rescuers," and Jews who rescued other Jews. The factors that motivated a specific individual or entire communities to harm Jews include, inter alia, greed, terror, religious hatred, national tensions, conflicts of interest, and yes—also antisemitism.[14]

In my opinion, examining the concept of "antisemitism" against the background of the Holocaust era highlights its importance. Anti-Jewish actions during World War II took place in the context of various ethnic and national tensions, but they nevertheless share a fingerprint that identifies Jews as preferred victims and objects of hate. Instances of the murder of Jews in different contexts were more similar to one another than they were to murders of non-Jews in the same contexts, and this demonstrates that Jews were in greater danger than others in a variety of periods and circumstances. Therefore, the alternative concepts that Engel proposes, as good as they are, can perhaps enrich the discussion, but they do not render the broader concept of "antisemitism" superfluous.

Moreover, use of the concept "antisemitism" in the context of the Holocaust is not the anachronistic conceptualization of scholars; the concept is used substantially and broadly in contemporary historical sources. For example, on August 15, 1920, Hitler gave a speech to supporters of the Nazi Party called "Why We Are Antisemites," which he later included in his book, *Mein Kampf*. Other senior Nazis also used this concept, and it appears in public opinion reports collected in Nazi Germany by German security services, as well as in the contemporary writings of Jews and non-Jews alike.[15] Engel is right that the concept of antisemitism in the eyes of these people is different from the one that crystallized in earlier periods and that sometimes contemporaries attribute different meanings to it. Thus, different studies attempt to give expression to this variation regarding the concept of antisemitism while addressing local patterns, different historical circumstances, and other unique characteristics.[16]

Those who view Engel as categorically disqualifying the very concept of "antisemitism" *ab initio* and not *ex post facto* actually adopt a simplistic and problematic perspective. Note that they do not call for liberation from the Judeocentric view and the examination of broader contexts beyond Jewish history;[17] rather, they assert that, *ab initio*, no step taken against Jews should be called antisemitism. This view does not substantively differ from one that attempts to classify within the concept of antisemitism any incident in which negative attitudes toward a Jew are expressed. These two approaches reflect an extreme attitude; there is no doubt that not every assault against Jews is a case of antisemitism, but there is also no substance in the claim that there is not even one incident that is worthy of being examined within the conceptual rubric of antisemitism.

Ultimately, our challenge as scholars is to focus on research and try to describe the whole without blurring its diverse and disparate components.[18] Just as blurring real differences between various parts of a whole impairs our understanding of it, so too does avoiding engagement with the whole. Therefore, I personally will continue to use the concept of antisemitism, albeit with precise awareness of its meaning: not only antisemitism, not always antisemitism, and certainly not antisemitism as a sole explanation. Understood in this way, the term antisemitism also has a place within the toolbox we have at our disposal as scholars of the modern history of the Jewish people.

NOTES

1. David Engel, "Away from a Definition of Antisemitism: An Essay in the Semantics of Historical Description," in *Rethinking European Jewish History*, ed. Jeremy Cohen and Moshe Rosman (Oxford: Littman Library of Jewish Civilization, 2009), 30–53.

2. Thus, the development of the Final Solution did not hinge solely on an ideology that called for the extermination of Judaism and Jews, but also on conditions in various fronts of the war. It is no coincidence that the mass murder of Jews began with Operation Barbarossa in June 1941, and there are some scholars who link the decision to murder all the Jews of Europe with the entry of the United States into the war.

3. For example, Nazi Germany's different ideological attitudes toward the peoples of eastern and western Europe influenced how Germans acted against Jews in those areas. This is true vis-à-vis both the policy of separating Jews from their surroundings through legislation or transfer to ghettos and the draconian collective punishment inflicted on those who aided Jews in eastern but not western Europe.

4. Christoph Dieckmann, *Deutsche Besatzungspolitik in Litauen 1941–1944* (Göttingen: Wallstein Verlag, 2011); Omer Bartov, *Anatomy of a Genocide: The Life and Death of*

a Town Called Buczacz (New York: Simon & Schuster, 2018); B. Engelking and J. Grabowski, eds., *Dalej jest noc: Losy Żydów w wybranych powiatach okupowanej Polski* (Warsaw: Centrum Badań nad Zagładą Żydów, 2018).

5. See, for example, Donald Bloxham, *The Final Solution: A Genocide* (Oxford: Oxford University Press, 2009), 139–43; Raz Segal, *Genocide in the Carpathians: War, Social Breakdown, and Mass Violence, 1914–1945* (Stanford, CA: Stanford University Press, 2016), 113–26; A. Dirk Moses, *Empire, Colony, Genocide: Conquest, Occupation, and Subaltern Resistance in World History* (New York: Berghahn Books, 2010). For Blatman's view of "uniqueness," see, for example, his talk titled "Beyond National Insights and Identities: Contemporary Historiography of the Holocaust in Poland," at a conference at the POLIN Museum of the History of Polish Jews, in Warsaw in 2015, www.youtube.com/watch?v=kzhPcSTa3O8 (from 1:04:45). It should be noted that the complicated views of leading Holocaust scholars vis-à-vis a variety of topics (antisemitism, the development of the Final Solution, relations between Jews and their environment, etc.) are often presented abstractly. This approach often calls their scholarly seriousness into question with arguments that easily become straw men. So, for instance, in the past some scholars (mainly Israeli) claimed that there is no historical event that can be compared to the Holocaust. Among its other flaws and limitations, this attitude mystified the Holocaust and undermined any possibility of analyzing specific aspects of it. Over the years, scholars—including Israeli scholars—have developed the more nuanced view that the Holocaust was an unprecedented event with unique features, but that it also shared common features with other genocidal tragedies.

6. For instance, Snyder describes the outbreak of terrible violence that inundated the territories between the Oder and Dnieper rivers—"Bloodlands"—from 1933 to 1945, bundling together fourteen million victims of both Nazi Germany and Soviet Russia. The murder of six million Jews—including those who, prior to the war, lived outside of the "Bloodlands" that he describes—is presented alongside the fate of the three million Ukrainians starved to death during the 1930s and millions of other European citizens. This geographical and chronological focus excludes, for instance, negative trends toward Jews that preceded 1933 and anti-Jewish steps taken by German occupiers and western European states themselves.

Blatman, by contrast, claims that the death marches were not an integral part of the Holocaust but instead belong to a different genocidal reality. Blatman claims that the death marches should be analyzed only in the context of German POWs in Russia and the Bataan Death March of American captives, not against the background of Europe's Jews in the Holocaust. Even though Blatman shows that inmates forced into death marches were often murdered by their captors and the local civilian population because they were seen as a threat—either an abstract demonic threat or the concrete threat posed by "Jews" (even if they were not Jews)—the event should not, according to him, be viewed as part of the Holocaust.

Another example comes from Raz Segal's study of the Carpathian Jews. Segal claims, based on the meticulous study of a range of sources, that the murder of the Carpathian Jews was not the product of antisemitism and that it should be understood not (only) in the context of the Holocaust, but specifically within more concrete contexts. According to him, this territory, in which numerous ethnic minorities, including Jews, lived, was replete with tensions. The various occupations and the radical attempts to reinforce Hungarian (Magyar) nationalism in their wake resulted in prolonged violence against different minorities. Segal therefore calls for examining the violence against Jews prior to the German invasion of Hungary in March 1944 against the backdrop of these ethnic and national tensions. See Timothy Snyder, *Bloodlands: Europe between Hitler and Stalin* (New York: Basic Books, 2010); Daniel Blatman, *The Death Marches: The Final Phase of Nazi Genocide* (Cambridge, MA: Harvard University Press, 2011); Segal, *Genocide in the Carpathians*. This approach also characterizes the essay "'Antisemitism' as a Question in Holocaust Studies," by Amos Goldberg and Raz Segal, in this volume, 299–318.

7. David Engel, "Patterns of Anti-Jewish Violence in Poland, 1944–1946," *Yad Vashem Studies* 26 (1998): 43–85. Also available via Yad Vashem's Shoah Resource Center, www.yadvashem.org/odot_pdf/Microsoft%20Word%20-%203128.pdf.

8. Ibid., 25 of the online version.

9. Nikolaus Wachsmann, *KL: A History of the Nazi Concentration Camps* (London: Little, Brown and Company, 2015), 29, 41–45; Kim Wünschmann, *Before Auschwitz: Jewish Prisoners in the Prewar Concentration Camps* (Cambridge, MA: Harvard University Press, 2015).

10. Barbara Engelking, *Such a Beautiful Sunny Day... Jews Seeking Refuge in the Polish Countryside, 1942–1945*, trans. Jerzy Michalowicz (Jerusalem: Yad Vashem, 2016), 293; Testimony of Yitzhak Lerner, 301.2802, Aug. 21, 1947 (Warsaw: Jewish Historical Institute).

11. Robert Rozett, *Conscripted Slaves: Hungarian Jewish Forced Laborers on the Eastern Front during the Second World War* (Jerusalem: Yad Vashem, 2013), 178–79.

12. Testimony of Yaakov Mallach, Pages of Testimony for Yitzhak Mallach, Yad Vashem, Hall of Names, 1157260 and 1956557. Another 2,800 Jews were deported on that transport from Greece. Of them, 417 men and 192 women were selected as inmates. The rest were murdered that same day.

13. Testimony of Jocelyne Benoliel, Pages of Testimony for Colette Allouche, Yad Vashem, Hall of Names, 1140564.

14. In addition to the studies already mentioned, see, for instance, Götz Aly and Susanne Heim, *Architects of Annihilation: Auschwitz and the Logic of Destruction* (Princeton, NJ: Princeton University Press, 2003); Christopher Browning, *Ordinary Men: Reserve Police Battalion 101 and the Final Solution in Poland* (New York: HarperCollins, 1992); Jan Grabowski, *Rescue for Money: Paid Helpers in Poland, 1939–1945* (Jerusalem: Yad Vashem, 2008).

15. For select examples, see Eberhard Jäckel, ed., *Hitler: Sämtliche Aufzeichnungen: 1905–1924* (Stuttgart: Deutsche Verlags-Anstalt, 1980), 448; Adolf Hitler, *Mein Kampf* (Boston: Houghton Mifflin, 1971), 560–61; Otto Dov Kulka and Eberhard Jäckel, eds., *The Jews in the Secret Nazi Reports on Popular Opinion in Germany, 1933–1945* (New

Haven, CT: Yale University Press, 2010), 96 (report from November and December 1934, Klein, Kassel) and 545 (report from September 30, 1941, Forchheim); Herman Kruk, *The Last Days of the Jerusalem of Lithuania* (New Haven, CT: Yale University Press, 2002), 175–76 (January 18, 1942), 523–24 (April 29, 1943); Rachel Feldhay Brenner, "The Anatomy of Rescue: The Wartime Diary of Aurelia Wyleżyńska, 1939–1944," *Yad Vashem Studies* 40, no. 1 (2012): 23–47.

16. For select examples, see Kamil Kijek, "Antysemityzm po polsku, 1905–1939: wprowadzenie," *Kwartalnik Historii Żydów* 258 (2016): 243–52; Shulamit Volkov, *Germans, Jews, and Antisemites: Trials in Emancipation* (Cambridge: Cambridge University Press, 2006); Saul Friedländer, *Nazi Germany and the Jews: Volume 1: The Years of Persecution, 1933–1939* (New York: HarperCollins, 1997), 93–136; Yehuda Bauer, "Ha antishemiyut baolam hamuslemi," in *Holocaust and Antisemitism: Research and Public Discourse—Essays Presented in Honor of Dina Porat*, [in Hebrew] ed. Roni Stauber, Aviva Halamish, and Esther Webman (Jerusalem: Yad Vashem, 2015), 275–96.

17. Richard Pipes, "Catherine II and the Jews: The Origins of the Pale of Settlement," *Soviet Jewish Affairs* 5, no. 2 (1975): 3–20; Israel Bartal, "The Other Story: Israeli Historians and Jewish 'Universalism,'" *European Review of History* 17, no. 3 (2010): 541–49.

18. Since the publication of the Hebrew version of this essay, the concept of antisemitism has come under a politically motivated attack that has echoes in this volume as well (including the essay by Goldberg and Segal noted above). See Scott Ury and Guy Miron, eds., *Antishemiyut: ben musag histori lesiah tsiburi* (Jerusalem: Shazar Center, 2020). In contrast to what emerges from their article, the International Holocaust Remembrance Alliance (IHRA) is an international government project established to promote the teaching, memorialization, and study of the Holocaust in various countries. The IHRA has published several working definitions devoted to museology (2012), Holocaust denial and distortion (2013), and anti-Roma discrimination (2020). This is the context in which the IHRA published its definition of antisemitism (2016). It is based on prior policy definitions and was formulated with the objective of providing policy makers in different countries with a tool to address the documented rise in Jew-hatred.

In the spring of 2021, a group of academics attacked the IHRA and its definition of antisemitism, and, in lieu of this definition published by a diplomatic body, offered an alternative academic definition in the so-called "Jerusalem Declaration on Antisemitism." This was a sad example of blurring the lines between history and politics. The document, which attempts to claim authority by using Jerusalem's name as part of its title, was not an open, academic, critical discussion. Rather, it brought together individuals from various disciplines who apparently share political views. Its purpose was not the advancement of knowledge in the field, but the formulation of a political agenda, and it should be seen as such. For the record, I have no affiliation whatsoever with the IHRA.

15

"Antisemitism" as a Question in Holocaust Studies

AMOS GOLDBERG *and* RAZ SEGAL

Dᴀᴠɪᴅ Eɴɢᴇʟ ɢʀᴀᴘᴘʟᴇs with a significant problem in his essay "Away from a Definition of Antisemitism." On the one hand, antisemitism is a very popular cultural and political concept in Jewish communities and throughout the Western world, and it also serves scholars of Jewish history and other realms. On the other hand, the concept is so flexible and signifies so many different and even contradictory phenomena that it seems to have lost, as Engel argues, its analytical power. Engel does not, of course, deny that Jews faced negative sentiments, discrimination, and violence throughout history. Rather, he claims that these phenomena are so different from one another that all they share is the word "antisemitism." Engel goes on to claim that it is necessary to develop a more distinct, subtle, and complex vocabulary to provide valid explanations for various phenomena in Jewish history. We maintain that this problem is not unique to this concept. Indeed, almost any major concept in the humanities and social sciences accumulates many, often contradictory, meanings. Nevertheless, Engel's question is important and urgent, as it helps clarify the different meanings of the concept of "antisemitism" and the various functions it carries out in a range of historical and political contexts.

Even though Engel has made significant contributions to the study of the Holocaust, his essay on antisemitism barely addresses the topic. The conspicuousness of the concept, however, is most clearly discernible in the context of the Holocaust. In popular discourse and in much scholarship, the connection between the Holocaust and antisemitism is unequivocal and undeniable; what could be more evident than Nazi antisemitism as a motivation to murder Jews?

Yet anyone who is even a bit familiar with the historiography of the Holocaust knows that things are far from simple. A series of questions about the concept of antisemitism and its analytical usefulness in understanding the Holocaust have in fact been raised since World War II. This constitutes a broad arena for polemics that were, and sometimes still are, emotionally charged.

Our article consists of three parts. In the first part, we present a survey of some of the questions that scholarship has raised concerning the explanatory power of the concept of antisemitism in the context of the Holocaust. The second part focuses primarily on one objection to the validity of this concept by examining more deeply the Holocaust in Romania and Bulgaria. In the third part of this article, we address the working definition produced by the International Holocaust Remembrance Alliance (IHRA), which defines antisemitism, and show why this particular definition, which emerged out of discussions of the Holocaust, is particularly problematic.

Antisemitism as an Open Question in the Study of the Holocaust

The extreme antisemitism of Hitler and the Nazi regime is often perceived as a self-evident explanation for the complex set of events and processes that together we call the Holocaust. According to this view, the Holocaust is not a historical riddle that demands deeper explanations, but rather self-explanatory—the (practically) inevitable result of the long history of antisemitism. This explanation is implied, for instance, by the permanent exhibit at Yad Vashem's Holocaust History Museum in Jerusalem.[1]

Yet how to explain the collection of events now known as the Holocaust is a problem that every historian of the Holocaust faces, and over which much ink has been and continues to be spilled. Almost all historians agree both that antisemitism is an important factor in explaining the Holocaust and that it is not the only factor. Historians disagree about the relative importance of antisemitism among other explanations for the Holocaust and the development of the "Final Solution," as well as about the very meaning of the concept of antisemitism and the extent to which antisemitism differs from or resembles other manifestations of othering.

We can use semiotic concepts to sort the issues surrounding the concept of antisemitism in the context of the Holocaust on two distinct planes. The first plane is diachronic; it allows us to examine the concept of antisemitism in the context of the Holocaust in relation to other historical phenomena, including in the modern period, that are called antisemitic. The second plane is synchronic; it allows us to analyze Nazi antisemitism and anti-Jewish policies in relation to other processes of mass violence and othering in the same period that were directed against other groups—or, more broadly, other modern phenomena that are not necessarily connected to Jews.

Let us begin with the diachronic axis on which the Holocaust could be linked to age-old antisemitic traditions in Europe. Shmuel Ettinger and David Nirenberg are examples of two very different scholars who made this connection. The former claims that anti-Jewish stereotypes circulated in Christian Europe for hundreds, even thousands of years—constantly changing their shape until culminating in the Holocaust.[2] David Nirenberg offers a more complex and updated version of this claim in his 2013 book surveying the history of anti-Judaism: "I do believe that the Holocaust *was inconceivable and is unexplainable* without that deep history of [anti-Jewish] thought."[3]

Perhaps Nirenberg is correct, but it is hard to prove such a claim; indeed, he himself uses the verb "believe." Yet this general history cannot provide a satisfactory explanation for the development of the mass murder of Jews. Two inevitable issues emerge in the diachronic context that make it difficult to understand how the age-old tradition of enmity toward Jews renders the Holocaust conceivable and explainable, to use Nirenberg's words: First, if the severe hostility toward Jews, as it developed in European Christian tradition, begat or even only explains the destruction, and this hostility is ancient, then why did the "Final Solution" only materialize in the mid-twentieth century? Second, even if we consider only modern antisemitism, which developed in eastern and western Europe during the nineteenth century primarily on the basis of ideas about race not religion, its connection to the "Final Solution," which was only implemented in the mid-twentieth century and, as Nirenberg notes, specifically by Germany, remains unclear.

A famous quip attributed (rightly or wrongly) to George Mosse expresses these problems very sharply: Had one been asked at the beginning of the century whether the annihilation of the Jews was possible, one would probably answer that indeed the French are capable of anything.[4] Indeed, in the period after the Dreyfus Affair and the appearance of the *Protocols of the Elders of Zion*, it seemed that acute political antisemitism characterized France, tsarist Russia, and Romania, but not Germany. It is thus difficult to link German antisemitic traditions directly with the destruction of Jews.[5] The historian Shulamit Volkov asked: Considering the terrifying results of the Holocaust, which went far beyond anything that had happened to Jews in Europe during the preceding century and a half, what is the degree of continuity or discontinuity within the phenomenon that we call antisemitism? In this case, Volkov answered that it was more discontinuous than continuous.[6]

This issue was also a main bone of contention between the "functionalist" and "intentionalist" schools in the study of the Holocaust and the "Final Solution." The functionalists, whose intellectual progenitor is considered to be the great Holocaust scholar Raul Hilberg, maintain that antisemitism was not the direct cause of the Holocaust; rather, local officials and bureaucrats responding to ad hoc problems and changing circumstances made murderous decisions that culminated in what we now call the "Final Solution." In the functionalist view, antisemitic ideology played only a secondary, contextual role in these developments.[7]

By contrast, advocates of the intentionalist school contend that antisemitic ideology constitutes the most important component for understanding the Holocaust. Most of these scholars focus on the short-term perspective (Nazi antisemitism and not on historical antisemitism) and argue that the radical antisemitism of Hitler and Nazi Germany led to the murderous policy against Jews. Many scholars maintain this view in one form or another, including Alon Confino, Eberhard Jäckel, Ian Kershaw, Yehuda Bauer, David Cesarani, and others, even though each of them offers a different understanding of the concept of antisemitism and its relationship with other explanatory factors.[8]

However, here, too, a question emerges: If antisemitism, as a fundamental ideological position, was the primary, unvarying motivation for Nazi anti-Jewish policies, then why did the mass murder of Jews begin only in the summer of 1941 and not in the preceding eight years, during which time the Nazis were in power in Germany, and after September 1939 in occupied Poland and most of western Europe? In fact, between 1933 and 1939 (and actually until October 1941), the Nazis made increasingly violent efforts to push Jews to emigrate. Later, between September 1939 and the summer of 1941, the Nazis considered several solutions involving the mass expulsion of Jews (to Poland's Lublin region, to Madagascar, and to deep inside the Soviet Union) after a German victory.

Ultimately, only when all of these solutions failed and the war continued longer than expected was the "Final Solution" developed gradually as a policy for the systematic mass murder of every Jew in areas controlled by and allied with Nazi Germany. Moreover, about a year before the onset of systematic mass murder, its two future architects and professed radical antisemites—Reinhard Heydrich and Heinrich Himmler—explicitly dismissed the possibility of annihilating a people.[9] It thus seems that there is no direct, simple, and inevitable link between antisemitism of one sort or another and the Nazi annihilation of Jews. Antisemitism may have been a necessary condition for the "Final Solution," but certainly not a sufficient, and perhaps not even the most central, condition. Any explanation that directly links antisemitism to the "Final Solution" must address other elements that explain the convoluted history of "the twisted road to Auschwitz."[10]

Weighty questions emerge also on the synchronic level—namely, the complex, reciprocal relationship of Nazi antisemitism as a murderous anti-Jewish policy and ideology with other ideological and violent policies in the same years, or during the modern era more generally. As many scholars have shown, the racial discourse that was central to Nazi antisemitism developed initially not against Jews, but rather against non-European peoples. Racial discourse had been used to justify terrible crimes, including genocide, mainly in European colonies outside of Europe.[11] Thus, one of the first anti-colonial thinkers, Aimé Césaire, described the Holocaust as representing the importation of colonial violence into the European continent.[12] It therefore makes less sense to view Nazi antisemitism as a *sui generis* form of radical exclusion that is completely different from other forms of exclusion and political violence than to agree with the historian Donald Bloxham, who writes in *The Final Solution* that "biological racism is only at the extreme end of a continuum of exclusionary beliefs that have the potential to attribute malign characteristics to all members of another group."[13] There is a large degree of contextual and explanatory continuity between the Holocaust and other genocides and instances of mass violence that occurred in the modern period with unprecedented intensity compared with the rest of human history.

Indeed, it seems that the "Final Solution" could not have emerged outside the context of nationalist and imperialist Nazi violence both within and beyond Germany. Much, for example, has been written about the Nazi euthanasia program—the mass murder of physically and mentally disabled people according to Nazi racial definitions— whose personnel developed their techniques in the killing facilities of the program and later formed the core of those building the annihilation camps of Operation Reinhard—Bełżec, Treblinka, and Sobibor.[14]

Likewise, many have identified the link between the mass murder of Jews in German-occupied areas of the Soviet Union—which began in the summer of 1941, mainly with the murder of Jewish men (whom the Nazis saw, collectively, as "commissars" and agents of the Soviet regime and ideology), and which became, within weeks or a few months, the murder of every Soviet Jew—and the murder of Soviet POWs, which was taking place at the same time (and sometimes in the same facilities). By the end of 1941, the Nazis had murdered about two million Soviet POWs, mostly through starvation, and around one million Soviet Jews.[15] A variety of studies have more broadly addressed the connection between the Holocaust, the Nazi starvation plan, and the General Plan of the East, in which the Nazis designed the mass murder of tens of millions of Slavs and the disappearance of entire national groups.[16] According to some scholars, then, the Holocaust, precisely because of its magnitude and extreme nature, demands a multidimensional explanation in which antisemitism constitutes context and background but not an immediate, concrete explanation for the development of the "Final Solution."[17]

Saul Friedländer's book *Nazi Germany and the Jews* exemplifies this tension. One of his central claims, developed in the book's first volume, is that Nazi antisemitism, which he refers to as "redemptive antisemitism," was unique and different from other types of antisemitism or racial hatred.[18] This antisemitism, which resulted from a mixture of religious traditions, romantic mysticism, and a particularly acute racial discourse, saw the redemption of Germany and all of Europe in the annihilation of Jews. This intense and extreme antisemitism, according to Friedländer, therefore renders the Holocaust unique.

However, when Friedländer comes to explain the timing of Hitler's decision on the "Final Solution," he gets caught in an internal contradiction, for he claims that Hitler made this decision in December 1941 after the United States entered the war, and that the decision was based on security considerations. Friedländer relies, inter alia, on an enigmatic entry in Himmler's appointment diary from December 18, 1941, after a meeting with Hitler: "The Jewish question | annihilate as partisans." This important but cryptic evidence has garnered a range of interpretations. Interestingly, Friedländer adopts here an interpretation in the spirit of Christian Gerlach, one of the most prominent historians to embed the Holocaust in the larger context of Nazi imperial violence and not in a unique, redemptive form of antisemitism.[19] According to Friedländer, "'partisans' associated maybe with the most general connotation used by Hitler in his declaration at the conference of July 16, 1941: All *potential enemies* within Germany's reach; it was understood . . . to include any civilians and entire communities at will."[20] It was only when Germany was thrown into a position of vast inferiority to the Allied Powers, Friedländer claims, that Hitler decided to take a firm stance against those whom he perceived to be the most dangerous internal enemy: Jews. In this focus on security anxieties, Friedländer's explanation of the "Final Solution" approximates explanations of other genocides, such as the Armenian genocide, and other cases of extreme mass violence. Once Friedländer needs to account for the actual genocide, he cannot help but refer to explanations about security, and not to "redemptive antisemitism": The murderers viewed and imagined their victims as a fifth column, an unrivaled danger especially at a time of fateful war, and therefore thought that they should be exterminated.[21]

The Cases of Romania and Bulgaria: Challenging Antisemitism as an Explanation for the Holocaust

The claim that Nazi antisemitism, as redemptive antisemitism, is a unique phenomenon—the core of an irrational ideology according to which the murder of all the Jews under German control and influence during World War II stood above every other consideration—obscures a basic feature of the Holocaust: It was not just a Nazi project, but a European project. Understanding the Holocaust in this way, as occurring beyond the areas occupied directly by Nazi Germany, reveals several problems with using the concept of antisemitism, and certainly "redemptive antisemitism," as a self-evident explanation for the mass murder of Jews and the destruction of Jewish communities.

For our purposes, the most important region beyond the areas occupied by Germany is southeastern Europe. Before the war, about 1.7 million Jews lived in this region, primarily in countries that ultimately became allies of Nazi Germany and remained independent throughout most of the war (Hungary, until the German invasion of the country in March 1944) or all of the war (Romania and Bulgaria). Addressing antisemitism in southeastern Europe demonstrates one of David Engel's claims: Sweeping, general treatments of antisemitism as a seemingly self-evident concept very often ignore the importance of broader historical contexts. In this case, a major twentieth-century political development is overlooked: the violent consolidation of the modern nation-state.

The vision of the nation-state of "Greater Romania" was the centerpiece of the policy of Ion Antonescu, the military dictator of Romania from January 1941 to August 1944. Antonescu strove to restore all the territories that Romania had lost in 1940—to the Soviet Union (northern Bukovina and Bessarabia in June), Hungary (northern Transylvania in August), and Bulgaria (southern Dobruja in September). These

Romanian territories were ceded within the framework of agreements imposed upon Romania by Germany and Italy as part of the diplomatic maneuvers meant primarily to prevent conflict between their allies. Thus, the "Greater Romania" of the aftermath of World War I became, within a year, a small country wounded by intense national humiliation. The loss of part of Transylvania especially stung the national consciousness, as nationalist leaders viewed—and continue to view— Transylvania as the cradle of the Romanian nation.[22]

Jews in Romania during World War II lived in a state with a history of anti-Jewish political and social discourse that stretched back almost a hundred years—since the establishment of modern Romania in 1859. This discourse intensified after World War I, in the context of a nationalist push to exclude from the Romanian nation Jews and other groups— those thought to be Bulgarians, Ukrainians, Germans, Roma, and especially Transylvanian Hungarians. The leaders of Romania relied on this vision when they accused Jews in northern Bukovina and Bessarabia of Soviet sympathies and abetting the Soviet takeover of these regions in the summer of 1940. This perception, which presented Jews as a security threat, prepared the ground for the mass murder and mass expulsion of Jews from these areas when the Romanian military joined the German attack on the Soviet Union in June 1941 and reoccupied them.

However, the mass violence was directed not only against Jews, but against anyone perceived as not belonging to, or endangering, the vision of "Greater Romania." As Antonescu declared before his ministers in September 1941: "[I demand] total purification of Jews and of all those who penetrated among us. I mean: Ukrainians, Greeks, Gagauzi [a Turkic-speaking group of Orthodox Christians], Jews, they all, row after row, will have to be evacuated."[23] Between 1941 and 1943, Antonescu considered three plans to realize this vision, which included the mass expulsion of 3.5 million people and the resettlement within Romania of about 2 million people whom the state considered Romanian and who lived primarily in Ukraine and the Northern Caucasus.[24] This was a broad national vision with colonial features. Even though much of this vision remained unrealized, it is essential for understanding the significance of antisemitism and the violent policies against Jews in Romania and the territories under its control during World War II.

Romanian state authorities expelled, plundered, and murdered over 350,000 Jews from Bessarabia, northern Bukovina, and Transnistria—the territory between the Dniester and Bug rivers that Hitler gave to Antonescu during the war to compensate him for the loss of northern Transylvania.[25] The Romanian authorities also expelled about 25,000 Roma to Transnistria; fewer than half of them survived the war.[26] However, starting in October 1942, Antonescu refused to hand over the rest of the Jews under Romanian control to the Nazis, who planned to murder them in the Bełżec annihilation camp. Thus, about 375,000 Jews remained alive in Romania until the end of the war. This drastic change in Romanian policy stemmed from Antonescu's assessment, starting in the summer of 1942, that Germany would lose the war—a forecast that required him to rethink Romanian anti-Jewish policy. In a postwar world dominated by the Allies, murdering Jews was likely to impede the fulfillment of the vision of "Greater Romania," especially in the struggle with Hungary over Transylvania. Indeed, about two years later, in August 1944, Romania switched sides and joined the Soviet attack on Hungary, during which it conquered northern Transylvania and reunified the territory under its control. As Holly Case has noted:

> The events of the Holocaust in Hungary and Romania were heavily influenced by the fact that the Jews were *not* the primary policy preoccupation in these states either before or during the war. Instead, the "Jewish Question" was frequently viewed in light of its relationship to territorial matters, and for that reason Hungarian and Romanian policy vis-à-vis the Jews was shockingly inconsistent.[27]

If the involvement of Romanian state authorities in the murder of Jews was rooted in a violent nationalist view against other groups as well, then not everyone who murdered Jews in Romania during World War II acted on the basis of anti-Jewish motivations. A group of German speakers in Transnistria (the Black Sea Germans) without any history of antisemitism, for instance, murdered tens of thousands of Jews. However, there was no discernible tension in their relations with the region's Jews before the war, and the high level of intermarriage with Jews attests to good relations.[28] The order to murder Jews came from the personnel of *Sonderkommando R*, the SS unit that governed regions of German-speaking settlements in German-occupied areas of the Soviet Union and in Romanian-controlled Transnistria. These SS men worked diligently to make these German speakers into loyal Nazis as part of a vision to build up the Nazi empire in eastern Europe. When Antonescu decided, in December 1941, that the Jews in and around Odessa constituted a security risk and must be expelled, the Romanian occupation authorities selected the area where the German speakers lived as their destination. The SS forces, who in the preceding months had murdered Jews as part of their efforts to "Germanize" the region, decided to use the German speakers to murder the expelled Jews.

The historian Eric Steinhart discusses two main reasons why German speakers in Transnistria carried out the orders of the SS: despoiling the property of the Jews they murdered and proving their loyalty to the occupiers from Berlin. However, in this case, demonstrating loyalty entailed a fateful element, as many German speakers in Transnistria had married not only Jews, but also local Slavic people. The German occupiers thus found a population that, as in other places in eastern Europe, filled an important role in the Nazi imperial vision, but the degree of its "Germanness" and the possibility of including it in the larger German "people's community" (*Volksgemeinschaft*) remained dubious. Participation in the mass murder of Jews thus allowed German-speaking Transnistrians to prove their "Germanness" in the eyes of the Nazis.[29] German speakers understood the advantages of this identity in a Nazi world. Steinhart's work thus joins a series of studies from the past decade that demonstrate the opposite of what is customarily presumed and taught: Identity, in many cases, does not motivate mass murder; rather, mass murder is a process that generates identities, both of the murderers and of the victims.[30]

The survival of around 50,000 Jews in Bulgaria is also relevant to our discussion, as there, too, we find no significant history of anti-Jewish social and political discourse. Still, state authorities persecuted, robbed, and expelled about 13,000 Jews from the border regions of Macedonia and Thrace, which Bulgaria occupied during the war. As in Romania, anti-Jewish policies in Bulgaria were inconsistent and stemmed from the vision of the nation-state of "Greater Bulgaria" and various possibilities of realizing this goal during the war.

However, it was Muslims and people identified as Greeks, not Jews, who topped the list of "others" in "Greater Bulgaria." Bulgarian national leaders had dreamt of controlling Macedonia and Thrace ever since the emergence of Bulgaria as an autonomous entity under Ottoman control after the Berlin Congress of 1878 and through the Balkan Wars of 1912–1913 and World War I. Bulgarian national leaders failed to realize this dream—despite the bloody wars against the Ottomans and against Greek and Serbian national leaders in Macedonia.[31] Like Transylvania for Romanian national leaders, Macedonia was seen as the cradle of the nation for Bulgarian national leaders. As in the Romanian case, Bulgaria viewed its alliance with Nazi Germany as a tool to realize the vision of "Greater Bulgaria." In April 1941, Bulgaria took the first step in that direction when the state joined Germany, Italy, and Hungary in attacking Yugoslavia and Greece, taking control of territories in western Thrace and eastern Macedonia.

The Bulgarian occupation authorities immediately began transforming these regions into parts of "Greater Bulgaria." In western Thrace, they closed Greek churches and schools and placed heavy restrictions on Greek business owners. In September 1941, Bulgarian authorities exploited the spontaneous uprising of Greeks in Drama to despoil and then expel about 100,000 Greeks to German-occupied areas in Greece and send tens of thousands of Bulgarian settlers to the region.[32] This is a crucial context for understanding the deportation of Jews from western Thrace and eastern Macedonia in March 1943 into the hands of the Nazis, who murdered them at the Treblinka annihilation camp.

The absence of a significant anti-Jewish discourse in Bulgaria before and during World War II has led scholars to emphasize the survival of some 50,000 Jews within the state's borders as of April 1941—a result of public outcry and protests by both Jews and non-Jews in the spring of 1943 against the state's plans to deport all Jews in Bulgaria into Nazi hands—while minimizing the role played by Bulgarian authorities in the arrest, plunder, and expulsion of 13,000 Jews from Bulgarian-occupied areas after April 1941.[33] Importantly, Jews had lived in western Thrace as Greek citizens before World War II, and Bulgarian state authorities therefore viewed them as Greeks—as did many of these Jews themselves—and treated them accordingly, that is, as a dangerous group in a key borderland region during a time of war. In the same way, the Bulgarian authorities treated the Jews of eastern Macedonia as Yugoslav citizens. As in the case of Romania, focusing on Jews in Bulgaria without considering the nation-state's territorial interests leads to a distorted view that assumes a clear, direct link between antisemitism or its absence and the fate of Jews during World War II.

Problematic Political Uses of the Concept of Antisemitism in Global Holocaust Memory

The analysis presented thus far not only demonstrates the problem with simplistically using the concept of antisemitism to describe and explain the persecutions, expulsions, and murder of Jews in Europe generally, and southeastern Europe particularly, during World War II. It also obligates us to address the problematic usage of the concept when discussing what are often called the "lessons" of the Holocaust, which, since the 1990s, have been institutionalized in global cultural and memorial frameworks in which the fight against antisemitism plays a central role.

Many organizations that deal with the Holocaust also fight against manifestations of antisemitism, racism, xenophobia, and the like. Perhaps the most important of them is the International Holocaust Remembrance Alliance (IHRA), an organization founded in 1998 that today unifies the official representatives—politicians, scholars, and educators—of thirty-five countries (almost all of them from Europe or the "West") and is very influential in the international arena. The IHRA fights antisemitism, but in contradistinction to Engel's call to turn away from defining antisemitism, the organization decided, in 2016, to adopt a rigid "working definition" of the concept that it has since relentlessly worked to apply in a wide range of contexts.

Our contention is that this move exemplifies Engel's fundamental claim that the use of antisemitism as an analytical category is not the result of "empirical observation but of a socio-semantic convention created in the nineteenth century and sustained throughout the twentieth for communal and political ends, not scholarly ones."[34] In the present case, it is easy to identify the political motives through a close reading of the IHRA definition, which has faced much criticism throughout the world and yet retains significant political power.[35]

The IHRA document focuses mainly on the fight against alleged antisemitism that masquerades, according to its drafters, as criticism of Israel. The word "Israel" appears nine times in the document. By contrast, the antisemitism spreading through the nationalist right in Europe and beyond, which is linked to other manifestations of racism and xenophobia, receives barely any attention. Moreover, countries where nationalist governments use blatantly antisemitic images, according to the IHRA definition itself, remain legitimate members of this organization, which, in effect, legitimizes their antisemitic, racist, and xenophobic policies.

Hungary, currently an IHRA member state, is a clear example of this situation. In recent years, the Hungarian government has made the Jewish billionaire and Holocaust survivor George Soros the target of political attacks using imagery that clearly meets the IHRA's definition of antisemitism. Soros often supports organizations that act against the nationalist and anti-democratic policies of Hungary. In the summer of 2017, the ruling party in Hungary, Fidesz, put up hundreds of billboards reading, "Don't let Soros have the last laugh." The billboards focused on the alleged international power of Jews—a classic antisemitic motif that Hitler and many other antisemites have used and still use to this day.[36] It is no wonder that some people added explicitly antisemitic messages to the billboards in graffiti, like "dirty Jew." Yet, Hungary continues to be a member of the IHRA, an organization that sees the struggle against antisemitism as one of its goals. The reality, however, is that IHRA's cooperation with Hungary actually legitimizes a government whose actions are antisemitic according to its own definition. This situation is thus a political performance that makes a completely cynical use of the term of "antisemitism."

Because it is an essentially political definition of antisemitism rather than a historical or an empirical one, the IHRA working definition also faces a basic contradiction in its characterization of the types of criticism of Israel that may be considered antisemitic. The document, for instance, lists "claiming that the existence of a State of Israel is a racist endeavor" as an example of antisemitism. However, this definition grants Israel a type of immunity from a common accusation of racism today regarding the nature of settler-colonial states.[37] Thus, discourse that is legitimate and reasonable with respect to the United States, Canada, France, and Australia, for example, is deemed antisemitic with respect to Israel and is made a moral taboo linked to the Holocaust—even though the IHRA working definition states that "criticism of Israel similar to that levelled against any other country cannot be regarded as antisemitic."

Moreover, due to its political essence, the IHRA document makes ahistorical determinations about statements that fall under the definition of antisemitism. In this context, we suggest returning to Shulamit Volkov's basic claim that the political and social context of antisemitic statements or actions are an integral part of the phenomenon. Therefore, the same statement that was uttered against powerless Jews in the 1930s or 1940s (for instance, "to boycott Jewish shops") has a completely different meaning when uttered against a sovereign state with significant military power relative to its neighbors and certainly relative to Palestinians under its control. While such a statement would be considered antisemitic in Nazi Germany in the 1930s, it is of a different nature, and perhaps even legitimate (if albeit controversial), when directed against Israel ("boycott Israel"). Any definition that tries to articulate a universal and unchanging truth will inevitably blur historical understanding so that it can serve, as Engel wrote, as a political tool.

This issue finds expression in another section of the IHRA definition as well. The document recognizes the legitimacy of criticizing Israel, but with the reservation that such criticism is only legitimate if it is "similar to that leveled against any other country." Here, too, the definition presents an ahistorical and thus distorted view, as though there is a fixed threshold within the public and international arena that only antisemites exceed. Yet there was no less criticism of South Africa during Apartheid, the Soviet Union during the Cold War ("Evil Empire"), the United States during the Vietnam War and the Trump presidency, France during the war in Algeria, and even Germany in the 2000s (in Greek discourse, for example, when the economic crisis hit) than there is against Israel today.

The overly broad IHRA definition and its vague examples make it possible for the IHRA working definition to categorize almost any harsh criticism of Israel or Zionism as antisemitism. Indeed, there is already a wealth of documentation that argues that the definition serves to silence legitimate criticism of Israel and Zionism.[38] It thus emerges that the fight against antisemitism based on Holocaust memory—which should protect Jews from discrimination and persecution by majority societies and nation-states—grants Israel, as a nation-state, and Jews, as the sovereign majority therein, the comparative privilege of discriminating against and even oppressing a minority, in this case Palestinians, without being censured for this behavior.

Just as Engel claimed about definitions of antisemitism, the working definition formulated by the IHRA is far more political than historical. We do not claim that an anti-Jewish opinion or statement cannot masquerade as anti-Israeli sentiment or as anti-Zionism. Nor do we claim that anti-Israeli attitudes or anti-Zionism are incapable of using patently antisemitic images or of sliding into overt antisemitism. However, in the spirit of Engel's criticism, we maintain that much conceptual, moral, and political damage is caused by such rigid and partial definitions that become fixed, ahistorically, as quasi-legal formulations that do not take into consideration the historical, social, and cultural contexts of those statements or actions that are perceived, according to such definitions, as antisemitic or not. Such formulations are absorbed into public discussions and easily enter historical research—and therein lies their danger.

Therefore, the authors of this article agree that using antisemitism as a concept with a fixed meaning and self-evident explanatory power in understanding the Holocaust specifically and modern Jewish history in general obscures more than it illuminates and does more harm than good. Moreover, in many cases, as Engel states, the concept of antisemitism is used politically, and sometimes even cynically. However, the two authors disagree about the status of the concept itself. While Goldberg views it as a necessary and important concept in understanding the history of Jews, albeit one that must be used with great caution and constant awareness of its different and varying meanings and its complex relationship with other factors in any historical context, Segal joins Engel in calling for the eschewal of its use and for seeking other ways of studying the past and speaking about the present.

NOTES

1. Amos Goldberg, "The 'Jewish Narrative' in the Yad Vashem Global Holocaust Museum," *Journal of Genocide Research* 14, no. 2 (June 2012): 187–213.

2. Shmuel Ettinger, *Haantishemiyut ba'et hahadashah* (Tel Aviv: Moreshet, 1978).

3. David Nirenberg, *Anti-Judaism: The Western Tradition* (New York: W. W. Norton, 2013), 458–59. Emphasis in the original.

4. Mosse put it a bit differently in his own words: "Before the First World War, it was France rather than Germany or Austria that seemed likely to become the home of a successful racist and National Socialist movement." George Mosse, *Toward the Final Solution: A History of European Racism* (New York: H. Fertig, 1978), 178.

5. Daniel Goldhagen argued for such a strong linkage, and his interpretation was rejected by many in the scholarly community. Daniel Jonah Goldhagen, *Hitler's Willing Executioners: Ordinary Germans and the Holocaust* (New York: Alfred A. Knopf, 1996).

6. Shulamit Volkov, *Germans, Jews, and Antisemites: Trials in Emancipation* (New York: Cambridge University Press, 2006), 67–81.

7. See Ian Kershaw, *The Nazi Dictatorship: Problems and Perspectives of Interpretation* (London: E. Arnold, 2000), 69–92; Richard Evans, *In Hitler's Shadow: West German Historians and the Attempt to Escape from the Nazi Past* (New York: Pantheon Books, 1989). See also Amos Goldberg, "The Holocaust and Modernity," *Moreshet: Journal for the Study of the Holocaust and Antisemitism* 12 (2015): 190–238.

8. Here we refer only to the highest levels of the Nazi leadership. We are not addressing the question of the degree to which the ranks tasked with implementing Nazi policies, the bureaucracy, and the general population acted out of antisemitic motives.

9. In May 1940, Himmler wrote Hitler a memorandum summarizing the demographic organization of Poland. In the document, he mentioned various methods to get rid of ethnic groups. Regarding Jews, he made clear his intent to deport them to Madagascar or another colony. Later in the same discussion he noted, in a slightly different context, that the "Bolshevik method of physically destroying a people must be rejected out of the inner recognition that this is an impossible and un-German act." See Helmut Krausnick, ed., "Denkschrift Himmlers über die Behandlung der Fremdvölkischen im Osten (Mai 1940)," *Vierteljahrshefte für Zeitgeschichte* 5, no. 2 (1957): 194–98, especially 196–97. According to the 1948 testimony of an audience member, in the summer of 1940 when speaking about the Madagascar plan, Heydrich stated: "We must get rid of [the Jews], but physical annihilation is unbecoming of Germans as a cultured nation." See Götz Aly, *"Final Solution": Nazi Population Policy and the Murder of the European Jews* (London: Arnold, 1999), 3.

10. Karl Schleunes, *The Twisted Road to Auschwitz* (Urbana: University of Illinois Press, 1970); Debórah Dwork and Robert Jan van Pelt, *Auschwitz: 1270 to the Present* (New York: W. W. Norton, 1996).

11. See Annegret Ehmann, "From Colonial Racism to Nazi Population Policy: The Role of the So-Called Mischlinge," in *The Holocaust and History*, ed. Michael Berenbaum et al. (Bloomington: Indiana University Press, 1998), 115–33; Jürgen Zimmerer, *Von Windhuk nach Auschwitz?* (Berlin: Lit Verlag, 2011). In a slightly different context, see James Q. Whitman, *Hitler's American Model: The United States and the Making of Nazi Race Law* (Princeton, NJ: Princeton University Press, 2017).

12. Aimé Césaire, *Discourse on Colonialism* (New York: Monthly Review Press, 1972).

13. Donald Bloxham, *The Final Solution: A Genocide* (Oxford: Oxford University Press, 2009), 6.

14. Henry Friedlander, *The Origins of the Nazi Genocide: From Euthanasia to the Final Solution* (Chapel Hill: University of North Carolina Press, 1995).

15. See, for instance, Karel C. Berkhoff, "The Mass Murder of Soviet Prisoners of War and the Holocaust: How Were They Related?," *Kritika: Explorations in Russian and Eurasian History* 6, no. 4 (Fall 2005) (New Series): 789–96.

16. See Christian Gerlach, *The Extermination of the European Jews* (Cambridge: Cambridge University Press, 2016), 215–60; Lizzie Collingham, *The Taste of War: World War II and the Battle for Food* (New York: Penguin, 2012), 32–48, 180–218; Mark Mazower, *Hitler's Empire: How the Nazis Ruled Europe* (New York: Penguin Books, 2008). See also the special edition of *Journal of Genocide Research* 19, no. 2 (2017).

17. Several studies over the past decade address, at the micro level, relations between Jews and their neighbors. These studies also identify the need to understand "antisemitism" and mass violence against Jews in the multidimensional context of social disintegration under German occupation and mass violence perpetrated against other groups. See Tomasz Frydel, "*Judenjagd*: Reassessing the Role of Ordinary Poles as Perpetrators in the Holocaust," in *Perpetrators and Perpetration of Mass Violence: Actions, Motivations and Dynamics*, ed. Timothy Williams and Susanne Buckley-Zistel (New York: Routledge, 2018), 187–203; Omer Bartov, *Anatomy of a Genocide: The Life and Death of a Town Called Buczacz* (New York: Simon & Schuster, 2018).

18. Saul Friedländer, *Nazi Germany and the Jews*, vol. 1, *The Years of Persecution, 1933–1939* (London: Weidenfeld and Nicolson, 1997), chap. 3.

19. See Christian Gerlach, "The Wannsee Conference, the Fate of German Jews, and Hitler's Decision in Principle to Exterminate All European Jews," *Journal of Modern History* 70, no. 4 (1998): 752–812.

20. Saul Friedländer, *Nazi Germany and the Jews: Years of Extermination, 1939–1945* (New York: HarperCollins, 2007), 280. Emphasis in the original.

21. Mark Levene, "'The Enemy Within'? Armenians, Jews, the Military Crises of 1915 and the Genocidal Origins of the 'Minorities Question,'" in *Minorities and the First World War: From War to Peace*, ed. Hannah Ewence and Tim Grady (London: Palgrave

Macmillan, 2017), 143–73; Isabel V. Hull, *Absolute Destruction: Military Culture and the Practices of War in Imperial Germany* (Ithaca, NY: Cornell University Press, 2006); A. Dirk Moses, *The Problems of Genocide: Permanent Security and the Language of Transgression* (New York: Cambridge University Press, 2021).

22. Holly Case, *Between States: The Transylvanian Question and the European Idea during World War II* (Stanford, CA: Stanford University Press, 2009).

23. Translation of this quote is from Vladimir Solonari, "'Model Province': Explaining the Holocaust of Bessarabian and Bukovinian Jewry," *Nationalities Papers* 34, no. 4 (2006): 487.

24. Vladimir Solonari, *Purifying the Nation: Population Exchange and Ethnic Cleansing in Nazi-Allied Romania* (Baltimore: Johns Hopkins University Press, 2009).

25. Jean Ancel, *The History of the Holocaust in Romania*, trans. Yaffah Murciano (Lincoln: University of Nebraska Press, 2011).

26. M. Benjamin Thorne, "Assimilation, Invisibility, and the Eugenic Turn in the 'Gypsy Question' in Romanian Society, 1938–1942," *Romani Studies* 21, no. 2 (2011): 177–205.

27. Case, *Between* States, 197. Emphasis in the original. On Hungary, see Raz Segal, *Genocide in the Carpathians: War, Social Breakdown, and Mass Violence, 1914–1945* (Stanford, CA: Stanford University Press, 2016).

28. Eric C. Steinhart, "Family, Fascists, and 'Volksdeutsche': The Bogdanovka Collective Farm and the Holocaust in Southern Ukraine, December 1941," *Holocaust Studies: A Journal of Culture and History* 16, nos. 1–2 (2010): 83–84.

29. Steinhart, "Family, Fascists, and 'Volksdeutsche,'" 87–88.

30. See Max Bergholz, *Violence as a Generative Force: Identity, Nationalism, and Memory in a Balkan Community* (Ithaca, NY: Cornell University Press, 2017); Lee Ann Fujii, *Killing Neighbors: Webs of Violence in Rwanda* (Ithaca, NY: Cornell University Press, 2011).

31. Marshall Lee Miller, *Bulgaria during the Second World War* (Stanford, CA: Stanford University Press, 1975), 2–3.

32. Miller, *Bulgaria during the Second World War*, 126–30; Theodora Dragostinova, *Between Two Motherlands: Nationality and Emigration among the Greeks of Bulgaria, 1900–1949* (Ithaca, NY: Cornell University Press, 2011), 250–54; Xanthippi Kotzageorgi-Zymari with Tassos Hadjianastassiou, "Memories of the Bulgarian Occupation of Eastern Macedonia: Three Generations," in *After the War Was Over: Reconstructing the Family, Nation, and State in Greece, 1943–1960*, ed. Mark Mazower (Princeton, NJ: Princeton University Press, 2000), 273–92.

33. The collection of texts and documents in Tzvetan Todorov, *The Fragility of Goodness: Why Bulgaria's Jews Survived the Holocaust* (Princeton, NJ: Princeton University Press, 2001) is symptomatic.

34. Engel, "Away from a Definition of Antisemitism," 53.

35. For a partial list, see Corey Balsam, "Who's Against Adopting the IHRA Anti-semitism Definition?," *Times of Israel* (blog), December 9, 2020, https://blogs.times ofisrael.com/whos-against-adopting-the-ihra-antisemitism-definition. On the polit-ical motivations behind the IHRA definition and the concept of the "New Anti-semitism," see Antony Lerman, *Whatever Happened to Antisemitism?: Redefinition and the Myth of the 'Collective Jew'* (London: Pluto, 2022), chap. 5. Also see Scott Ury, "Strange Bedfellows? Anti-Semitism, Zionism, and the Fate of 'the Jews,'" *American Historical Review* 123, no. 4 (October 2018): 1151–71.

36. Shimon Stein and Moshe Zimmermann, "The 'Laughing Jew': The Nazi Backstory of Hungary's Anti-Soros Poster Campaign," *Haaretz*, July 13, 2017, www.haaretz.com /opinion/2017-07-13/ty-article/the-laughing-jew-the-nazi-backstory-of-hungarys -anti-soros-poster-campaign/0000017f-e397-d9aa-afff-fbdfd4e10000.

37. The question of whether Israel is a settler-colonial state or at least has charac-teristics of settler colonialism lies beyond the scope of this article. It is sufficient to note that this approach is accepted by many in the scholarly community. See the comprehensive survey in Areej Sabbagh-Khoury, "Settler Colonialism, the Indige-nous Perspective, and the Sociology of Knowledge Production in Israel," [in Hebrew] *Theory and Criticism* 50 (Winter 2018): 391–418. Even Anita Shapira, a senior Zionist historian, sees significant colonial elements in the Zionist project. See Anita Sha-pira, *Land and Power: The Zionist Resort to Force, 1881–1948* (Stanford, CA: Stanford University Press, 1999), 57–67, 155–56, 355–56.

38. For examples, see "IRHA Definition at Work," *Independent Jewish Voices Canada*, September 4, 2020, www.ijvcanada.org/ihra-definition-at-work.

16
Is There Christian Antisemitism? The History of an Intra-Catholic Debate, 1965–2000

KARMA BEN-JOHANAN

"The hatred for Judaism is at bottom hatred for Christianity."
SIGMUND FREUD, Moses and Monotheism

*"In a broader sense, modern anti-Semitism turned out to be a
continuation of the premodern rejection of Judaism by Christianity."*
JACOB KATZ, From Prejudice to Destruction

THE HISTORIOGRAPHY devoted to relations between the Catholic Church and Jews in late modernity has dealt with the Holocaust at length. Historians have focused on clarifying the attitudes of Pope Pius XII (1939–1958) toward the destruction of Europe's Jews. The Christian roots of Nazi antisemitism have also garnered significant scholarly attention.

A smaller number of historical studies have been devoted to the process by which the Catholic Church purged itself of antisemitism in the wake of the Holocaust, a process that peaked with the Second Vatican Council (1962–1965), whose purpose was to achieve reconciliation between the church and the modern world. The Council addressed relations between the church and Jews in Article 4 of *Nostra Aetate*, "Declaration on the Relation of the Church to Non-Christian Religions."[1] In this section, the Council decries antisemitism and proclaims that the Jewish people bear no collective guilt for the murder of Jesus. This declaration is considered revolutionary, bringing the centuries-old Christian-Jewish debate to a "conciliatory close."[2]

The tendency to identify hostility as the center of gravity in Christian-Jewish relations throughout history has led to a situation in which the aftermath of Vatican II's conciliatory move garnered very little historiographic attention. Even though *Nostra Aetate*, Article 4 left open questions, and even though it sparked an enduring, polyphonic, and penetrating discussion within the Catholic world about antisemitism and Europe's Christian past, historians have tended to devote only a few paragraphs to the subject, generally in epilogues and prefaces as a sort of addendum to the main discussion—one that often puts the church and its leaders on trial for their part in the fate of European Jewry.[3] Existing treatments of the church debate on antisemitism mainly assess whether the church's change of heart about Jews was authentic and sufficient.

However, scholarship that puts the subject of study on trial suffers from a lack of curiosity about foundational historical topics. Of interest is not only whether the church got rid of its antisemitism (a question that presumes that the church was infected with antisemitism), but also why and how it did so. Moreover, there is no reason to assume that when church leaders and theologians speak of "antisemitism" they are referring to the same thing that Jews, historians, or other groups speak about. Therefore, we must also ask what antisemitism is in the eyes of theologians and leaders of the Catholic Church, and how the decision about what to include in and exclude from the category of "antisemitism" is itself part of the church's engagement with it.

These questions are the focus of the present article, in which I trace the motives of popes, members of the church hierarchy, and Catholic theologians after Vatican II who invoke the term "antisemitism." I examine the meanings with which they invested this term and how using it helped them conceptualize and promote political and cultural objectives beyond the realm of relations between the church and Jews. As I will show below, the discussion of antisemitism, which became an important part of the church's agenda in the context of Vatican II and remained central for more than three decades, was intrinsically linked to the general yet fraught attempt of the Catholic Church to reconcile with and reposition itself in relation to the modern world.

The Question of Antisemitism at the Second Vatican Council

Pope John XXIII (1958–1963) convened Vatican II because he thought that the church needed "updating" (*aggiornamento*) to enable it to begin a fruitful dialogue with the modern world. One aspect that demanded such fine-tuning was the traditional Catholic view of Jews and Judaism, which saw the Jewish people as Christ-killers and the church as superseding the rebellious Jews as God's chosen people. These views were considered by many to be unsuitable after the Holocaust, and the pope decided that the program for modernizing the Catholic Church should include their revision.[4]

Two specific accusations motivated church leaders to formulate a document concerning Jews (*Decretum de Judaeis*) in the context of the Council: The first was laid out before John XXIII by the Jewish historian Jules Isaac, namely, that Europe's Christian heritage is not unrelated to the Holocaust. In other words, the "Teaching of Contempt," on which generations of Christians were raised, paved the way for Nazi antisemitism.[5] The other accusation, which caused a controversy after the Council had already begun, was that of the (Protestant) playwright Rolf Hochhuth, whose work *The Deputy* (*Der Stellvertreter*) first kindled the debate about Pope Pius XII's "silence" in the face of the destruction of European Jewry.[6] Hochhuth and Isaac, each in his own way, raised the question of the link between modern antisemitism and the Nazi death industry, on one hand, and "traditional" Christian hostility toward Jews, on the other.

In response to these accusations, the members of the subcommittee that worked on *Decretum de Judaeis* defended Catholic doctrine from slanderers and distinguished it from antisemitic views:

Although the Church is the new people of God, the Jews should not be presented as rejected or accursed by God, as if this followed from the Holy Scriptures. All should see to it, then, that in catechetical work or in the preaching of the word of God they do not teach anything that does not conform to the truth of the Gospel and the spirit of Christ.

Furthermore, in her rejection of every persecution against any man, the Church...decries hatred, persecutions, displays of anti-Semitism, directed against Jews at any time and by anyone.[7]

Nostra Aetate, Article 4 does not provide a positive model for how to present Jews in a manner consistent with scripture and does not bother to square the church's self-perception as the "new people of God" with the "updated" view that Jews—the old people of God—were not rejected by God. It is content to assert that scripture is not the source of the prevalent Christian view, according to which Jews are "rejected or accursed by God," but rather that the prevalent Christian view distorts scripture. To repair the Catholic perception without causing a rupture with tradition, the drafters of *Decretum de Judaeis* made efforts to show that a positive approach toward Jews does not demand forsaking tradition; on the contrary, it demands reconnecting with that tradition. This approach is embedded deeply within tradition, and it must be recovered by means of returning to the sources.[8]

Post-Council Discourse on Antisemitism

The question of whether the goal of *Nostra Aetate*, Article 4 to extract from Christian tradition a more positive approach toward Jews than the one that had prevailed for centuries was indeed realistic, or whether hostility toward Jews was irreparably embedded in that tradition, continued to occupy theologians and church leaders long after Vatican II was over. This complex issue must be understood within the broader context of the reception of Vatican II, a subject that engages the Catholic public to this day.[9]

When it came to the Catholic world's internalization and interpretation of the legacy of Vatican II, differences of opinion erupted among theologians and church leaders concerning the nature of the reforms presented. Some of the most prominent theologians viewed Vatican II as the beginning of a new era and sought to take the "spirit" of the Council further by proposing additional reforms in many other realms of Catholic life and thought. Others were concerned that presenting Vatican II as a revolution within church history could cause a rupture within Catholic tradition and amounted to an uncritical surrender to modernity. They preferred to relate to the Council as a natural development of stances that preceded it—a "clarification" of existing attitudes, not a complete novelty.

Like this broader interpretive discussion, the discussion of Christian antisemitism also dealt with the dichotomy of continuity and rupture and the balance between the church's loyalty to tradition and its modernization.[10] If Christian doctrine, from the New Testament onward, was indelibly stamped with the seal of antisemitic views, then the role of *Nostra Aetate*, Article 4 was to discard these elements of the tradition and turn a new leaf. If, however, the phenomenon of antisemitism was external to Christian tradition and not an organic part of it, then *Nostra Aetate*, Article 4 merely granted renewed validity to an existing tradition by distinguishing doctrinal principles from distortions that occurred over centuries. In other words, the question of the connections between Christianity and modern antisemitism had ramifications for the question of the perfection and morality of the Catholic tradition as a whole. If the church erred so terribly vis-à-vis Jews, what other errors did it make?

The Progressive Position

During the two decades after Vatican II, "progressive" theologians began to question *Nostra Aetate*, Article 4's presentation of antisemitism as something external to Christianity and its acquittal of the New Testament of harboring it.[11] The church's treatment of the new Judeo-Christian fraternity as something that had always been present within mainstream Christian tradition helped the church—according to these theologians—absolve itself from responsibility. In the 1970s, Gregory Baum, himself one of the drafters of *Nostra Aetate*, Article 4, renounced his earlier view that the Christian Gospel is free of Jew-hatred. Baum confessed that he understood the sources themselves as hostile toward Jews and the idea that the church superseded the Jews as God's chosen people as fundamental to Christianity. Therefore, the call by *Nostra Aetate*, Article 4 to cling to "the truth of the Gospel and the spirit of Christ" was nothing more than a cosmetic treatment of the diseases plaguing a tradition that required fundamental change.[12]

Baum was one of the few Catholic intellectuals, alongside the American theologian Rosemary Radford Ruether, who dared to identify the New Testament as a source of antisemitic views.[13] Yet even theologians who hesitated to criticize the New Testament shared the sense that comprehensive theological reform—reform that would not spare even fundamental Catholic doctrine—was necessary to uproot the traces of Jew-hatred from Catholic tradition. Catholic thinkers claimed that relating to Jews and their historic fate as a theological category within a Christian metahistorical conception introduces the seeds of antisemitism because it strips Jews of their realness and turns them into a sort of abstraction. The prominent theologian Edward Schillebeeckx, for example, claimed that the dogmatization and Hellenization of the Christian Gospel during the first centuries of the Common Era (peaking with the Council of Chalcedon) alienated Christianity from its Jewish heritage. Schillebeeckx also hinted that the church's dogmatic heritage transformed this estrangement from Jews into a principle, and that this, in turn, is the source of Christian antisemitism.[14] Johann Baptist Metz claimed that the traditional attitude of the church toward Jews attests to the degree to which ("bourgeois") Christian theology is indifferent to history. According to him, the church must jettison the series of "memoryless" (*gedächtnislose*) abstractions through which Catholics considered Jews and replace it with unmediated encounters with real Jews.[15] What Metz viewed as a series of ahistorical abstractions was in fact the traditional way to do theology.

This view that Christianity is plagued by Jew-hatred—a view that does not spare the central pillars of Catholic tradition, perhaps not even scripture, of this charge—characterizes, in general, Catholic thinkers belonging to the group that promoted a radicalization of Vatican II. This group was concerned with a broad range of burning issues, from contraception to papal infallibility. Metz is considered the (Western) spiritual father of liberation theology, a progressive ideological movement striving for radical socioeconomic change by synthesizing theological ideas with Marxist principles. Ruether became one of the world's most important feminist theologians, and also a prominent pro-Palestinian liberation theologian. Baum integrated the ideas of the Frankfurt School into Catholic theology and promoted liberal ecumenical initiatives. Schillebeeckx was a pioneer in the theological use of biblical criticism and was even summoned for inquest by the Congregation for the Doctrine of the Faith (the body entrusted with defining doctrine, formerly called the Supreme Sacred Congregation of the Roman and Universal Inquisition), as it was suspected that his ideas challenge the dogmas of the Chalcedon Council. In the eyes of these thinkers and their colleagues, the question of Christian antisemitism demonstrated everything problematic about Catholic theology. Their attitudes toward Jews and Judaism were integrally linked to their broader programs to reform the church.

The Conservative Position

As mentioned above, conservative forces within the Catholic world were concerned about the radicalization of theology in "progressive" directions, and presented a much narrower interpretation of the Council, viewing it as a continuation rather than a revolution. This interpretation also applied to the church's attitude toward Jews and Judaism. Authoritative theologians and members of the church hierarchy continued the process of reconciliation that began with *Nostra Aetate*, Article 4, but without leveling such pointed criticism at central Catholic doctrines. Applied to the Council, the hermeneutics of continuity demanded a description of *Nostra Aetate*, Article 4's sympathetic approach that was continuous with the long history that preceded it—a history filled, at least *prima facie*, with hostility toward Jews. Theologians and church officials who identified with this stance drew inspiration from a small group of Catholic thinkers (including, most prominently, Henri de Lubac, Jacques Maritain, Johannes Oesterreicher, and Karl Thieme) who wrote about Jews during the three decades preceding the Council and updated their ideas to meet the needs of the hour.[16]

Grounding the positive Catholic approach toward Jews and Judaism within the centuries-old Catholic tradition was therefore part and parcel of the effort to root Vatican II within the teachings of the preconciliar church. The theological strategy chosen to produce a narrative of continuity between Judaism and Christianity presented their relationship as one of "fulfillment" rather than "supersession" (based on Matthew 5:17: "Do not think that I have come to abolish the Law or the Prophets; I have not come to abolish them but to fulfill them").[17] "We should be careful to avoid any transition from the Old to the New Testament which might seem merely a rupture," states the 1985 declaration of the Pontifical Commission for Religious Relations with the Jews (CRRJ).[18] "The Old Testament and the Jewish tradition founded upon it," the CRRJ continues, "must not be set against the New Testament in such a way that the former seems to constitute a religion of only justice, fear and legalism, with no appeal to the love of God and neighbor." Rather, it is necessary to have a more refined conception of the relationship between the two Testaments, one based on Jesus as the "fulfilment and perfection of the earlier Revelation."[19] This means that Judaism remained valid as a promise still awaiting fulfillment in Christ. The concept of "fulfillment," that Jesus fulfills the promise of the Old Testament, was seen as better representing continuity between the two covenants because it does not arouse a sense of paradigmatic rupture.

Conceiving of the Christian Gospel as the fulfillment of Judaism also served these thinkers by exonerating the tradition of interpreting the Old Testament in light of the New Testament from accusations of supersessionism (the view that the church inherited the status of God's people when the Jewish people rejected Christ and completed their role in history). Distinguishing the traditional reading of scripture from the concept of supersession aimed to improve the moral reputation of typology (which identifies prophecies about Jesus and the church within the Old Testament), whose importance to the Catholic exegetical tradition cannot be exaggerated.[20]

This distinction was not self-evident. Traditionally, the typological method created a wedge between Hebrew scripture and its Jewish exegetes. In the words of de Lubac: "The church takes [the book from] the synagogue. The synagogue, which has become blind and sterile, is merely her librarian."[21] The fact that the church included Hebrew scripture in its canon was not linked to a pro-Jewish view or to respect for Jewish exegesis of the Bible.[22] On the contrary, typology rendered Jewish exegesis of the Old Testament superfluous. The role of Jews was to attest to Christian truth with their mistaken interpretations. Now, however, the church adopted the opposite argument: Typological readings of scripture attested to the existential decision of maintaining an ongoing, intimate connection with the Jewish people. If the Old Testament was vital to Christian faith, it was now claimed, then contemporary Jews were also vital to it.

In this ideological context, church representatives frequently posited the church's proto-Orthodox rejection of the Marcionite heresy as evidence of its ongoing fealty to its Jewish heritage. In the second century CE, Marcion of Sinope maintained that Hebrew scriptural sources are the work of a materialistic, cruel God who created the world and is fundamentally different from the God who appears in New Testament writings—the heavenly father who sent his son to redeem mankind from the material world. Marcion sought to dissociate the Hebrew sources from Christian scripture and to eschew completely any connection to Judaism and its cruel God. The church opposed Marcion's doctrines and chose to include the books of the Hebrew Bible—the Old Testament—in its sacred canon. It viewed both Testaments as Gospels of the one and only God and of his plans for humankind—and it excommunicated Marcion as a heretic.

Debates regarding Marcionite heresy and its influence on the development of Christian antisemitism appeared even prior to the Council in a polemic by Catholic theologian Hans Urs von Balthasar written in response to Martin Buber's 1950 work *Two Types of Faith*.[23] After Vatican II, theologians and conservative church officials agreed with Buber that the "temptation" of Marcion still lurks at the door of Christianity. However, following Balthasar, they maintained that the Catholic tradition never submitted to it.[24] According to these theologians and church officials, those who questioned the place of the Old Testament in the Catholic canon were, in fact, never Catholics. For example, the Lutheran idea of justification by faith alone (*justificatio sola fide*) cast Judaism as a religion of law in opposition to Christianity as a religion of grace. Lutheran theologian and Bible scholar Adolf von Harnack took this further and argued in favor of completing what Luther failed to do, discarding the Old Testament once and for all.[25] Conservative Catholic thinkers argued that these attitudes are what ultimately led to the claim, accepted in certain Protestant circles during the 1930s and 1940s, that Jesus was Aryan.[26] According to Cardinal Jean-Marie Lustiger, the dichotomous prism through which most people are used to reading patristic and medieval literature as antisemitic is anachronistic, inspired by Martin Luther and, even more so, by Hitler's *Mein Kampf*.[27] Moreover, according to Cardinal Joseph Ratzinger, contemporary liberal theologians who vilify typology as anti-Jewish appropriation of the Bible are guilty of the same sins as the greatest antisemites, for it was the splitting of the Old Testament and the New Testament that led Germany to adopt Nazi ideology and attempt to destroy Judaism.[28]

This claim, which connected antisemitism to unorthodox Christian views, was applied in the reverse as well: If it was the rejection of the canonic link between the Old Testament and the New Testament that provoked, perhaps even created, modern antisemitism, then antisemitism was fundamentally aimed against the Catholic faith. Because Jews, ever since *Nostra Aetate*, Article 4, were no longer defined as Christ-killers but considered, instead, Jesus's kin, it became inconceivable that murderousness toward Jews grew out of Christian vengefulness; on the contrary, it reflected an anti-Christian impulse to kill Christ. That is, even if antisemitism occasionally disguised itself as Christianity, it was fundamentally anti-Christian, an atheistic or pagan sin, aimed not only against Jews but also against the church, and perhaps even against God himself. After all, it aspires to erase belief in God entirely and wipe away the divine election of the Jewish people and of Christ from the annals of history.[29] Thus, Christian antisemitism is, in the words of Cardinal Johannes Willebrands, head of the CRRJ, self-contradictory.[30]

This view remains the primary theological position through which the church has understood the Holocaust since the 1980s:[31] "The threat against you is also a threat against us," declared Pope John Paul II (1978–2005) in Warsaw in 1987.[32] The shared fate of Jews and Christians, the pope emphasized, is what gives Jewish tragedy its significance as a herald of redemption, and it is of decisive importance for all of Europe. John Paul II returned to this theme in Vienna in 1988: "Exposed here is the fearsome face of a godless, perhaps even anti-God, world, whose murderous intent was clearly directed against the Jewish people, but also against the faith of those who worship a Jew, Jesus of Nazareth, Redeemer of the world."[33] And, at the Vatican in 1989 he declared:

The new paganism and the systems related to it were certainly directed against the Jews, but they were likewise aimed at Christianity, whose teaching had shaped the soul of Europe. In the people of whose race "according to the flesh, is the Christ" (Rom. 9:5), the Gospel message of the equal dignity of all God's children was being held up to ridicule.[34]

John Paul II clearly wanted to deepen the process of Christian-Jewish reconciliation. Yet he did not share the hopes of progressive theologians to completely uproot problematic doctrines for the sake of modernizing the tradition. On the contrary, for the conservative John Paul II who wished to restore order to the church, it was important to present Christian-Jewish friendship as an established principle of Catholic tradition and as something that had always stood as a bulwark against the ethical deterioration of human culture, a deterioration symbolized most prominently by Auschwitz.[35] Within the context of the Christian ethos that he presented to European society, Auschwitz represented the unbridled cruelty of modern atheism, whether led by Nazis or Communists. It was the "Golgotha of the modern world," he noted when he visited the extermination camp in 1979, the absolute abrogation of human rights. However, it was also the symbol of the victory of Christian love over godless hatred.

Just as liberal theologians saw antisemitism as a symbol for the church's need for moral and theological reform, so John Paul II and his favored thinkers tended to view it as a symbol of the dangers of secularism. The Holocaust, in this conception, did not occur because of Europe's Christian heritage, but, on the contrary, because Europe eschewed its Christian heritage (under blatantly Protestant inspiration). Theologians and members of the church hierarchy holding this view condemned antisemitism in the context of criticizing secularization. They anchored their vision for the church—reconnecting secularized Europe with its Christian roots—with the idea that the Catholic tradition was rooted in Judaism and never renounced its ties to the Jewish people. The Catholic hermeneutic of continuity was formulated not only as a response to the rebukes of progressive thinkers but also as a broad cultural and political vision. At its center stands the claim that an enduring ethical alternative for the West after World War II must take the Christian (Catholic) heritage of Europe into consideration, for only a worldview that respects tradition can also include the respect due to Jews. Catholic Christianity stands on a continuum with Judaism, whereas modern paganism, with its Protestant roots, is the source of the rupture from which modern antisemitism issued.

Therefore, the official view of antisemitism that crystallized within the church during the papacy of John Paul II should be understood within a dual context: both that of the struggle to interpret Vatican II and the scope of its reforms, and that of the "New Evangelization" movement, the church's effort to promote a new Christian vision for secular Europe.

The Church Apologizes

Jewish scholars and leaders protested against identifying antisemitism with hatred of Christianity and what was perceived in the Jewish world as the "appropriation" of Jewish suffering into a Catholic metanarrative that failed to take any real responsibility for the part of Christians in the development of antisemitism or the behavior of Pope Pius XII during the Holocaust. Though their ire focused on a few main incidents (most prominently the controversy over the Carmelite convent at Auschwitz [1984–1993] and the beatification of Edith Stein [1987]), it resulted directly from the deep chasm between Christian and Jewish thought about the Holocaust and antisemitism. The pope's frequent and public addressing of these subjects made this chasm especially palpable.

The church insisted on identifying antisemitism with modernity in a way that did not dovetail with the dominant contemporary Jewish narrative. According to this narrative, Nazi antisemitism was not an essentially different category than Christian hostility toward Jews; it stood apart only in its magnitude. The gun that had appeared in the First Act—the accusation of the Jews of deicide—was fired in the Third

Act—the "Final Solution." These opposing views of antisemitism also served contradictory political and cultural visions. While the Catholic leadership was busy with its revindication of Europe as a "Judeo-Christian" culture free of hatred toward Jews and Christians alike, Zionism was using the conception of antisemitism as a fixed, integral component of Jewish life in the Diaspora to justify the State of Israel as the exclusive solution to the problem of antisemitism.[36] As a result, many Jews did not see Christians as potential partners in the construction of a shared culture, but instead as those who created the need for a Jewish national home in the first place. These Jews expected Christians to accept responsibility and apologize for Christian antisemitism.

The heads of the church were not indifferent to these Jewish sensitivities, and in the early 1990s they agreed to respond gradually to some of the claims that Jewish representatives brought before them. Indeed, the pope and his representatives in Jewish-Christian dialogues began a long series of apologies for the part played by Christians in generations of Jewish suffering in Europe.

Still, the willingness of church leaders to apologize does not mean that they adopted the dominant Jewish narrative, according to which there is no essential difference between traditional Christian hostility toward Jews and modern antisemitism, and which rejected the equation of antisemitism with anti-Christianity. On the contrary, this identification allowed church leaders to define antisemitism as a grave sin, not only against the Jewish people, but even against God himself.[37] The technical vindication of the Catholic Church and its tradition from the accusation of antisemitism allowed the heads of the church to confess to the obstinate existence of an "anti-tradition" that stemmed from "erroneous and unjust interpretations of the New Testament" and nourished generations of Catholic believers.[38] "The spiritual resistance and concrete action of [many other] Christians [during the Holocaust] was not that which might have been expected from Christ's followers," states "We Remember: A Reflection on the Shoah."[39] "For Christians, this heavy burden of conscience of their brothers and sisters during the Second World War must be a call to penitence."[40] Yet this hostility toward Jews in Christian milieus, even if terribly strong, was not defined as antisemitism or accepted as part of the legacy of the church itself, that is, of the Catholic truth that always remains distinct from the contingencies of history.

These apologies directly responding to the prevailing Jewish narrative that blamed the persecution of Jews on Christians were eagerly accepted in the Jewish world and calmed passions to a large extent.[41] When John Paul II personally apologized at Yad Vashem for "displays of anti-Semitism directed against the Jews by Christians at any time and in any place," he ended the debate of thirty-five years, both among Catholics and between Catholics and Jews.[42] Of course this debate can be reopened, not because the Catholic Church is or is not irredeemably antisemitic, but because both Christian and Jewish conceptions of the past continue to change and adjust to historical circumstances.

Alternate Narratives in Context

The post–Vatican II intra-Catholic debate about the nature of anti-semitism and its connection to Christianity was, to a large extent, a debate about Christianity's attitudes toward modernity and its place in secular Europe. Some judged Christian tradition from a "progressive" perspective and called on the church to jettison that which is no longer compatible with modern circumstances. In their opinion, antisemitism was part of the church's dark, obsolete past. Others judged "progress" and "modernization" from a traditional perspective; they criticized modern culture as causing antisemitism through its unchecked impulse of replacing the old with the new.

Within Jewish discourse as well, different conceptions of anti-semitism involve different understandings of history and differently shape how Jews navigate the world around them. It is worth noting that the "progressive" Catholic view is exceedingly similar to the "traditional" Jewish view, which sees the Christian world (and perhaps the non-Jewish world more generally) as irreparably antisemitic. By contrast, the conception of antisemitism as a clear result of modernity, which in the Catholic world is deemed a conservative view, is considered more critical and "progressive" within the Jewish world, as it allows for the liberation of Jewish existence from the burden of ontological, ahistorical isolation from the rest of humankind, and it transforms the Holocaust into a universal story that pertains to a specific chapter of history. The story that one community tells itself about antisemitism can indeed shed light on the story of a different community, even today, in the age of Jewish-Christian reconciliation.

NOTES

1. Second Vatican Council, "Declaration on the Relation of the Church to Non-Christian Religions: *Nostra Aetate*, Proclaimed by His Holiness Pope Paul VI, October 28, 1965." Vatican website, www.vatican.va/archive/hist_councils/ii_vatican_council /documents/vat-ii_decl_19651028_nostra-aetate_en.html/.

2. Israel J. Yuval, *Two Nations in Your Womb: Perceptions of Jews and Christians in Late Antiquity and the Middle Ages*, trans. Barbara Harshav and Jonathan Chipman (Berkeley: University of California Press, 2006), 20.

3. An example of this is David Kertzer's offhand discussion of the 1998 statement by the Catholic Commission for Religious Relations with the Jews, *We Remember: A Reflection on the Shoah*. (I will discuss this issue further below.) See David I. Kertzer, *The Popes against the Jews: The Vatican's Role in the Rise of Modern Anti-Semitism* (New York: Alfred A. Knopf, 2001), 5-6, 10-11. A similar discussion appears in the concluding chapter of Susan Zuccotti, *Under His Very Windows: The Vatican and the Holocaust in Italy* (New Haven, CT: Yale University Press, 2000), 324-25.

4. On Pope John XXIII's vision for convening an ecumenical council, see Peter Hebblethwaite, *John XXIII: Pope of the Century* (London: Continuum, 2000), 156-73; Alberto Melloni, *Papa Giovanni: Un cristiano e il suo concilio* (Turin: Einaudi, 2009). On his sensitivity to the Jewish issue, see Dina Porat, "Tears, Protocols and Actions in a Wartime Triangle: Pope Pius XII, Roncalli and Barlas," in *Cristianesimo nella storia* 27, no. 2 (2007): 599-632.

5. See Jules Isaac, *L'enseignement du mépris: Vérité historique et mythes théologiques* (Paris: Fasquelle, 1962). On his meeting with Pope John XXIII, see Norman C. Tobias, *Jewish Conscience of the Church: Jules Isaac and the Second Vatican Council* (Cham, Switzerland: Palgrave Macmillan, 2017), 185-86.

6. Rolf Hochhuth, *Der Stellvertreter: ein christliches Trauerspiel* (Reinbek bei Hamburg: Rowohlt, 1963). See also John Connelly, *From Enemy to Brother: The Revolution in Catholic Teaching on the Jews, 1933-1965* (Cambridge, MA: Harvard University Press, 2012), 263-64.

7. *Nostra Aetate*, Article 4.

8. See Connelly, *Enemy to Brother*, 242.

9. There is a sprawling literature on the reception of Vatican II. See, for example, Matthew L. Lamb and Matthew Levering, eds., *The Reception of Vatican II* (New York: Oxford University Press, 2017); Massimo Faggioli, *Vatican II: The Battle for Meaning*

(New York: Paulist Press, 2012); Alberto Melloni and Giuseppe Ruggieri, eds., *Chi ha paura del Vaticano II?* (Rome: Carocci, 2009).

10. Within scholarly literature there is a common distinction (which the church has adopted, as will be discussed below) between "anti-Judaism" as a religious hatred of Jews, which prevailed in the premodern Christian world, and the racial hatred called "antisemitism," which characterizes modern secular society. I have not adopted this distinction because in church and theological sources, the distinction between Christian hatred and secular hatred or between traditional hatred and modern hatred is itself part of the discussion of the nature of antisemitism and of its continuity or discontinuity with the Christian tradition. Therefore, this distinction is unsuitable as a basis for this discussion.

11. My use of the term "progressive" adopts the term as used in the Catholic world to refer to the group that promoted the reforms of Vatican II. This group is also called "liberal." However, it overlaps only partially with how the word "liberalism" is used in other social and political contexts today.

12. Gregory Baum, "Introduction," in Rosemary Radford Ruether, *Faith and Fratricide: The Theological Roots of Anti-Semitism* (New York: Seabury, 1974), 6.

13. Ruether, *Faith and Fratricide*.

14. Robert Schreiter, "Christology in the Jewish-Christian Encounter: An Essay-Review of Edward Schillebeeckx *Jezus Het Verhaal van een Levende*," *Journal of the American Academy of Religion* 44, no. 4 (December 1976): 693–703.

15. Johann Baptist Metz, *Jenseits bürgerlicher Religion: Reden über die Zukunft des Christentums* (Mainz: Matthias-Grünewald, 1980), 32.

16. On Oesterreicher and Thieme, see Connelly, *Enemy to Brother*. Maritain's most important essay was "Le mystère d'Israël," in *Le mystère d'Israël et autres essais* (Paris: Desclée de Brouwer, 1965), 19–62. De Lubac did not devote any systematic theological thought to the subject, but he vehemently claimed that the church's attitude to the Old Testament requires its opposition to antisemitism. See Henri de Lubac, *Résistance chrétienne à l'antisémitisme: souvenirs 1940–1944* (Paris: Fayard, 1988), 111–25.

17. For example, Franz Mussner, *Tractate on the Jews: The Significance of Judaism for Christian Faith*, trans. Leonard Swindler (Philadelphia: Fortress, 1988), 114; Jean-Marie Lustiger, *La Promesse* (Paris: Parole et Silence, 2002), 15–30.

18. Commission for Religious Relations with the Jews (CRRJ), "Notes on the Correct Way to Present the Jews and Judaism in Preaching and Catechesis in the Roman Catholic Church," 1985, www.christianunity.va/content/unitacristiani/en/commissione-per -i-rapporti-religiosi-con-l-ebraismo/commissione-per-i-rapporti-religiosi-con-l -ebraismo-crre/documenti-della-commissione/en2.html.

19. CRRJ, "Guidelines and Suggestions for Implementing the Conciliar Declaration Nostra Aetate, Article 4," 1974, www.christianunity.va/content/unitacristiani/en /commissione-per-i-rapporti-religiosi-con-l-ebraismo/commissione-per-i-rapporti -religiosi-con-l-ebraismo-crre/documenti-della-commissione/en3.html.

20. In the language of CRRJ, "Notes": "Typology...makes many people uneasy and is perhaps the sign of a problem unresolved." CRRJ, "Notes on the Correct Way to Present Jews and Judaism."

21. Henri de Lubac, *Medieval Exegesis: The Four Senses of Scripture*, vol. 3, trans. Marc Sebanc (Grand Rapids, MI: Eerdmans, 1998), 242.

22. The sermons of Cardinal Faulhaber are a blatant example of this. In them he defended the dignity of the Old Testament while refusing to defend contemporary Jews, claiming that they do not continue ancient Judaism. See Michael von Faulhaber, *Judaism, Christianity and Germany*, trans. George D. Smith (New York: Macmillan, 1934).

23. Martin Buber, *Two Types of Faith*, trans. Norman Goldhawk (Syracuse, NY: Syracuse University Press, 2003); Hans Urs von Balthasar, *Einsame Zwiesprache: Martin Buber und das Christentum* (Köln: Hegner, 1958).

24. [West] German Bishops' Conference, "The Church and the Jews: Bonn, April 28, 1980," in *Bridges: Documents of the Christian-Jewish Dialogue*, vol. 1, *The Road to Reconciliation (1945–1985)*, ed. Franklin Sherman (New York: Paulist Press, 2011), 240.

25. See Harnack's well-known book on Marcion: Adolph von Harnack, *Marcion: Das Evangelium vom fremden Gott* (Leipzig: J. C. Hinrichs, 1924).

26. Susannah Heschel, *The Aryan Jesus: Christian Theologians and the Bible in Nazi Germany* (Princeton, NJ: Princeton University Press, 2008).

27. See Jean-Marie Lustiger, *Le choix de Dieu: Entretiens avec Jean-Louis Missika et Dominique Wolton* (Paris: Fallois, 1987), 81–88; Jean Duchesne, ed., *Cardinal Jean-Marie Lustiger on Christians and Jews* (New York: Paulist Press, 2010), 80–82.

28. Joseph Ratzinger, "Preface" to the Pontifical Biblical Commission, "The Jewish People and Their Sacred Scriptures in the Christian Bible" (Rome: Vatican Press, 2001).

29. See Duchesne, *Lustiger*, 80–82; Lustiger, *Le choix*, 81–88; Lustiger, *La Promesse*, 162.

30. Johannes Willebrands, *Church and Jewish People* (New York: Paulist Press, 1992), 18.

31. On the attitudes of John Paul II and Benedict XVI to the Holocaust, see also Adam Gregerman, "Interpreting the Pain of Others: John Paul II and Benedict XVI on Jewish Suffering in the Shoah," *Journal of Ecumenical Studies* 48 (2013): 443–56.

32. John Paul II, "Discorso di Giovanni Paolo II ai Rappresentanti della Comunità ebraica Polacca" (speech, Warsaw, June 14, 1987), Vatican website, www.vatican.va /content/john-paul-ii/it/speeches/1987/june/documents/hf_jp-ii_spe_19870614_com unita-ebraica.html.

33. John Paul II, "Meeting with the Representatives of the Jewish Communities in the Apostolic Nunciature in Vienna" (speech, Vienna, June 24, 1988), Vatican website, www.vatican.va/content/john-paul-ii/it/speeches/1988/june/documents/hf _jp-ii_spe_19880624_comunita-ebraica.html.

34. John Paul II, "Message of His Holiness John Paul II on the Occasion of the

50th Anniversary of the Beginning of the Second World War" (August 27, 1989), in *L'Osservatore Romano: Weekly Edition in English* 36 (1989): 1–3.

35. On John Paul II's use of Auschwitz as a symbol, see Jonathan Huener, *Auschwitz, Poland, and the Politics of Commemoration, 1945–1979* (Athens: Ohio University Press, 2003), 185–245.

36. Zionism also justified the State of Israel with the idea of "negation of the exile," which views Diaspora Jewish life as a "lachrymose" story. See Amnon Raz-Krakotzkin, "Exile within Sovereignty: Critique of 'the Negation of Exile' in Israeli Culture," in *The Scaffolding of Sovereignty*, ed. Zvi Ben-Dor Benite et al. (New York: Columbia University Press, 2017), 393–99.

37. Edward Idris Cassidy, *Ecumenism and Interreligious Dialogue: Unitatis Redintegratio, Nostra Aetate* (New York: Paulist Press, 2005), 190.

38. John Paul II, "Address of His Holiness John Paul II to a Symposium on the Roots of Anti-Judaism" (speech, October 31, 1997), Vatican website, www.vatican.va/con tent/john-paul-ii/en/speeches/1997/october/documents/hf_jp-ii_spe_19971031_com -teologica.html, quoted in CRRJ, "We Remember: A Reflection on the Shoah," March 16, 1998, www.christianunity.va/content/unitacristiani/en/commissione-per-i-rapporti -religiosi-con-l-ebraismo/commissione-per-i-rapporti-religiosi-con-l-ebraismo-crre /documenti-della-commissione/en1.html.

39. CRRJ, "We Remember."

40. CRRJ, "We Remember."

41. Nevertheless, many criticized the contents of the apologies as insufficient for various reasons, e.g., distinguishing between the church and historical details and refusing to condemn Pius XII. See, for instance, Sergio I. Minerbi, "Pope John Paul II and the Jews: An Evaluation," *Jewish Political Studies Review* 18, nos. 1–2 (2006): 15–36.

42. John Paul II, "Speech of John Paul II: Visit to the Yad Vashem Museum" (speech, Jerusalem, March 23, 2000), Vatican website, www.vatican.va/content/john-paul-ii /en/speeches/2000/jan-mar/documents/hf_jp-ii_spe_20000323_yad-vashem -mausoleum.html.

VI
CONCLUDING
EXPLANATIONS

17
Can the Circle Be Broken?

DAVID ENGEL

The editors have invited me to close this engrossing volume with some thoughts about what the scholarly discussion reflected in its pages has accomplished and how it might proceed productively in the future. In doing so, they have added to the honor they and my colleagues have given me by treating a piece of my writing as worthy of serious debate. I am particularly gratified by the changes some of the authors have made to their own contributions following my response to their original iterations in the Hebrew-language volume in which this discussion began.[1] In recognition of those changes I shall not repeat what I said there. Instead, I shall concentrate upon what seems to me one outstanding issue, broached in different ways by many of the contributors, that I did not address adequately in the initial go-round—a tension between thinking about "antisemitism" as the thought or behavior of "antisemites" and thinking about it as a feature of Jews' own experience. Examining that tension will also lead to some observations about how a scholarly discussion focused upon it might productively inform broader public consideration of the matters at its heart.

First, a clarification. The Hebrew-language volume in which this discussion began was reported on in the Israeli press. Some readers of the newspaper accounts took my argument, likely on the basis of those accounts alone, as a claim that the hostility Jews have faced throughout their history and continue to face today are figments of the Jews' own collective imagination. They had either not read or not understood a key passage in the final paragraph of my original essay:

> [T]hroughout the centuries many people have behaved violently towards Jews. Many have depicted them verbally or artistically in

derogatory fashion, agitated publicly for their subjection to legal discrimination, discriminated against them socially, or privately felt varying degrees of prejudice towards or emotional revulsion from them. However, no *necessary* relation among particular instances of violence, hostile depiction, agitation, discrimination, and private unfriendly feeling across time and space *can be assumed*.[2]

In other words, by pointing to problems with "antisemitism" as a concept I do not make light of the serious threats and injuries, sometimes calamitous, that Jews have endured over the centuries, nor do I denigrate the role those threats and injuries have played in shaping Jews' lived experiences and their sense of what being Jewish involves.[3] I do, however, dissent from the assumption, noticeable among scholars and pervasive among the broader public, that all these troubles stem from a single source. I also dispute two corollaries of this belief: first, that *all* instances of adversity Jews have ever faced are best understood as members of a single set; second, that the relation among the members of that all-inclusive set is such that what is true for one member can be presumed true for all.[4] That is what I mean by the words I have italicized in the selection quoted above.

A softer way of stating my claim is that the probability of identifying any single, empirically demonstrable, intrinsic attribute of *all* phenomena habitually designated as "antisemitism" in common discourse seems extremely low. By "intrinsic attribute" I mean a property that can be demonstrated to be present without dispute in all supposedly "antisemitic" phenomena. I say this because, to date, the many proposed answers to the question "What is 'antisemitism'?" have failed to resolve the issue to universal satisfaction.

To be sure, it *has* proven possible to identify such common attributes for *some* such phenomena. It has also proven possible to identify what appears to be a common *extrinsic* attribute of virtually all "antisemitic" manifestations, meaning one whose sense can be established only in relation to some quality not inherent in the purported manifestation itself (like "poison" or "inspiration," words defined by their effect upon others). However, inferring that an intrinsic attribute present in *some* expressions of "antisemitism" is present in *all* such expressions requires deliberately selecting particular phenomena that meet predefined criteria and restricting the designation to them. That practice produces a circular argument.[5] Similarly, seeking the meaning of "antisemitism" via its universal extrinsic attribute in practice renders moot virtually any proposition that such circular arguments generate. Understanding why each possibility leads where it does may help elucidate the tension I noted at the outset.

Consider, for example, the article by Susannah Heschel in this volume—the only one among them, on my reading, that actually claims a *necessary* connection linking *all* instances of "antisemitism." She locates that connection in an "affect" purportedly "underlying" all cases: "Antisemitism...is a regime of emotion demanding gratification," one that "stimulates pride, a sense of superiority, and the thrill of creating a new and revolutionary movement" and "is about creating a fear of being vulnerable to...degeneracy" so powerful that "antisemites...are relentlessly obsessed with Jews."[6] No doubt those statements are true for *some* acts and individuals who have borne the label "antisemitic." But they would seem prima facie to exclude, among others, many of the things Eli Lederhendler has termed the "low wattage" "nonlethal" forms of antagonism toward Jews and their symbolic projection, 'the Jews'" that commonly go by the name "antisemitism" in contemporary Western democracies.[7] Think of the characters in Laura Hobson's 1946 novel *Gentleman's Agreement*, who exhibit behaviors to which the book explicitly applies that label: the genteel patricians who use expressions like "Jew him down," the doctor who praises a Jewish colleague for not overcharging the way some of "them" do, the editor who assumes a Jewish writer must have been a correspondent during the recent war instead of a combat soldier, the personnel manager who systematically rejects applications from people with Jewish-sounding names, or the Jew who doesn't "look especially Jewish" who changes her name to get a job, only to object when her employer announces a new hiring policy she fears may open the door to "the kikey ones."[8] Heschel's assertions entail a claim that *all* persons who do *any* of these things can be assumed a priori to be driven by a search for emotional gratification and to experience the emotions she enumerates. Yet it hardly seems obvious that use of a derogatory figure for a Jew in casual conversation or prejudicial assumptions about a Jew's military record invariably indicate that someone is "relentlessly obsessed with Jews" or feels exhilaration from being part of a "revolutionary movement" aimed at "expulsion of the dangerous people."[9] Surely sometimes a boorish remark can be nothing more than a boorish remark.

In theory, Heschel's approach permits two ways to treat such mildly untoward verbal behavior—either insist that makers of such remarks actually *do* harbor the motives and feelings that animate all "antisemites" (even if they do not voice them or admit them consciously) or declare that they are not really "antisemites" in the "true" sense of the word at all. Because neither Heschel nor anyone else has direct access to the emotions of everyone who has ever said "Jew him down" or disparaged "yids" as cheap, self-centered duty shirkers, the first possibility is not susceptible to empirical proof. The second can be true only if "true antisemites" are defined *in advance* as people of a certain emotional makeup—a classic logical circle.[10]

Heschel appears to take the first direction, arguing that "motivations may not be verbalized and thus elude the most careful empiricist historian."[11] Perhaps. But perhaps not. Some things (like the philosopher's stone, the emperor's new clothes, or evidence of widespread voter fraud in the 2020 US presidential elections) can't be seen not because they are invisible to the unaided eye but because they don't exist in the first place. Heschel's approach doesn't provide a way to distinguish reliably between the hidden and the nonexistent. Whereas "careful empiricist historians" know how to examine context for circumstantial evidence that may help assess whether a given boorish remark, made in a certain time and place, was more probably a faux pas or something more egregious, her insistence that the motivations she associates with "antisemitism" are *always* present in every instance identified as such obviates the need not only for contextual investigation but for any evidence at all.

Eschewing empirical checks on theoretical pronouncements leads easily to the fallacy of equivocation (in which an argument depends upon using a single word or expression in multiple senses). By giving "antisemitism" multiple distinct referents—"the foundation of white supremacist ideology," "a reservoir of possibility waiting to be activated by the present," "the spontaneous murder of Jews in...Jedwabne," the "seducti[ve]...strategy of *Mein Kampf*," "secret knowledge," and more—as well as by conflating propositions about "antisemitism" with propositions about "racism," "religiocide," and "Afropessimism"[12] and slipping regularly between claims concerning medieval religious polemics, sexual violence, Joseph Goebbels, and lynchings of African Americans, among others, Heschel's argument seems to rest largely on (no doubt unintentional) linguistic and logical legerdemain.[13]

Other articles avoid such sleight of hand by pursuing the second direction. They assert that not everything that has ever been called "antisemitism" is "antisemitism" in fact. By doing so, they effectively give up the search for an intrinsic attribute shared by *all* of the term's disparate referents. Thus, according to Havi Dreifuss, "not every assault against Jews...is antisemitism," even though there are at least some "incident[s]...worthy of being examined within" that "conceptual rubric."[14] Unfortunately, her article neither enumerates those incidents nor provides any vehicle for distinguishing among "assault[s] against Jews" that do or don't merit the label.

Gershon Bacon is more explicit: He reserves the term for expressions displaying only certain specific characteristics—belief that (quoting Amos Funkenstein) "being Jewish is a *character indelibilis*," fear of "a Jewish conspiracy to take control of the world through economics and culture," and intent to act "specifically against Jews."[15] This approach— advocating "cautious use" of the term and the concept it signifies, "with precise awareness of its meaning"—has a history at least a century old.[16] So far, though, it has failed to generate any consensus among scholars about which of the various "antisemitisms" adduced has the strongest claim to the title.

Indeed, it is difficult to imagine what sort of argument could compel Youval Rotman or Tzafrir Barzilay to forgo their preferred differentiae in favor of Bacon's, or Bacon to abandon his in favor of Fritz Bernstein's or Gavin Langmuir's. These differentiae generate nonidentical subsets of "antisemitic" manifestations.[17] Determining which subset has a prior claim on the "antisemitic" label seems an impossible task. True, each subset shares some members with the full set of utterances and incidents habitually called "antisemitism," but determining the degree to which every conceivable subset intersects with the full set, even if theoretically possible, would surely in practice be a prohibitively exhausting undertaking. Most likely it would lead to the discovery that the proportions have varied widely over time and space. It hardly seems feasible, then, to award the title, as it were, on a quantitative basis to the one that has intersected most for more years in more places than any other. Similarly, virtually all contemporary scholars have rejected historical criteria, such as the suggestion that the designation be confined to actions by the self-styled "antisemitic" organizations that attracted public attention in Germany between the 1880s and the First World War. I have seen no significant coalescence among students of "antisemitism" around any alternative delimitations to guide their use of the term in their scholarly work. I doubt I shall see one in my lifetime.[18]

The situation might be different if scholars, taking a cue from physicians' current practice for diabetes, would distinguish each set using modifiers like "antisemitism type 1," "antisemitism type 2," et cetera.[19] But just as what links the different types of diabetes is not any common intrinsic attribute of their causative agents but a common extrinsic effect of different causative agents upon the human body (interference with a body's ability to metabolize glucose), so too it appears that the various subcategories of "antisemitism" would likely be linked in practice not by an element they all share inherently but by a common way in which Jews respond to them.

An anecdote will clarify. On February 26, 2017, police were summoned to the Mt. Carmel Jewish cemetery in Philadelphia, Pennsylvania, to investigate the toppling of headstones. To date (November 2022) the perpetrators have not been located.[20] As a result, the perpetrators' motives cannot be known. Nevertheless, the press, Jewish spokesmen, and local political and civic leaders spoke of the incident more often than not as part of a "wave of anti-Semitic attacks" displaying "a concerted effort with intent" to harm Jews.[21] Most significantly, the Anti-Defamation League (ADL) listed and counted the occurrence in its "2017 Audit of Anti-Semitic Incidents,"[22] as did Tel Aviv University's Moshe Kantor Database for the Study of Contemporary Antisemitism and Racism in its summary of "violent antisemitic cases" for the same year—its claim that it reports only instances with "proven antisemitic motivation" notwithstanding.[23]

There were, however, several reasons to dispute that ascription of intent. The superintendent of a large Philadelphia cemetery who first noticed the damage ventured that, judging by the "unreal...amount of trash" from "parties and stuff" that he found on site, the perpetrators were most likely "just kids with ants in their pants."[24] So too did the director of a local Jewish funeral home: In his experience, "it happens; kids go rushing through cemeteries pushing over headstones."[25] Statistically these were sound guesses. A private company that tracks cemetery vandalism worldwide recorded 127 such incidents in the United States in 2016, of which three (2.36 percent) occurred in Jewish cemeteries—a distribution consistent with the proportion of Jews in the overall US population at the time (and hence with random target selection).[26] Moreover, similar attacks were noted two weeks earlier at a nearby Catholic cemetery and six weeks before at a different Catholic cemetery in a Philadelphia suburb.[27] Investigators examining the full range of available evidence might thus reasonably have determined that the crime's motive could not be established.[28]

On what basis, then, did the ADL decide to count the incident among the 1,986 "anti-Semitic incidents" it noted for 2017? It turns out that for the ADL, motives and emotions weren't the only factors that determined which incidents were included in its 2017 list and which were not:

> Incidents are defined as vandalism of property, or as harassment or assault on individuals or groups, where *either*...circumstances indicate anti-Jewish animus on the part of the perpetrator, *or*... the victim(s) could plausibly conclude that they were being victimized due to their Jewish identity. *Any* vandalism against Jewish religious institutions or cemeteries is also included [whether or not the motive is known, DE]. Although some incidents are hate crimes, many incidents included in the Audit include non-criminal acts that rise to the level of an anti-Semitic incident as we define it above.[29]

In other words, in the ADL's understanding in 2017, an expression of "antisemitism" did not have to reveal any *intrinsic* characteristic at all.

Even the most commonly imagined intrinsic feature of "antisemitism" in public discourse—"hatred or hostility toward Jews"—did not need to be visibly present in an incident that the ADL defined as "antisemitic" in that year; it was sufficient for Jews reasonably to *perceive* such hatred for an act to be counted. Moreover, the ADL deemed that perception was justified in *all* incidents of cemetery vandalism, with or without evidence of motive. In the most recent audit (2021), the organization made the point more succinctly: "853 incidents were categorized as vandalism, defined as cases where property was damaged in a manner that incorporated evidence of antisemitic intent *or* which had an antisemitic impact on Jews."[30] Although it did not define the phrase "antisemitic impact on Jews" directly, contextual clues appear consistent with a reading of "striking Jews as having an adverse impact on their interests or their sense of security and wellbeing"—making any act of vandalism that so strikes Jews an instance of "antisemitism" even in the absence of "antisemitic intent."

In this fashion, the ADL appears to have affirmed the direction taken in 2006 by Britain's All-Party Parliamentary Inquiry into Antisemitism (examined in the article by David Feldman in this volume), according to which "it is the Jewish community itself that is best qualified to determine what does and does not constitute antisemitism."[31] That determination effectively rendered "any remark, insult or act the purpose *or effect* of which is to violate another [Jewish] person's dignity or create an intimidating, hostile, degrading, humiliating or offensive environment for him [*sic*] ... antisemitic."[32] In short, a defining attribute of "antisemitism" in the eyes of some of the major bodies that have shaped public discourse about it in the English-speaking world is an *extrinsic* quality—something "antisemitism" purportedly does *to* Jews.

This development echoes several themes sounded in the chapters of this volume. It chimes, for instance, with the observation of Adi Ophir and Ishay Rosen-Zvi concerning the Hellenistic era, in which "Judeophobia" was "in the first place a Jewish phobia ... express[ing] the self-consciousness of a minority culture."[33] It also illustrates Arie Dubnov's point that scholars and the general public tend to use words to do different sorts of work (although in the case of "antisemitism" the distinction is often blurred, as David Feldman has suggested and as I shall illustrate further shortly).[34] In this regard, it appears telling that none of the contributors to this volume has *expressly* followed the ADL and the Parliamentary Inquiry in speaking mainly about extrinsic attributes of "antisemitism" or in allowing the word to signify whatever Jews collectively use it to signify in practice at any moment. On the other hand, several contributors seem to have come close to doing so *implicitly*: They have called for retaining "antisemitism" as an analytical tool in scholarly discussions of Jewish history and contemporary affairs because the concept has been an integral part of the way in which Jews have understood their situation for many generations.

Each of these motifs reflects aspects of the tension between the two different ways of thinking about "antisemitism" that I noted at the outset of my remarks. Exploring them further can, I think, deepen understanding about how the concept has actually functioned past and present, both in the academy and in the public arena, and how it might be translated in a way that allows its multiple referents to figure fruitfully in both realms in the future.

The tension and the possibilities both seem clearest in the argument that the *concept* "antisemitism" (as distinct from its referents) is inseparable from lived Jewish experience. The claim appears true for the interval beginning around 1880; for earlier eras it can be true only if "antisemitism" is conflated with some earlier concept Jews used to understand their environment. The extent to which such conflation is empirically justifiable is a question for research of the type some contributors to this volume have undertaken.

Meanwhile, for generations since 1880, the claim might actually preclude apprehending "antisemitism" through its purported intrinsic qualities. Granted, it is a primary task of historical scholarship to get into the heads of past actors, as it were, and to see the world through their eyes. But that obligation does not obviously entail a concomitant duty to *express* their worldviews in the same terms they would have employed. People who lived through the Great Plague of London in 1665 attributed it not to the bacterium *Yersinia pestis*, of whose existence they were ignorant, but to a miasma polluting the air. Survivors in the city who experienced the Great Fire of the following year understood that event as a massive escape of an element called "fire" into the atmosphere. By 1728, when Copenhagen experienced a similar conflagration, a new explanation referred to a mysterious "principle" called phlogiston, which was not detectable by the senses but was nevertheless supposed to make all combustible material burn.

History is replete with similar examples of views of the world that eventually failed basic empirical tests. People who held those views behaved in accordance with them; hence historians seeking to explain their behavior must try to comprehend the ideas in their minds. But that seems rather different from using "miasma" or "phlogiston" to explain why Londoners died or Copenhagen residents were rendered homeless. In any event, it seems to me that scholars committed to using their subjects' language as their own ought now, for precisely that reason, to abandon the search for universal intrinsic attributes of what their subjects routinely call "antisemitism" in favor of an approach more consonant with that of the ADL.

That approach is not as dubious as it might first sound; actually, it turns out to present intriguing possibilities for breaking the largely circular character of arguments about "antisemitism" in contemporary academic discourse. For although "What is antisemitism?" is a question that can't be answered in a manner true for *all* uses of the word in common parlance, at least by reference to any empirically verifiable, essential intrinsic quality, "What things have struck Jews in different times and places as having an adverse impact on their interests or on their sense of security and well-being?" is easily amenable to empirical investigation.

Various sources exist for investigating the latter question with regard to at least some Jewish communities. Much contemporary information comes from public opinion research. For example, in a 2018 survey by the European Union Agency for Fundamental Human Rights, thirty-nine percent of respondents reported that they had "experienced some form of antisemitic harassment" once or more during the previous five years. The most commonly reported experiences were "offensive or threatening comments in person" (twenty-seven percent) and "offensive gestures or inappropriate staring" (twenty-three percent). Only four percent noted vandalism against their property "because they are Jewish," while three percent had "personally experienced a physical attack" for the same reason. Yet more than one-third of respondents indicated that they "have considered emigrating in the past five years because they did not feel safe as a Jew in the country where they live."[35]

The situation appears similar in the United States. A 2020 study by the Pew Research Center showed fifty-one percent of respondents having encountered "antisemitism" at least once during the previous year, where "antisemitism" included seeing "anti-Jewish graffiti or vandalism" (thirty-seven percent), being "made to feel unwelcome because they are Jewish" (twenty percent), "called offensive names" (fifteen percent), "harassed online" (eight percent), or "physically threatened or attacked" (five percent). Nevertheless, a slightly greater number (fifty-three percent) indicated that they felt less safe than they did five years before.[36] That feeling appears to have prompted growing numbers of American Jews to "think the unthinkable" about their prospects in their country, to the point where, by October 2022, the director of the ADL observed that "among the most frequently asked questions ... I get" is where Jews might move if they no longer feel safe in America.[37]

No comparable data are available for Jewish communities before the Second World War. However, other sources suggest that Jews have historically required considerably harsher expressions of adversity to make them fear actively for their future in their countries of residence. Jews in Poland in the 1930s felt their physical security severely threatened by, among other things, government-sanctioned discrimination, student groups throwing Jews out of lecture halls or forcing them to sit on back benches, and mobs trying to beat them up. When such occurrences grew in frequency and force in the context of a protracted economic downturn that made many worry for their livelihood, and when growing numbers came to perceive them as part of a systematic campaign of "national oppression," against which they could mount no effective defense, waged against them by all levels of state and society in order to drive them from the country, demand for emigration rose sharply. In that setting, hearing themselves or others called *parszywy Żyd* (mangy Jew), or even Christ-killers, hardly seemed significant in isolation; absent far more ominous political and economic trends, such verbal behavior likely had little bearing on Jews' collective sense of safety.[38]

Some Jews in late Weimar Germany appear to have displayed an even higher anxiety threshold. In a single week following the July 1932 Reichstag elections that made the Nazis Germany's largest political party, the bulletin of the *Centralverein* (a defense organization roughly analogous to the ADL) noted, among other violent acts, an assassination attempt upon its representative in Königsberg, a bomb planted at a synagogue in Kiel, a hand-grenade attack on a Jewish shop in Upper Silesia, and a bloody beating of a Jewish merchant in East Prussia.[39] Yet in the bulletin's next issue, the organization's director, noting that "the state has not yet failed," advised small-town Jews, who felt most directly threatened by such acts, to remain in place, for their situation would soon improve.[40] At the time, Jewish leaders worldwide generally did not see German Jewry facing greater threats than Jews in countries farther east.[41] Nor did Weimar Jews themselves contemplate emigration to nearly the degree that European and American Jews reported more than eight decades later, despite far more severe threats to life and limb.[42]

It is moot whether Weimar Jews *should* have been more inclined to leave. To be sure, "security" can refer to both a perception and a condition, and, given adequate evidence, historical research can reveal gaps between the two in specific situations. It may indeed be that, in evaluating their situation in 1932, Jews in Germany had their eyes on less portentous things than they might have. More important for present purposes, however, is that both perceptions and actual conditions have historically depended upon far more than the presence of attitudes or actions commonly taken today as indicators of "antisemitism." Indeed, it seems that until the last several decades there has been little correlation between a community's overall sense of safety and variations in the frequency or intensity of the behaviors and attitudes monitored by the ADL. For example, Jews in early modern Poland who wrote about such things generally expressed stronger feelings of security than did their counterparts in the Holy Roman Empire, even though Jews in both places were exposed to similar day-to-day expressions of hostility from similar sources to similar degrees. In each location Jews attributed their different situations to differences in legal, political, and economic arrangements, not to any ostensibly greater or lesser hatred toward them in one place or another. And in fact, those differences do appear generally to have worked to Polish Jews' comparative benefit.[43]

The studies that have yielded this knowledge indicate that exploring, through detailed local investigations, the full range of factors that have made for greater or lesser degrees and senses of security among Jews over the centuries and across the globe, including but not limited to the many disparate referents the word "antisemitism" has assumed over the decades in popular and scholarly literature, may offer a rich research agenda leading to fruitful comparisons across eras and locations. This agenda can, I think, yield significant new insights into Jewish history (and into the history of intergroup relations more broadly) in a way that studying an abstract "antisemitism" presumed to display the same essential intrinsic qualities independently of time and place is unlikely to reveal. Indeed, "antisemitism" appears historically to have taken on meaning for Jews only in relation to all of those factors taken together.

On the basis of preliminary observations, I would propose as an opening hypothesis that since the 1880s Jews have employed "antisemitism" largely to designate those aspects of non-Jews' attitudes and behavior toward them that they regarded as potentially most threatening in their own circumstances. I would also suggest two corollaries: first, that historians who have referred to "antisemitism" before the 1880s have similarly used the term to denote aspects of the environment that seem to them retrospectively most injurious to the security of the Jews they study, and second, that not only for the logical reasons I detailed earlier but also because different communities' perceptions have often been different, inferences from supposed general attributes of "antisemitism" to particular situations often prove unreliable. To be sure, all of these propositions require careful empirical testing. Such empirical work will doubtless lead to more refined, less sweeping generalizations. Meanwhile, though, sufficient sources exist for enough times and places to make prospects for discovery sufficiently enticing to recommend it to scholars.

Taking up such an agenda involves far more than substituting a more felicitous word for "antisemitism." Indeed, I do not wish to join the sort of terminological debate others have dismissed as futile. I seek rather a new conceptual language, one that permits me to designate separately the multiple factors that have made for greater or lesser levels and feelings of security and danger for Jews in particular historical contexts instead of requiring me to subsume all under a single rubric—in short, a language capable of precisely those differentiations that one centered about "antisemitism" (according to Yehuda Bauer, for one) is not.[44] I recognize that acquiring such a new language demands a degree of effort that others doubt justifies the payoff.[45] But that objection merely echoes the protests by eighteenth- and nineteenth-century chemists (among them some of the world's most accomplished scientists) who continued to proclaim the "absolute existence" of phlogiston even as they acknowledged the superiority of the oxygen theory of combustion. Because phlogistic chemistry offered satisfactory explanations for most day-to-day experiences of fire, they argued, its imperfections (including the inability to define it precisely) could be safely overlooked.[46] As it turned out, those imperfections could be ignored for only so long.

True, the comparison is inexact, among other reasons because the phlogiston versus oxygen debate had little resonance among the general public and stood to affect public behavior in the face of fire but little. Current scholarly discussions of "antisemitism," by contrast, are deeply embedded in a public discourse that, as David Feldman puts it, "not only classif[ies] … actions" as "antisemitic" but "declare[s] … them … unjust and unacceptable."[47] Feldman is correct: The negative branding campaign begun in the late nineteenth century continues strongly into the present. That campaign has routinely spurned precisely the sort of differential tools whose absence I and others have noted, favoring instead a strategy that represents verbal slights and mass murder as parts of a single continuum on which all points are equally dangerous. "It starts with hate mail, name calling and grave desecrations," proclaimed a full-page advertisement by the New York Jewish umbrella organization, UJA-Federation, in September 1990, above a large photograph of Yad Vashem's Hall of Remembrance, with the names Dachau, Bergen-Belsen, Majdanek, and Auschwitz-Birkenau centered. The text continued: "We all know how it ends. And now, it looks like it's starting all over again in the Soviet Union," for newspapers had recently reported "the outbreak of anti-Semitism" in the

USSR. Hence, it concluded, Soviet Jews, in mortal danger, needed to be moved immediately to Israel "before history repeats itself."[48]

The advertisement did not make known that after 1989 the USSR no longer restricted Jewish emigration as it had in the past or that in 1990 nearly as many Jews left the country as had during the previous two decades.[49] Nor did it mention that, according to the same newspaper reports to which it evidently referred, between eighty-eight and ninety percent of respondents in a recent survey agreed that the government should enforce equal opportunity in education and employment for Jews, that "President . . . Gorbachev's program has freed many Soviet Jews to observe their faith," and that "anti-Semitism was growing *while Jewish cultural and other activities had increased considerably*."[50] For the advertisement's purposes, the complexities of the Soviet Jewish situation were irrelevant; as long as "antisemitism" was present in any form to any degree, Jews faced the real prospect of imminent slaughter.

For decades that message has been advanced not only by major Jewish organizations worldwide but also by a global cultural elite that helped designate any behavior Jews might find upsetting—physical, legal, social, or verbal—as beyond the pale of social acceptability. Since the end of the Second World War their work has arguably accomplished much. Job discrimination, for one (a central concern of *Gentleman's Agreement*), seems no longer to worry American Jews sufficiently for the ADL to include in its annual "Audit of Anti-Semitic Incidents."[51] Similarly, admissions quotas for Jewish students, still evident in the United States in the 1950s, have lately become a source of shame for universities that implemented them.[52] Such apparent successes may well make scholarship that highlights the doubtful history upon which the branding campaign rests appear to undermine efforts from which Jewish scholars benefit together with society as a whole. Perhaps here is a deterrent to abandoning the language of what has been a highly effective public undertaking.

In the third decade of the twenty-first century, however, prospects for continued success may be fading. The notion that "it [the Nazi Holocaust] started with words" originated as a branding tactic, but growing numbers of Jews appear to accept it as historical truth. That belief, in turn (along with the practice of reporting Jews' fears as statistics to be feared in their own right), has made post-Holocaust Jews increasingly alarmed over the persistence of hostile words, to the point where, for all the tactic's achievements, more and more seem to feel less and less secure. In Israel, for example, a well-known television personality and former Knesset member, commenting on a destructive May 2021 mob attack by non-Jewish Israeli citizens upon Jewish property in Lod (Lydda), likened the events to the murderous 1938 Kristallnacht riots in Nazi Germany. He even wore a six-pointed yellow star to the television studio, as if to draw a direct line between dangers facing Jews then and now.[53] Context offered him no comfort; all assaults upon Jews were, it seems, potentially lethal to the same degree. Even Jewish political sovereignty and control of military and police forces evidently did not make him feel safe.

Moreover, in the age of social media, the cultural elites that have been assigned a central role in the dominant security strategy no longer control public discourse to nearly the extent that they did for six decades after 1945. Jewish planners today thus face a major problem: how to fill the function those elites are now unable to perform adequately. Solving that problem demands engagement not only with the tactical question of how to "combat antisemitism" but also with the strategic challenge of ascertaining how the broad gamut of political, economic, social, cultural, and religious variables that together have shaped conditions for Jews in different times and places in the past are doing so today.

Earlier Jewish generations faced a similar challenge. For the most part, with some fleeting exceptions, they assumed they would always face an irreducible core of hostility that they could at most hope to render harmless in practice. In recent decades, however, Jews seem increasingly to have confused branding "antisemitism" as socially unacceptable with eliminating all expressions of hostility altogether, as if only by doing so can Jews ever be truly secure.[54] That belief directs attention away from the myriad other factors that affect Jewish security, thereby undermining the very goal it claims to serve. In any event, public and academic discussions that reduce threats to Jewish security to a single uniform "antisemitism" seem to me inadequate to the weighty tasks now confronting both the academy and the world beyond.

NOTES

1. Scott Ury and Guy Miron, eds., *Antishemiyut: ben musag histori lesiah tziburi* (Jerusalem: Shazar Center, 2020).

2. David Engel, "Away from a Definition of Antisemitism: An Essay in the Semantics of Historical Description," in *Rethinking European Jewish History*, ed. Jeremy Cohen and Moshe Rosman (Oxford: Littman Library of Jewish Civilization, 2009), 53. Emphasis added.

3. I also believe that Jews today have reason to be concerned for their security. I shall elaborate below. Meanwhile, note that my use of quotation marks around "antisemitism" is meant only to clarify that I refer to a word and to the concept it commonly signifies instead of to ideas or actions. It should not be taken to imply that I regard the occurrences commonly thought of as manifestations of "antisemitism" as imaginary.

4. I originally formulated these claims in response to a question by Shmuel Ettinger, longtime professor of modern Jewish history at the Hebrew University of Jerusalem: "Do all of the various manifestations of hatred and rejection of Jews and Judaism throughout the ages, which since the final quarter of the nineteenth century have been called antisemitism, constitute a single phenomenon, or is [antisemitism] merely a common label for a range of social, political, and psychological phenomena that have been lumped together for terminological convenience?" Shmuel Ettinger, *Haantishemiyut ba'et hahadashah* (Tel Aviv: Moreshet, 1978), ix. Ettinger saw a single phenomenon. However, he reached his conclusion via a circular argument that appears frequently in efforts to define what he and others have called the single phenomenon's "essence." On this argument, see below. In any event, as is evident from, inter alia, the complaint by Yehuda Bauer that closes the first paragraph of the introduction to this volume, the "common label" has brought not "terminological convenience" but widespread terminological despair. Scott Ury and Guy Miron, "Antisemitism: On the Meanings and Uses of a Contested Term," 1–2.

5. An example: In response to the Hebrew-language volume, a scholar claimed that there is "absolutely" a connection between "all expressions of antisemitism": "The common denominator...is the image of the Jew...as responsible for every ill under the sun." Dina Porat, "Ein kesher hechrahi bein kol bituyei haantishemiyut? Yesh, behehlet yesh," *Haaretz*, October 19, 2020. The statement can be true only if "antisemitism" is defined a priori as expressions or behavior conveying or motivated by such an image. Ironically, the writer served for many years as head of a research institute that maintains a database of "antisemitic incidents" worldwide. The listings include numerous entries for incidents in which such an image is not evident.

6. Susannah Heschel, "Erotohistoriography: Sensory and Emotional Dimensions of Antisemitism," 68, 71, 76, 77. Her corresponding Hebrew article expressed the idea more succinctly: "[A]ntisemitism is *invariably* expressed with passion, both verbally and in physical attacks." Emphasis added. Susannah Heschel, "Likrat historiyografiyah erotit: Heker hamemadim hahushiyim shel haantishemiyut," in *Antishemiyut: ben musag histori lesiah tsiburi*, ed. Scott Ury and Guy Miron, 82.

356 · DAVID ENGEL

7. Eli Lederhendler, "America and the Keyword Battle Over 'Antisemitism'," 214.

8. Laura Z. Hobson, *Gentleman's Agreement* (New York: Simon & Schuster, 1946), 155, 154.

9. Heschel, "Erotohistoriography," 68, 76, 77.

10. Actually, the first possibility rests on a circular argument as well because its conclusion (John Doe harbors certain motives and feelings) is inferred syllogistically from a major premise (all antisemites harbor certain motives and feelings) and a minor one (John Doe is an antisemite), both assumed to be true in advance.

11. Heschel, "Erotohistoriography," 70.

12. At least one of those propositions—that "scholars of racism would never... claim" that "no necessary relations of particular instances of violence...can be assumed"—is false; the article by Stefanie Schüler-Springorum in this volume, for one, cites scholars of racism who do indeed make such a claim. But even if it were true, and even if we accept that "the enslavement of Black Africans by American whites in the eighteenth and nineteenth centuries has a clear and essential relationship to the lynching of Emmett Till in 1955," it remains unclear how a fact concerning one incident in the history of race relations in the United States demonstrates that all instances of violence against Jews everywhere and at all times, let alone all acts or utterances routinely called expressions of "antisemitism," are *necessarily* related to one another. Some are, some aren't, and the relations (or their absence) can be uncovered only by empirical research. See Heschel, "Erotohistoriography," 65, and Stefanie Schüler-Springorum, "Toward Entanglement," 87–101.

13. Another example: Deborah E. Lipstadt, *Antisemitism: Here and Now* (New York: Schocken Books, 2019), 14–19. The author explains that Jews perceive "antisemitism" intuitively in moments of recognition (called "Click!" moments) that others are less likely to experience. Such moments may be triggered when a person indicates resentment of another in a manner that identifies the other as a Jew: "Complaining about that 'crooked real-estate developer' is one thing. Complaining about that 'crooked Jewish real-estate developer' is—Click!—antisemitism." Later, the author, reasoning from a different definition of "antisemitism" as "a persisting latent structure of hostile beliefs towards Jews as a collective," concludes that "antisemitism...has an internal coherence" expressed in a set of "themes and tropes" that appear consistent with one another only to people convinced absurdly that "Jews are not *an* enemy but *the* ultimate enemy." The author appears thereby to permit the inference that a person who notes the Jewishness of a certain adversary can be presumed a priori to regard *all* Jews as "*the* ultimate enemy." Here is the fallacy of equivocation. The author has at best only partial knowledge of what the person in question thinks about one particular Jew in one specific situation, yet she seems prepared to include that person among delusional conspiracy theorists (see page 7, where "antisemitism" is placed in the larger category of "conspiracy theories") without any empirical evidence. The success of such a move depends upon conflating disparate definitions of a single word.

14. Havi Dreifuss, "In Defense of the Concept of 'Antisemitism' in Holocaust Studies," 294.

15. Gershon Bacon, "Cautious Use of the Term 'Antisemitism'—for Lack of an Alternative: Interwar Poland as a Test Case," 189, 190, 193.

16. Dreifuss, "In Defense of the Concept," 294.

17. For that matter, each of Bacon's three criteria generates different sets. The writer Julian Ursyn Niemcewicz, whom Bacon suggests deserves the "antisemitic" label for his fear of a Jewish takeover of Warsaw, did not regard Jewishness as indelible. See, for example, his 1821 novel *Lejbe i Siora*, in which the protagonists illustrated possibilities for emancipation and integration into Polish society *as Jews*. See also Artur Eisenbach, *Kwestia równouprawnienia Żydów w Królestwie Polskim* (Warsaw: Książka i Wiedza, 1972), 280; Artur Eisenbach, *Emancypacja Żydów na ziemiach polskich 1785–1870 na tle europejskim* (Warsaw: Państwowy Instytut Wydawniczy, 1988), 162–63.

18. The debates of the last decade surrounding the alternative definitions of "antisemitism" offered by, among others, the International Holocaust Remembrance Alliance (IHRA) and the Jerusalem Declaration on Antisemitism (JDA) center around the *normative* question of what sorts of actions and utterances should be deemed unacceptable and subject to sanction in the public sphere. The competing definitions have no *descriptive* value. In any event, they reveal discord, not consensus.

19. What were once commonplace modifiers of "antisemitism," used to distinguish between purported "political," "economic," "religious," "cultural," and "social" forms, do not appear serviceable to me. Space does not permit me to explain why in full. Suffice it to say that problems of definition similar to those regarding "antisemitism" as a whole have regularly appeared in literature devoted to explaining the ostensible differences among the various subcategories.

20. The incident was reported internationally. For a partial list, see Emily Babay, "News of Weekend Vandalism at a Jewish Cemetery in Philadelphia Has Generated Headlines around the World," *Philadelphia Inquirer*, February 27, 2017, www.inquirer .com/philly/blogs/real-time/Vandalism-at-Jewish-cemetery-in-Philadelphia-makes -news-worldwide.html.

21. Emmanuelle Saliba and Corky Siemaszko, "Philadelphia Jewish Cemetery Vandalized in Wave of Anti-Semitic Attacks," *NBC*, February 27, 2017, www.nbcnews .com/news/us-news/philadelphia-jewish-cemetery-vandalized-wave-anti-semitic -acts-n726321. Only the CEO of the local Jewish Federation warned that "'maybe we'll never know if this was an anti-Semitic act.'" Ralph Ellis and Eric Levenson, "Jewish Cemetery in Philadelphia Vandalized; 2nd Incident in a Week," *CNN*, February 27, 2017, www.cnn.com/2017/02/26/us/jewish-cemetery-vandalism-philadelphia/index .html.

22. Anti-Defamation League, "2017 Audit of Anti-Semitic Incidents" (New York: Anti-Defamation League, February 25, 2018).

23. Kantor Center for the Study of Contemporary European Jewry, "Antisemitism Worldwide, 2017: General Analysis, Draft," (copy available at cst.tau.ac.il), 5, 59.

It appears that the text reporting incidents of cemetery vandalism in the United States was taken verbatim from the ADL audit. For the original entry in the Moshe Kantor Database, see https://tau-primo.hosted.exlibrisgroup.com/permalink/f/jim 576/972TAU_ALMA71203726880004146.

24. Stephanie Farr, "Vandalism at Jewish Cemetery Predated Reports, Superintendent Says," *Philadelphia Inquirer*, February 28, 2017, www.inquirer.com/philly/news /Vandalism-at-Jewish-cemetery-predated-reports-superintendent-says.html.

25. Debra Nussbaum Cohen, "Philadelphia Jews Reeling After Hundreds of Graves Vandalized," *Haaretz*, February 27, 2017, www.haaretz.com/us-news/2017-02-27/ty -article/.premium/philadelphia-jews-reeling-after-hundreds-of-graves-vandaliz ed/0000017f-e3b3-df7c-a5ff-e3fb951d0000.

26. Emily Ford, "The Year in Cemetery Vandalism: 2016," *Oak and Laurel* (blog), December 30, 2016, www.oakandlaurel.com/blog/the-year-in-cemetery-vandalism-2016# _ftn2. In only eighteen percent of cases was a perpetrator apprehended.

27. Ashleigh M. Albert, "'Disgusting' Vandalism at Cherry Hill Cemetery Leaves Trail of Headless Statues," *Philadelphia Inquirer*, April 18, 2017, www.inquirer.com /philly/news/new_jersey/Vandalism-at-Calvary-Catholic-Cemetery-disgusting-to -some-repairs-upcoming.html; Ralph Ellis and Eric Levenson, "Jewish Cemetery in Philadelphia Vandalized."

28. One bit of evidence appeared to cut in the other direction: an adjacent Christian cemetery was not touched that day.

29. Methodology section of "Audit of Anti-Semitic Incidents: Year in Review 2018" (New York: Anti-Defamation League, 2019), www.adl.org/audit2018#methodology. Emphasis added.

30. "Audit of Anti-Semitic Incidents 2021" (New York: Anti-Defamation League), www.adl.org/resources/report/audit-antisemitic-incidents-2021/. On the other hand, it modified its treatment of vandalism: "Vandalism against Jewish religious institutions or cemeteries *may* also be included." Emphasis added. Note the absence of "all," which was present in 2017. The conditions under which attacks on cemeteries "may" be included were not specified.

31. David Feldman, "A Retreat from Universalism: Opposing and Defining Antisemitism and Islamophobia in Britain, ca. 1990–2018," 258–60.

32. All-Party Parliamentary Group Against Antisemitism, "Report of the All-Party Parliamentary Inquiry into Antisemitism" (London: The Stationery Office, 2006), 1. Emphasis added. See Feldman, "A Retreat from Universalism."

33. Adi M. Ophir and Ishay Rosen-Zvi, "Separatism, Judeophobia, and the Birth of the 'Goy': The Chicken and the Egg," 117.

34. Arie M. Dubnov, "'Fog in Channel—Continent Cut Off'?: Remarks on Antisemitism, Pride, and Prejudice in Britain," 227–50.

35. European Union Agency for Fundamental Human Rights, *Experiences and Per-*

ceptions of Antisemitism: Second Survey on Discrimination and Hate Crime against Jews in the EU (Luxembourg: Publication Office of the European Union, 2018), 31, 49, 51.

36. Pew Research Center, *Jewish Americans in 2020* (n.p.: Pew Research Center, 2021), 124, 126.

37. Dana Milbank, "American Jews Start to Think the Unthinkable," *Washington Post*, October 28, 2022, www.washingtonpost.com/opinions/2022/10/28/american-jews-exile-fears.

38. See, most recently, Kenneth B. Moss, *An Unchosen People: Jewish Political Reckoning in Interwar Poland* (Cambridge, MA: Harvard University Press, 2021), 57–83, esp. 15 (for the phrase "national oppression").

39. "Nach der Wahl: Statt Burgfrieden—Gewalttaten und Blutvergießen," *CV-Zeitung*, August 5, 1932, 1.

40. L. H. [Ludwig Holländer], "An die Freunde im Lande," *CV-Zeitung*, August 12, 1932, 1.

41. David Engel, "The Jewish World Under Nazi Impact, 1930–1939," *Cambridge History of the Holocaust* (forthcoming).

42. Doron Niederland, *Yehudei germaniyah—Mehagrim o pelitim: iyun bidefusei hahagirah bein shetei milhamot haolam* (Jerusalem: Magnes Press, 1996), 22, 65–66.

43. See, inter alia, Adam Teller, "Telling the Difference: Some Comparative Perspectives on the Jews' Legal Status in the Polish-Lithuanian Commonwealth and the Holy Roman Empire," *Polin* 22 (2010): 109–41; Moshe Rosman, *Categorically Jewish, Distinctly Polish: Polish Jewish History Reflected and Refracted* (Oxford: Littman Library of Jewish Civilization, 2022), 129–39.

44. Scott Ury and Guy Miron, "Antisemitism: On the Meanings and Uses of a Contested Term," 1–2.

45. For example, Gershon Bacon maintains that "using the term 'antisemitism' does not necessarily contribute to historical analysis," but it "does not necessarily detract from it"; hence he won't eliminate it from his professional vocabulary but will merely resolve to employ it "cautiously." No doubt a skilled scholar of the first rank like Bacon can in theory restrict his own use of the term to clearly defined, logically and empirically consistent referents and explain the restriction with such lucidity that no reader will ever misunderstand. In practice, however, even Bacon himself has not used the term in this way. Using "antisemitism" may not *"necessarily* detract from . . . historical analysis," but I am hardly alone in pointing out that all too often it does so in fact. Gershon Bacon, "Cautious Use of the Term 'Antisemitism'—for Lack of an Alternative," 195.

46. Victor D. Boantza and Ofer Gal, "The 'Absolute Existence' of Phlogiston: The Losing Party's Point of View," *British Journal for the History of Science* 44, no. 3 (2011): 317–42.

47. Feldman, "A Retreat from Universalism," 252.

48. *New York Times*, September 10, 1990, B12. The newspaper reports that most likely informed the advertisement noted a recent survey, according to which eighteen percent of the Soviet population "disliked" Jews, with eighteen percent "liking" and sixty-four percent "neutral" (Frank J. Prial, "Upheaval in the East: Survey in Moscow Sees a High Level of Anti-Jewish Feeling," *New York Times*, March 30, 1990, A8); distribution of hostile propaganda by Russian nationalist groups (Joel Brinkley, "Soviet Emigres to Israel Tell of Hate Back Home," *New York Times*, February 4, 1990, A24; Anonymous, "Article in Pravda Says Anti-Semitism Is Rife," *New York Times*, July 24, 1990, A8); and "anti-Semitic assaults and insults" mentioned by "several" of two hundred former Soviet Jews then seeking asylum in East Germany (Henry Kamm, "Evolution in Europe: Soviet Jews in East Berlin Tell of Intolerance," *New York Times*, June 25, 1990, A10; see Henry Kamm, "Upheaval in the East: Soviet Rabbi Tells of New Anti-Semitism," *New York Times*, February 21, 1990, A11).

49. Mark Tolts, "A Half Century of Jewish Emigration from the Former Soviet Union: Demographic Aspects" (speech, Cambridge, MA, November 20, 2019), Davis Center for Russian and Eurasian Studies, https://daviscenter.fas.harvard.edu/events/half-century-jewish-emigration-former-soviet-union-demographic-aspects.

50. See *New York Times*, September 10, 1990, B12. Emphasis added.

51. See the ADL's methodological statement above, www.adl.org/audit2018#methodology.

52. Chris Peacock, "Stanford Apologizes for Admissions Limits on Jewish Students in the 1950s and Pledges Action on Steps to Enhance Jewish Life on Campus," *Stanford Report*, October 12, 2022, https://news.stanford.edu/report/2022/10/12/task-force-report-jewish-admissions-and-jewish-life.

53. Rogel Alpher, "Mi she-oned al atsmo telai tsahov...," *Haaretz*, May 25, 2021, www.haaretz.co.il/gallery/television/tv-review/.premium-1.9839791. Actually, no requirement for Jews to wear the yellow star was in force at the time of Kristallnacht. It was first imposed in part of Nazi-occupied Poland in November 1939 and introduced into Germany proper only in September 1941.

54. An international scholars' conference held in Vienna in 2018, entitled "An End to Antisemitism," claimed it would "develop effective strategies for the eradication of Jew-hatred." "General Information: About: An End to Antisemitism!," accessed January 24, 2023, https://anendtoantisemitism.univie.ac.at/general-information/about.

Select Bibliography

Adams, Jonathan, and Cordelia Hess, eds. *The Medieval Roots of Antisemitism: Continuities and Discontinuities from the Middle Ages to the Present Day.* New York: Routledge, 2018.

Adorno, Theodor W., Else Frenkel-Brunswik, Daniel J. Levinson, and Nevitt Sanford. *The Authoritarian Personality.* With an introduction by Peter E. Gordon. London: Verso, 2019.

"AHR Roundtable: Rethinking Anti-Semitism." Jonathan Judaken, guest editor. *American Historical Review* 123, no. 4 (October 2018).

Almog, Shmuel, ed. *Antisemitism through the Ages.* Translated by Nathan H. Reisner. Oxford: Pergamon, 1988.

Anidjar, Gil. *Semites: Race, Religion, Literature.* Stanford, CA: Stanford University Press, 2008.

Arendt, Hannah. *The Origins of Totalitarianism.* New York: Harcourt Brace Jovanovich, 1973.

Bauer, Yehuda. "In Search of a Definition of Antisemitism." In *Approaches to Antisemitism: Context and Curriculum*, edited by Michael Brown, 10–23. New York: American Jewish Committee, 1994.

Bauman, Zygmunt. "Allosemitism: Premodern, Modern, Postmodern." In *Modernity, Culture, and "the Jew,"* edited by Bryan Cheyette and Laura Marcus, 143–56. Cambridge: Polity, 1998.

Baumgarten, Murray, Peter Kenez, and Bruce A. Thompson, eds. *Varieties of Antisemitism: History, Ideology, Discourse.* Newark: University of Delaware Press, 2009.

Becker, Adam H., and Annette Yoshiko Reed, eds. *The Ways That Never Parted: Jews and Christians in Late Antiquity and the Early Middle Ages.* Minneapolis: Fortress Press, 2007.

Beller, Steven. *Antisemitism: A Very Short Introduction.* New York: Oxford University Press, 2007.

Bemporad, Elissa. *Legacy of Blood: Jews, Pogroms, and Ritual Murder in the Lands of the Soviets.* New York: Oxford University Press, 2019.

Berger, David, ed. *History and Hate: The Dimensions of Anti-Semitism.* Philadelphia: Jewish Publication Society, 1997.

Birnbaum, Pierre. *The Anti-Semitic Moment: A Tour of France in 1898.* New York: Hill and Wang, 2003.

Blobaum, Robert, ed. *Antisemitism and Its Opponents in Modern Poland.* Ithaca, NY: Cornell University Press, 2005.

Bunzl, Matti. *Anti-Semitism and Islamophobia: Hatreds Old and New in Europe.* Chicago: Prickly Paradigm, 2007.

Carroll, James. *Constantine's Sword: The Church and the Jews: A History*. Boston: Houghton Mifflin, 2001.

Chazan, Robert. *From Anti-Judaism to Anti-Semitism: Ancient and Medieval Christian Constructions of Jewish History*. New York: Cambridge University Press, 2016.

Cohen, Jeremy. *Living Letters of the Law: Ideas of the Jew in Medieval Christianity*. Berkeley: University of California Press, 1999.

Cohen, Mark R. *Under Crescent and Cross: The Jews in the Middle Ages*. Princeton, NJ: Princeton University Press, 1994.

Cohn, Norman. *Warrant for Genocide: The Myth of the Jewish World-Conspiracy and the Protocols of the Elders of Zion*. Chico, CA: Scholars Press, 1981.

Connelly, John. *From Enemy to Brother: The Revolution in Catholic Teaching on the Jews, 1933–1965*. Cambridge, MA: Harvard University Press, 2012.

De Michelis, Cesare G. *The Non-Existent Manuscript: A Study of the Protocols of the Sages of Zion*. Translated by Richard Newhouse. Lincoln: University of Nebraska Press, 2004.

Dinnerstein, Leonard. *Antisemitism in America*. New York: Oxford University Press, 1994.

Dundes, Alan. *The Blood Libel Legend: A Casebook in Anti-Semitic Folklore*. Madison: University of Wisconsin Press, 1991.

Efron, John M. *Defenders of the Race: Jewish Doctors and Race Science in Fin- de-Siècle Europe*. New Haven, CT: Yale University Press, 1994.

Elukin, Jonathan M. *Living Together, Living Apart: Rethinking Jewish-Christian Relations in the Middle Ages*. Princeton, NJ: Princeton University Press, 2007.

Engel, David. "Away from a Definition of Antisemitism: An Essay in the Semantics of Historical Description." In *Rethinking European Jewish History*, edited by Jeremy Cohen and Moshe Rosman, 30–53. Oxford: Littman Library of Jewish Civilization, 2009.

Ettinger, Shmuel. *Haantishemiyut ba'et hahadasha*. Tel Aviv: Moreshet, 1978.

Feldman, David. "Toward a History of the Term 'Anti-Semitism.'" *American Historical Review* 123, no. 4 (October 2018): 1139–50.

Feldman, David, and Marc Volovici, eds. *Antisemitism, Islamophobia and the Politics of Definition*. Cham, Switzerland: Palgrave Macmillan, 2023.

Frankel, Jonathan. *The Damascus Affair: "Ritual Murder," Politics, and the Jews in 1840*. Cambridge: Cambridge University Press, 1997.

Friedländer, Saul. *Nazi Germany and the Jews*. 2 vols. New York: HarperCollins, 1997–2007.

Gager, John G. *The Origins of Anti-Semitism: Attitudes Toward Judaism in Pagan and Christian Antiquity*. New York: Oxford University Press, 1983.

Gilman, Sander L. *Jewish Self-Hatred: Anti-Semitism and the Hidden Language of the Jews*. Baltimore: Johns Hopkins University Press, 1986.

———. *The Jew's Body*. New York: Routledge, 1991.

Goldberg, Sol, Scott Ury, and Kalman Weiser, eds. *Key Concepts in the Study of Antisemitism*. Cham, Switzerland: Palgrave Macmillan, 2021.

Goldhagen, Daniel Jonah. *Hitler's Willing Executioners: Ordinary Germans and the Holocaust*. New York: Alfred A. Knopf, 1996.

Goldstein, Phyllis. *A Convenient Hatred: The History of Antisemitism*. Brookline, MA: Facing History & Ourselves, 2012.

Gross, Jan T. *Fear: Anti-Semitism in Poland after Auschwitz: An Essay in Historical Interpretation*. New York: Random House, 2006.

Hammerschlag, Sarah. *The Figural Jew: Politics and Identity in Postwar French Thought*. Chicago: University of Chicago Press, 2010.

Hanebrink, Paul. *A Specter Haunting Europe: The Myth of Judeo-Bolshevism*. Cambridge, MA: Harvard University Press, 2018.

Herf, Jeffrey, ed. *Anti-Semitism and Anti-Zionism in Historical Perspective: Convergence and Divergence*. London: Routledge, 2014.

Heschel, Susannah. *The Aryan Jesus: Christian Theologians and the Bible in Nazi Germany*. Princeton, NJ: Princeton University Press, 2008.

Hilberg, Raul. *The Destruction of the European Jews*. New York: Holmes & Meier, 1985.

Hoffmann, Christhard, Werner Bergmann, and Helmut Walser Smith, eds. *Exclusionary Violence: Antisemitic Riots in Modern German History*. Ann Arbor: University of Michigan Press, 2002.

Horkheimer, Max, and Theodor W. Adorno. *Dialectic of Enlightenment: Philosophical Fragments*. Stanford, CA: Stanford University Press, 2002.

Hsia, R. Po-chia. *The Myth of Ritual Murder: Jews and Magic in Reformation Germany*. New Haven, CT: Yale University Press, 1988.

International Holocaust Remembrance Alliance (IHRA). "What Is Antisemitism? The Working Definition of Antisemitism." https://holocaustremembrance.com /resources/working-definitions-charters/working-definition-antisemitism.

Isaac, Benjamin H. *The Invention of Racism in Classical Antiquity*. Princeton, NJ: Princeton University Press, 2004.

"The Jerusalem Declaration on Antisemitism" (JDA). https://jerusalemdeclaration. org.

Judaken, Jonathan. *Jean-Paul Sartre and the Jewish Question: Anti-Antisemitism and the Politics of the French Intellectual*. Lincoln: University of Nebraska Press, 2006.

———. "Rethinking Anti-Semitism." *American Historical Review* 123, no. 4 (2018): 1122–38.

Kalman, Julie. *Rethinking Antisemitism in Nineteenth-Century France*. New York: Cambridge University Press, 2010.

Kalmar, Ivan Davidson, and Derek J. Penslar, eds. *Orientalism and the Jews*. Waltham, MA: Brandeis University Press, 2005.

Karp, Jonathan, and Adam Sutcliffe, eds. *Philosemitism in History*. New York: Cambridge University Press, 2011.

Katz, Jacob. *From Prejudice to Destruction: Anti-Semitism, 1700–1933*. Cambridge, MA: Harvard University Press, 1980.

Kertzer, David I. *The Popes Against the Jews: The Vatican's Role in the Rise of Modern Anti-Semitism*. New York: Alfred A. Knopf, 2001.

Klier, John D., and Shlomo Lambroza, eds. *Pogroms: Anti-Jewish Violence in Modern Russian History*. Cambridge: Cambridge University Press, 1992.

Klug, Brian. "Interrogating 'New Anti-Semitism.'" *Ethnic and Racial Studies* 36, no. 3 (2013): 468–82.

Langmuir, Gavin I. *Toward a Definition of Antisemitism*. Berkeley: University of California Press, 1990.

Lassner, Phyllis, and Lara Trubowitz, eds. *Antisemitism and Philosemitism in the Twentieth and Twenty-First Centuries: Representing Jews, Jewishness, and Modern Culture*. Newark: University of Delaware Press, 2008.

Lerman, Antony. *Whatever Happened to Antisemitism? Redefinition and the Myth of the "Collective Jew."* London: Pluto Press, 2022.

Levy, Richard S., ed. *Antisemitism: A Historical Encyclopedia of Prejudice and Persecution*. Santa Barbara, CA: ABC-CLIO, 2005.

Lindemann, Albert S., and Richard S. Levy, eds. *Antisemitism: A History*. Oxford: Oxford University Press, 2010.

Lipstadt, Deborah E. *Antisemitism: Here and Now*. New York: Schocken Books, 2019.

Lipton, Sara. *Dark Mirror: The Medieval Origins of Anti-Jewish Iconography*. New York: Metropolitan Books, 2014.

Litvak, Meir, and Esther Webman. *From Empathy to Denial: Arab Responses to the Holocaust*. London: Hurst, 2009.

Löwe, Heinz-Dietrich. *The Tsars and the Jews: Reform, Reaction, and Anti-Ssemitism in Imperial Russia, 1772–1917*. Chur, Switzerland: Harwood Academic, 1993.

Mack, Michael. *German Idealism and the Jew: The Inner Anti-Semitism of Philosophy and German Jewish Responses*. Chicago: University of Chicago Press, 2003.

Marcus, Kenneth L. *The Definition of Anti-Semitism*. New York: Oxford University Press, 2015.

Michlic, Joanna B. *Poland's Threatening Other: The Image of the Jew from 1880 to the Present*. Lincoln: University of Nebraska Press, 2006.

Mosse, George L. *Towards the Final Solution: A History of European Racism*. Madison: University of Wisconsin Press, 1985.

Nirenberg, David. *Anti-Judaism: The Western Tradition*. New York: W. W. Norton, 2013.

———. *Communities of Violence: Persecution of Minorities in the Middle Ages*. Princeton, NJ: Princeton University Press, 1998.

Ophir, Adi, and Ishay Rosen-Zvi. *Goy: Israel's Multiple Others and the Birth of the Gentile*. Oxford: Oxford University Press, 2018.

Porter-Szűcs, Brian. *Faith and Fatherland: Catholicism, Modernity, and Poland*. New York: Oxford University Press, 2011.

Pulzer, Peter G. J. *The Rise of Political Anti-Semitism in Germany & Austria*. Cambridge, MA: Harvard University Press, 1988.

Renton, James, and Ben Gidley, eds. *Antisemitism and Islamophobia in Europe: A Shared Story?* London: Palgrave Macmillan, 2017.

Rose, E. M. *The Murder of William of Norwich: The Origins of the Blood Libel in Medieval Europe*. New York: Oxford University Press, 2015.

Rubin, Miri. *Gentile Tales: The Narrative Assault on Late Medieval Jews*. Philadelphia: University of Pennsylvania Press, 2004.

Ruether, Rosemary Radford. *Faith and Fratricide: The Theological Roots of Anti-Semitism*. New York: Seabury Press, 1974.

Sartre, Jean-Paul. *Anti-Semite and Jew*. New York: Schocken Books, 1995.

Schäfer, Peter. *Judeophobia: Attitudes toward the Jews in the Ancient World*. Cambridge, MA: Harvard University Press, 1997.

Schechter, Ronald. *Obstinate Hebrews: Representations of Jews in France, 1715-1815*. Berkeley: University of California Press, 2003.

Schroeter, Daniel J. "'Islamic Anti-Semitism' in Historical Discourse." *American Historical Review* 123, no. 4 (2018): 1172-89.

Shain, Milton. *The Roots of Antisemitism in South Africa*. Charlottesville: University of Virginia Press, 1994.

Stern, Menahem, ed. *Greek and Latin Authors on Jews and Judaism*. 3 vols. Jerusalem: Israel Academy of Sciences and Humanities, 1974-1984.

Stow, Kenneth. *Alienated Minority: The Jews of Medieval Latin Europe*. Cambridge, MA: Harvard University Press, 1992.

Tal, Uriel. *Christians and Jews in Germany: Religion, Politics, and Ideology in the Second Reich, 1870-1914*. Ithaca, NY: Cornell University Press, 1975.

Teter, Magda. *Blood Libel: On the Trail of an Antisemitic Myth*. Cambridge, MA: Harvard University Press, 2020.

Trachtenberg, Joshua. *The Devil and the Jews: The Medieval Conception of the Jew and Its Relation to Modern Anti-Semitism*. Philadelphia: Jewish Publication Society, 1983.

Ury, Scott. *Barricades and Banners: The Revolution of 1905 and the Transformation of Warsaw Jewry*. Stanford, CA: Stanford University Press, 2012.

———. "Strange Bedfellows? Anti-Semitism, Zionism, and the Fate of 'the Jews.'" *American Historical Review* 123, no. 4 (October 2018): 1151-71.

Ury, Scott, and Guy Miron, eds. *Antishemiyut: ben musag histori lesiah tsiburi* (Antisemitism: Historical Concept, Public Discourse). Jerusalem: Shazar Center, 2020.

Veidlinger, Jeffrey. *In the Midst of Civilized Europe: The Pogroms of 1918-1921 and the Onset of the Holocaust*. New York: Metropolitan Books, 2021.

Volkov, Shulamit. "Antisemitism as a Cultural Code: Reflections on the History and Historiography of Antisemitism in Imperial Germany." *The Leo Baeck Institute Year Book* 23, no. 1 (January 1978): 25-46.

———. *Germans, Jews, and Antisemites: Trials in Emancipation*. New York: Cambridge University Press, 2006.

Volovici, Leon. *Nationalist Ideology & Antisemitism: The Case of Romanian Intellectuals in the 1930s*. Oxford: Pergamon, 1991.

Webman, Esther. "From the Damascus Blood Libel to the 'Arab Spring': The Evolution of Arab Antisemitism." *Antisemitism Studies* 1, no. 1 (2017): 157-206.

Weeks, Theodore R. *From Assimilation to Antisemitism: The "Jewish Question" in Poland, 1850-1914*. DeKalb: Northern Illinois University Press, 2006.

Wistrich, Robert S. *A Lethal Obsession: Anti-Semitism from Antiquity to the Global Jihad*. New York: Random House, 2010.

————. *From Ambivalence to Betrayal: The Left, the Jews, and Israel.* Lincoln: University of Nebraska Press, 2012.

Yavetz, Zvi. "Judeophobia in Classical Antiquity: A Different Approach." *Journal of Jewish Studies* 44, no. 1 (1993): 1–22.

Yerushalmi, Yosef Hayim. *Assimilation and Racial Anti-Semitism: The Iberian and the German Models.* New York: Leo Baeck Institute, 1982.

Zimmermann, Moshe. *Wilhelm Marr: The Patriarch of Anti-Semitism.* New York: Oxford University Press, 1986.

Contributors

GERSHON BACON retired in 2017 from the Department of Jewish History and Contemporary Jewry at Bar-Ilan University, where he held the Marcell and Maria Roth Chair in the History and Culture of Polish Jewry. His research and publications focus on the social, political, and religious history of Polish Jewry in the nineteenth and twentieth centuries. He is the author or editor of numerous monographs and articles in the field, most notably *The Politics of Tradition: Agudat Yisrael in Poland, 1916–1939* (Magnes Press, 1996; Shazar Center, 2005, in Hebrew). He currently serves as editor in chief of *Gal-Ed: On the History and Culture of Polish Jewry.*

TZAFRIR BARZILAY is a senior lecturer in history at Bar-Ilan University. He is the author of *Poisoned Wells: Accusations, Persecution, and Minorities in Medieval Europe, 1321–1422* (University of Pennsylvania Press, 2022) and co-editor of *Jewish Daily Life in Medieval Northern Europe, 1080–1350: A Sourcebook* (Medieval Institute Publications, 2022). He is currently investigating religious practices pertaining to water in Jewish and Christian life in High and Late Medieval Europe.

KARMA BEN-JOHANAN teaches at the Department of Religious Studies at the Hebrew University of Jerusalem. She is the author of *Jacob's Younger Brother: Christian-Jewish Relations after Vatican II* (Harvard University Press, 2022); "Uncensored: Recovering Anti-Christian Animosity in Contemporary Rabbinic Literature," *Harvard Theological Review* 114, no. 3 (2021): 393–416; and "From the State of Israel to the Election of Pope John Paul II, 1948–1978," in Edward Kessler and Neil Wenborn, eds., *A Documentary History of Jewish-Christian Relations: From Ancient Times to the Present Day* (Cambridge University Press, forthcoming).

HAVI DREIFUSS is a professor in the Department of Jewish History at Tel Aviv University and director of both the Institute for the History of Polish Jewry and Israel-Poland Relations at Tel Aviv University and the Center for Research on the Holocaust in Poland at the International Institute for Holocaust Research, Yad Vashem. Her research deals with various aspects of everyday life during the Holocaust, including the relationship between Jews and Poles, religious life during the Holocaust, and Jewish existence in the face of extermination. She has published a number of books and articles; the latest, *Ghetto Warsaw: The End* (Yad Vashem, 2018, in Hebrew), is currently being translated into Polish and English.

ARIE M. DUBNOV is an associate professor of history and the Max Ticktin Chair of Israel Studies at the George Washington University. His expertise includes modern Jewish political thought, intellectual history, and the history of the British Empire in the Middle East. His publications include the intellectual biography *Isaiah Berlin: The Journey of a Jewish Liberal* (Palgrave Macmillan, 2012) and three edited volumes, *Zionism: A View from the Outside* (Mosad Bialik, 2010, in Hebrew), *Partitions: A Transnational History of Twentieth-Century Territorial Separatism* (Stanford University Press, 2019), and *Amos Oz's Two Pens: Between Literature and Politics* (Routledge, 2023).

DAVID ENGEL is Greenberg Professor Emeritus of Holocaust Studies and professor emeritus of Hebrew and Judaic Studies at New York University. For many years he was also a fellow of the Goldstein-Goren Diaspora Research Center at Tel Aviv University, where he edited the series *Gal-Ed: On the History and Culture of Polish Jews*. He is the author of nine books and more than one hundred articles on various aspects of Jewish history, Jewish historiography, and the Holocaust, including most recently a co-authored work entitled *War, Conquest, and Catastrophe: Jews in the Soviet Union 1939–1945* (New York University Press, 2022).

DAVID FELDMAN is a professor of history at Birkbeck, University of London where he is also director of the Birkbeck Institute for the Study of Antisemitism. His most recent book is a co-edited volume, *Antisemitism, Islamophobia and the Politics of Definition* (Palgrave, 2023). He has written on antisemitism for *The Guardian, Financial Times, Haaretz, History Workshop Online, The Independent*, and *The Political Quarterly*, and is currently writing a history of anti-antisemitism in the nineteenth and twentieth centuries.

AMOS GOLDBERG is an associate professor at the Department of Jewish History and Contemporary Jewry and the head of the Research Institute of Contemporary Jewry at the Hebrew University of Jerusalem. He is the author of *Trauma in First Person: Diary Writing during the Holocaust* (Indiana University Press, 2017) and co-editor of *The Holocaust and the Nakba: A New Grammar of Trauma and History* (Columbia University Press, 2018). His forthcoming book *Five Critical Readings in Holocaust Memory* (Resling, 2023, in Hebrew) includes a chapter on the IHRA definition of antisemitism. He was among the initiators and drafters of the Jerusalem Declaration on Antisemitism (JDA).

SUSANNAH HESCHEL is Eli M. Black Distinguished Professor and chair of the Jewish Studies Program at Dartmouth College. She is the author of *Abraham Geiger and the Jewish Jesus* (University of Chicago Press, 1998), *The Aryan Jesus: Christian Theologians and the Bible in Nazi Germany* (Princeton University Press, 2008), and *Jüdischer Islam: Islam und jüdisch-deutsche Selbstbestimmung* (Matthes & Seitz, 2018). Her next book project is a co-authored book titled *Jewish Studies and the Woman Question*.

OFRI ILANY is a historian and journalist and also editor in chief of the Van Leer Jerusalem Institute's *Hazman hazeh* magazine. He is the author of *In Search of the Hebrew People: Bible and Nation in the German Enlightenment* (Indiana University Press, 2018). Ilany's research interests include intellectual history, the history of sexuality, and theological aspects of the Anthropocene. His column "Under the Sun" is published as part of *Haaretz Weekly Supplement*.

ELI LEDERHENDLER is the Stephen S. Wise Professor Emeritus of American Jewish History and Institutions at the Hebrew University of Jerusalem. His major publications include *The Road to Modern Jewish Politics* (Oxford University Press, 1989), *New York Jews and the Decline of Urban Ethnicity, 1950–1970* (Syracuse University Press, 2001), *Jewish Immigrants and American Capitalism* (Cambridge University Press, 2009), and *American Jewry: A New History* (Cambridge University Press, 2017). He is a co-editor of the annual journal *Studies in Contemporary Jewry* and director of the Leonid Nevzlin Research Center for Russian and East European Jewry at the Hebrew University.

GUY MIRON is the vice president for academic affairs at the Open University of Israel, where he is also a professor of Jewish history. His research focuses on German and Central European Jewish history in the twentieth century, Hungarian Jewish history, and Jewish and Israeli historiography. His publications include *German Jews in Israel: Memories and Past Images* (Magnes Press, 2004, in Hebrew), *The Waning of the Emancipation: Jewish History, Memory, and the Rise of Fascism in Germany, France, and Hungary* (Wayne State University Press, 2011; Shazar Center, 2011, in Hebrew), and *Space and Time under Persecution: The German-Jewish Experience in the Third Reich* (Magnes Press, 2021, in Hebrew; University of Chicago Press, 2023).

AMOS MORRIS-REICH holds the Geza Roth Chair of Modern Jewish History at Tel Aviv University, where he is director of the Stephen Roth Institute for the Study of Contemporary Antisemitism and Racism and professor in the Cohn Institute for the History and Philosophy of Science and Ideas. His research brings together modern Jewish history with the history of science and technology. His most recent book is *Photography and Jewish History: Five Twentieth-Century Cases* (University of Pennsylvania Press, 2022).

ADI M. OPHIR is professor emeritus at Tel Aviv University and a visiting professor at the Cogut Institute for the Humanities and the program for Middle East Studies at Brown University. Among his recent publications are *In the Beginning Was the State: Divine Violence in the Hebrew Bible* (Fordham University Press, 2022), *On Ruling Power* (Resling, 2022, in Hebrew), and *Goy: Israel's Multiple Others and the Birth of the Gentile* (Oxford University Press, 2018).

ISHAY ROSEN-ZVI is professor of rabbinic literature and chair of the Department of Jewish Philosophy and Talmud at Tel Aviv University. His publications include *Demonic Desires: Yetzer Hara and the Problem of Evil in Late Antiquity* (University of Pennsylvania Press, 2011), *Body and Soul in Ancient Jewish Thought* (Modan, 2012, in Hebrew), *The Mishnaic Sotah Ritual: Temple, Gender and Midrash* (Brill, 2012), *Goy: Israel's Multiple Others and the Birth of the Gentile* (Oxford University Press, 2018), and *Between Mishnah and Midrash: The Birth of Rabbinic Literature* (Open University, 2020, in Hebrew).

YOUVAL ROTMAN is professor of history at Tel Aviv University. He is the author of *Byzantine Slavery and the Mediterranean World* (Harvard University Press, 2009), *Insanity and Sanctity in Byzantium: The Ambiguity of Religious Experience* (Harvard University Press, 2016), and *Slaveries of the First Millennium* (ARC Humanities Press, 2021). He is also co-editor of the *Mediterranean Historical Review*. His current research integrates new methodologies in the social sciences into historical research on the Middle Ages, in particular in regard to modern slavery, forced migration, child labor, religious violence, and monotheism.

STEFANIE SCHÜLER-SPRINGORUM, a historian by training, was director of the Institute for the History of the German Jews in Hamburg from 2001 to 2011. Since 2011, she has been director of the Center for Research on Antisemitism, and since 2012 co-director of the Selma Stern Center for Jewish Studies, both in in Berlin. Her main fields of research include Jewish, German, Spanish, and gender histories. Her recent publications include the co-edited volumes *Football and Discrimination: Antisemitism and Beyond* (Routledge, 2021) and *Four Years After: Ethnonationalism, Antisemitism and Racism in Trump's America* (Winter, 2020), as well as the recent article "Gender and the Politics of Anti-Semitism," *American Historical Review* 123 (2018): 1210–22.

RAZ SEGAL is associate professor of Holocaust and genocide studies and endowed professor in the study of modern genocide at Stockton University, where he also serves as director of the Master of Arts in Holocaust and Genocide Studies. He has held a Harry Frank Guggenheim Fellowship, a Fulbright Fellowship, and a Lady Davis Fellowship at the Hebrew University of Jerusalem. His major publications include *Genocide in the Carpathians: War, Social Breakdown, and Mass Violence, 1914–1945* (Stanford University Press, 2016), *Days of Ruin: The Jews of Munkács During the Holocaust* (Yad Vashem, 2013, in Hebrew), and, as guest editor, a special issue of *Zmanim: A Historical Quarterly* 138 (2018, in Hebrew).

SCOTT URY is an associate professor in the Department of Jewish History and director of the Eva and Marc Besen Institute for the Study of Historical Consciousness at Tel Aviv University (TAU), and also senior editor of the journal *History and Memory*. Previously, he was director of TAU's Stephen Roth Institute for the

Study of Contemporary Antisemitism and Racism. He is the author of *Barricades and Banners: The Revolution of 1905 and the Transformation of Warsaw Jewry* (Stanford University Press, 2012) and co-editor of several volumes, including *Cosmopolitanism, Nationalism and the Jews of East Central Europe* (Routledge, 2014) and *Key Concepts in the Study of Antisemitism* (Palgrave Macmillan, 2021).

Index

academic publications, popular publications *versus*, 50
Adorno, Theodor, 9
Afro-Pessimism, 77–78
agency, questions regarding, 65, 247–48
Ahimeir, Abba, 175
Ajax soccer team, 168
Alderman, Geoffrey, 257
Alexander, Jeffrey, 60
Alexandria, 113, 115
Ali, Nadya, 269
allosemitism, 173–74, 175, 179–80
Allouche, Colette, 288, 291
All-Party Parliamentary Group Against Antisemitism (APPGAA), 258, 263–64, 269, 275n51
All-Party Parliamentary Group on British Muslims (APPGBM), 266–69
All-Party Parliamentary Inquiry into Antisemitism (APPIA), 258–60, 262, 263, 346
Almog, Shmuel, 173
American Historical Review (*AHR*), 4, 14, 17, 212, 216
American Jewish Committee (AJC), 9, 12, 218, 221, 260–61
anarchism/anarchists, 287
Anidjar, Gil, 90
anti-Black racism, 11, 22, 24, 66–68. *See also* race/racism
Anti-Defamation League (ADL), 220, 344–46, 348
anti-Judaism, 7, 17, 23, 93, 111, 123n37, 146n65, 148–49, 156, 158–61, 161n3, 267n71, 301, 334n10
Anti-Judaism (Nirenberg), 61, 156–57
Antiochus VII Sidetes, 114
anti-philosemitism, 170. *See also* philosemitism

antisemitic harassment, 34, 68, 196, 197, 348–49
antisemitism: anti-Jewish animus and, 6–7, 24, 345; in antiquity, 105, 106, 128, 190; assumptions regarding, 5–6; attributes of, 340–41; avoiding use of term, 55–56; branding of, 36–37; as category, 49–61; characteristics of, 76; comparisons with, 9; conceptualization regarding, 281–82; as cultural code, 76; current approaches to, 6–21; debates regarding, 6–21; definitions of, 1, 258–64, 270; dominant approach to, 5; essence of, 38; essentialization of, 65; eternal, 7; expansive concept of, 251; functions of, 71; historical context of, 192–95; historical continuity of, 7; historical term use of, 36–37; history regarding, 36–37, 281–82; in Israeli public discourse, 16, 209, 346, 352; manifestations of, 262; medieval, 74, 127–30; misconceptions regarding, 340–41; as modern phenomenon, 189–92; motivations for, 66, 70, 342; "new antisemitism," 5, 13, 15, 16, 19, 200; open questions regarding, 6–21; overview of, 1–2; as phenomenon, 49–61; politics of, 139–41; in the public square, 219; referents regarding, 342–43; as scholarly category, 147; as seduction, 75–78; significance of, 66; as signifier, 49–61; subcategories concept for, 344; tensions regarding, 6; term limitations of, 2, 37–38, 65, 209–12, 233, 247; as unique phenomenon, 12; as useful category of historical analysis, 21–26; vernacular usage of, 231–32, 233; word usage regarding, 231–35; and Zionism, 19–20, 212, 247, 314, 331
Antisemitism Studies (Indiana University Press), 12

373

Antisemitism Through the Ages, 9–10
anti-Zionism, 13, 14, 15, 16, 18–20, 200, 212–13, 247, 257, 261–62, 314, 331. *See also* Israel; new antisemitism
Antonescu, Ion, 306, 307, 308, 309
Antoninus Pius, 109
Apion, 110, 115
Arab-Israeli conflict, 257. *See also* Israeli-Palestinian conflict
Aragon, Kingdom of, 155–56
Arendt, Hannah, 7, 15, 69–70, 172, 176, 215, 224n22
Aristeas, 109–10, 112
Aryan race/blood, 75, 238, 328
assimilation, of Jewish people, 180
Astashkevich, Irina, 73
astronomy, 48, 49
Auschwitz, 288, 329, 330
Australia, 313
Austro-Hungarian empire, 194
"Away from a Definition of Antisemitism" (Engel), 33, 105, 177, 187–88, 251–52, 299

Barnai, Jacob, 13
Baron, Salo, 151–52, 160
Bauer, Bruno, 236
Bauer, Yehuda, 1–2, 26, 188–89, 302, 352
Baum, Gregory, 323–24, 325
Bauman, Zygmunt, 98, 173–74, 175
Beauvoir, Simone de, 76
Beloff, Max, 257
Bełżec, 304, 308
Bernstein, Fritz, 33–34, 37, 38, 343
Berthelot, Katell, 112
Bessarabia, 306, 307, 308
Bettelheim, Bruno, 9
Bialik, Hayim Nahman, 74
Bible: Esther, Book of, 110, 112, 114, 115, 117; Jewish separation accounts within, 111, 112–13, 114, 115; New Testament, 26, 179, 323, 324, 326, 327, 328, 331; Old Testament, 25, 326–27, 328
biologization and racialization of society, 57–58, 60, 89, 97, 238, 304
Birkbeck Institute for the Study of Antisemitism, Birkbeck, University of (London), 11, 12

Bismarck, Otto von, 97
Black Americans, 65, 68, 70
Blair, Tony, 264
Blatman, Daniel, 284, 295n6
Bloch, Ernst, 173, 176
Bloodlands, 295n6
blood libel, 39, 110
blood purity laws, 88–91
Bloxham, Donald, 284, 304
Bohak, Gideon, 106, 122n31
Bolshevik Revolution, 191
Bolsheviks, 80
Book of Maccabees, 110, 112–16, 117
Bossong, Georg, 89–90
Bourne, Lord, 265
Braungart, Georg, 177
Brenner, Michael, 174
British Union of Fascists, 231, 240
Buber, Martin, 327
Bukovina, 306, 307, 308
Bulgaria, 306–11
Butler, Judith, 15–16, 19, 82
Butterfield, Herbert, 238
Byzantium: antisemitism politics within, 139–41; Christianization within, 128, 134; conversions within, 134, 136–38; hagiography in, 133–35; heretics within, 136–38; historiography in, 130–33; iconoclasm within, 128, 129, 132–33, 135–36, 139; Islamophobia politics within, 139–41; Jewish-Christian conflict within, 134; Jewish conversion within, 134, 136–37; Jewish stereotypes within, 129; Muslim-Christian conflict within, 134; Muslim conversion within, 137–38; religiopolitical crises within, 128; religious rivals within, 130–35

Canada, 11, 217, 313
capitalism, 77, 190
career discrimination, 34, 88–89, 218, 353
Carpathian Jews, 295–96n6
Case, Holly, 308
Catholic Church/Catholicism: apology from, 330–32; conservative position of, 325–30; Frankfurt School and, 325; in Great Britain, 93–94, 236–37;

historiography of antisemitism in, 319–20; progressive position of, 323–25, 334n11; reconciliation and, 319, 325, 329; Second Vatican Council (Vatican II), 319, 320, 321–23, 324, 325, 327, 330. *See also* Christians/Christianity

Catholic Emancipation Act (Great Britain), 93

Caunt, James, 242

cemeteries, vandalism of, 344–46

censorship, 243

Center for Research on Antisemitism, Technical University (Berlin), 11

Césaire, Aimé, 304

Cesarani, David, 302

Chamberlain, Houston Stewart, 69, 231

Cheruvallil-Contractor, Sariya, 269

Christian antisemitism: apology regarding, 330–32; conservative position regarding, 325–30; overview of, 319–20; progressive position regarding, 323–25, 334n11; reconciliation and, 329; Second Vatican Council and, 321–23. *See also* Catholic Church/Catholicism

Christian Gospel, 70, 321, 323, 324, 326, 329

Christians/Christianity: alienation from Jewish sources, 324; Jews' relationship with, 154, 155, 158, 160–61, 175–76; replacement theology of, 179; shared culture between Jews and, 153, 331; supersession, 326; violence by, 155–56

Christian Zionism, 168, 177

church, 154, 217, 230, 310, 319–33

Churchill, Winston, 239–40

civil rights movement (United States), 216–17. *See also* anti-Black racism

Clark, Christopher, 173

Clinton, Bill, 264

Cohen, Daniel, 241

Cold War, 6, 13, 218, 313

colonialism, 67, 318n37. *See also* settler colonialism

communism, 191, 210, 213, 289

Communities of Violence (Nirenberg), 61, 155–56

Community Security Trust (CST), 258, 260, 262

concentration camps, 70, 287

conceptual history (*Begriffsgeschichte*), 188, 233, 235

Confino, Alon, 302

Constantine, 130

Constantine V, 135

conversion: to Christianity, 128, 174; circumcision and, 109; forced, 93, 157, 172; to Islam, 130, 132; overview of, 134, 136–38

Copenhagen, Denmark, 348

Corbyn, Jeremy, 199–200

Coughlin, Charles, 69

Council for the Advancement of Arab-British Understanding, 245

Crewe, Ivor, 257

Cross-Government Working Group on Anti-Muslim Hate Crime, 270

Crown Prosecution Service, 268

crucifixion, 131, 132, 135, 173

Cuffel, Alexandra, 77

cultural sociology, 60

Czech Republic, 290

Daily Express, 242

Dalal, Farhad, 71

Dark Mirror (Lipton), 155

Daston, Lorraine, 56

death marches, Holocaust, 295n6

Decretum de Judaeis, 321, 322

de-idealization, 52–53, 54–55, 61–62

Delumeau, Jean, 97–98

demagogues, 81

Diner, Dan, 176

Dinur, Ben-Zion, 13

Diodorus Siculus, 107, 114, 121n23

discrimination: education, 88–89, 195, 218, 349, 353; legal, 122n30, 236, 340; social, 224n22

disease, 37, 81, 244

Donne, John, 80

Dracula, 72

Dubnow, Simon, 13

ecclesiastical history, 130

The Education of the Human Race (Lessing), 179, 180–81

Efron, John, 91–92

Egypt, 107, 113–16, 119n9, 134
Eichmann, Adolf, 69–70
elections, 192–93, 342, 350
Elukin, Jonathan, 158, 160
emancipation, 92, 95, 236–37
emotions: gratification of, 67, 68, 71, 81,
341; in history of Israel, 19; in history
of Zionism, 19; influence of, 19, 20;
regarding antisemitism, 4, 19–20; as
response to the trauma of history, 82;
soundscape and, 78, 80
Engel, David: "Away from a Definition of
Antisemitism," 33, 45, 46–49, 51–61, 105,
177, 187–88, 251–52, 299; critique of, 151;
de-idealization by, 52–53; *Historians of the
Jews and the Holocaust*, 191–92; influence
of, 2, 148, 213–14; "Patterns of Anti-Jewish
Violence in Poland," 285–86; quote of,
65, 87, 311–12; viewpoint of, 1, 2–3, 18, 21,
24, 26, 65, 105–6, 147, 177, 188, 195, 201, 207,
219, 228, 233, 246–47, 281, 282, 291, 293, 299,
314–15, 351–52; warnings from, 200–201;
writings of, 33–40, 339–54
Engelking, Barbara, 199
English Civil War, 236
English language, 210, 228, 229–30, 233–36,
246
Enlightenment, 90, 98, 179, 180
Equality Act, 263
equivocation fallacy, 342, 356n13
erotic fantasy, 71, 78
erotohistoriography, 67, 68, 75, 79
Esther, Book of, 111, 112, 114, 115, 117
eternal antisemitism, 7, 97. *See also*
antisemitism
Ettinger, Shmuel, 3, 9–11, 13–14, 15, 301, 355n4
eugenics, 57, 238
Europe, 97–98, 254. *See also specific locations*
European Jewish Congress, 260
European Union Monitoring Commission
on Racism and Xenophobia (EUMC),
260–63, 264
Eusebius, 130
euthanasia, 304
evangelical movement, 92–93, 168. *See also*
Christians/Christianity
Exodus, from Egypt, 107, 115, 117, 119n10

expulsion, 88, 147, 149, 150, 190, 303, 307,
310, 342
extermination, of Jews, 8, 112–16, 117, 286, 289,
292, 294n2, 295n6. *See also* Final Solution;
Holocaust, the/Holocaust Studies

fascism, 66, 209, 219
Faulkner, William, 18, 76
Federation of Student Islamic Societies,
270
Feldman, Louis, 106
feminism, 67, 95, 96, 97
Fidesz, 312
Final Solution: antisemitism as purpose
of, 8, 303, 304; the church and, 330–31;
decision of, 305; development of, 294n2,
295n5, 300–301, 302; explanation for, 305;
influences to, 231
First Crusade, 149, 150, 154, 156
Fischer, Eugen, 58, 59, 60
Fischer, Lars, 177–78
Ford, Henry, 69, 221
The Formation of a Persecuting Society
(Moore), 154
Forster Garbett, Cyril, 241–42
France, 236, 285, 290, 291, 313
Frankel, Jonathan, 237
Frankfurt School, 66, 325
Freeman, Elizabeth, 67
Freud, Sigmund, 319
Friedländer, Saul, 57, 305–6
Frye Jacobson, Matthew, 216
fulfillment concept, 326
functionalism, 283, 302
Fundamental Rights Agency (FRA), 264,
275n51
Funkenstein, Amos, 189–90, 343
The Future of Multi-Ethnic Britain
(Runnymede Trust), 265

Geertz, Clifford, 87
gender: antisemitism and, 67, 68, 76; of
emotions and, 77; exclusion and, 97;
sexuality and, 74–75, 78, 98; study of, 4
genocide, 13, 25, 110, 220, 283, 284, 303–54.
See also Final Solution; Holocaust, the/
Holocaust Studies

gentile gaze, 208–9
Gentleman's Agreement (Hobson), 341, 353
Gerlach, Christian, 305
German American Bund rally, 79
German language/concepts in German, 56, 236
Germany/Nazi Germany: allies of, 306; antisemitism word usage within, 36, 251; Bible and, 328; ghetto concept within, 282; influence of, 285; invasion by, 58; legislation within, 194, 215; nationalism of, 72; overview of, 94–97, 350; public opinion within, 293; radical antisemitism of, 302–3; redemptive antisemitism and, 305; riots in, 354; Sephardic culture within, 91; struggle against, 243; war developments and, 283; Week of Brotherhood, 171. *See also* Final Solution; Holocaust, the/Holocaust Studies; Nazis
ghetto, ghettoization, 195, 196, 197, 198, 282
Gilman, Sander, 96
Gilroy, Paul, 265
Goebbels, Joseph, 77, 343
Gold, Ben-Zion, 196
Golders Green together Facebook page, 255
Goldhagen, Daniel, 315n5
Goldstein, Eric, 217–18
Grabowski, Jan, 199
Graetz, Heinrich, 149, 151–52, 158
Grant, Robert, 236
Great Britain/United Kingdom: anti-Jewish incidents within, 242; antisemitism overview of, 230, 233–34; antisemitism reconceptualization within, 245; antisemitism working definition within, 258–64, 270; black-white binary within, 265; categorical identification within, 244–45; Catholic Emancipation Act within, 93; Catholicism within, 93–94, 236–37; censorship within, 243; Continental nationalism and, 229–30; empire and, 238–40; evangelical movement within, 92–93; historical overview of, 227–29; internationalization and, 237; Islamophobia working definition within, 265–69; Israel and, 263; Jewish experience within, 253–54, 255; Jewish political allegiance within, 254; Jewish question within, 235–37; Jews' Civil Disabilities Bill within, 236; Jews within, 91–94, 97; Labour Party within, 244; legislation within, 245–46; minorities within, 235; Minority Treaties and, 234; Muslim experience within, 253–54, 255; Muslim political experience within, 254–55; nationalism within, 244; Notting Hill riots within, 245; papacy within, 93–94; political interests within, 265; postwar moment within, 240–46; subjective feelings of minorities within, 59; violence within, 242; "Whig" perception of, 238; Zionism within, 238–40
Great Depression, 194
Great Fire of London, 347–48
Great Plague of London, 347
Greece, 107, 288, 291, 310
Greeks, 307, 310–11
Green, Abigail, 237
Grimm, Marc, 170
Gross, Jan Tomasz, 199
Gulf War, 253

HaCohen, Ruth, 78
hagiography, 133–36, 138, 139
Halevi, Judah, 149
Harari, Yuval Noah, 50–51
Hartman, Saidiya, 66, 69, 81, 82
Hebrew scripture, 326–27
Hebrew University of Jerusalem, 11
Hecataeus of Abdera, 107, 108
Hellenistic era, 107, 346
Hellenistic writers, 106, 107, 109, 115
Heng, Geraldine, 89, 161n3
Heraclius (Emperor), 134
heresy, 153–54, 327
heretics, in Byzantine literature, 136–38
Hering Torres, Max, 89
Herzl, Theodor, 36, 239
Heydrich, Reinhard, 303
Higham, John, 214, 218, 219
Hilberg, Raul, 302
Himmelfarb, Gertrude, 171

Himmler, Heinrich, 303, 305, 315n9
historians: dilemmas of, 47–48; educational role of, 47, 51, 52, 53; historiography and, 130–33; justification by, 48; professional language of, 48–49; training of, 53; values of, 51; writing process of, 46–47, 49–50
Historians of the Jews and the Holocaust (Engel), 191–92
historiography, religious rivals in Byzantine, 10, 130–33. *See also* Zionism/Zionists
Hitler, Adolf: devotion to, 72, 79; Final Solution decision of, 305; Holocaust and, 300; influence of, 243; *Mein Kampf*, 75–76, 293, 328; memorandum to, 315n9; motif of, 312; policies from, 302; policies of, 77; speech of, 293; territory given by, 308; viewpoint of, 221
Hobson, Laura, 341
Hochhuth, Rolf, 321
Holmes, Colin, 230
Holocaust, the/Holocaust Studies: antisemitism and, 5, 8–9, 81, 282–85, 292–94, 300–306, 311–15; assumption regarding, 5; Bulgaria case, 306–11; causes of, 329, 353–54; children's deaths within, 290; Christian inaction during, 331; commonality within, 282, 286, 288, 290, 292–94; death marches within, 295n6; decision making regarding, 283–84; diachronic plane regarding, 301; functionalist school, 8, 283, 302; as general category, 285–92; geographical borders of, 284–85; intentionalist school, 8, 283, 302; Jewish fates within, 291; periodization of, 284–85; philosemitism and, 168, 170; Romania case regarding, 306–11; short-term perspective regarding, 302; synchronic plane regarding, 301, 303–4; time frame for, 303; victim profiles within, 286–92; writings regarding, 191–92. *See also* Final Solution; genocide
Horkheimer, Max, 9
Hungary, 191, 287, 291, 296n6, 306, 308, 310, 312

iconoclasm, 128, 129, 132–33, 135–36, 139
idealization, 53–54

Im Anfang war Auschwitz (Stern), 173
immigration/anti-immigration sentiment, 220
imperialism, 67
Indiana University, Bloomington, 11
Inquisition, 89, 90, 93, 97, 150, 325
International Holocaust Remembrance Alliance (IHRA), 239, 260, 264–66, 270, 297n18, 311–15, 357n18. *See also* "Jerusalem Declaration on Antisemitism" (JDA)
International Jews, 239
Interwar Period, 192–99
intimacy, and antisemitism, 71–73, 74
Isaac, Benjamin, 106
Isaac, Jules, 321
Ishmaelites, 132
"Islamic antisemitism," 17, 18
Islam/Muslims: Arabs, 90, 128, 133; in Bulgaria, 310; in Byzantium, 130, 132–33, 134, 136–38; demographics in Britain, 254; identity of, 267; Jewish commonality with, 270–71; Muslimness as defined by, 267; racism experience of, 255; in Spain, 88–90; stereotyping of, 138
Islamophobia, 127, 139–41, 252–53, 256–57, 259, 265–71
Islamophobia (Runnymede Trust), 256
Islamophobia Defined (APPGBM), 266–69, 270
Israel: as the "collective Jew," 15; condemnation of, 67; criticism of, 15, 263, 312; debates regarding, 5–6; Jewish society within, 213; Jewish studies in, 11; Jewish viewpoints within, 19, 59; Jewish viewpoints within, 19, 59; mob attack within, 354; new antisemitism and, 15, 16, 200; protests against, 19; settler colonialism and, 318n37; as solution to antisemitism, 331; support for, 168, 181; viewpoints regarding, 245. *See also* Israeli-Palestinian conflict; Zionism
Israeli-Palestinian conflict, 14, 17–18, 199, 212–13, 254, 257, 258, 261–63, 264
Italy, 307, 310

Jäckel, Eberhard, 302
Jacobs, Joseph, 238

Jacobson, Matthew Frye, 216
Jakobovits, Lord, 257
Jazz Age, 221
Jensen, Uffa, 78
Jerusalem Declaration on Antisemitism
  (JDA), 271n4, 297n18, 357n18. *See also*
  International Holocaust Remembrance
  Alliance (IHRA)
"Jerusalem school" of Jewish history, 10
Jesus, 68, 72, 77, 80, 173, 179, 326, 328
Jew-hatred: antisemitism term *versus*,
  190, 234; in Catholic tradition, 324; in
  Christian Gospel, 323, 324; defined,
  127, 128, 210, 218; in England, 230, 238;
  extreme expressions of, 106; Hasmonean
  struggle and, 114; rise in, 297n18; self-
  separation and, 110, 111; sociocultural
  hierarchy and, 139; term use of, 105, 140,
  189, 211. *See also* antisemitism
Jewish communal organizations, 160–61,
  259, 263
Jewish exile, 150, 158, 197
Jewish nationalism, 15–16, 239, 240, 244, 282
Jewish national project, 150
Jewish question, 33, 35, 175, 235–37, 305, 308
A Jewish Renaissance in Fifteenth-Century
  Spain (Meyerson), 157–58
Jewish self-hatred, 177
Jewish War, 108
Jews: ancient writings regarding,
  107–12, 130–31; blaming of, 67; categorical
  identification of, 244–45; characteristics
  of, 108; Christians' relationship with,
  154, 155, 158, 160–61, 175–76; coding of, 76;
  conspiracies regarding, 190; criticism of,
  107; denouncing of, 67; differentiation
  of, 107; divine commandments and,
  86n55; envy of, 77; as eroticized object,
  76; God's choosing of, 179; harms of,
  207–8; historical periods regarding,
  149–50; hostility toward, 38; influence
  of, 34; justifications by, 220; as "killers
  of God," 135, 173; as kin of Jesus, 328;
  loathing of, 77; as minorities, 59; murder
  of, 70; Muslim commonality with,
  270–71; Polish, 34; population growth
  of, 254; as race of traitors, 172; rights for,
252; sameness of, 180; self-segregation/
  separatism of, 107, 109–12, 115–17,
  172–77; shared culture of, 153; societal
  discrimination of, 172; soundscape and,
  78–79; subjectivity regarding, 59–60;
  uniqueness of, 180; violence against, 149,
  150, 154
The Jews (Lessing), 178–79
Jews' Civil Disabilities Bill (Great Britain),
  236
job discrimination, 34, 88–89, 218, 353
John Paul II (Pope), 328–29, 330, 332
John XXIII (Pope), 321
Josephus, 109, 110, 112, 119–20n12
Judaism: attacks against, 74–75; Byzantium
  and, 129; Catholicism and, 321,
  325–28; Christianity and, 77, 80, 176, 319;
  conversion to, 170–71; Great Britain
  and, 91–93; hostility toward, 71; Muslim
  iconoclasm and, 132–33, 135–37; negative
  portrayal of, 140; as phenomenon, 157;
  philanthropy and, 112; reduction of, 181
Judaken, Jonathan, 4, 14, 19, 176, 212, 216
Judenfrage, 231, 236, 237
"Judeo-Bolshevism," 191
Judeophobia, 39, 91, 95, 97, 105, 106–12, 117,
  228, 346. *See also* antisemitism
Julian (the Apostate), 131, 132
Julius, Anthony, 8, 230
justification by faith, 327–28
Justinian (Emperor), 131

Kant, Immanuel, 80, 181
Karaski, Jan, 198
Karp, Jonathan, 176–77
Katz, Jacob, 319
Kershaw, Ian, 302
Kishinev, pogrom of 1903, 73–74
Klatzkin, Jakob, 175
Koselleck, Reinhart, 56, 60
kosher slaughter, 194
Kossak-Szczucka, Zofia, 198
Kot, Stanisław, 34, 35, 36
Kristallnacht, 354, 360n53
Krugman, Paul, 199
Ku Klux Klan, 221
Kushner, Tony, 242

Labour Middle East Council, 245
Labour Party (Great Britain), 199, 200, 244, 254, 266
Langmuir, Gavin, 38, 39, 97, 151, 343
Lawrence, Stephen, 259
Left (political left, left-wing politics), 15, 67, 81, 170, 244, 254, 265
Lerman, Antony, 257, 261
Lerner, Miriam and Hannah, 287, 289–90, 291
Lessing, Gotthold Ephraim, 169, 177–81
Lessing, Theodor, 177
Letter of Aristeas, 109–10, 116
Leutheuser, Julius, 72
Levenson, Alan, 176
Lévi-Strauss, Claude, 140
liberal philosemitism, 171, 175
Lipman, Barbara, 216
Lipton, Sara, 155, 157, 160
Living Together, Living Apart (Elukin), 158
Livne, Zipora, 196
London, 255, 259, 347–48
London Society for the Promotion of Christianity, 92–93
love, 72, 74, 167, 170, 173
Lubac, Henri de, 325, 326
Lustiger, Jean-Marie, 328
Luther, Martin, 80, 327–28
Luxemburg, Rosa, 239
lynching, of African Americans, 65, 70, 343

Macedonia, 309, 310, 311
Macpherson, William, 259, 264, 268
MacShane, Denis, 258
Mahler, Raphael, 192
Maimonides, 149
Malalas, John, 131, 132
Mallach, Yitzhak, 288, 291
Manifestation of Antisemitism in the EU, 260
Marcion of Sinope, 327
Marcus, Kenneth, 261
Maritain, Jacques, 325
Marr, Wilhelm, 36
Marranos, 93
Marshall, Louis, 221
Martínez, María Elena, 89
martyrologies, Christian, 133

Marx, Karl, 236, 239
Massey, Irving, 174–75
Mbembe, Achille, 78
McCaul, Alexander, 94
Mehring, Franz, 170
Mein Kampf (Hitler), 75–76, 293, 328. See also Nazis/Nazism
Mendelsohn, Ezra, 195
Mendelssohn, Moses, 178
The Merchant of Venice (Shakespeare), 76, 80, 220, 235
Messianism, 132
Metz, Johann Baptist, 324
Meyerson, Mark, 157–58, 160
Middle Ages, 1, 7, 23, 89, 133, 147, 148–51, 153–54, 155–57
Middle East, 256, 258, 262. See also Israel; Israeli-Palestinian conflict
Mill, John Stuart, 268
Mills, Charles W., 66
minoritization, defined, 234–35
Minority Treaties, 234
misanthropy, 107, 109, 115, 119n10
misogyny, 66, 78, 97
missionary philosemitism, 171. See also philosemitism
modernity, 7, 9, 77, 88, 89, 98, 175, 323, 330, 332
Modood, Tariq, 265, 267, 268, 276n73
Mohamad, Mahathir, 199, 200
Montefiore, Moses, 237
Moore, Robert I., 153, 154, 159, 160
Mosley, Oswald, 231, 240
Mosse, George, 302, 315n4
Motzkin, Gabriel, 172
Mt. Carmel Jewish cemetery (Philadelphia, Pennsylvania), 344–46
Mühsam, Erich, 287, 289, 291
Muñoz, José Esteban, 68
Muslims. See Islam/Muslims

Nagler, Neville, 257
Narutowicz, Gabriel, 193
Nathan the Wise (Lessing), 178–79
nationalism, 15, 67, 75, 96, 172, 229, 230, 239, 244, 282, 295–96n6
National Jews, 239, 240

natural language, challenges of, 46, 48–49

Nazi Germany and the Jews (Friedländer), 57, 305

Nazis/Nazism: antisemitism of, 70, 293, 301–6, 319, 321, 330–31; in Bulgaria, 310; ideology of, 283, 294n3; mass murder by, 1, 25, 254, 310; in Poland, 199; rise of, 9, 241; vision of, 309

Neighbors, 199

Netanyahu, Benzion, 91

Neuberger, Julia, 257

new antisemitism, 5, 13, 15, 16, 19, 200. *See also* antisemitism

New Evangelization movement, 330

New Testament, 26, 153, 179, 323, 324, 326–28, 331

New York Times, 47, 49

Nicetas of Byzantium, 138

Nicolson, Harold, 227, 235

Niemcewicz, Julian Ursyn, 191, 357n17

Nietzsche, Friedrich, 68, 232

Nirenberg, David, 5, 61, 155–57, 159, 201, 205–6n45, 301. *See also* anti-Judaism

Nolte, Ernst, 80, 86n55

Nostra Aetate, 319, 320, 322, 323–25, 328

Notting Hill riots, 245

Nussbaum, Perry, 217

Odessa, 309

Oesterreicher, Johannes, 325

Old Testament, 25, 326–27, 328

Oliver Twist (Dickens), 235

On the Civil Improvement of the Jews (Dohm), 180

Operation Barbarossa, 294n2

Operation Reinhard, 304

Organization for Security and Co-operation in Europe (OSCE), 264

Orientalism, 91, 174, 209

The Origins of Totalitarianism (Arendt), 7, 172

Orwell, George, 240–41, 243–44

Ottoman Empire, 90, 310

Oxford English Dictionary, 233

Pagans, 23, 128, 131, 328

Parkes, James, 235

Parting Ways (Butler), 15

"Patterns of Anti-Jewish Violence in Poland" (Engel), 285–86

Paz, D. G., 93

Penslar, Derek, 19

Pentagon, attack on, 253

persecution, of Jews, 88–90, 92, 113, 149, 151–52, 157, 332. *See also* anti-Judaism; antisemitism; Holocaust, the/Holocaust Studies

Persians, 131

Persson, Göran, 264

Petschauer, Attila, 287–88, 290, 291

Peyrère, Isaac La, 170

Philo, 109, 110, 112

philosemitism: from antagonism to esteem regarding, 169–72; antisemitism *versus*, 178; awakening of, 168; critique of, 172–77; defined, 167; Gotthold Ephraim Lessing as test case for, 177–81; growth of, 241; as independent phenomenon, 177; overview of, 167–69; term use regarding, 170; types of, 171; Utilitarian, 171; writings regarding, 168, 171–72

Philosemitism in History (Karp and Sutcliffe), 176–77

Philo-Semitism in Nineteenth-Century German Literature (Massey), 174–75

phlogiston, 348, 352

Piłsudski, Józef, 195

Pinsker, Yehudah Leib (Leon), 200

Pius XII (Pope), 319, 321, 330

Pluto, 48, 49

pogroms, 66, 71, 73, 74, 75, 79, 82, 194, 214

Poland: anti-Jewish pogroms within, 194–95; discrimination within, 203n14; economic policy within, 193; elections law within, 192–93; establishment of, 234; Interwar Period within, 195–99; Jews within, 34, 190–91, 194–95, 199–200, 349, 350–51; military conscription within, 193–94; murder of Jews within, 285–88; *numerus clauses* within, 195; public service within, 194; Sunday Rest Law within, 194; violence within, 195, 199, 286–88

Poliakov, Léon, 150–51

politics, of antisemitism and Islamophobia, 139–41
politics, of Israel/Palestine, 263
Pontifical Commission for Religious Relations with the Jews (CRRJ), 326
popular publications, academic publications *versus*, 50
Porat, Dina, 8, 260–61, 355n5
POWs, 295n6, 304
Procopius, 131
pro-philosemitism, 170
proteophobia, 98
The Protocols of the Elders of Zion, 191, 221, 302
Prussia, 180, 350
Ptolemy IV Philopator, 113
public service, 194

rabbinism/rabbinic Judaism, 93–94
race/racism: acts of, 65–66; anti-Black, 11, 22, 24, 66–68; antisemitism compared to, 9, 13, 66, 215–16, 217, 265, 312; appeal of, 71; defined, 215–16; erotics of, 71; intimacy of, 71–73, 74; Jewish experience of, 255; Muslim experience of, 255; religion and, 4–5, 89, 91, 238; study of, 11; vulnerability and, 68; Zionism as, 261
Race Relations At, 259
racialization, 57, 58, 59, 216
Ragussis, Michael, 91, 92
rallies, antisemitic, 79–80
rape, 73–74, 75
Ratzinger, Joseph, 328
reconciliation, 319, 325, 329, 333
refugees, 17, 99n19, 195, 197, 248
Relations between Jews and Poles during the Holocaust (Dreifuss), 196–97
relevance, of scholarship, 46–47
religiocide, 74–75, 343
religion, 36, 77, 89, 91, 128, 130. *See also* conversion; *specific religions*
renaissance, 157–58
replacement theology, 179
research centers of antisemitism, 11–12, 13
revelation, 179, 180, 326
reverse racism, 239
Roma, 307, 308
Roman Catholic Relief Act, 236

Romania, 300, 302, 306–11
Romanus the Neomartyr, 135
Rome, 119n11
Rosenfeld, Alvin, 8, 17, 19
Rowling, J. K., 199
Rozin, Orit, 19
Rubinstein, William and Hilary, 171–72
Ruether, Rosemary Radford, 324–25
Runnymede Trust, 253, 256, 260, 264, 266
Runnymede Trust Commission on Antisemitism, 256, 257
Ruppin, Arthur, 58, 60
Russia/tsarist Russia, 191, 234, 238, 295n6, 302. *See also* Soviet Union

Said, Edward, 91, 174
salons, 95
Sapiens (Harari), 50–51
Sasanian Empire, 131, 132
Sayyid, Salman, 267, 269
Schallmayer, Wilhelm, 57–58, 59
Schapkow, Carsten, 91–92
Schillebeeckx, Edward, 324, 325
Schoeps, Hans-Joachim, 167–68, 170–71
Schreiner, Stefan, 90
Schroeter, Daniel, 17, 18
"Science as a Vocation" (Weber), 52
scientific work, idealization within, 53–54
Scott, Joan Wallach, 87
Sebeos, 132–33
Second Vatican Council (Vatican II), 319, 320, 321–23, 324, 325, 327, 330
security and insecurity, Jews' sense of, 36–37, 213, 305–6, 346, 348–54
self-segregation/separation of Jews, 107–9, 110–12, 114, 115–18, 120n22
Sepharad, 88–91, 92, 94
September 11, 2001, attacks on, 253
settler colonialism, 313, 318n37
sexual laws, 74–75
Shakespeare, William, 76, 80, 220, 235
shared culture, of Jews and Christians, 153, 331
silence, violence of, 69–71
Sithole, Tendayi, 77
Sivanandan, Ambalavaner, 265
Skinner, Quentin, 56

slavery, 65, 68, 69, 71, 77, 81, 82, 114, 281–82

Sobibor, 288, 304

A Social and Religious History of the Jews (Baron), 152

Social Darwinism, 238

social history, of the Jews, 152–53. *See also* historiography, religious rivals in Byzantine

socialism, 176, 180

Socrates Scholasticus, 130–31, 132

Sonderkommando R, 309

Sonderweg thesis, 246

Soros, George, 312

soundscape, antisemitism as, 78–80

Southall Black Sisters, 267–68, 269, 276n73

Soviet Union, 14, 34, 197, 303, 304, 306, 307, 309, 313, 352–53. *See also* Russia/tsarist Russia

Sozomenos, 131, 132

Spaeth, Johann Peter, 170–71

Spain: blood purity laws within, 88–89, 91; early modern era within, 88; Expulsion and, 147, 149, 157–58; as historical laboratory, 91; Inquisition and, 90; Jewish Renaissance within, 157–58; violence within, 150

Stallaert, Christiane, 89

Stangl, Franz, 70

Stein, Edith, 330

Steinhart, Eric, 309

The Stephen Lawrence Inquiry, 259

Stephen Roth Institute for the Study of Contemporary Antisemitism and Racism (Tel Aviv University), 11, 261

Stern, Frank, 173

Stern, Kenneth, 261, 262

Stillman, Norman, 17

Studies in Antisemitism (Indiana University Press), 12

Studies in Prejudice (American Jewish Committee), 9, 12

Sunday Rest Law (Poland), 194

Sutcliffe, Adam, 176–77

Tacitus, 107–9, 115, 119n11, 120n17

Technical University (Berlin), 11

Tel Aviv University, 11, 261, 344

Theisohn, Phillipp, 177

Theophanes the Confessor, 132–33

theoretical-academic (analytic usage) of words, 50–51, 56, 140, 148, 207, 210, 212, 232, 233, 299–300, 311, 347

theoretical concepts, 232–33, 247, 252, 267, 281–94, 299–303, 306, 311, 314

Thieme, Karl, 325

Thrace, 309, 310

Till, Emmett, 65, 356n12

Titus, 107

tolerance, 159, 176, 179, 180, 235, 241

Torah, 11, 122n30

Tottenham soccer team, 168

Toury, Jacob, 236

Transnistria, 308, 309

Transylvania, 307, 308

Treblinka, 304, 310

Trotsky, Leon, 239

tsarist Russia, 191, 234, 302. *See* Russia/tsarist Russia

UJA-Federation, 352–53

Ukraine/Ukrainians, 295n6, 307, 309

uniqueness: of antisemitism, 10, 13, 25, 284; of Jews, 175, 180. *See also* antisemitism; Jews

United Kingdom. *See* Great Britain/United Kingdom

United States: antisemitism statistics within, 211, 345, 349; civil rights movement within, 217; Israel and, 168, 261, 313; Jazz Age within, 221; Jewish experience within, 212, 214–15, 218, 349, 353; Jewish social integration within, 215; populism within, 218–19; racism within, 66, 68; socially institutionalized barriers within, 218, 353; violence within, 216

universalism, 169, 256, 258, 263, 269–70

USSR, 352–53

Utilitarian philosemitism, 171

Vakil, AbdoolKarim, 267

Valman, Nadia, 93

vandalism, 36, 242, 344–46, 348

Vatican II (Second Vatican Council), 319, 320, 321–23, 324, 325, 327, 330

verbal assaults, 68, 69, 78, 87, 213, 227, 242, 342, 349, 352, 353
vernacular usage of words, 231–32
A Very Light Sleeper (Runnymede Trust), 253, 256, 257, 258
Vidal Sassoon International Center for the Study of Antisemitism (Hebrew University), 7, 10
violence: by Christians, 149–50, 154–56; in Germany, 350; in Great Britain, 242; homophobic, 98; against Jews, 33, 65, 66, 71, 149, 150, 154, 194, 213; Kingdom of Aragon and, 155–56; local causes of, 156; motivations for, 70, 116; in Poland, 195, 199, 286–88; sexual, 73; of silence, 69–71; social processes and, 156; in Spain, 150; understanding, 156; in the United States, 216. *See also* extermination, Jewish; Holocaust, the/Holocaust Studies
visual art, 155
Volkov, Shulamit, 66, 231, 302, 313
von Balthasar, Hans Urs, 327
von Braun, Christina, 78
von Dohm, Christian Wilhelm, 180
von Harnack, Adolf, 327–28
von Luschan, Felix, 58, 59, 60
von Treitschke, Heinrich, 69, 169–70, 173
von Wilamowitz-Moellendorff, Ulrich, 182n6
Voss, Bettina, 90

Wagner, Richard, 69, 78
Warsaw, 191
Warsi, Baroness Saveeda, 265
Weber, Max, 52
Week of Brotherhood (Germany), 171
Weimar Jews, 350
Weininger, Otto, 78

Weizmann, Chaim, 240
Whitehall Government Working Group, 269
white nationalism, 67
whiteness, 67, 215–17
white privilege, 215, 217
white supremacy, 67, 68, 342
Whitham, Ben, 269
Wilderson, Frank B., III, 77
Willebrands, Johannes, 328
Winkler, Beate, 260, 261
Wistrich, Robert S., 3, 7–8, 11, 14–15, 16–17, 18–19, 61
Wolf, Lucien, 234
women: Jewish, 76, 78, 92–93, 94–98; rape of, 73–75, 82; violence against, 287–91; violence by, 70. *See also* feminism
World Trade Center, attacks on, 253
World War II, 34, 196, 198, 240, 290, 293, 306, 307, 308, 310–11, 331. *See also* Holocaust, the/Holocaust Studies
World Zionist Organization, 14, 168

Xenophobia, 97, 106–12, 116, 211, 229, 246, 247, 311, 312

Yad Vashem, 300, 332, 352
Yale University, 11, 12
Yazid II, 132, 136
yellow star, 77
Yerushalmi, Yosef H., 91
Yugoslavia, 310

Zangwill, Israel, 239
Żegota, 198
"Zionism Versus Bolshevism" (Churchill), 239–40
Zionism/Zionists, 14, 150, 238–40, 261, 314, 331. *See also* antisemitism; Israel